THE CHURCH'S CONFESSION UNDER HITLER

by

ARTHUR C. COCHRANE

THE WESTMINSTER PRESS
Philadelphia

LIBRARY OF CONGRESS CATALOG CARD No. 62–7939

PRINTED IN THE UNITED STATES OF AMERICA

THE CHURCH'S
CONFESSION
UNDER HITLER

BOOKS by ARTHUR C. COCHRANE
Published by The Westminster Press

THE CHURCH'S CONFESSION UNDER HITLER

THE EXISTENTIALISTS AND GOD

To
Karl Barth, theologian
Martin Niemöller, churchman
Wilhelm Niemöller, historian
of
Barmen
this book is gratefully dedicated

Contents

Foreword

∟ The Barmen Declaration was unanimously adopted by the First Confessional Synod of the German Evangelical Church, held in Barmen, May 29–31, 1934, in order to withstand the errors of the " German Christians " and the Reich Church government. It was the theological basis of the true evangelical Church, commonly called the " Confessing Church." It was the point of departure for the subsequent synods held in Dahlem (1934), Augsburg (1935), and Bad-Oeynhausen (1936). Its decisions were binding upon the Church's Council of Brethren and administrative boards in their conduct of the practical work of the Church in the fight against the Reich Church bishop and the Church committees appointed by the Government. It was adopted by the Second Free Reformed Synod, in Siegen, March 26–28, 1935, and is still numbered among the historic Confessions of the Reformed Church in Germany.[1]

In the constitutions and Church orders that have been issued since 1945 by the Evangelical Church in Germany, the United Evangelical Lutheran Church in Germany, the Evangelical United Church, and by thirteen of the provincial Churches (*Landeskirchen*), the Barmen Declaration has been incorporated with varying degrees of acceptance. The United Church and its member Churches in the Rhineland, Westphalia, Brandenburg, and Saxony have adopted Barmen along with the Confessions of the Reformation. Article I, Section 6, of the Church order of the Church in the Rhineland is typical: " It affirms the Theological Declaration of the Confessional Synod of Barmen as a Scriptural and binding testimony to the gospel for the Church's ministry." Likewise the Evangelical Church in Hesse and Nassau, of which Dr. Martin Niemöller is the present

Church president, professes the Barmen Declaration in its basic articles of faith.

On the other hand, there has been a strong tendency in the Lutheran provincial Churches to subordinate Barmen to the old Lutheran Confessions and to restrict its significance to the historical "event" of the Synod of 1934.[2] This tendency is reflected in the amendment made to the original draft of the constitution of the Evangelical Church in Germany. The original text read as follows: "The foundation of the Evangelical Church in Germany is the gospel of Jesus Christ, as it is attested in the Holy Scriptures of the Old and New Testaments, brought to light again as authoritative in the Confessions of the Reformation period, and confessed anew as obligatory in the Barmen Theological Declaration." In the constitution of July 13, 1948, Barmen was not adopted in the confessional preamble but was included in Article I, Section 2, as follows: "With its member Churches the Evangelical Church in Germany affirms the decisions reached in the first Confessional Synod in Barmen. As a confessing Church, it recognizes that it is obligated to implement the insights gained in the Church Struggle concerning the nature, task, and order of the Church." In his commentary on the constitution of the Evangelical Church in Germany, Dr. Heinz Brunotte explains this change as follows: "The Evangelical Church in Germany and its member Churches do not affirm [what Brunotte strangely refers to as] Barmen 'theories' but Barmen *deeds,* the decisions taken there against the errors of the 'German Christians,' the Church government of Ludwig Müller, and Jäger, and in the last analysis against the religious policies of the totalitarian State at that time." Significantly, the constitutions of the Lutheran Churches in Mecklenburg, Thuringia, and Saxony contain no reference to Barmen at all.

Quite apart from its legal recognition or nonrecognition, Barmen continues to exert an enormous influence upon the Church life of Germany. It is the point of reference for tackling issues facing the Church today, namely, the rearmament of Germany with atomic weapons, the chaplaincy service, and the Dibelius controversy about the interpretation of the State in Romans, ch. 13. For instance, the statement issued by representatives of the Church Brotherhoods, meeting in Frankfurt, October 2–4, 1958, in answer to the question, "What does it mean to confess Jesus Christ in the atomic threat to the world? " was directly and deliberately tied into the first, second, and fifth articles of the Barmen Declaration.[3] It is no accident that precisely those men who unswervingly adhered to Barmen throughout the Church Struggle under Hitler are the same men who today in loyalty to Barmen are opposing the rearmament of Germany!

In view of the crucial role that the Barmen Declaration has played and is still playing in the face of issues that concern all of us, it is most unfortunate that since the end of the war, the history of the Confessing Church has been almost completely neglected by English-speaking Church historians. Prior to and during the war, a number of books by C. S. Macfarland, A. S. Duncan-Jones, Hermann Stewart, Adolf Keller, and Arthur Frey kept us remarkably well informed about what was going on inside Germany. Unfortunately these books — with the exception of the translation of Frey's *Cross and Swastika* — for the most part looked upon the Church Struggle as a struggle for religious liberty under a totalitarian State, whereas it was essentially a struggle of the Church against itself for itself — a struggle, as Prof. Ernst Wolf has rightly observed, for the Barmen Declaration,[4] and a struggle for the Church to remain faithful to the Declaration in its preaching and actions. In 1943, two papers read at a summer conference at Newnham College, Cambridge, England, were published in a pamphlet entitled *The Significance of the Barmen Declaration for the Ecumenical Church,* with a foreword by the Bishop of Chichester. To my knowledge this is the only attempt made in English to assess the theological significance of the Synod of Barmen. Thanks to the industry of German scholars we are today in a much better position to appraise its importance.

For some strange reason the Church Struggle has been almost completely neglected by American and British historians. In a paper delivered before the American Society of Church History, April 8, 1960, Prof. Franklin H. Littell cited two typical examples of this neglect. "In the Harper Historical Series under the editorship of Guy Stanton Ford we find a major history by Chester V. Easum, chairman of the History Department of the University of Wisconsin. In *Half-Century of Conflict,* Dr. Easum, author of several books in German history and for a time Cultural Attaché at Bonn, covers the first half of the twentieth century. In over nine hundred pages of military and political history, with large chapters devoted to Nazism

and World War II, there is no reference to the Church Struggle!
The names of von Bodelschwingh, Dibelius, Niemöller, and Wurm
are not even found in the index.[5] For the second example, take the
study unit in the D. C. Heath Series ' Problems in European Civilization ' in *The Nazi Revolution* [6]: In a one-hundred-page study unit for
university students, covering many phases of the Nazi Party and
the Third Reich, no mention is made of the Church Struggle and
its significance to internal German politics and to international relations during and since the war. The entire dimension of the true historical significance of Nazism as a ' post-Christian ' phenomenon,
of the Church Struggle itself as illuminating whole pages of nine-
teenth- and twentieth-century European civilization, is studiously
neglected." William L. Shirer's history of Nazi Germany, *The Rise
and Fall of the Third Reich,* runs over twelve hundred pages, of
which seven meager pages are devoted to the persecution of the
Christian Churches.[7]

Perhaps it is the nature of the case, however, that secular historians
should ignore the Church Struggle. The Church's resistance to Hitlerism, viewed politically and sociologically, did not really amount to
very much and had little apparent effect upon the course of events.
Why should these historians pay much attention to the protests of a
relatively tiny minority? Even the persecution of the Church was
light in comparison with the unspeakable sufferings of the Jews and
the miseries inflicted upon neighboring peoples by the Nazis. Perhaps too, it is the nature of the case that secular historians should fail
to discern the theological significance of what Hermann Rauschning
called "the revolution of nihilism," and to perceive the spiritual
bankruptcy and the abyss of evil into which our generation had
fallen — revealed not in the fiendish atrocities committed by the
Nazis, which were merely symptomatic, but in the truths confessed
and the long-standing errors rejected by the Confessing Church. But
it *is* surprising that Church historians have failed to see in the
Church Struggle a clue to the deepest cause of the sickness of our
age, and to search out the lessons which those appalling twelve years
from 1933 to 1945 have to teach us.

In Germany itself there has been a long delay in collecting and
cataloging the primary sources indispensable to a comprehensive,
accurate history of the period. It was not until 1955 that the Council

of the Evangelical Church in Germany, recognizing that the National Socialist period had brought about a revolutionary change in the history of the Church, appointed a Commission for the History of the Church Struggle in the National Socialist Period under the chairmanship of Professor K. D. Schmidt, of Hamburg. The Commission is composed of men who took an active part in the Church Struggle and have subsequently written on its history and meaning: Dr. Heinz Brunotte, of Hanover; Dr. Wilhelm Niemöller, of Bielefeld; Prof. Günther Harder, of Berlin; President Joachim Beckmann, of Düsseldorf; and Prof. Ernst Wolf, of Göttingen. The Commission has contracted to publish some forty-two specialized studies, of which about one fourth have appeared to date, the first being Otto Diehn's bibliography of the Church Struggle listing nearly six thousand separate items.

Indicative of the rising interest in the period, not only in Germany but in other lands, was the First International Conference on the History of the Church Struggle held in Tutzing, Bavaria, August, 1959. The conference met under the auspices of the Commission at the suggestion of Prof. Franklin Littell, of Southern Methodist University, in Dallas, Texas. It attracted scholars from Britain, Denmark, Switzerland, Italy, and the United States. A second such conference was held in Bielefeld, Germany, July, 1961. Following the first conference, the seven delegates from the United States, including the present writer, constituted themselves an "American Committee," with Professor Littell as secretary, to further research in the field.

My own interest in the Church Struggle, and in the Synod of Barmen in particular, goes back to the year 1936. Upon the suggestion of Dr. John Macconachie, of Dundee, Scotland, then the leading exponent of the theology of Karl Barth in the English-speaking world, and with the permission of the senate of Edinburgh University, I began work on the doctoral thesis: "The Relation of Karl Barth to the Historic Creeds and Standards of the Church." The first part of the thesis explored the formal question of the nature of a Confession of Faith; the second ventured an analysis and comparison of the Barmen Theological Declaration with the standards of the Reformed Church. Most of the research was done while I was a guest in the home of Dr. Hermann Hesse, who at that time was Moderator of the Alliance of Reformed Churches in Germany and director of the

seminary in Elberfeld. I enjoyed the inestimable advantage of ex-
periencing something of the Church Struggle at first hand, and of
having the wise counsel of Dr. Hesse and his four sons who were
preparing for the Christian ministry: Theodor, Friedel, Helmut, and
Eduard. The first two were killed on the Russian front, Helmut died
in Dachau Concentration Camp, and Eduard, the namesake of our
eldest son, is at present minister in Hoerstgen, Kreis Moers, Germany.

In 1957–1958 a fellowship from the American Association of Theological Schools enabled me to take a year's leave of absence to resume
my study of the Synod of Barmen. Already fully persuaded that the
Barmen Declaration is the most significant Church document that
has appeared since the Reformation Confessions and Catechisms of
the sixteenth and seventeenth centuries, and oppressed by the knowledge that the present generation of theological students was completely ignorant of it, and indeed of the Church Struggle itself, I resolved this time to concentrate upon the history and prehistory of the
synod. It seemed to me hardly worth-while, especially for English
readers, to discuss the doctrinal content of the Barmen Declaration
until first we had understood the situation in which it arose and the
factors that produced it. To my mind, Barmen is important not
merely because in its six brief articles it represents a radical break by
the Church itself — and not just by an individual theologian — with
the modernist Protestant theology of the nineteenth century, not
merely because, while seeking to remain faithful to the various Reformation Confessions, it succeeded in clarifying, supplementing, and
even correcting certain Reformation doctrines, but primarily because
after a silence of more than three hundred years the Church again
learned what it means to confess Christ as a Church before men and
what is the nature of a true Confession of Faith. Barmen broke
through a fundamentalist confessionalism on the one hand and a
liberal confessionlessness on the other. It is the fact of Barmen, the
act of confession, and the circumstances that attend it which will engage our attention in this book.

As a fairly exhaustive account of the prehistory of Barmen, I have
provided a sort of opening chapter to the history of the German
Church Struggle which, I trust, will be taken up and completed by
historians much more competent than I. It takes the reader up to the

date of the synod, May 29–31, 1934. A concluding chapter, " The Nature of a Confession of Faith, Illustrated from the Theology and
History of Barmen," touches upon some of the highlights of the
Church Struggle between 1934 and 1945, but in no sense does it attempt to cover the history of the period. Even this introduction to
the Church Struggle by no means gives a full picture of all fronts on
which the struggle was waged up until May, 1934. Only a brief account is given of the part played by the Roman Catholic Church. No
account is given of the Free Churches and sects, and no account of
the relations of the Confessing Church to the Ecumenical Church,
World Lutheranism, and the Presbyterian World Alliance. This is
not because these were unimportant themes but because they were
not immediately relevant to a history of Barmen.

The opening chapter, on National Socialism, is obviously only a
rough sketch intended to give the reader a background for the history of the Church. A much more serious omission is any thorough
treatment of the causes of National Socialism and of the apostasy and
failure of the Church prior to and during the Hitler regime. It was
my original intention to include a chapter on the roots of National
Socialism, but for a number of reasons I decided against it. In the
first place, a single chapter would have been woefully inadequate,
and anything more than this would have deviated from the main
purpose of the book. It would have involved an investigation of Germany's cultural and institutional history, its philosophy and theology,
in the eighteenth and nineteenth centuries, and even in the Reformation period itself.[8] Moreover, if the history of Germany from 1933 to
1945 was not an isolated and anomalous phenomenon but was symptomatic of a deep-seated sickness of the so-called Christian West,
then the investigation would have taken us farther afield. In any
case, the causes of the misery of Germany and our Western world
would be best seen *after* the story of the Church Struggle had been
told and therefore in the light of the theological and ethical insights
gained from it. Following the war, German and European scholars
did, in fact, engage in serious self-examination.[9] But this needs to be
done again in the light of the historical studies now being carried on
and from the perspectives gained with the passage of the years.

The present work, less ambitious, begins around 1917, when the
theological climate first showed signs of change. On the one hand it

describes the theological transformation " between the times " that paved the way for the Synod of Barmen, and on the other it traces the rise of the " German Christians," whose errors were rejected at Barmen. Three chapters are then devoted to the events in Church and State that led to the calling of the synod. A separate chapter deals with the history of the synod itself, about which fortunately we have fuller information than we have of any other important synod or council in the history of the Christian Church. A final chapter endeavors to gather together what Barmen has to teach concerning the nature of a genuine Confession of Faith.

Two things need to be borne in mind by a student of the history and nature of a Confession of Faith. First, a Confession of Faith involves a conflict not merely between theological schools *within* the Church but a conflict between the true and the false Church, a conflict that *divides* the Churches. While love for the erring brethren may still prevail, the division is extremely painful and deep wounds are inflicted. This explains the enflamed passions and often bitter polemic that accompany a Confession — so alien to the spirit of the debate among various schools in our Churches in America. A Confession of Faith is a consuming fire, and it is a fearful thing for those who approach too closely to it. Those among us who glibly call for a new Confession know not what they ask. My book would not be a faithful account of the Barmen Declaration if it did not reflect something of the intense personal conflicts that attended it. Secondly, a Confession of Faith is a decision in which " the first shall be last, and the last shall be first," and none may glory save in the Lord! The true story of the Church in Germany is not an unrelieved epic of faith and courage; it is to a large extent a sad tale of betrayal, timidity, and unbelief. Even among those most faithful to the gospel, there were " none righteous, no, not one." I have therefore striven to set down without fear or favor what was said and done *at that time* in the belief that God's amazing grace is praised not only *in excelsis* but also *ex profundis* of human sin and error. I would ask readers of this book to bear in mind that the views of the Church leaders and theologians herein set forth were the views they held at the time in question and may not be their views today. Many of the men who in this volume are described as " German " or " half-German " Christians today hold positions of prominence in the German Church and enjoy the deep respect of scholars throughout the world. Some of them I count among my personal friends.

Of special importance for the study of Barmen is a new transcription of the rediscovered stenographic text of 1934 of the minutes of the synod. The transcription of 1934 had been lost either through fire or confiscation by the Nazis. Fortunately Dr. Karl Bode, a chief administrative adviser for the Government who had been a member of the synod, survived the war and was able to make a new transcription at the end of 1952. In June, 1934, immediately following the synod, Pastor Karl Immer was authorized by the Synod's Council of Brethren to publish two reports on its proceedings: the first, *Bekenntnissynode der deutschen evangelischen Kirche Barmen 1934. Vorträge und Entschliessungen,* and the second, *Die Kirche vor ihrem Richter. Biblische Zeugnisse auf der Bekenntnissynode der deutschen evangelischen Kirche.* Additional important material is contained in the files of the Office of the President of the Confessional Synod of the German Evangelical Church. These had been in the possession of President Karl Koch in Bad-Oeynhausen. When after the war the British Occupation Forces compelled him to leave his house, he took the files to Bielefeld. Because of the housing shortage at that time he had decided to have them destroyed. At Dr. Wilhelm Niemöller's request he handed them over to him and they are now safely lodged in the Bielefeld Archive of the Confessing Church. The letters, papers, and records in the files of Hermann Hesse, Wilhelm Jannasch, Karl Lücking, and Martin Niemöller, all preserved in the Bielefeld Archive, also afford invaluable source material. Further sources are indicated in the notes and in the bibliography.

Here I must record my tremendous indebtedness to Dr. Wilhelm Niemöller. Dr. Niemöller, pastor of the Jakobuskirche in Bielefeld, who is certainly the foremost authority on the history of the Church Struggle, placed at my disposal the resources of the Bielefeld Archive, of which he is the founder and director. He furnished me with a heated room in the Archive so I could examine the various documents in the comfort we Americans seem to require, and he patiently answered the hundred and one questions with which I plied him. Much more than that: he extended to me the warmth of his friendship and hospitality.

Special thanks are also due to his son, Dr. Gerhard Niemöller, who permitted me to read the manuscript of his then unpublished two-volume work on Barmen: *Die erste Bekenntnissynode der deutschen evangelischen Kirche zu Barmen. I. Geschichte, Kritik und Bedeutung der Synode und ihrer theologischen Erklärung;* II. *Text-Dokumente-Berichte.* Göttingen, 1959. Although I took pains to check his findings with the sources in the Archive, they greatly facilitated my research for the chapter on the synod itself. Unless further source material is discovered — which is highly unlikely — Dr. Niemöller's two volumes will undoubtedly remain the definitive work on the history of the Synod of Barmen. My own book differs from Dr. Niemöller's in that I have devoted much more space to the prehistory and background of the synod, whereas he has added a survey of the criticism of the Barmen Declaration.

Prof. Ernst Wolf's book, *Barmen. Kirche zwischen Versuchung und Gnade* (Munich, 1957), is different again in character. Building in part upon the historical data gathered by Dr. Niemöller, he has written the first systematic exposition of the articles of the Theological Declaration and has assessed their importance in the history of Christian thought, and for the life of the Church today. My thanks are due to Professor Wolf, and also to Prof. Karl Barth, with whom I visited, for their assistance in clearing up certain obscure points in the history of the text of the Declaration and certain difficulties in its translation.

In addition, I wish to record my indebtedness to the following persons for their helpful criticisms and suggestions: Dr. Calvin Schnucker, Dean of The Theological Seminary of the University of Dubuque, for his encouragement and assistance; Dr. George B. Ehlhardt, librarian of the seminary, for securing certain invaluable source material; Prof. Franklin Littell, of the Perkins School of Theology, Southern Methodist University, Dallas, Texas; and Dr. Paul L. Meacham, of The Westminster Press.

ARTHUR C. COCHRANE

The Theological Seminary,
University of Dubuque
Dubuque, Iowa

I

National Socialism
— a Sinister Background

THE SUBJECT of this present volume is the history of the First Confessional Synod of the German Evangelical Church held in Barmen, May 29–31, 1934. The Church's struggle in Germany was in
part a struggle against the National Socialist State, but even more a
struggle against the heretical " German Christian " party. But from
its inception it was essentially a struggle of the Church against itself
for itself. It was a struggle to recover the confession of faith and a
struggle to remain faithful to it in the preaching and actions of the
Church. Nevertheless, the ideology and politics of Hitlerism formed
the dark and somber background against which the Church Struggle was played out. It was the historical setting for the Church's recovery of and struggle for faith. It will therefore be necessary to
sketch in this sinister background and to give some account of the
rise of National Socialism in Germany.

National Socialism is the name of a movement that was founded
by Adolf Hitler in Germany in 1919. Its full title was the Nationalsozialistische Deutsche Arbeiterpartei (NSDAP). So intimately was
this movement identified with the personality of its founder that it
could also be described as Hitlerism. Adolf Hitler, born April 20,
1889, in the Austrian town of Braunau am Inn, was surely one of the
most astonishing, inscrutable, and evil figures in all of history. It is
doubtful whether the ordinary categories of thought can account for
the career of a man whom Sir Winston Churchill once described as
" a monster of wickedness," of a man whose name became a byword
for infamy and horror all over the world. Perhaps he belonged to a
dimension of the demonic that is ultimately irrational and inexplicable. Who was this man who rose from miserable circumstances

and, with but the slightest formal education, became the ruler and destroyer not only of Germany but of Continental Europe? What are the political ideas to which he owed his rise to power?

Hitler's father was Alois Schicklgruber, the illegitimate son of Maria Anna Schicklgruber, who changed his name at the age of thirty-five to the name of the man who was probably his father, namely, Hitler. Alois Schicklgruber (Hitler) was a shoemaker who became a customs inspector. His third marriage was to Klara Poelzl, a girl twenty-three years his junior, who was a maid in his first wife's home. To this union was born Adolf Hitler and a second son, Edward, who died in childhood. Although quite intelligent, the young Hitler was a shiftless student. At the age of nineteen he moved to Vienna to study art. The Academy of Art rejected him twice because of his failure to meet the standards and he was unable to enter the School of Architecture because he had not made his *Abitur*. Frustrated in his ambition to become an artist, he was forced to take a job as a day laborer. Yet these years in Vienna were formative for his whole life. Here he conceived his theory of a Germanic master race destined to rule the world, his intense hatred of the Jews as the archenemies of mankind, of democracy, liberalism, and humanism, and his cynical disdain of Christianity. Here the seeds of what Hermann Rauschning called "the revolution of nihilism" were sown in the mind of Hitler.

World War I was for Hitler a joyous release. Here he experienced a sense of mission and purpose in life. He thanked God that he was privileged to live in "heroic" times and to participate in the "noble" deeds of pan-Germanic, Wagnerian splendor. He was twice wounded and was awarded an Iron Cross, but he never rose to a higher rank than corporal. The end of the war found him convalescing from the effects of a gas attack at Ypres. With the defeat of Germany, his world lay in ruins. In *Mein Kampf* (My Struggle), he relates that he wept for the first time since the death of his mother and experienced the paradox of despair and hatred. His soul was filled with a loathing for the founders of the Weimar Republic and he referred to them as the "November criminals" who had stabbed Germany in the back. He entered politics with the fanatical purpose of "regenerating" his fellow Germans and of "saving" them from Jews, Marxists, capitalists, democrats, and Masons. His first field of activity was in Munich, the capital of Bavaria. In June, 1919, he joined a small German Workers' Party. " It was," he wrote, " the most fateful decision of my life." Later he changed its name to the " Nationalsozialistische Deutsche Arbeiterpartei." He gathered around him a group of disgruntled soldiers who were afterward to become the top officials in his government: Ernst Röhm, the head of the Reich Army; Rudolf Hess, the student of geopolitics; Hermann Göring, a former air force officer; Alfred Rosenberg, a Baltic emigrant; the Jew-baiting Julius Streicher and the brothers Gregor and Otto Strasser. Rosenberg became the author of *The Myth of the 20th Century,* the most widely read book of the movement besides Hitler's own *Mein Kampf.* Hess helped Hitler write *Mein Kampf* during their internment in the fortress in Landsberg am Lech in 1924 and later became his personal representative; Röhm organized the brown-shirted SA (*Sturmabteilung*) and was purged from the Party in June, 1934; Göring organized the air force and headed the industrial mobilization; and Streicher edited the anti-Semitic weekly *Der Stürmer.* Others who subsequently played a prominent part in the movement were Joseph Goebbels, the minister of propaganda and enlightenment; Heinrich Himmler, organizer and commander of the black-uniformed SS (*Schutzstaffel*), Hitler's personal elite guard, and of the Gestapo (*Geheime Staats Polizei*), the dreaded secret police; and Robert Ley, the leader of the " German Workers' Front."

The National Socialist ideology was actually a political religion. Its basic concept was the race. It was held to be the primary factor in all historical events and in the formation of states and nations. By race was understood a biological substance that inheres in the blood of every man and determines him not only physically but intellectually and spiritually. This element accounts for higher and lower races and peoples. The highest and best race is the so-called " Aryan " race because it alone is capable of culture. Of course, the Nazi theory of race is not supported by any scientific study of biology or sociology, and the Government was obliged to set up its own chairs in the universities to propagate its tenets and to give to them the aura of academic respectability. Biologists have never discovered any quality in the blood of man by which racial differences are determined, nor has it been possible for sociologists to draw hard and fast distinctions among the races of mankind. Indeed, it is doubtful whether there exists anywhere in the world today such a thing as a pure race. Thus the whole structure of National Socialism was built upon a pseudo science, a myth. From the basic premise of blood and race it was deduced that the Germanic race, and in particular the German people, was destined to play a special role. Germany had the task of being the "*Herrenrasse*," the ruling race among the lesser nations of the world; the others were to work and obey or be exterminated.

One might argue that anti-Semitism was an outgrowth of a belief in racial superiority. Theologically, it is perhaps truer to say that the National Socialist theory of blood and race was the peculiar form that anti-Semitism took in Germany and that therefore anti-Semitism, and not any particular theory of blood and race, was in reality the fundamental principle of the National Socialist State. If this is so, then it is apparent that the phenomenon of National Socialism is ultimately explicable only on theological grounds, namely, man's natural hatred of God's chosen people as the witnesses to the God who exercises grace in judgment. Anti-Semitism is always a sign of man's enmity to the grace of God that has appeared just in the one Jew, Jesus of Nazareth. Moreover, precisely because of its anti-Semitism it was inevitable that National Socialism would attack the Christian Church, and then all human justice and freedom. If Israel was the root from which the Church had its life, if Israel's Messiah was the Lord of the Church, then it was inevitable that those who hated the Jews would also hate the Church. And once the right to exist was denied to Christians and Jews, the rights of all men and nations were in jeopardy.

Whether one regards a theory of the racial superiority of the "Aryan" race or anti-Semitism as the basic principle of National Socialism, the fact remains that from the beginning it looked upon the Jews not merely as an inferior race but as the "*Gegenrasse*" whose main objective was to overthrow the "Aryan" race. The Jews were parasites to be exterminated. The Jew was the source that was poisoning all mankind, the incarnation of all that was evil and wicked. In *Mein Kampf*, Hitler wrote that "the Jew today is the great agitator for the complete destruction of Germany. Wherever we read of attacks made against Germany, the Jews are the authors of them, just as in times of peace and during the war the Jewish financial papers and the Marxist press systematically stirred up hatred against

Germany. It was the Jews who plotted the First World War, and they are the power behind Germany's two archenemies: international capitalism and international Bolshevism."

According to Hitler, Germany would become a great power capable of vanquishing its enemies only when it had first been welded into a powerful military nation. Such an iron society, he taught, can be realized only through discipline and authoritarianism. The State must be organized as a hierarchy in which the "leader" is clothed with final and absolute power. All local groups and committees are working committees but devoid of voting powers. Individualism, liberalism, and democracy are incompatible with this *Führerprinzip*. To achieve his ideal of a thoroughly military State, Hitler prescribed the necessary steps to be taken: purification of the race, elimination of class distinctions, the removal of divisive elements such as political parties, ideologies, and religious denominations, and, finally, a new system of education in the schools and universities. Only when this internal reformation would be accomplished would Germany be able to turn its attention to foreign policy. Then the chief task of a new foreign policy would be the creation of *Lebensraum* (living space) for the German people. Only through territorial expansion could the future of Germany be guaranteed. Since this could not be realized without displacing the peoples already settled in neighboring lands, war was the only means by which Germany could achieve its goal. Unlike the old colonial imperialism, Hitler looked to Eastern Europe for *Lebensraum* rather than to overseas colonies.

All these ideas are to be found in Hitler's autobiography, which was published in 1925. But few people took such a program seriously in Germany, or even in Europe. Indeed, the strange blindness and inertia that possessed the Western nations between the two wars enabled Hitler to push through his program. He subscribed to a crass Darwinian doctrine of the survival of the fittest. Men and nations, he believed, are condemned to an unceasing struggle in which the strong triumph and the weak perish. "Conflict has made man great. . . . Whatever goal man has reached, he owes to his creative powers and to his brutality. . . . All life may be summed up in three propositions: conflict is the father of all things, virtue is a matter of blood, and leadership is primary and decisive." Here in Hitler's own words we have the substance of National Socialist ideology. The principle that "might is right" was founded upon a supposed law of nature.

On November 9, 1923, Hitler, supported by Field Marshal Erich Ludendorff, made his first attempt to gain power. The "beer hall Putsch," as it was called, was a dismal failure. Hitler was sentenced to prison but was pardoned in December of the following year. The Party was reorganized in February of 1925. Since Germany was enjoying years of artificial prosperity from 1924 to 1929, it was not a fruitful period for the radical ideas of a demagogue. At the end of 1928, Hitler's Party numbered only sixty thousand members and the elections of that year gave him only twelve seats in the German Reichstag. The world-wide depression that set in in 1929 changed the picture completely. Hitler attracted to his ranks the unemployed, the disgruntled, and the uprooted, as well as political opportunists, idealists, and adventurers. All who were dissatisfied with the democratic republic, with the innumerable small parties, with the policies of the victorious allied powers and their enforcement of the iniquities of the Treaty of Versailles, and, of course, with the mounting unemployment and poverty, flocked to his banner. Hitler took advantage of the widespread discontent, confusion, and despair. To the farmers he promised higher prices; to the industrialists, support against the trade-unions; to the workers, social security and higher wages; to nationalists, the hope of a greater Reich; to former officers, a new, powerful army. A master of propaganda and mass psychology, he employed flags, bands, uniforms, torchlight parades, military discipline, martial songs, and huge Party congresses to kindle the hopes, fire the imaginations, and strengthen the wills of young and old alike. The storms of rage, the hysterical speeches, and the hypnotic appeal of this strange ascetic, vegetarian, and teetotaler with the wild eyes, unruly forelock, and "Charlie Chaplin" mustache, created in the minds of many the impression that he was indeed a heaven-sent messiah. As Göring expressed it: "We love Adolf Hitler because we believe deeply and unswervingly that God has sent him to us to save Germany."

By September, 1930, Hitler's Party received six and a half million votes and gained 107 seats in parliament to become the second strongest faction. Since the Communists had also made big gains, the democratic work of the Reichstag was undermined by the two parties which, though bitterly opposed to each other, were united in their antidemocratic principles and tactics. When no one party could obtain an over-all majority, Germany was faced with the threat of being governed by orders-in-council by the aging president of the Reich, Field Marshal von Hindenburg. At first Hindenburg was minded to uphold the constitution. But he was a monarchist at heart. Thanks to the election of July, 1932, which gave Hitler thirteen and three quarter million votes and made his Party the strongest in the Reich, and thanks to the political intrigues of Franz von Papen, Baron von Schroeder, Fritz Thyssen, and Alfred Hugenberg, who used Hindenburg as their tool, Hitler was named chancellor on January 30, 1933, and was called upon to head a coalition government composed of National Socialists and members of the conservative and nationalistic right. While the conspirators were not averse to undermining democracy, they foolishly imagined that they could " use " Hitler to serve their own purposes. They were soon to discover their folly. Meanwhile Hitler's *Weltanschauung* was looked upon as mere political propaganda. No one dreamed that he would actually put into practice the fantastic and dangerous ideas outlined in his book.

At first, Hitler gave the appearance of being a peace-loving, sensible, and statesmanlike chancellor. He refrained from speaking of a National Socialist " revolution " but spoke of a " national uprising." His policy of deferring to President von Hindenburg attracted to his side millions of conservative and monarchist citizens. His immediate purpose was to consolidate and increase his power. With a view to extending the basis of his government he dissolved the Reichstag and ordered new elections to be held in March, at which he hoped his Party would achieve an over-all majority. During the weeks preceding the election, the SA and SS terrorized political opponents. In order to discredit the Communists and to recommend himself as the strong man to deliver the nation, he hit upon the terroristic ruse of burning the Reichstag building in the night of February 27. This fire was interpreted by the Nazis as a sign of an imminent plot on the part of the Communists to overthrow the government. It is known today that the Communists had planned neither a revolt nor the burning of the Reichstag; that the Nazis themselves had organized it; and that Göring and Goebbels were chiefly responsible. Details concerning this arson are still shrouded in mystery, and it has not been shown whether it was committed with Hitler's knowledge. The feeble-minded Dutch Communist van der Lubbe was executed as the guilty person, but he was obviously just a scapegoat.[1] For on the same night the fire occurred, Communist party leaders and members of the Reichstag were arrested and the publications of the leftist parties banned. Moreover, the Reichstag burning was made the excuse for issuing a *Decree of the Reich President for the Safety of the Nation and State* the morning of the following day. This lengthy document must have been prepared well in advance of the alleged Communist revolt! With this emergency order the civil rights, upon which the democracy was based, were virtually abolished. It became the most important instrument by which Hitler wielded dictatorial powers. It was to remain in force "until further notice" and this lasted until May 8, 1945 — the date of the collapse of the Hitler Reich. Article 48, section 2, of the Weimar constitution did provide for such an emergency decree. Thus with a show of legality Hitler used this provision, not to defend the constitution, but to overthrow it. As Walther Hofer has observed,[2] the door was wide open for the ruthless destruction of those liberties for which European man had struggled for four hundred years to achieve. The police could now arrest anyone without a hearing and keep him in prison for an indefinite period without a trial. Private dwellings could be searched, property seized, newspapers censored or prohibited, telephones tapped, organizations and parties dissolved, and meetings forbidden — all on the pretext of the existence of an emergency situation. With one blow human and civil rights were crushed.

In spite of the propaganda use Hitler made of the Reichstag fire and the regime of terror he initiated, he failed to secure an absolute majority in the elections of March 5. Only with the fifty-two seats of his coalition partner, the DNVP (German National Union Party), led by Hugenberg, was Hitler able to command a majority of 340 seats out of a total of 647 seats in the Reichstag. In this last partially free election the German people gave Hitler only 44 per cent of the vote. Actually Hitler was not too disturbed by the outcome of the election, for he now possessed other than constitutional means to put through his revolution. The Party took over power in the various German states or provinces by sending out Reich commissars who placed the power of the police in the hands of the SA and SS leaders. Hitler himself issued an appeal to the SA and SS to arrest anyone opposed to the movement on the pretext of rooting out Communism. Thus Heinrich Himmler and Reinhard Heydrich quickly became the chiefs of police in Bavaria, and Hermann Göring in Prussia. It is significant that the Army did not aid Hitler's rise to power. But it did send General von Blomberg as its representative in the Government. Since the General was quite sympathetic to Hitler, the Government had nothing to fear from that quarter. Indeed, the Army recognized in Hitler the man who would restore to it its former glory.

When the new Reichstag met in the garrison church in Potsdam on March 21, 1933, it proceeded to pass — on March 24 — the so-called " enabling " law whereby the legislative powers of the Reichstag were reduced to a sounding board for the Party. The necessary majority for the passage of this bill was secured by the arrest of certain members and terrorizing the other parties. The few remaining democratic parties took the line that it was now hopeless to oppose the Chancellor's will. Only the Social Democrats dared to withstand Hitler. Their leader, Wels, raised his voice — the last in the Reichstag — in a courageous appeal for democracy, humanity, and justice. But it was too late and only served to bring down upon him and his party the wrath of the tyrant.[3] On June 22 the Social Democratic Party was banned, as well as its newspapers and publications, and its property was confiscated. The official justification given for this action was that the leaders of the Social Democratic Party were sympathetic to Communism and were treasonably hostile to the best interests of the German people. Hitler capitalized on the bugaboo of the Communist menace to gain complete dictatorial powers. The abolition of all other political parties was soon to follow, including the very ones that had given him the necessary majority to pass the " enabling law." The next month — on July 14 — Hitler declared the National Socialist Party to be the only party in Germany. Anyone who tried to perpetuate an existing party or to organize a new one would be liable to imprisonment up to three years.

The next victims were the trade-unions. On May 1, Hitler proclaimed a national holiday to celebrate the new regime. That night the offices and buildings of all trade-unions throughout the country were occupied by the police. Their files and office equipment were confiscated. Prominent labor leaders were arrested by the Gestapo and placed in prison. Thus in a single night the powerful unions were smashed and Hitler was free to set up his own labor organization. One by one those groups which could challenge his authority were eliminated.

However, the most serious challenge to Hitler's power came from within his own Party — from Ernst Röhm, the leader of the brown-shirted SA, which had done so much to put him at the head of a totalitarian State. Röhm and his associates felt that they had not received their proper share in the spoils of victory, and were agitating for a " second revolution " in which the middle class in Germany would be exploited. But Hitler was not interested in a social revolution. His one concern was to enhance his own power, and he needed the support of the industrialists and military personnel if he was to have a strong Army and a self-sufficient economy. Moreover, Röhm wanted to merge the Reich Army into his brown-shirted people's army with himself as commander-in-chief. Needless to say, this was not pleasing to the generals or to the other leading Nazis in Hitler's cabinet. Röhm had to be rubbed out. With typical recklessness and brutality Hitler ordered the " blood purge " of June 30 and July 1 in which hundreds were massacred. Not only were Röhm and other leaders of the SA murdered, but also Jews, former enemies, and many who might have led a possible conservative counterrevolution. Among those who were shot were General von Schleicher and his wife, General von Bredow, and Gregor Strasser. It was explained to the nation that the purge was an act of national self-defense and therefore legal. Justice had now become nothing more or less than the arbitrary will of the dictator. Henceforth the SA played no political role. Instead, the black-uniformed SS under Himmler and Heydrich became the chief instrument for a ruthless enslavement of Germany. With the death of Hindenburg on August 2, 1934, the last conservative obstacle disappeared. The presidency was abolished and Hitler proclaimed himself Reichsführer (Leader) and Chancellor. All generals, soldiers, and State officials were compelled to take an unconditional oath of personal allegiance to Hitler. Thus at a Party congress held in September, Hitler could proudly announce that the revolution had been accomplished. The Third Reich was now ready to inaugurate the " new order," which was to last for a thousand years.

The concentration of all power in his own hands gave Hitler the chance to mold Germany according to his own will. He himself admitted that the realization of the National Socialist program was a thousand times more difficult than gaining power. His intention was to create a totalitarian State that would be the exact opposite of liberal democracy and in which the individual citizen would be only a pawn. The State was to control and direct every area of life. All social, cultural, and economic life was supervised by the Party. Industry and finance were organized in the interest of a State preparing for war, even though the capitalistic structure of the national economy was retained. Indeed, the whole society was mobilized as if a state of war already existed. All citizens were obliged to belong to some organization of the State, so that their working hours and free time were dominated by the Government. By far the largest of these organizations was the "German Workers' Front." The idea back of it was to abolish the distinction between employers and employees. It had nothing in common with free trade-unions. It was, in fact, an arm of the State. Headed by Robert Ley, a man of extremely radical views, its purpose was to achieve the highest efficiency and productivity of the German people. In the place of former educational and recreational branches of the labor movement came "Kraft durch Freude" (Strength Through Joy) an organization to provide recreation and trips during evenings, weekends, and vacations when, of course, the participants would be subjected to a ceaseless barrage of National Socialist propaganda. Trips and tours within and outside Germany were provided at very low rates, so that many workers were enabled to enjoy the pleasures of sight-seeing formerly restricted to more prosperous classes. Thus the Party could plausibly point to its deep concern for the laboring class.

The youth were organized into the "Hitler Youth," so that they were directly subject to the control of the State. Here the "re-education" program was carried on most successfully, and it is not surprising that Hitler's most fanatical disciples and warriors were drawn from the rising generation. Children were taught that their first allegiance is not to the family or to the Church but to the Führer. The schools and universities offered no opposition to this enslavement of young minds and soon lost their independence. Teachers and professors unsympathetic to the movement were discharged or fled the country, to be replaced by those who adhered to the Party line. Perhaps the most illustrious of these exiles was Albert Einstein, whose theory of relativity was rejected as Jewish speculation. Literature and art, music and the theater, the radio, press, and movie films were transformed in keeping with the prevailing ideology. Naturally the press and radio were immediately placed under the strictest State control. Indeed, virtually all news articles and editorial comment emanated from Goebbel's Office of National Enlightenment, so that the daily newspapers were marked by a drab sameness. A so-called "Law for Editors," proclaimed October 4, 1933, was the legal pretext for getting rid of all Jewish editors (and all "Aryans" married to Jews) as well as any persons "unfriendly" to the aims of the new Germany. A Reich Chamber of Culture was created in which all artists were required to be members. Hitler frequently set himself up as an art and music critic. He denounced all modern music and art because of their "Bolshevist" tendencies. Naturally Jews were excluded from cultural activities, and music by Jewish composers, notably that of Felix Mendelssohn, was banned. Books and pictures were publicly burned, as in the Middle Ages. Many authors, composers, and artists left Germany of their own volition or because they were forced to if they were to escape the fate of innumerable of their colleagues: the concentration camp.

Mention has already been made of the collapse of justice in Germany. In its place was set up a so-called Germanic justice that consisted in the legalizing and codification of arbitrariness. Dr. Frank, who headed the ministry of justice, announced that the National Socialist *Weltanschauung* and especially utterances by the Führer were guides for judges and the basis for the interpretation of all justice. The famous German jurist, Prof. Karl Schmitt, ascribed to Hitler the capacity to create justice immediately in virtue of his leadership and as being the highest court of appeal. Thus the arbitrary will of a megalomaniac was in the last analysis the basis of German jurisprudence. The terrifying symbol of this arbitrary justice was the "People's Court," set up in 1934.

Hand in hand with this supposed "justice" went a process whereby the Jews were deprived of all legal rights. A series of laws were passed that were but the prelude to the actual persecution and extermination of German and later of European Jews. The mass murdering of Jews, which increased in fury as National Socialism neared its end, was not, however, a deterioration of the system. Anti-Semitism was intrinsic to its very nature. But it was necessary first to rear up a generation that would take it for granted. It is doubtless true that the great majority of Germans and even of the Party members failed to realize that the biological anti-Semitism taught by Hitler and made the official stand of the Government would inevitably lead to the physical extermination of Jewry, and reports of the worst massacres were withheld lest the still-existing Christian and humanistic conscience of the public be shocked. Nevertheless, Hitler made it plain in *Mein Kampf* and again before the outbreak of the war that another war would result not in the destruction of Germany but of Judaism in Europe. For in Hitler's mind the struggle for *Lebensraum* for the *Herrenrasse* included the physical removal of the Jews. As long as the political situation in Germany had not been stabilized, and in order to allay the fears of foreign powers, Hitler was obliged to go easy at first in his persecution of the Jews. At the start of his regime it took the form of discrimination; Jews were excluded from public office, from the arts, and from schools and universities. Jewish shops were forced to carry a sign: " This is a Jewish store." Walther Hofer distinguishes four stages in the development of the severity of the Jewish persecutions: 1933 to 1935, when isolated measures were taken against the Jews on the basis of emergency orders and the " enabling law," lending an air of pseudo legality; 1935 to 1938, the period of the Nuremberg laws and the decrees based on them; 1938 to 1941, the pogroms and the first mass deportations to the Polish camps; 1941 to 1945, mass extermination by gas chambers and shootings.[4]

The first official anti-Jewish measure by the Government was the one-day boycott of Jewish businesses on April 1, 1933. It was represented as an answer to the " boycott " and slanderous agitation of Jews inside and outside of Germany. Hindenburg protested in a letter against discriminatory actions taken against Jewish officials who had been wounded in the war. When six days later a law was issued retiring all Jewish officials, a concession was made to Hindenburg's protest by making exceptions in the case of those who had rendered signal war service. Once Hindenburg was removed by death, the " patriotic services " of Jews no longer counted. The second phase was ushered in by the adoption of the " Nuremberg laws " by " acclamation " at a Party congress in Nuremberg in September of 1935. German citizens were divided according to their nationality and their Reich citizenship. Jews were branded as second-class citizens. Marriages between Jews and " Aryans " were forbidden, and sexual intercourse between the races outside marriage was subject to heavy penalties — even the death sentence. Up until the outbreak of the war more than 250 anti-Jewish decrees were promulgated. On November 14, 1935, all Jews were discharged from public office. From then on they were banned from one field of endeavor after the other: from the Army, the legal and medical professions, from the schools. They were permitted to carry on private business enterprises up until 1938. But the pogrom of November 9–10 of that year, which opened the third phase, changed even that. This violent sudden attack upon the Jewish population was represented by the official propaganda as a spontaneous act of expiation by the German people for the murder of a member of the German embassy in Paris by a Polish Jew. It was obvious, however, that the attack had been carefully organized and carried out by the SA. Throughout the whole country hundreds of Jewish stores, houses, schools, and, above all, synagogues were set on fire, and thousands of Jews were mistreated and beaten. Heydrich reported thirty-six dead. Two hundred and fifty synagogues were burned to the ground and twenty thousand Jews were arrested. Damages amounted to several hundred million marks. This attack was followed by an order excluding Jews from all business enterprises. In addition to this they were forced to pay a billion marks, later one and a quarter billion, to the Reich to cover the damages and " to make atonement." For thousands of Jewish families this meant economic ruin and the loss of a means of livelihood. In January of 1939, Hitler commissioned Heydrich to solve the Jewish " problem " by emigration or evacuation, and he reiterated his threat that in the event of war it would be finally solved by their extermination. Nevertheless, by the outbreak of hostilities on September 1, 1939 — the attack against Poland — there were still 375,000 Jews in Germany. Only a quarter of the original five-hundred thousand had managed to escape. Forbidden to hold any position, or even to appear in public, they were confined to a " ghetto without walls." Forced labor was imposed upon the Jews of Poland as early as October, 1939, and this policy was introduced in Germany itself two years later. At the conclusion of the Polish campaign, mass deportations of Jews from Austria and Bohemia were carried out. Huge ghettos were established in Lodz and Warsaw in which Polish and later other European Jews were confined. With the conquest of other European countries the Jews were harassed and driven from one land to another.

The last phase of Jewish persecution began with the invasion of Russia. Four special commands of the SS and of the police were formed, each from five hundred to one thousand men strong, which were detailed to comb the vast area from the Baltic Sea to the Black Sea with orders to exterminate Jews, gypsies, and political enemies in the conquered territories. These SS groups " liquidated " an estimated million men by mass executions. There was no letup in the number of blood baths and massacres until the Russian army drove the invaders back into their own country. In the fall of 1941, the first series of deportations of Jews from Germany itself to ghettos and concentration camps in the East began. Men, women, and children were herded like cattle into boxcars without heat, without food, and without room to sit down — with the result that thousands perished en route. By the end of May, Germany was declared to be " free of Jews," though this was not entirely true to the facts. Likewise in the fall of 1941 the first gas chambers were set up in Ausschwitz, a name that became the terrible symbol for mass murder. Another was built in Chelmno near Posnania. Thither were shipped Jews from Belgium, France, Holland, Norway, Hungary, the Baltic countries, and even from Italy. It has been estimated that a million Jews perished in Ausschwitz alone. But Ausschwitz was only one among many such death camps: Chelmno, Belzec, Sobibor, Treblinka, and Maidanek, as well as the concentration camps inside Germany: Sachsenhausen, Belsen, Oranienburg, Dachau, Buchenwald, Theresienstadt, Flossenbürg, and Mauthausen. Here large masses succumbed from outright execution, malnutrition, disease, and suicide. A conservative estimate of the total number of the Jews who were murdered is between 4,194,200 and 4,851,200. The Anglo-American Committee of April, 1946, put the figure at 5,721,500.[5] These figures stagger the human imagination, especially when one reflects upon the enormity of human pain and suffering, fear and despair, that lie concealed beneath these bare statistics. Words fail when we try to describe the indescribable misery of Israel. " When the allied troops entered Germany and discovered the concentration camps with their instruments of torture, crematoriums, with their thousands of skeletons and unburied corpses, and with their still surviving but emaciated prisoners, a cry of horror and revulsion went through the whole civilized world. Thanks to the measureless crimes of the National Socialist regime the German name was disgraced and despised as no other nation has ever been." [6]

As we observed in our discussion of the National Socialist ideology, it was inevitable that an anti-Semitic regime would also vent its wrath upon the Church that was built upon Jewish prophets and apostles and upon the chief cornerstone, Jesus the Christ of Israel. But we should observe an important difference between the persecution of Jews and Christians. Christians were persecuted because of their *confession* of the Jew Jesus Christ, whereas Jews were persecuted simply because they were born Jews or part Jew. They were persecuted indiscriminately, regardless of whether they were good or bad Jews, Orthodox or Reformed, Christian or atheistic Jews. It is a mistake to assert that they were persecuted because of the Judaistic religion. Of course, so-called " moral " charges were laid to the Jews as a race. But even granting that these charges were true in the case of some Jews or even of the majority, this would not account for the blind hatred against *all* Jews. The Jews suffered because of their very existence as Jews. " He was oppressed, and he was afflicted, yet he opened not his mouth; like a lamb that is led to the slaughter, and like a sheep that before its shearers is dumb, so he opened not his mouth." (Isa. 53:7.) This unreasoning and demonic hatred of the Jews and their consequent suffering can have ultimately only a theological explanation, namely, that as the chosen people of God they are the sign of *the* Suffering Servant, of Jesus Christ who endured the hatred of all men and the wrath of God *against* all the ungodliness and unrighteousness of men *for* all men — Jews and Gentiles. Christians in all European lands suffered immeasurably less than their Jewish brethren. The Church does well to be very humble when it speaks about its tribulation, for it was insignificant in comparison with Israel's. Moreover, the Church has reason to be ashamed that it was not counted worthy to suffer more, especially since — with noble exceptions — it failed to identify itself with its Jewish brethren and did not register an unequivocal protest against all forms of anti-Semitism.

As already indicated, the Church Struggle was a struggle waged against the background of National Socialist theory and practice. To that background belongs also the story of the National Socialist attempt to subjugate Christianity to its own purposes. Subsequent chapters will afford an account of the relations between the Hitler Government and the Evangelical Church. A similar account could be given of the role played by the Roman Catholic Church, but it does not fall within the scope of the present work. In these pages we are concerned with a Church struggling within itself for the recovery of the true faith in its witness to the nation. In its altercations with Hitler's regime the Roman Church was always in a better tactical position. It had the advantage of an authoritarian institutionalism and well-established dogmas. Accordingly, the struggles of the two communions took on a different character. Rome fought to preserve its ecclesiastical organization and to defend its venerated traditions and teachings, whereas the Protestants struggled to regain their faith. But what is important for us here is to understand that Hitler did strive to bend the Christian Churches to his will. He had silenced the political parties, trade-unions, press, radio, schools, and universities. Would he succeed in subduing the Churches too? The broad outlines of that story should now be told without anticipating the details of the struggle of the German Evangelical Church itself.

At first Hitler set out to deceive Church people as to the real goals and intentions of his Party. In *Mein Kampf* he stressed that the Party would be neutral with respect to the confessional or denominational differences. A confessional schism in Germany, he warned, would only serve the interests of international Judaism. He patronizingly referred to Roman Catholicism and Protestantism as equally valuable supports for the continuance and well-being of the nation. He maintained that Church and State should be strictly separated, and he condemned political parties that owed allegiance to any particular denomination, such as the Catholic Center Party. According to Hitler, the Church was to concern itself with the life after death, whereas the State had to do with the temporal affairs of men. The Party program guaranteed the freedom of all religious denominations but with the significant qualification: " so far as they do not endanger the existence of the State or do not offend the moral and ethical conscience of the Germanic race." The notion of race was thus set above and against Christianity — certainly for a Christianity which acknowledged that in Christ there is no difference between Jew and Gentile and that both may be baptized. Unfortunately at the beginning few churchmen detected the warning signal. Few realized that an anti-Semitic racialism was utterly irreconcilable with Christianity. They were blinded by Hitler's repeated assurances that he stood for " positive Christianity " against " godless Bolshevism." It is to the lasting credit of Prof. Hermann Sasse, of the University of Erlangen, that he was the first to declare that because of this one plank in the Party's program the Church could in no way approve of Nazism. It had to be categorically repudiated. The fact that Sasse eventually broke with the Confessing Church in the interest of a narrow Lutheran confessionalism, and thereby greatly weakened the Church's opposition to National Socialism, must not obscure the prophetic role he played at the outset.

After Hitler had seized power, he continued to throw dust in the eyes of the Christian population. He declared that " the National Socialist government sees in the two Christian Confessions the most important factors in the preservation of our national life. . . . They are the unshakable foundations of the moral and spiritual life of our peoples." At the same time he was privately telling his intimate associates that the two Churches no longer had a future; that he would destroy Christianity in Germany, root and branch, and that for the German people everything depends upon whether it has the Jewish Christian faith with its weak morality of compassion or a strong heroic faith in God, in nature, in one's own people, in one's own destiny, and in one's own blood. " One is either a Christian or a German. One cannot be both." [7]

It ought to have been obvious from the start that when Hitler proclaimed his ideology as a political *faith* with totalitarian claims upon the whole life of man, and demanded for himself absolute obedience, National Socialism and Christianity were mutually exclusive. It was a clear case of " either-or." National Socialism was in fact a religion that sought to replace Christianity by rendering it superfluous.

Under the pretext of removing the influence of denominationalism and sectarianism from public life, Hitler had two goals in mind: the elimination of political Catholicism by an agreement with the Vatican, and the establishment of a National German Evangelical Church. The first of these objectives was quickly achieved with the signing of a concordat between the Holy See and the German Reich on July 20, 1933.[8] The Holy See agreed to " prescribe regulations that will prohibit clergymen and members of conventional orders from membership in political parties and from working on their behalf." In return for this concession the State promised to guarantee the rights and privileges of the Church. The advantages that Hitler saw in the Concordat, revealed in the minutes of a meeting of the Reich Government,[9] were: the refutation of the charge that National Socialism is unchristian and opposed to the Church; the unqualified recognition of the new regime by the Vatican; and the destruction of Christian trade-unionism and the Center Party. Hitler, of course, had no intention of keeping his part of the bargain any longer than it served the purpose of consolidating his power.

The clash between the State and the Evangelical Church began with Hitler's espousal of the " German Christian " party within the Evangelical Church. Stated briefly, the " German Christians " were the group that sought to combine Christianity with the tenets of National Socialism. State interference in the controversy that arose within the Church took the form of the appointment of commissars for the Evangelical Church (Dr. Jäger on June 24, 1933, in Prussia), of the appointment by Hitler of his confidant, Ludwig Müller, as Reich bishop, September 27, 1933, and of " German Christian " bishops for various territorial Churches on October 5. New elections of Church officers were forced through, Church finances were placed under State control, and Church committees were named by the Government to administer Church affairs. State interference culminated in the formation by Hitler of a Reich Ministry for Church Affairs in 1935 with far-reaching supervisory powers. Usually the edicts issued by Reich Minister Kerrl were enforced by the Gestapo. While the Church was engaged in withstanding the State's encroachment upon its offices and government, it also had to combat the neopaganism of the " German Faith Movement " which the Government, at first secretly and later openly, espoused, as well as the nationalist and racial ideology of the Party propounded by men like Alfred Rosenberg. Thus when the Confessional Synod of the Old Prussian Union passed a resolution March 5, 1935, that expressly condemned a " national, racial Weltanschauung " with its deification of an eternal Germany, and which was read the following Sunday from all pulpits, over seven hundred ministers were arrested and taken into custody.

The Church Struggle reached its peak in 1937 when ministers and prominent Church laymen were imprisoned or placed in concentration camps. Others were fined, relieved of their passports, or forbidden to preach. Congregations were forbidden to take up collections, theological schools and seminaries were closed, and the publication of innumerable religious books and Church periodicals was stopped. On July 1, 1937, Pastor Martin Niemöller, the organizer of the Pastors' Emergency League and the outstanding leader of the Confessing Church, was arrested. Though subsequently acquitted by a court, he was kept in a concentration camp until the end of the war as Hitler's personal prisoner, in spite of repeated appeals and protests by Church bodies.

The year 1937 also witnessed the height of the conflict between the Roman Catholic Church and the Hitler State. For some time the Nazis had blatantly disregarded the terms of the Concordat. The rights of the Catholic schools were ignored and the work of the religious orders was curtailed. The Catholic youth organizations were at first undermined by the Hitler Youth Movement and in 1936 were banned. The humanitarian work of the Caritas Society was hindered in every way and was also suppressed in the same year. The Nazis could not tolerate any charity that did not enrich the coffers and the prestige of the Party! By a decree of Dr. Ley, Reich leader of the German Workers' Front, July, 1936, all Catholic workers' organizations were outlawed. The Church press was first hampered and then shut down. Many theological books were banned, as well as literature aimed at combating the Rosenberg "myth." In spite of many such provocations, the Roman Church was slow to reach an open break with the State.[10] But Cardinal Faulhaber, of Munich, and Graf von Galen, Bishop of Münster, were particularly outspoken in their condemnation of the Government's policies toward the Church schools. Finally, a strong delegation of bishops, consisting of three cardinals — Faulhaber, of Munich; Schulte, of Cologne; and Bertram, of Breslau — and Graf von Galen, Bishop of Münster, and Graf von Preysing, Bishop of Berlin, interviewed the pope himself and persuaded him that Bolshevism was not the only enemy. At last the pope broke his silence and issued the encyclical "*Mit brennender Sorge*" (With Burning Anxiety) on March 4, 1937. It constituted an outright break with Nazism. It outlined the innumerable infractions of the Concordat and charged the Hitler Government with attempting to exterminate Christianity. It condemned the deification of race, nation, and State as unchristian and protested the obstacles placed in the way of the Church's work.[11] The State's answer to this criticism was to do all that it could to discredit the Church in the eyes of the public. This was done by hundreds of trumped-up charges against religious orders of smuggling currency out of the country. Wide publicity was given to a long series of trials for alleged violations of currency regulations. This was followed by "immorality trials" of priests and monks, which were played up in the daily press so as to appeal to the basest instincts of the populace. Newspaper headlines conveyed the impression that all priests were immoral and good Germans would have nothing to do with them. Goebbels referred to the Catholic Church as a "moral morass." Then a series of "treason trials" was staged. The upshot was that hundreds of clergymen found their way into concentration camps, and innumerable monasteries and Catholic schools were closed as well as many of the theological *Hochschulen* and faculties.

The persecution of Christianity abated somewhat with the outbreak of war. Hitler was intent upon closing his ranks in an all-out war effort. But plans were being laid to root out Christianity once the war was victoriously concluded. A circular letter written in 1942 by Martin Bormann, one of the most fanatical of the Nazi leaders, marked "strictly confidential," reveals the intention of the Party to silence the Churches completely.[12] Organized resistance by both Protestant and Catholic Churches was virtually impossible during the war, since many of the clergy were compelled to go into the armed forces. Nevertheless, leaders like the Lutheran Bishop Wurm and the Catholic Bishop Graf von Galen were outspoken in their condemnation of Hitler's frightful brutality and inhumanity. Both men condemned the mass murders of the so-called "worthless lives" of the physically and mentally ill, the mass executions in occupied territories, and the extermination of the Jews. The struggle for the faith of the Church and for the Church's ecclesiastical and religious rights became more and more a struggle for bare human rights and political justice. It was not surprising, therefore, to find Roman Catholic and Protestant clergymen among the leaders of the Resistance Movement that culminated in the attempt to assassinate Hitler on July 20, 1944, and to overthrow his government.

Even if it is all too tragically true that the Church of Jesus Christ — Protestant and Catholic — was unable to prevent the rise of National Socialism, and if the Church's primary concern during the twelve years of Nazi rule was for its own spiritual and physical existence rather than a concern for a just State, and even if it was unable to prevent the dreadful crimes committed by National Socialist Germany, the fact remains that the Church was the one group within the nation which Hitler failed to quell. Only the Church offered to Hitler the resistance of a large section of the population. Let us hear the testimony of two very different witnesses. Prof. Albert Einstein, the Jewish physicist and discoverer of the theory of relativity, wrote in exile:

> Being a lover of freedom, when the [Nazi] revolution came, I looked to the universities to defend it, knowing that they had always boasted of their devotion to the cause of truth; but no, the universities were immediately silenced. Then I looked to the great editors of the newspapers, whose flaming editorials in days gone by had proclaimed their love of freedom; but they, like the universities, were silenced in a few short weeks. . . .
>
> Only the Church stood squarely across the path of Hitler's campaign for suppressing the truth. I never had any special interest in the Church before, but now I feel a great affection and admiration for it because the Church alone has had the courage and persistence to stand for intellectual and moral freedom. I am forced to confess that what I once despised I now praise unreservedly.[13]

Karl Barth, writing in June, 1945, declared:

> In 1933 and the years immediately following — at the time the National Socialists " seized power " — there was no struggle of the German universities and schools, of the German legal profession, of German business, of the German theater and German art in general, of the German Army, or of the German trade-unions. Many individuals, it is true, went down to an honorable defeat. But in no time at all, those large groups and institutions were subdued and made to conform. On the other

hand, from the very first months on there was a German
Church struggle. Even it was not a total resistance against
totalitarian National Socialism. It restricted itself to repelling
the encroachment of National Socialism. It confined itself to
the Church's Confession, to the Church service, and to Church
order as such. It was only a partial resistance. And for this it
has been properly and improperly reproached: properly — in so
far as a strong Christian Church, that is, a Church sure of its
own cause in the face of National Socialism should not have
remained on the defensive and should not have fought on its
own narrow front alone; improperly — in so far as on this admittedly all too narrow front a serious battle was waged, at
least in part and not without some success. At any rate, the substance of the Church was rescued and with a better understanding of it than it had had before. If at least as much had been
done in other areas as was done at that time in the Church,
National Socialism would have had a hard time of it in Germany right from the start. In proportion to its task, the Church
has sufficient reason to be ashamed that it did not do more; yet
in comparison with those other groups and institutions it has
no reason to be ashamed; it accomplished far more than all
the rest.[14]

In discussing the ideology of National Socialism, we have already
alluded to the fact that the conception of racial superiority was basic
to the imperialistic and militaristic policies of the Nazi Government.
The conquest of more *Lebensraum* was the objective of its foreign
policy. Hitler concerned himself with this question in the last chapter
of his book, *Mein Kampf.* He made no secret of the fact that in his
opinion such expansion is possible only through a bloody war. A man
who had no respect whatever for the rights of Jews, Christians, and
liberals within his own country was certainly not going to be concerned for the rights of other nations. But as Walther Hofer has
pointed out,[15] it was never clear exactly *what* or *how much Lebensraum* Hitler believed was necessary for his *Herrenrasse.* The indefi-
niteness of his imperialism doubtless appealed to his fanatical followers who longed to see the Swastika raised in far-off lands. On the
other hand, it served to deceive the other great powers as to Hitler's
real and far-reaching ambitions. In *Mein Kampf,* Hitler referred to
Russia and France as Germany's two main enemies: Russia, because

it was the champion of Bolshevism; France, because it had always
been Germany's sworn enemy. He thus played upon the two fears
that have been latent in the consciousness of the German people. Although he was confident that with a rearmed Germany he would
have no difficulty in vanquishing these two ancient foes, he was not
averse to acquiring allies. In *Mein Kampf,* he looked upon England
and Italy as likely partners. Naturally Russia and France, as well as
all those countries with German minorities within their borders, had
reason to be alarmed when Hitler assumed power in January, 1933.
In order to calm their fears and to conceal his ultimate objectives,
Hitler did a rightabout-face after he had gained power. In his public
utterances he reiterated that the peace of the world is the primary
concern of National Socialism. He repudiated imperialism in any
form and any interference in the internal affairs of any nation. He
declared that all nations should enjoy equal legal status in the community of nations, and that international disputes, including revision
of the Treaty of Versailles, should be settled by peaceful negotiations
and without resort to arms. By means of this propaganda line Hitler
succeeded in gaining valuable time in which to rearm Germany for
war. Millions of people inside and outside Germany believed his
protestations of peaceful intentions. Indeed, even to this day there
are those who claim that Hitler at first acted in a sensible and statesmanlike fashion and then later — perhaps after his meeting with
Chamberlain in Munich — he lost all sense of proportion and set his
heart upon world conquest. Secret government papers, dating from
1933 and released to the public since 1945, prove conclusively that in
reality Hitler never swerved from his original purposes: the creation
of *Lebensraum* for a German *Herrenrasse* at the expense of other nations. Contributing to the astounding success of Hitler's foreign policy during this period was the disunity of the other powers, American isolationism, mistrust between England and Russia, the wave of
pacifism and disarmament feeling that gripped the democracies, and
the breakdown of the system established at Versailles and of the authority of the League of Nations. The League had suffered a severe
blow when it failed to take measures against Japan after its invasion
of Manchuria in 1931 and again when Mussolini's Italy had attacked
Ethiopia. Indeed, the Japanese conquests in Asia, the Italian invasion,
and the Spanish civil war were " opening skirmishes " in the tremen-

dous world-wide conflict that began in 1939. All these warlike actions followed a logical progression of, first, a disregard for treaty obligations, and later, open violation of existing pacts. In each case, the aggression was unopposed by military action on the part of the principal powers.[16]

Under the pretext of contending for Germany's position of equality among the nations, Hitler insisted upon Germany's moral right to have an army with which to defend itself. He demanded that the military (not the territorial) clauses of the Versailles Treaty be revised. When the Allies hesitated to take action, Germany withdrew from the League of Nations and from the Disarmament Conference. That was in October, 1933. About this time Germany secretly began to rearm. No doubt the British secret service was aware of it, but the Government seemed to be indifferent. In order to pacify an uneasy Poland, Hitler made a friendship pact with that country in January, 1934. Walther Hofer regards this pact as the smartest move in Hitler's diplomacy.[17] It gave the appearance of seeking peaceful relations with neighboring states, quieted a potentially dangerous enemy, made a serious breach in France's eastern European alliances, and protected Hitler's northern (Polish) flank as he later made his moves toward the southeast. When this mock friendship with Poland no longer served his purposes, it quickly turned into a fierce enmity that became the immediate cause of the outbreak of World War II.

In March, 1935, Germany reintroduced universal military service and a year later occupied the demilitarized Rhineland. Europe stood on the brink of war. France was prepared to do battle, but when England withheld support, France was unwilling to act alone.[18] Having acquired military freedom of action, Hitler turned his attention to securing allies among the nations alienated from the League of Nations: Italy, Franco Spain, and Japan. Thus was created the " Berlin-Rome-Tokyo Axis." The basis of their agreement was of course a common opposition to the Communist International and its interference in the internal politics of nations.

It was toward the end of 1937 that Hitler felt strong enough to revert to the foreign policy outlined in his book, namely, the gathering of all Germans into one great Reich. The first victims to fall were Austria and Czechoslovakia. On March 12, 1938, Hitler's troops marched into Austria to be greeted, not with bullets, but with bou-

quets of flowers from the populace. This success spurred Hitler on.
Next he demanded that the German Sudetenland be separated from
Czechoslovakia on the moral grounds that a people or race should
have the right of self-determination. Czechoslovakia was a new nation carved out of Austria-Hungary by the Treaty of Versailles, and
its independence was guaranteed by pacts with France, and indirectly
by Britain. The issue was whether the postwar system of collective
security was to be maintained or whether Hitler's claim to racial
solidarity was to be appeased. The policy of " appeasement " is associated with the name of Neville Chamberlain, who became Britain's
prime minister in 1937. In a speech delivered September 26, 1938,
Hitler issued a virtual ultimatum to President Beneš, of Czechoslovakia: either return of the Sudetenland or war. At the same time he
gave a solemn assurance that " if this problem were solved, there
would be no more territorial problems for Germany in Europe. . . .
We don't want any Czechs! " In a sudden dramatic move Chamberlain communicated with Hitler in Berchtesgaden and Godesberg,
and then flew to Munich to meet with Hitler, Mussolini, and Premier
Daladier, of France. By an agreement signed on September 9, 1938,
the Sudetenland, with its strong defenses and the Skoda war industries, was sacrificed, and Chamberlain returned home with a promise
from Hitler of " peace in our time." While most Churches throughout the world held special thanksgiving services for peace, Karl Barth
had written his famous letter to Professor Hromádka in Prague in
which he stated: " Every Czech soldier who then fights and suffers
will be doing it also for us, and — I say it today without reserve —
he will also be doing it for the Church of Jesus Christ." [19] Barth was
among the few who perceived the truly demonic nature of Hitlerism
and who knew that only war would satisfy his cruel appetite. For
Hitler, the Munich Pact was just a scrap of paper. The ink was
scarcely dry when three weeks later he was issuing secret orders for
the " settlement of the rest of Czechoslovakia." [20] And just six months
later, following a sudden revolt of Slovakia, Czech President Hácha
was summoned to Berlin to confer with Hitler. On March 15, 1939,
Hácha issued a statement making Czechoslovakia a " protectorate "
of Germany.

Even though Hitler excused the annexation of Bohemia on the
ground that it had belonged to Germany's *Lebensraum* for a thou-

sand years, the argument no longer deceived the Western allies. The flagrant violation of the Munich Pact made an indelible impression on them, all the more so since Hitler himself had signed it. Britain and France now set about rearming as fast as possible. Britain gave Poland and Romania, and later Greece, assurances that in the event of attack it would come to their assistance, and France also subscribed to these guarantees. Meanwhile, Hitler was demanding of Poland the return of the free city of Danzig to Germany in return for a twenty-five-year nonaggression pact. The Poles, remembering Hitler's hollow promises to Czechoslovakia and strengthened by the assurances of Britain and France, refused to comply. In April of 1939, Britain and France entered into negotiations with their erstwhile Communist enemy Russia — for so Russia was regarded then as today by the capitalistic Western democracies — with a view to forming a defensive alliance against Germany. Russia was reluctant to enter into such an alliance, being skeptical of the West's desire and will to fight in view of the weakness and vacillation the West had shown in the League of Nations and at Munich. Then on August 23 came the announcement that shocked the world — a German-Soviet nonaggression pact. The archenemies — Bolshevism and National Socialism — had concluded a friendship treaty! How was such a development possible? The Western powers had demanded that Stalin guarantee the independence of the eastern States threatened by Hitler, that is, Poland and Romania. But Hitler offered to share spheres of interest with Russia. In accordance with secret clauses of their nonaggression pact the Baltic countries were assigned to Russia, Poland was divided by the Narew-Weichsel-San river line, and Bessarabia was denoted a Soviet sphere of influence. Thus in order to crush Poland and to secure a free hand for later action in the direction of the West, Hitler, who had posed as the great opponent of Bolshevism, surrendered most of Eastern Europe to his enemy. Stalin, on the other hand, who entertained no illusions about Hitler, was reasonably satisfied as he had extended his defensive frontiers against the one enemy that could menace him, Germany. Russia annexed Latvia, Estonia, and Lithuania (which had at one time belonged to Russia), and in the winter of 1939 conquered Finland against heroic resistance. Thus Russia secured its western flank and had an outlet to the North Sea.

The demarcation line in Poland at the Narew-Weichsel-San river line implied the acknowledgment of the famous " Curzon Line " which in 1919 was established as the boundary between Poland and Russia, but which was sharply rejected by the Poles. The agreement between Hitler and Stalin was the basis for the later demands of Stalin on Roosevelt and Churchill. Stalin insisted upon the " Curzon Line " in 1945 just as he had done with Hitler in 1939. Since the Western powers after the war wanted to make Poland a strong state again, Churchill proposed to shift Poland toward the West, at the expense of Germany, and this led to the Oder-Neisse line.

No sooner had the Russian-German nonaggression pact been signed than the British Government notified Hitler that it would honor under all circumstances the guarantees it had given Poland. But Hitler wanted war and was not to be dissuaded. Actually he wanted to start the attack on August 26, and between that date and the early-morning hours of September 1, when the German soldiers invaded Poland, there was feverish diplomatic activity, which we will not go into. For weeks prior to the outbreak of hostilities the German press and radio were filled with inflammatory propaganda against Poland. On the evening of August 31, members of the SS, dressed in Polish uniforms, made a mock attack upon the radio station at Gleiwitz. This was the " moral " justification for " repelling " the Poles. With this act of gangsterism the Second World War began. Britain and France demanded that Germany withdraw its troops from Poland. When this was not done, they declared war on Germany on September 3. It is reported that when the declaration of war was brought to Hitler he sat as if turned to stone and stared into space. And Göring said, " If we lose this war, may heaven be merciful to us."

It is not our task to describe the campaigns of this bloodiest and most vicious of wars in the history of mankind. One has only to recall the unprovoked and unannounced invasions of neutral Denmark and Norway, the utterly callous attacks upon the friendly countries of Holland and Belgium, the brutal air bombardment that leveled much of Rotterdam to the ground, the swift crushing of France, the evacuation of Dunkirk by the British forces, the Battle of Britain of 1940 in which the Germans indulged in the wholesale wanton destruction of British cities — Coventry, Southampton, Sheffield, Bristol, Birmingham, Liverpool, and London — killing 23,081 civilians and wounding 32,296, yet failing to break the British will to fight on under the stirring leadership of Winston Churchill. Then came the campaigns in North Africa, the Balkans, Crete, and the Near East, the Russian campaigns, the Japanese attack upon Pearl Harbor on December 7, 1941, the battles waged in the Pacific, the invasion of France on June 6, 1944, Germany's unconditional surrender on May 7, 1945, followed by that of Japan on August 15.

Statistics concerning World War II supplied by the 1955 edition of *The Encyclopedia Americana* stagger the imagination. Of the 14,000,-000 men mobilized by the United States, over 1,000,000 casualties were suffered, including 433,000 dead or missing. The military force of the British Commonwealth numbered 12,000,000; and casualties mounted to 1,200,000. Germany mustered 17,000,000 (13,000,000 before September, 1944), many of whom were boys fifteen and sixteen years old. Of these, 2,500,000 were killed and 1,500,000 listed as missing. (Hofer put the figure of enlisted men killed at 3,500,000.) It has been estimated that Japan's casualties numbered another 1,500,000. But by far the greatest losses were sustained by Russia. Although no definite figures have ever been released, it is estimated that Russia mobilized 22,000,000 men. Russia's dead is put at 15,000,000, but this includes a large number of citizens, victims of persecution and deportation. The figures given above do not include civilian losses through air raids and sinking of merchant and fishing ships. In Germany 500,000 were killed as the result of tons of explosives dropped on its cities. Hiroshima alone suffered 306,545 casualties, with 78,150 dead from the A-bomb dropped on that city on August 5, 1945. Add to that the devastation wrought by an A-bomb on Nagasaki four days later and by other air raids on Japan and the total of Japan's civilian dead numbered 360,000. Needless to say, casualty lists do not include the millions of ill-clad, undernourished, and homeless refugees. They do not include the enormous damage done to homes, churches, schools, and hospitals. Nor do they include the demoralizing and dehumanizing effect of the war not only upon all who took part in it but upon the children born and reared during years of terror and neglect.

The suicidal end of National Socialism was typical of a nihilistic movement. When at Casablanca in January, 1943, Churchill and

Roosevelt agreed to a policy demanding Germany's unconditional surrender, it suited Hitler perfectly. For he never had any intention of surrendering. The more hopeless and senseless the war became for Germany, the more stubborn became Hitler's will to continue the struggle even if it meant the annihilation of the nation. He believed that a Germany which could not be victorious deserved to be extinguished, not by the might of the enemy, but by the will of its own commander-in-chief and dictator. It became obvious that Hitler really had no concern for the German people. When the Allied armies were at the German borders, he ordered the formation of a sort of "national guard" (*Volkssturm*) composed of small boys and old men. Lest the enemy derive any advantage from them, he ordered the destruction of all military, transportation, and communication establishments, all industries and supply centers inside Germany. When Albert Speer, then Minister for Armaments and Munitions, protested in a memorandum that Germany's defeat was inevitable, that a policy of destroying Germany's remaining resources could not affect the final outcome, and that it was the duty of Germany's rulers to ensure that the people would have some means of reconstruction after the war, Hitler replied that " if the war is lost, the nation will also perish." Toward the end, Hitler seemed possessed by a fiendish will to self-destruction and to dragging the whole nation down with him.

As the fighting drew to a close, Hitler rarely left the Chancellery building in Berlin, a vast pile of stone now surrounded by the ruins of a bombed city. During the last month, he lived almost entirely in a cement air-raid shelter deep beneath the Chancellery. From there he issued his senseless orders and, strange as it may seem, still managed to find men to carry them out — men like Goebbels, Göring, Himmler, Bormann, and Ribbentrop, who clung to the desperate hope that *der Führer* by some stroke of magic would discover a way out. But there was no way out. On April 22 the Russians had broken through the outer defenses of Berlin, and the city itself was a holocaust. The Nazi inner circle pleaded with Hitler to escape to the "National Redoubt" at Berchtesgaden. Hitler, however, had resolved to remain in the bunker until the end. With his mistress, Eva Braun, to whom he was married in the early hours of April 29, he joined in a suicide pact. On the afternoon of the next day he shot himself through the mouth, and Eva Braun swallowed poison.

Shortly before he took his life he dictated his will and political testament. As Alan Bullock observes, in his biography of Hitler: " From first to last there is not a word of regret, nor a suggestion of remorse. The fault is that of others, above all, that of the Jews. . . . Word for word, Hitler's final address to the German nation could be taken from almost any of his early speeches of the 1920's or from the pages of *Mein Kampf*." [21] The last paragraph of this document is a final testimony that the essence of National Socialism was its hatred of God's chosen people. " Above all, I charge the leaders of the nation and those under them to scrupulous observance of the laws of race and to merciless opposition to the universal poisoner of all peoples, international Jewry." The testament was witnessed by Goebbels and Bormann. Following Hitler's explicit instructions concerning the disposal of the bodies, they were carried into the garden of the Chancellery and burned.[22]

The end of Hitler's accomplice in tyranny, Benito Mussolini, was just as inglorious and just as appalling, news of which was received by Hitler the night before he blew his brains out. Attempting to flee to Switzerland in disguise after the German collapse, Mussolini and his last mistress, Clara Petacci, were captured by Partisans near Como and after a summary court-martial were shot on April 28, 1945. Their bodies, brought to Milan, were strung up half naked in the public square and then buried in a pauper's grave.

Thus was the curtain rung down upon a segment of human history unparalleled for evil and wanton destructiveness. Yet this history was not only the sinister background for the history of the Church of Jesus Christ; it was the stage, the external presupposition of that history. World history from 1933 to 1945 occurred for the sake of the Church and its witness and ultimately for the glory of God. As God raised up Pharaoh for the purpose of showing His power in Him and proclaiming His name in all the earth (Rom. 9:17), so God raised up Hitler for the sake of the Church's proclamation of the name of Christ. Only from the standpoint of the inner history of the Church do the terrible events of 1933–1945 make sense. Only in the light of the history of Christ with His people is this " sinister " history seen within the good, merciful, and sovereign will of God.

II

Between the Times: 1917–1933

KARL KUPISCH has rightly observed that from the standpoint of world history the year 1917 was epoch-making.[1] It was the year in which the United States of America entered World War I, and Lenin led the Bolshevist Revolution in Russia. The war that was " to end all wars " was instead the initial bloody phase of a series of convulsions that ended in the catastrophe of World War II. This second bloodletting resulted in turn in the world's being divided by an " iron curtain " dropped right down in the middle of Germany between East and West, between Russia and America. But 1917 was also important because it was roughly the date at which a new theological period was being ushered in, a period that broke radically with the nineteenth century and culminated in the Declaration of the Synod of Barmen. The period itself, however, was theologically (as well as politically) " between the times " — between the modern liberal and orthodox Protestantism and the new direction indicated by Barmen.

Although World War I left, as we shall presently see, an indelible impression upon the sensitive theological souls of that generation, it had little or no effect upon the Church as a whole. The so-called " Christian " nations that engaged in the war all identified God with their own cause and prayed to him for victory. The union of Christianity, nationalism, and militarism was taken for granted. Patriotic sentiments were equated with Christian truth. Flags and patriotic songs were introduced into church services with no qualms of conscience. In Germany the defeat of 1918 did nothing to change this. On the contrary, it was the start of a new nationalism within the Church, which eventually blossomed forth in the movement of the

" German Christians." Most ministers took the position that a churchman should be conservative in political affairs. Secretly they rejected democracy. In the minds of the people the old union of " throne and altar " was replaced by a union of " nation and altar." Karl Kupisch is doubtless correct when he declares that " these nationalistic, religious tendencies did more to handicap the genuine renewal of the Church than the old liberalism had ever been able to do . . . especially when appeals were made to a heroic conception of Luther." [2]

In the midst of this nationalistic enthusiasm, a book appeared that created something of a sensation. Otto Dibelius, who was already a prominent Church leader, published his book, *Peace on Earth*. It was the first time in the history of the Evangelical Church that a leading churchman took a stand on the question of the relation of Christianity to military service. To the question of whether war is according to the will of God, he replied with an unconditional No. On the other hand, he refrained from preaching absolute pacifism. He spoke of a " pacifism of a higher order," a pacifism of " faith and moral force." Even if the Church itself will never advocate that Christians should refuse to render military service, it will " give Christian pacifists its blessing even when it does not approve of their stand."

Sometime later — November, 1928 — a sober and restrained lecture on the subject " The Church and the Reconciliation of the Nations," delivered by Günther Dehn to a Magdeburg congregation, provoked a storm of protests and touched off what later became known as the " Dehn Case." Ernst Bizer speaks of the Dehn Case as " a prelude to the struggle of the Confessing Church in the Third Reich." [3] Dehn, a minister in Berlin, who for a time had been a member of the Social Democratic Party and had advanced from religious socialism to the Dialectical Theology in his theological development, attempted to set forth the Biblical teaching about war. Like Dibelius, Dehn also asserted that war is contrary to " God's gracious will for life." " At best, war is a stern necessity, an act of self-defense. . . . As an act of self-defense . . . it must be admitted that even for Christians there is the possibility of engaging, not in a holy or perhaps not even in a just war, but in a necessary war in defense of life given by God." Dehn declared that the decision to take part in even a " necessary war " is enormously difficult, and there always remains the chance that one has made a wrong decision. Because there is the possibility of a necessary war, Dehn argued against unconditional pacifism. But he advised Christians to co-operate with all friends of peace to abolish war. War should never be glorified or romanticized. Moreover, since persons killed in war were also intent upon killing, there is a world of difference between the martyr-death of Christians and the sacrifice of those killed in war. For this reason the honoring of the fallen should be left to the " civil community," and war memorials should not be placed in churches. Dehn was immediately accused of calling the fallen war heroes " murderers." The accusation was shown to be false, but the Brandenburg Consistory attached greater weight to the testimony of two young girls than to Dehn. He was rebuked for " having used language that led to regrettable misunderstandings." It was his duty " to weigh his words carefully "; instead, he employed a " harshness that cannot be condoned in a minister at such a time." The Consistory never bothered to examine the theological content of Dehn's lecture.

Unfortunately, the affair did not end there. When, toward the end of December of 1930, Dehn received a call to be Professor of Practical Theology at Heidelberg, the Magdeburg incidents were revived by an outsider, and the Heidelberg Theological Faculty withdrew the call. Only Martin Dibelius opposed the opportunism of the faculty. When Dehn was then called to Halle by the Prussian Minister of Culture, the National Socialist students seized the opportunity to make it a test of their strength. They threatened to leave Halle en masse for Jena or Leipzig. The situation deteriorated when certain National Socialist professors of theology took a public stand against Dehn. Dehn was subjected to indignities in the classrooms and was forbidden to preach in the chapel. At the height of the controversy the professors Karl Barth, K. L. Schmidt, Martin Dibelius, Otto Piper (now at Princeton Seminary), and Georg Wünsch declared that they stood solidly behind Dehn.[4] In an article that appeared in the *Frankfurter Zeitung* on February 15, 1932, Barth observed that Dehn was only the accidental and easy victim of a fundamental attack upon the Dialectical Theology which repudiated mixing nationalistic tendencies with concern for evangelical preaching. He urged that if passions have to be involved in the debate, let it be carried on at an academic level of theological opinions. To Otto Piper's question, "Why does the Church keep silent?" Otto Dibelius, then General Superintendent, replied that he saw in the whole thing "only a problem of academic pedagogy" that was not a concern of the Church. Needless to say, Dehn was among the first of the professors to be discharged after Hitler came to power. Later he suffered imprisonment and banishment to the upper country of Württemberg. From there he was called to the Chair of Practical Theology in Bonn in 1946.

For a Church that was so consciously bound up with the nation, the defeat of Germany in 1918 was a severe blow. The Church too had suffered defeat. Yet, instead of undertaking a sober rethinking of the Church's prophetic ministry within the State, the Church consoled itself and the nation with the thought: "We have lost the war, but Germany is not lost. We still have the Reich." Instead of questioning the fatal line from Frederick the Great to Bismarck and then to Kaiser Wilhelm, the Church thanked God for its political leaders. Moreover, the Church continued to pursue a reactionary policy toward labor, which it accused of materialism. It frowned upon socialism and thereby alienated large numbers of the working class.

The Church's principal concern at the conclusion of hostilities was for its own legal status in the new political order. The Church feared that through the anticipated separation of Church and State, it would be reduced to a voluntary religious society, a "free church" or sect, deprived of the financial support of the State.[5] Actually its fears on both scores proved to be unfounded. The constitution of the German Reich, promulgated on August 11, 1919, marked the end of the State Church. Article 137 guaranteed to all religious bodies complete freedom of association and equal rights before the law. Every denomination had the right to administer its own affairs and appoint its own officials without the co-operation of the State. But Article 137 also provided that "religious societies which are incorporated are entitled to raise taxes on the basis of the civil tax roll according to the regional civil regulations." This meant that a citizen could enroll voluntarily with the tax authorities as a member of the Roman Catholic Church or Evangelical Church, and his tax would be collected by the State for the Church. Of course, free churches, such as the Methodist and Baptist Churches, were not financed in this way. They were completely independent of State assistance and were supported only by the free-will offerings of their members. This difference between "established" and "free" churches does not, however, contradict the fact that "all citizens enjoy complete liberty of faith and conscience" (Article 135). The constitution guaranteed the unhindered practice of religion. No one was forced to take part in religious exercises or to take a religious oath. In fact, no one was obliged to disclose his religious convictions except for the purpose of taking a census prescribed by law.[6]

Negotiations begun at Church conferences held in Dresden and Stuttgart in 1919 and 1921 respectively resulted in the formation of the German Evangelical Federation of Churches in Wittenberg in 1922. While not restricting the independence of the twenty-eight regional Churches (*Landeskirchen*), it enabled the Churches to act in concert in matters of common interest. These regional Churches were represented at a German Evangelical Church Conference, which was held every three years. The mind of the whole Church was reflected in official pronouncements issued by these conferences, as, for example, the so-called "Social Message" of 1924. It was certainly an advance over the customary conservatism of previous deliverances, but it came about twenty years too late. "Now it was like a sort of ecclesiastical echo of achievements that had been realized without the Church's co-operation."[7] Actually the Church found it difficult to address itself to the social, economic, and political problems of the day. It wanted to be a "peoples' Church," but the weight of tradition prevented it from abandoning its neutrality in social and political matters and its fastidiously correct relations with the government. The burning question of the political responsibility of a Christian in a democracy was never raised in any concrete fashion. The reform of the Church's constitution, therefore, was not accompanied by an inner spiritual reform. Instead, as has so often been the case in Church history, the Church turned its attention to ecclesiastical and liturgical questions. Many regional Churches, whose constitution required that a clergyman be the leader, introduced the office of bishop: Saxony, Hanover, Brunswick, Nassau, and Schleswig-Holstein. The Synod of the Old Prussian Union Church rejected the office of bishop, placing administrative powers in the hands of general superintendents. Friederick Heiler and Oscar Mehl were the leaders of a High Church Movement in Lutheranism that sought to renew the sacramental character of the church service. Karl Bernhard Ritter and Wilhelm Stählin led an earlier school that sought to cultivate the liturgical character of the Church service, but they looked upon it as giving expression to a renewal of the whole of Christian life. Side by side with these movements went an effort to reform hymn-singing by reviving the hymns of the Reformation, by a return to Johann Sebastian Bach, and by opposing the subjectivism of pietism and romanticism. The liturgical movement was largely confined to a relatively small circle of followers who were frequently accused of borrowing from Catholic rites. The movement to reform congregational singing, on the other hand, continued to grow and was most prominent during the Church Struggle. The Confessing Church was a singing Church.

Although World War I had little effect upon the militaristic and nationalistic sentiments within the Church, it did stimulate certain movements that were to challenge the mounting nationalism. Upon the express invitation of President John R. Mott, German delegates attended the international conference of the Student Christian World Federation that was held in Peking in April, 1922. Chief among the German delegates were the theologian Karl Heim and the chairman of the Student Christian Movement, Georg Michaelis, Reich Chancellor for a few months during 1917. When Michaelis spoke candidly about the imputation of war guilt to Germany and expressed the hope that here among Christian brethren there would be a sympathetic understanding of Germany's feelings in the matter, representatives of the Allied nations declared that it was their Christian duty to work for the revision of the Treaty of Versailles. This spirit of good will paved the way for the German Church's active participation in the growth of the ecumenical movement and in the Stockholm and Lausanne conferences. Important is the fact that the ecumenical movement broadened the horizons of the German Church. International relations were established that were to be a source of inspiration and hope both during and following the Church Struggle. Moreover, through ecumenical channels have flowed to Churches in other lands the lessons that the German Church has learned since the end of the First World War.

By far the most important aspect of the period "between the times" was, of course, the theological awakening. Without it the

Synod of Barmen and its Declaration could not have taken place. There is a primary and a secondary presupposition of any genuine Confession of Faith. The primary presupposition is the sovereign will of God, or more concretely, the simple fact that Christ, the Lord of the Church, wills that at a given time he be confessed before men by his own members. The secondary presupposition is that the Confession must be the culmination of a long and strenuous period of theological reflection. Karl Barth was well aware of these indispensable prerequisites of a Confession and gave voice to them in a report to the conference of the World Presbyterian Alliance held in Cardiff, Wales, in June and July, 1925, and delivered at a meeting of the Federation of Reformed Churches in Germany at Duisburg-Meiderich, June 3, 1925. The lecture was entitled " The Desirability and Possibility of a General Reformed Confession of Faith." [8] It is immensely important, not only because it was delivered nine years before the Synod of Barmen convened and definitely belongs to its prehistory, but because it defined the nature of a true and a false Confession and outlined the factors that would make possible a Confession. A document that so definitely prepared the way for the Barmen Declaration needs to be considered in some detail.

Barth began his paper with the following definition of a " Reformed Confession of Faith ": " A Reformed Confession of Faith is a statement of an insight provisionally granted to the universal, Christian Church into God's revelation in Jesus Christ, which is testified to only in Holy Scripture. This statement is spontaneously and publicly formulated by a Christian community that is locally circumscribed. Until further notice, it is authoritative for its outward character, and, until further notice, affords direction for its own doctrine and life." The elements of this definition were then discussed under nine points.

1. The Reformed Confession of Faith seeks to be the statement of a particular insight into God's revelation in Jesus Christ. Because of the ultimately inexplicable character of this explanation of a Confession, Barth refrained from saying more about it.

2. That which the Reformed and early Lutheran views of a Confession have in common and which distinguishes them from Catholicism and modern Protestantism is the clause about God's revelation " which is testified to only in Holy Scripture."

3. The Confession is the statement of " an insight granted " to the Church. It is possible and actual only through the Holy Spirit. Consequently the Confession does not consider itself to be a statement of opinions or convictions but as dogma, that is, as a human insight yet one that is determined by its object and its origin.

4. The Confession desires to be the Confession of the one, holy, catholic Church and not of any particular " ism " or denomination. It does not call itself Zwinglian or Calvinist, but Christian.

5. The assertion that the insight is " provisionally given " emphasizes the fact that it must be granted by God and received by the Church ever again. Here Barth stressed the dynamic character of a Confession.

6. Unlike the Lutheran view of its Confession of Faith, the Confession cannot be authoritative for the Church's doctrine and life *ad omnem posteritatem* but only " until further notice." The Confession is debatable, improvable, and replaceable. Reformed dogma is in a fluid state; it is dogma only in an act of knowledge that is to be renewed ever again.

7. The Confession is at best a human and fallible statement! It makes a sharp distinction between its own authority and the incomparably superior authority of Scripture. It looks upon itself as a temporary action that must be taken here and now for the sake of the Church on earth. In this respect Barth believed that the Congregationalists, with their horror of all Church authority as such, represent a genuine aspect of the Reformed conception of a Confession.

8. In the last analysis the Confession is made by the congregation and not by an ecclesiastical office or by the clergy. It is the fruit of open disputation and voting. If a synod draws up a Confession, it does so only as the authorized agent of the congregation. No clerical order may come between Christ and the local congregation.

9. The Confession has practical significance not only for the Church's own doctrine and life but for all who come to hear it. Accordingly, a Reformed Confession does not shrink from dealing with basic issues in society and the State. A Confession does not usurp Scripture as the law or norm of doctrine and life. It is a commentary upon Scripture. It loses its authority when Scripture itself demonstrates that the commentary is false, or when a knowledge of Scripture no longer takes place.

Barth wrote that if the Church contemplated drawing up a Confession of Faith that would be in keeping with the character of a Reformed Confession, it would have to correspond to these nine points. A Confession that amounted to nothing more than an unobligatory, lyrical religious effusion or that was simply intent upon documenting the " genius " of the Reformed faith would definitely not be a Reformed Confession.

The particular question with which the Council in Cardiff was concerned was the desirability and possibility of a general Confession that would embrace all Reformed Churches in the world. Barth drew attention to the fact that originally the Reformed congregations, say at Basel, Geneva, or Zurich, drew up their own confessions with an astonishing independence of others. Corresponding to the particularity of the Confession was the Reformed conception of the Church as a visible society. Theoretically, of course, the concrete observability of a Christian community could be extended over land and sea. But the more extensive it becomes, the more improbable is a genuine Confession. One can believe with the *coetus oecumenicus,* but one can confess one's faith only with one's immediate fellow believers. Geographically the place of confession can be extended, but it must remain a place where " human beings can stand, meet, weep, and rejoice with one another." Thereupon Barth raised the question as to whether the proposed world-wide Confession would not be just a vague generalized resolution or pronouncement.

Assuming, however, that the Reformed Churches of that day (1925) were in a position to draw up a truly Reformed Confession of Faith, having met all the requirements of the definition, and assuming that the special requirement of a Reformed Confession, namely, the particularity and concreteness of the confessing community, did not stand in the way of making a general Confession, Barth urged that there are then certain essential presuppositions of a Christian Confession that are decisive for the question of its desirability and possibility. First among these is the consciousness of being obedient to the will of God.

> God preserve us and all concerned from all conceivable and practicable machinations, from all undertakings which in this age of the airplane and the radio technically lie within the realm of the possible, but behind which there was not the

Christian need and the Christian compulsion — the earnest, desperate discovery and recognition of their inevitability in the will of God. There are things which one may and can do only then when one *must* do them. Among these things belongs a Christian Confession of Faith. No enthusiasm, no amount of good will, no practical brotherly love, no consideration for Church politics, could replace this " must," this inevitability of the Creed that is recognized in despair. One says, " *Credo* " only when all other possibilities have been exhausted, when, utterly confounded, one can say nothing else than just, " *Credo.* " Every other " *Credo* " is a humbug and of the devil, even if it were literally the Apostles' Creed. The Reformed Church cannot afford to utter such another " *Credo.* "

Barth went on to explain that there is a dogmatic and an ethical presupposition of a Confession which follows from the basic presupposition concerning the will of God. The Church is persuaded that it has gleaned certain insights from Scripture in the hard struggle against theological lies and half-truths. A Confession that was not the outcome of a long history between the Bible and the Church, the conclusion of protracted, earnest theological debates, could never be anything but boring, unoriginal, conciliatory, and ineffectual. " If it were only a document for a unity based on brotherly love or the expression of a common aspiration or ideal or a compromise formula between schools behind which there was no longer any vital Christian thought, and which were uniting in a Confession only because they no longer knew what they had once fought about; or a preamble to a Church constitution because a Church constitution has to have a preamble with a confessional ring to it — all that sort of thing would certainly not be a Confession of Faith."

Barth himself confessed that he entertained grave doubts about the possibility of a genuine Confession at that time — eleven years before the Synod of Barmen. " Where has there been in the theology of our time," he asked, " the erection of a great truth by which the Church felt itself seriously claimed or of a great heresy by which it felt itself gravely and intolerably attacked? Where is there an Athanasius, a Luther among us, not to speak of phenomena like an Augustine, a Thomas, and a Calvin who were not only stimulating and moving but who also shaped the movements they founded? What would be the special cause to which the Church would have to bear public witness today? Let us not delude ourselves. We are not living in a classical period in Protestant theology whose potentialities would warrant our opening our mouths too much. On the contrary, the fact is that we are living *between the times,* burdened with the fatal pietistic-rationalistic inheritance of the last two centuries and faced with a future which we, armed with a few very modest beginnings, can approach only with great uneasiness." Consequently, Barth saw no possibility of a Confession in Germany at that time and he doubted whether the situation was any different in France, Holland, England, and North America.

In a final train of thought, Barth invited his readers to suppose for a moment that the dogmatic presupposition had been fulfilled, that men no longer stood *between* the times but were already victoriously at the *turn* of the times when they again knew what theological exegesis and dogmatics were, when the Trinity, predestination, and Christology were discussed among theological professors and students and at ministers' conferences. Let us even suppose, he said, that a Confession of Faith had been able to put its finger on the great heresy of the day, say that of Schleiermacher. Yet there would still remain the question of whether the other presupposition, the ethical, had been fulfilled, whether the Church had something to say to the concrete life of men.[9] What, Barth asked, has the Church to say to the rise of Fascism and Nationalism in various countries? to the emergence of anti-Semitism? Does the Church affirm war as a matter of principle or does it condemn the militarism that it had condoned in all countries in 1914? Here again Barth expressed his doubts, whether at that time — 1925! — the Church wanted or had anything to say to the dangerous issues of the day. It seemed to him that the Church was even more vacillating in the area of ethics than in the area of dogmatics — to be sure, full of good will to everyone, but certainly not a prophetic voice among the chaos of other voices.

Barth concluded with a reference to the sharp " either-or " which had been apparent throughout his paper. He stated that it was not his intention to make it any easier. If the question concerning the desirability and possibility of a genuine Confession could not be answered in the affirmative, there should be radical reflection upon what was lacking. Let there be a confession of sin by the modern

Reformed Churches and a sober acknowledgment that they are not the Church of Pentecost but must humbly wait for the Holy Spirit.

Thus did Barth accurately describe the period "between the times" in Germany as well as the absolute need for earnest theological work before any Confession of Faith worthy of the name could be produced. Fortunately the years between 1917 and 1933 did yield the most vigorous theological activity. Particularly important was the "Luther Renaissance" ushered in by the Berlin Church historian and pupil of Adolf Harnack, Karl Holl (1866–1926), who published a volume of essays on the Reformer. Instead of writing a biography, he seized upon certain problems in Luther's theology and with his thorough acquaintance with the sources presented Luther's teaching concerning conscience, morality, and the doctrines of Scripture and of the Church in a new light. This method of studying Luther was enthusiastically received by the younger generation, who saw in the struggles of the younger Luther the daring of faith in a day when the old authorities had collapsed. Luther's view of the world, the State, society, and calling, growing out of his experienced paradoxes of faith, was for many a rousing challenge.[10]

Karl Kupisch has pointed out that Holl's book on Luther also had an apologetic interest. It was directed not so much against the Catholic polemic as against a criticism that came from the camp of modern *Kulturprotestantismus,* especially against the views of the religious philosopher Ernst Troeltsch (1865–1922), who had relegated Luther and the basic elements of his faith to the late Middle Ages and had blamed Luther's conservative and patriarchal thought for the exaggerated importance attached to the civil magistrate and the State in German Lutheranism. Holl's book, and the Luther renaissance it stimulated, had the effect of shaking the liberal Protestant understanding of Luther and of opposing the individualism of the day. Holl had the effect of calling in question Troeltsch's theological and philosophical presuppositions. However, it is doubtful whether he succeeded in refuting Troeltsch's criticisms of specific weaknesses in Luther's theology. Nevertheless, Holl himself was still too much a child of his time to sound the prophetic note so urgently needed. Moreover, it was too much to expect that a renewal of the Church would result by means of a direct return to Luther. A mere imitation or repetition of Luther could lead only to sterile confessionalism, just as an uncritical return to Calvin has led to an arid orthodoxy in other countries. A literal reproduction of Luther is as foreign to the spirit of the Reformer as the tendency to regard everything he said as sacrosanct. Luther and Calvin claimed obedience not to themselves but to God's Word revealed in Jesus Christ. A genuine rediscovery of the Reformers should serve as a guide to the Scriptures for God's answer to the questions the Church faces in the present.

An immediate result of the renewed interest in Luther was the publication of new editions of his works. Luther's sermons and expositions of the Scriptures, as well as his polemical works, were avidly read. Parallel to the Luther revival was a rediscovery of John Calvin. Wilhelm Niesel and Peter Brunner edited a new edition of select works of the Genevan Reformer and this was accompanied by numerous separate studies of aspects of Calvin's thought. At the same time, the voices of the nineteenth-century conservative theologians such as August Fr. Chr. Vilmar (1800–1868) and Hermann Friedrich Kohlbrügge (1803–1875) were heard again.

Kohlbrügge is of special importance because of the high esteem in in which he was held by Barth and because of the positive influence he had upon Barth. In the *Prolegomena zur christlichen Dogmatik* (1927), Barth spoke of Kohlbrügge as one in whose company he felt at home. Kohlbrügge was anything but a systematic theologian and his writings consisted almost exclusively of sermons — mostly upon Old Testament texts. His one academic effort was a doctoral thesis for the University of Utrecht, and it was an exegesis of Ps. 45. Actually, Kohlbrügge's theological perspective was quite limited. He concentrated upon four main themes: the sovereignty of God's grace in man's salvation, a Christological exposition of the Old Testament, the problem of suffering, and the doctrine of the law. Kohlbrügge became an outstanding exception to the prevailing subjectivism of the nineteenth century by proclaiming the justification not of the religious or moral man but of the godless man. He was acutely conscious of the secret pride and Pharisaism, even of the Christian, and insisted — against the pietists of his day — that the converted, bornagain man is " carnal, sold under sin." In opposition to an experiential interpretation of regeneration, he taught that man had been born again " on Golgotha." Later, Barth criticized Kohlbrügge's teaching on the ground that (1) it rested upon a mechanical doctrine of verbal inspiration and (2) that the grace of sanctification threatened to disappear in the grace of justification, obedience in faith.[11] Nevertheless, Kohlbrügge's sermons were widely read — especially in Reformed circles — and were a source of comfort and strength to the Confessing Church in its trials and persecutions.[12]

Apart from Karl Barth the most influential theologian "between the times" was Karl Heim. Heim was born in Württemberg in 1874. From 1899 to 1902 he was secretary of the Student Christian Movement in Germany and attended conferences as far distant as China and America. Later he gave himself to the study of philosophy and theology and was appointed Professor of Systematic Theology at the University of Münster in 1914. Since 1920 he has held this chair at Tübingen. His first book to attract attention, *Das Weltbild der Zukunft* (The Idea of the Universe in the Future), was published in 1904 and was indicative of his life's work. Heim has been regarded as an apologist who wanted to ground Christian faith philosophically. Actually it is probably more accurate to say with Karl Kupisch that he endeavored to carry on a conversation with questioning modern man who stands outside the Christian Church and Christian tradition. He was particularly interested in epistemology and in modern science. His apologetic took the form of an invitation to his non-Christian partner to think things out to the end at which emerges the "either-or": relativism or Christ. Heim's six-volume lifework, begun in 1931, is entitled *Der evangelische Glaube und das Denken der Gegenwart: Grundzüge einer christlichen Lebensanschauung* (Protestant Belief and Modern Thought: Outlines of a Christian View of Life).[13] His contention is that "if Christianity is not to allow itself to be relegated to the ghetto, if it is convinced that it has a universal message for the entire world and that like Paul it is 'debtor both to the wise and to the unwise,' . . . then there is no avoiding discussion between the upholders of the Christian faith and the students of the physical universe."

While Karl Heim was certainly one of the most stimulating thinkers during a period of intense theological ferment, it cannot be said that his type of theology was best suited to prepare the Church for a struggle, not against the "earnest searchers after truth," but against a heresy within the Church that posed as the truth. Heim, somehow assuming a knowledge of the truth of the gospel by the Church, wished to communicate the gospel to his alienated contempories.[14] Karl Barth and his associates in the "Dialectical School of Theology" on the other hand, strove to recover the truth of the gospel for the Church in a time of confusion, uncertainty, and error.

The Dialectical Theology was the dominant movement in theology "between the times." It began with the publication in 1919 of the first edition of Karl Barth's commentary on the epistle to the Romans. The second, completely reworked, edition appeared in 1921.[15] About the same time, Friedrich Gogarten published his book *Die religiöse Entscheidung;* Emil Brunner, *Erlebnis, Erkenntnis und Glaube;* and Eduard Thurneysen his study, *Dostojewski.* In the fall of 1922, Barth, Gogarten, and Thurneysen founded the periodical whose title *Zwischen den Zeiten* was prophetic for the whole period. Georg Merz acted as editor in chief, and later Brunner and Bultmann co-operated in the venture. An outsider called the group the "Dialectical School." It was also described as "The Theology of Crisis," the title of one of Brunner's earliest works in English (1931). Often it was labeled simply "Barthianism." Barth himself never wished to be known as the founder or representative of any particular "theological school." He wanted his theology to be understood as "Church dogmatics."[16] Brunner also explained that neither Barth nor he nor any other member of their group had conferred these titles on their theology. "Our only possible name for it would be 'The Theology of the Bible' or 'Christian Theology.'"[17] Yet he admitted that "dialectic" and "crisis" were terms fitted to bring out what it stood for. The word "dialectic" was used, not in the Hegelian sense of a thesis and an antithesis united in a higher synthesis, but in the Kierkegaardian dialectic of an absolute paradox. "It is only by means of the contradiction between two ideas — God and man, grace and responsibility, holiness and love — that we can apprehend the contradictory truth that the eternal God enters time or that the sinful man is declared just. Dialectical theology," Brunner wrote, "is the mode of thinking which defends this paradoxical character, belonging to faith-knowledge, from the nonparadoxical speculation of reason."

The "dialectical" theologians were at first united in their opposition to the traditional liberal Protestantism which presumed to speak about God in terms of religion and piety in general, human psychology, and religious history. Consequently they stressed the transcendence of God over against every form of man's knowledge and good works, including that of religion. They emphasized the sovereignty of God's revelation in Jesus Christ and the authority of Holy Scripture, and insisted that sinful man, even as a believer, always stands before God with empty hands. Thus, as the French Jesuit Henri Bouillard has rightly observed, the Dialectical Theology adapted the thought of the Reformers of the sixteenth century without returning to early Protestant orthodoxy.[18]

In combating the prevailing liberalism, Barth and his associates were influenced by a number of thinkers. In their brochure *Zur inneren Lage des Christentums* (1920), Barth and Thurneysen drew attention to Franz Overbeck, Professor of Critical Theology at the University of Basel from 1872 to 1897, and especially to his little work *Christentum und Kultur*. They asserted that the question Overbeck had addressed to all theologians remained unanswered, namely, that all theology is unchristian and satanic, for it has drawn Christianity down into the sphere of civilization and culture, and has thereby denied its essentially eschatological character. They took seriously the attacks made upon Christianity by Nietzsche and Feuerbach, especially the latter who, in the words of H. Richard Niebuhr, " translates all statements about God into statements about man." [19] From Dostoevsky they learned about the crisis and ambiguity of human life, even of the Christian life. Barth and Thurneysen were also influenced by Johann Christoph Blumhardt (1827–1891), who believed, as a consequence of his miraculous healings of the sick, quite unpietistically that Jesus is victor, and that the healings were signs of the concrete reality of the sin-forgiving power of the Kingdom of God that has come nigh and were pledges of a new, great outpouring of the Holy Spirit before Christ comes again. The biography that Friedrich Zündel (1827–1891) had written about Blumhardt was republished during this period. Zündel's own books, *Jesus* and *Aus der Apostelzeit,* which had received scant attention during his lifetime, were reissued by Georg Merz, and now found a hearing as testimonies to the coming Kingdom of God. Hermann Kutter (1863–1931) also played his part, particularly with his book *Sie müssen!,* which depicted socialism and the labor movement as " God's left hand," as a movement of the Kingdom of God, because it served God without knowing it or wanting to know about it.

It was, however, the works of Sören Kierkegaard, translated into German during the 1920's, that played the dominant role in the theological movement of that period. Their influence upon the " dialectical theology " was decisive. Barth admitted in the preface to the second German edition of his commentary on the epistle to the Romans (1921) that " if I have a system, it is limited to a recognition of what Kierkegaard called the ' infinite qualitative distinction ' between time and eternity, and to my regarding this as possessing negative as well as positive significance: ' God is in heaven, and thou are on earth.' The relation between such a God and such a man, and the relation between such a man and such a God, is for me the theme of the Bible and the essence of philosophy." Although Barth's exegesis of Scripture was colored by Kierkegaardian dialectics, and especially his view of eschatology, it would be a mistake to understand his theology, even in that early period, solely from the standpoint of the antithesis between time and eternity. He who would grasp the consistent concern of Barth's teaching, from its inception and throughout all his writings, must see that it arises out of the need of the preacher who from Sunday to Sunday must mount the pulpit to preach God's word to men. He declared that he wished his theology to be regarded as a " marginal note," a question mark, and as a " corrective " to all existing theology. To be sure, that " marginal note " has grown into many thick volumes of the *Church Dogmatics*. But his chief concern has always been that the message of the gracious and holy God revealed in Jesus Christ be the heart and core of the Church's proclamation, as opposed to the historic relativism, the rational orthodoxy, and the pietistic experientialism of the day. Not man with his desires, longings, and needs but God's promise and commandment: that should be the theme of theology and the task of the Church. Therefore Barth hammered away at this theme: God is not man, and man is not God. God is the wholly Other, the *totaliter aliter* who must not be identified with anything human, with nature, history, conscience, or experience. He wrote in tantalizing paradoxes: God touches our world without touching it, as a tangent touches a circle. His revelation is like a volcanic eruption, leaving an empty crater. It meets us like a " stroke of lightning " — " straight down from above " and at the " point of death."

The note of judgment and crisis in Barth's theology led many of his critics to view it as a purely negative and pessimistic view of history and culture stemming from the disillusionment consequent upon World War I. Paul Althaus saw in the " theology of crisis " a denial of the meaning and purpose of history, as God's judgment not only upon human guilt but upon all creatureliness as such. Althaus wanted to complement the divine No with a divine Yes to man and to history.[20] But as G. C. Berkouwer has rightly observed,[21] both Barth and Brunner were concerned, not with interpreting " a deplorable historical situation," but with showing that crisis was related to salvation and grace. The crisis consists in God's No, God's judgment upon man's highest and best righteousness, especially upon man's religiousness, in order that in the No, God's righteousness, God's forgiveness, might appear as man's salvation. Barth recognized that man makes his most refined and cunning effort to establish his *own* righteousness and to secure himself against the divine judgment precisely in the area of religion. Consequently the crisis consists in the fact that man with all *his* endeavors stands under the radical condemnation of the living and true God, and that there faith apprehends the new possibility of God's mercy. But faith is not a human contrivance, not a virtue or an achievement. It is the sober acknowledgment of God's No. But man may hear God's No as a divine Yes because it is God's No. In the No of his wrath we perceive the Yes of his mercy. Yet here we do not have, as Berkouwer has correctly discerned, " a strange and peculiar dialectical balance between Yes and No, but a conquest of the Yes *in* and *through* the No, because the triumph of Yes becomes manifest exactly at that point where judgment is pronounced over man's *own* righteousness. *In* the crisis, grace is the issue; in judgment, forgiveness." Consequently Berkouwer realizes that when the predominance of the Yes over the No is not fully recognized and understood, it might be thought that in the course of his development Barth had substituted an optimistic, triumphant theology for an earlier pessimistic theology of despair. The truth is rather that in his later writings Barth has simply underscored the triumphant character of grace that was already present in the *Römerbrief*. " Barth's theology must, *from its inception,* be characterized as triumphant theology which aims to testify to the overcoming power of grace. . . . And the triumphant note in Barth's theology stands in direct connection with both God's *judging* and his *gracious* action in Jesus Christ." [22]

At the outset there was marked similarity between Barth's thought and that of the other representatives of the Dialectical Theology. Gogarten wrote that the idea of God " signifies the absolute crisis of everything human and that includes every form of religion." [23] Bultmann, writing in a similar vein, declared: " God signifies the complete abolition of man, his negation, his questionableness, his judgment." [24] In his polemical book against Schleiermacher, *Die Mystik und das Wort,* Brunner also taught: " Grace can appear as grace . . . only in the crisis where man has come to his end." All agreed that revelation and faith transcend historical knowledge and religious experience, that God reveals himself in Jesus Christ as the " wholly Other," that God's Yes to man is accompanied by a radical No, and that the justified man remains a sinner. Yet underneath this measure of agreement there were scarcely perceptible rifts — rifts that widened and came to the surface as the time of the Church's Confession and Struggle drew closer. It seemed as if in the Spirit's providential cultivation of the theological ground upon which a Confession of Faith alone was possible, the representatives of the Dialectical Theology had to contend against one another and even come to a parting of the ways. Their respective positions had to be more narrowly defined before the issues which the Synod of Barmen faced in 1934 could be seen and understood by the Church.

The debate among the " dialectical " theologians came about largely through what Barth later referred to as a " deepening " in his own thinking and through his faculty for self-criticism. This deepening process occurred roughly during the transition from the *Prolegomena zur christlichen Dogmatik* of 1927 to the appearance of the completely reworked *Prolegomena zur kirchlichen Dogmatik, Die Lehre vom Wort Gottes,* I, 1, in 1932. Positively, it consisted in a " Christological concentration " of his theology according to which all Christian doctrine is centered in Jesus Christ.[25] Negatively, it consisted in an abstention from any anthropological, philosophical basis for theology. " To the best of my ability I have cut out in this second issue of the book (the *Prolegomena*) everything that in the first issue might give the slightest appearance of giving to theology a basis, support, or even a mere justification in the way of existential philosophy. . . . In the former undertaking I can see only a readoption of the line Schleiermacher-Ritschl-Herrmann and . . . in any thinkable continuation of this line I can see only the plain destruction of Protestant theology and the Protestant Church." [26] Barth looks upon his book on Anselm as the decisive turning point in his development, *Fides quaerens intellectum. Anselms Beweis der Existenz Gottes* (1931). It reflected the Christological concentration. This deepening or cleansing of Barth's own thought was a real anticipation of the stand taken by the Church at Barmen, and it brought him into conflict with Gogarten. Gogarten had criticized Barth for not developing an anthropology.[27] Barth replied that he regretted having gone too far in the direction of letting an " existential philosophy " provide the basis for dogmatics. " There is a way from Christology to anthropology," he wrote. " There is no way from an anthropology to Christology." [28]

Bultmann also thought that theology could speak about God only when it spoke about man at the same time. For Bultmann this did not mean speaking about the *one* man who is identical with God — the man Christ Jesus; rather, it presupposed an independent view of man. Since 1928 Bultmann had taken this " *Vorverständnis* " over from the philosopher Martin Heidegger. The being of man is historical. In Bultmann's words, man's being " is at stake in the concrete situations of life, and consists of decisions in which man . . . chooses himself as his possibility." [29] Thereupon Barth asked whether for Bultmann " theology and anthropology were really interchangeable concepts." He asserted that the revelation of which the First Commandment speaks becomes secondary and subordinate when in theology a more or less shrewd analysis of our existence or some principle derived from creation is regarded as a special, prior revelation.[30]

According to Emil Brunner, even the unbeliever was capable of a knowledge of himself, and this knowledge had its place within a theological anthropology and was the " point of contact " for revelation in man's reason. Brunner (mistakenly) appealed to Kierkegaard for justification of his own eristic theology. Kierkegaard, he admitted, was not a dogmatic theologian, but he was an eristic theologian second to none in the history of Christian thought. The old apologetics, he said, made the mistake of placing itself on the same ground as that of the opponent, that of theory, giving the impression that Christian truth is a theoretical proposition like the theoretical propositions of reason. Thus apologetics was not only untrue to the gospel but set itself the impossible task of proving the gospel as speculative truth. Brunner spoke of Pascal, Hamann, and Kierkegaard

as the three great eristic theologians of modern times simply because they avoided this error. Instead they forced their opponents to
raise " the existential question, the question about the understanding
of one's own life," as preliminary and preparatory to the question of
Christian faith. This is how Brunner viewed eristics as " the other
task of theology." [31] Consequently he was led to affirm anthropology,
man's view of himself, as the common ground of faith and unbelief,
and he hailed Gogarten as the successor to Kierkegaard because of
his profound interest in anthropology and existentialism. Brunner
agreed that the self remains the point in existence at which one is
passionately, that is, existentially, interested, that it is possible to
demonstrate to a man apart from faith that he lives in contradiction
to himself and is not able to extricate himself from this contradiction. Man knows that he is not what he would like to be. Hence he
is brought to despair and is driven to ask the question about God.
Here, Brunner believed, is to be found " the point of contact " in
man for divine revelation. Pelagianism erred, not in establishing a
point of contact in man, but in seeking it in something positive
rather than negative. Actually it consists in the negativity and ambiguity of human existence. The task of eristics is to make man
aware of the contradiction in which he is involved. Brunner, however, linked this sense of contradiction and despair in man with an
imperfect, natural knowledge of God. Man's relatedness to God gives
rise to his question about God, and this is the *imago Dei* which has
not been destroyed by sin. Man is " a creature who somehow knows
about God. His knowing about God is his humanity — however perverted and questionable this knowledge may be." [32]

Three years later — 1932 — Brunner addressed himself to the question of the point of contact again, and insisted: " It is senseless to
dispute the significance of a natural knowledge of God. Debatable
is not the fact itself but its quality. Religion is — even when it is the
wildest heathenism — the undeniable sign of man's relationship to
God, and at the same time the necessary point of contact for the true
knowledge of God." [33] The natural man is related to God but in
this relationship he stands under the divine wrath and judgment.
And this is " objectively the same as that which is subjectively an
evil conscience or despair." [34]

Barth had rejected Brunner's other eristic task of theology and his teaching about the point of contact in the *Prolegomena* to Church Dogmatics and in his article in *Zwischen den Zeiten*, "The First Commandment as a Theological Axiom." At that time — it was March, 1933 — Barth regarded his protest against the line taken by Gogarten, Bultmann, and Brunner as a theological protest *within* the Church and not as a protest that would *divide* the Churches. But the heresy implicit in the teachings of Barth's erstwhile colleagues was coming to a head: indeed, it had come to a head in the tenets of the heretical "German Christian" party within the German Evangelical Church which identified Christianity and National Socialism, and which saw in race, folk, and nation natural orders by which God was revealing his will to the German people.[35] The "Dialectical School" broke up, and the periodical *Zwischen den Zeiten* ceased publication, when Gogarten joined the ranks of the "German Christians" and Barth resigned from the editorial board. Bultmann, however, never aligned himself with the "German Christians," and Gogarten withdrew from the movement in November, 1933. In a farewell statement, Barth set down his reasons for terminating their literary venture. He perceived in Gogarten's step "the unequivocal expression of what he had always thought and wanted," and its inevitable consequence. "I can see in the German Christians," Barth wrote, "nothing else than the final, most complete, and worst offspring of the essence of modern Protestantism which, unless it is overcome, will have to make the evangelical Church ripe for Rome. I regard Stapel's statement about God's law (that it is identical with the nomos of the German people) as treason against the gospel. I think that this proposition amounts to setting up the Man-God of the eighteenth and nineteenth centuries in a form that is much worse than in the Harnack-Troeltsch era because it is much more axiomatic and much more concrete." [36]

Emil Brunner, being a Swiss, did not, of course, go over to the ranks of the "German Christians," and it would be unfair to suggest that he would have identified himself with them. But his pamphlet *Nature and Grace,* published in 1934 after the Synod of Barmen, in which he attacked Barth's categorical rejection of all natural theology, amounted to a denial of the first thesis of the Barmen Declaration. What provoked Barth's reply *No!* with its "angry introduction" was the fact that Brunner's tract had won the "loud applause of K. Fezer, O. Weber, P. Althaus, and all the other half or three-quarter 'German Christians.' " [37] The *Deutsches Pfarrerblatt* called it "a mine of treasure, a veritable gold mine." [38] Barth was angered with Brunner because he had afforded comfort to the enemy at the very time the Church was fighting for its life. Barth's polemic against Brunner was more acute than against Emanuel Hirsch, the theologian of the "German Christians," [39] because, being closer to the truth, he was "much more dangerous," and because he regarded Brunner as a "classical precursor" of a future theology of compromise. Consequently he rejected Brunner's contention that there is a second revelation in creation, in nature and history, by which "men somehow know the will of God, though but distortedly and dimly"; that there is a special preserving grace apparent to us in God's preservation of the world; that there are "ordinances" of creation and preservation, such as marriage and the State, which may be imperfectly known and "to some extent realized" even by the natural man; and that the natural man's confused and distorted knowledge of God, of the law, and of his own dependence upon God is "the necessary, indispensable point of contact for divine grace." Barth insisted that Brunner's doctrine of the point of contact "has to be most categorically opposed on the score that it is incompatible with the third article of the Creed. The Holy Ghost . . . does not stand in need of any point of contact but that which he himself creates." [40]

Consequently Barth argued that the natural man's so-called knowledge of the wrath of God is not the wrath *of God;* that His judgment is the judgment of grace, and that hence it is by no means identical with any fundamental condition or "negative point" of our existence. Man's consciousness of the ambiguity, uncertainty, and contradiction of his existence and his consequent despair, anxiety, or dread is not a factor which co-operates with the judgment of God and which therefore is indispensable for its execution. Nor is it indirectly identical with the judgment of God, as being its subjective manifestation. He wrote:

> *That* sorrow which really is possible to us is always that sorrow of which it is said in II Cor. 7:10, that it "worketh death. . . ." It can never be the sorrow "after a godly manner" which works "repentance not be repented of," which leads to salvation. . . . That loss of certainty of the natural knowledge,

that destruction of the " fictions of *Weltanschauungen* " which I can with my little piece of despair undertake and carry out, is bound to issue in the worst of all idols, namely, a so-called " truth, from the throne of which *I* consider myself able to see through all gods and to unmask them as idols. The better I succeed in despairing, the more certainly this must be the end. The world which *I* have cleared of gods is truly neither the Kingdom of the living God nor even a preparation for it, but probably the worst of all forms of diabolism, by which I can oppose that Kingdom. . . . Is there any form of pride worse than that of a certain type of Kierkegaardianism? Has there ever been a more explicit Prometheanism than that of the philosophy of an existence despairing of itself? [41]

The words with which Barth concluded his message of resignation in *Zwischen den Zeiten* were prophetic of accusations that were to be repeatedly hurled against him in the days ahead. He warned against attributing his position in the present crisis of the Church to the opposition of his Reformed Confession to the Lutheran. He admitted that he belonged to the Reformed Church. But the modern Protestantism that culminates in the " German Christian " movement, he wrote, is destructive of both the Lutheran and Reformed Confessions. Good Lutherans stand with us in opposing the " German Christians," just as bad Reformed churchmen stand halfway or altogether with them. And he added that if there ever was a time when good Lutheran and Reformed churchmen should unite in a new fighting Confession, it is today. The fronts run straight across the boundaries of the historic Confessions of the two Churches. Secondly, he warned against thinking that his political views determined his theological position. And finally, he warned against explaining his position on the ground that he is a Swiss and not " from head to foot " a German. Time and again throughout the Church Struggle and even since 1945, attempts have been made to dismiss Barth on the grounds of his denominational, political, and national affiliations. It is a pity that the Church in Germany — and not only in Germany — has used these as pretexts to evade Barth's salutary witness.

III

The Rise of the "German Christians"

THE "FAITH MOVEMENT OF 'GERMAN CHRISTIANS'" (*Glaubensbewegung deutscher Christen*) was born June 6, 1932, with the publication of guiding principles for the movement.[1] The principles set forth the "methods and goals for a new order for the Church." Virtually ignoring theological questions, the principles echoed the main points of the National Socialist Party propaganda: positive Christianity; the fight against Marxism, the Jews, internationalism, and Free Masonry; preservation of the purity of the race; and defense of the people against degeneration. As we look back now upon the phenomenon of the "German Christians," especially in the light of the infamy of the whole Nazi era, it is difficult to understand, particularly for English readers, how such a movement could have been a serious temptation for the Church. It is necessary, therefore, to treat the history of the rise of the "German Christians" as sympathetically as possible.

The "German Christians," regarded from the standpoint of Christian faith, were a liberal, nationalistic sect which, at the initiative of the National Socialist Party, formed a union of various schools and groups. These schools and groups, in spite of all differences, were united in their nationalistic tendencies and liberal Christianity. The movement owed its existence to the fact that the National Socialists in 1931–1932 were intent upon carrying their fight against the Weimar Republic into the Churches. It disappeared with the collapse of the Hitler regime at the end of World War II. Unlike the Church, the "German Christian" party was dependent upon historical and political factors. When these changed, it ceased to exist.[2]

The earliest forerunner of the "German Christians" was the

League for a German Church (*Bund für deutsche Kirche*), which strove to reform the Church along nationalistic lines and to free it from its " Judaistic " characteristics. It was founded in June, 1921, by Joachim Kurd Niedlich and a Pastor Bublitz who edited *Die Deutschkirche* — a fortnightly Sunday paper for the German people. Others prominent in the League were Prof. Adolf Bartels and Pastor Friedrich Andersen, of Flensburg. The latter is typical of how many ecclesiastics turned from Protestant orthodoxy to a radical liberalism. As early as 1907 and 1913, Andersen was an avowed critic of the Old Testament and " all Jewish blurring of the pure teaching of Jesus "; and in defending himself, he liked to appeal to Adolf von Harnack's book *Marcion*. Coming under the influence of the writings of Houston Stewart Chamberlain, Andersen eventually became a member of the Hitler Party and an enthusiastic advocate of its racial theories, even defending Rosenberg's *Myth of the 20th Century*! As Hans Buchheim has observed, Andersen is a classic example of the transformation of liberal, historical theology into an intolerant German nationalistic dogmatism.[3]

The League for a German Church demanded that the Old Testament no longer be accepted as canonical; that Paul's rabbinic principle of redemption be done away; and that Jesus' death be presented as a heroic sacrifice in line with Germanic mysticism. Although the League was not a party within the Church and merely sought to influence the old parties with its philosophy, it did unite with other nationalistic movements, notably with the German League of Christians. Thus there emerged in February, 1926, the German Christian Working Community (*Deutsch-christliche Arbeitsgemeinschaft*).[4]

The most radical group was the " Thüringian 'German Christians.' " It was the work of two pastors, Julius Leutheuser and Siegfried Leffler. To the very last these two men believed in Hitler's mission without ever ceasing to believe in Christ. They thought they could convert their fellow-citizens to Christ when they freed themselves from the teaching of the Church and when a new Church emerged out of the National Socialist peoples' community.[5]

Leutheuser and Leffler were originally members of the Youth Movement.[6] As they began to study theology in Bavaria in the years following the war, they became convinced that the Church had failed in the political and national need of the people because it had thought that a dead orthodoxy was more important than a love for the people. They saw in the systematic theology offered at the universities a symptom of the fact that the official Christianity of the Churches was divorced from the real life of the nation. The Church had become a bureaucracy for the propagation of stale doctrines unrelated to the practical needs of men. In a revolt against theology the two men stressed life and work — a Christian activism. They sought to win the disinterested to Christianity by adopting the jargon of the day and by interpreting the Christian message in terms of current events. Leutheuser and Leffler did not err in endeavoring to make the Christian gospel relevant. Their fault lay in thinking that the traditions of the evangelical Churches and all theology are opposed to the demands of a vital concern for the needs of people. Instead of allowing theology to be the basis for a sound pastoral theology, the aspirations and desires of the people became normative. When these became increasingly nationalistic in character, it was a short step to preaching the divine election of the German people and the saving work of Adolf Hitler and to finding God's revelation, not in the text of Scripture, but in the events of history. As Hans Buchheim has said, historical events can be divine indices which can be understood and interpreted by an already existing faith, but they cannot be the revelation itself that creates faith. Leutheuser and Leffler failed to distinguish between sacred and profane history. The history of the German people was, for them, *Heilsgeschichte.*

The two pastors further erred in the belief that they had first experienced genuine human fellowship in the National Socialist Party rather than in the Church. They were persuaded that within the struggle of the Party they had been confronted with an ultimate " either-or," and that they had been challenged in the depths of their being to lay down their lives as a daily sacrifice on behalf of their people. One, therefore, cannot fail to recognize a high idealism motivating these " German Christian " leaders, nor will one be able to deny that their criticism of the German Church and theology was not without justification. Theology had become so systematic and academic, so far removed from the spiritual life of the Church, that it had little in common with true dogmatics. Christian ethics to a large extent resembled philosophic moral principles and seemed more concerned about abstract theories than about men. Indeed, one will observe a certain similarity between the protest of these "German Christians" and existentialists who deny that there are any timeless principles, values, ideals, and rules to which the Christian can appeal. But the solution grasped by Leffler was that Christian conduct should arise out of love of one's neighbor and out of the concrete situation. That situation was, for them, the dire need of Germany, and the National Socialist struggle to meet that need. Furthermore, one cannot deny the charge that the Church had become divorced from real life. When Leffler demanded that the Church be renewed in the light of the concrete situation in the nation, and when he spoke of the German people as the new people of God, he was guilty of an outrageous perversion of Christianity. Yet the element of truth underlying these demands was the desire for a Church that was addressing itself to the actual needs of men and understood that there are no spheres of human society outside of the sovereign grace of Christ. Unfortunately the "Thüringian 'German Christians'" virtually went to the length of putting the *Volk* in the place of Christ.

The immediate forerunner of the National Socialist "Faith Movement of 'German Christians'" was the Christian-German Movement. This group pursued political objectives and looked upon Christianity as an intellectual and moral force in stabilizing the body politic. It sought to conserve the political influence that Protestantism had exercised until 1918. It lacked the reforming zeal that stamped the "League for a German Church" and the "Thüringian 'German Christians.'" It was founded in 1930 by Werner Wilm; and later Bishop Heinrich Rendtorff, of Mecklenburg, succeeded to the leadership. The Christian-German Movement opposed the politics of the Catholic Center Party and the Social Democrats and urged its members to align themselves with the "rightist" parties. It condemned the "war-guilt lies" and "enslaving peace treaties," and fought for Germany's liberation. It argued for equality for Reformed and Lutheran Churches and professed to believe in ecumenicity while insisting that "God had created the nations of the earth, each with its special stamp." Nevertheless, its conception of the nation (*Volk*) was conservative and historical. It avoided a racial definition of nationality, and this was the reason few National Socialists joined the movement.[7]

Among the numerous scholars in the universities who joined the

Christian-German Movement, the most prominent were Paul Althaus
and Emanuel Hirsch. Hirsch in particular was one of the men to
whom the " Christian Germans " and later the " German Christians "
liked to appeal whenever they wanted to find a theological justification for their tenets. He himself took an active part in Church politics although he was by nature a pure theorist with little comprehension of practical politics.[8] Althaus later was outspoken in his
criticisms of the Theological Declaration of the Synod of Barmen.

Until the year 1930, Hitler's Party refrained from any direct interference in Church affairs. Point 24 of the Party program declared
that the Party took " the standpoint of ' positive Christianity ' " without being " bound to any particular Confession of Faith." To be sure,
the article guaranteeing freedom for all religious bodies in the State
was qualified by the sentence: " so far as they do not endanger the
existence of the State or do not offend the moral and ethical conscience of the Germanic race." As already reported, Hermann Sasse
was among the very few who recognized the utter incompatibility
of this article with Christian faith. He wrote:

> This article makes any discussion with the Church impos-
> sible. . . . For the Evangelical Church would have to begin a
> discussion about it with the frank admission that its doctrine is
> an intentional and permanent offense to the moral and ethical
> feelings of the Germanic race. . . . Let it be said that the Evan-
> gelical doctrine of original sin — in contrast to the Catholic —
> does not admit of the possibility of the Germanic, Nordic, or
> any other race being able by nature to fear and love God and
> to do his will, that on the contrary a newborn child of the most
> noble Germanic descent with the finest racial characteristics of
> an intellectual and physical sort is just as liable to eternal dam-
> nation as a half-breed born of two decadent races and with
> serious hereditary defects. Moreover, we have to confess that
> the doctrine of the justification of the sinner *sola gratia, sola
> fide* is the end of Germanic morality as it is the end of all hu-
> man morality.[9]

Any discussion with National Socialism would therefore have to
begin with the repeal of this article.

Unfortunately there were few who saw in a Nazi victory a threat
to the Church. Most churchmen, while critical of National Socialism,

recognized merits in it and looked upon it as offering great opportunities for the Church in the future. For example, H. Schreimer wrote in 1931: "Out of the depth of its nature [National Socialism's] there comes to us a will which is pointing us to a divine commission." On the other hand, Schreimer insisted that Hitlerism was not the proper means for carrying out this commission, and that "to show that National Socialism and Christianity belong inseparably together . . . is almost all a betrayal of the gospel." [10] D. H. Kremer, the president of the Evangelical Alliance, saw it as "our Christian task in the face of this movement" to preserve it from naturalism and from Rome.[11] The publisher, Leopold Klotz, a layman, published two volumes in 1932 under the title *The Church and the Third Reich. Questions and Demands of German Theologians.* Klotz appealed to "the German conscience not yet confused by catchwords of the street" and sought to create through the free expression of opinion a platform for an initial debate with National Socialism. The contributors to the first volume — among them Ernst Bizer, Emil Fuchs, Friedrich Heiler, Ferdinand Kattenbusch, Friedrich Niebergall, Otto Piper, Martin Rade, K. B. Ritter, Gotthilf Schenkel, Hermann Strathmann, Paul Tillich, Heinrich Weinel — were for the most part critical of the movement. Bizer insisted that the racial theories of National Socialism are irreconcilable with Christianity. Fuchs and Heiler were unequivocal in their repudiation of the Party. Said Heiler: "In the twelve years in which I have been active in German Protestantism, nothing has stirred and shocked me so much as the fact that broad sections of evangelical Churches and societies have quite uncritically thrown themselves into the arms of a movement which in its ideological principles and in its practical effects stands in irreconcilable opposition to the New Testament gospel." [12] Otto Piper took the position that "as a political movement it has its right and its limits like any other political party. . . . But the Church has to take it seriously as a religious movement, as an important question addressed to her." [13] Paul Tillich formulated ten theses, in which he articulated his opposition to Hitlerism. At that time Tillich viewed the situation as a struggle between socialism and Nazism, and warned that a Protestantism that opened its arms to the latter and rejected the former would betray its commission to the world. It "must lead to the future dissolution of German Protestantism."

" To the extent to which it justifies nationalism and an ideology of blood and race by a doctrine of divine orders of creation, it surrenders its prophetic basis in favor of a new manifest or veiled paganism and betrays its commission to be a witness for the *one* God and the *one* mankind." [14] Some of the writers were inclined to see in National Socialism a judgment upon the Church for having held aloof from the Marxist movement. But Schenkel was very clear in his mind that whereas religious socialism was inspired by Christian faith, hope, and love, Nazism was the outgrowth of base natural instincts. It " brings no new insights, neither economic nor historical nor religious. . . . It is the embodiment of the will to power." [15] Unfortunately, alongside these critical utterances were statements by scholars who welcomed the fact that " the National Socialist wave is forcing Church and theology to consider the ideas of nationalism and Germanism."

A copy of the first volume was sent to Hitler. A professor, J. Stark, supposedly the founder of a " German physics," who worked in Hitler's Office on Church Affairs, was charged with passing judgment upon it. He declared: " The book in question affords a valuable commentary on the intellectual level of numerous ' evangelical ' academic theologians. Never have I seen such an accumulation of ignorance, superficiality, presumption, and malicious enmity to the German Freedom Movement." The second volume escaped such harsh treatment, for it was largely a compilation of articles by younger men who were destined to become leaders in the " German Christian " Movement. It also contained the first " Ten Directives of the Faith Movement of the ' German Christians ' " and a commentary on them by Dr. Friedrich Wieneke. Klotz's two volumes, taken together, pointed up the tremendous confusion of conflicting views that prevailed in the Church.

Alfred Rosenberg's *Myth of the 20th Century,* which was a blasphemous attack upon Christianity, was treated as a private publication by the official organs of the Party for which the author alone was responsible. Naturally Rosenberg's book did not go unanswered, though it is significant that answers were not forthcoming until three to five years after its publication in 1930.[16] It was not until Hitler entrusted Rosenberg with the entire intellectual and ideological education of the Party in January, 1934, that the Party's endorsement of Rosenberg's paganism was fully evident. At the start Hitler was intent on impressing upon the populace that his Party was Christian. To this end, Party members were encouraged to attend church in uniform and to parade to church in a body. For the Church authorities the question arose whether the Church was not being made into a stage for political demonstrations and whether Church members with other political affiliations were not being discriminated against. While the attitude of the Church leaders in Mecklenburg and Württemberg was favorable, the Council of the Old Prussian Union circulated a somewhat vague decree which, nevertheless, condemned demonstrative visits to Churches by National Socialists.[17] This action spurred Wilhelm Kube, the leader of the National Socialist faction in the Prussian Landtag, and the editor of the weekly paper called *Der Märkische Adler,* to repudiate the agreement that had existed between the Prussian Church and the Prussian State, and to form a National Socialist party within the Prussian Church. The Church elections were to be held in the fall of 1932. As early as January of that year he initiated a propaganda campaign. But at that time he did not have a united organization to serve his purposes. During the preceding year he had managed to gather around him in Berlin a circle of evangelical National Socialists.

At the same time, a National Socialist Pastors' League was being formed by Dr. Friedrich Wieneke, of the Cathedral at Soldin, and Joachim Hossenfelder, minister of Christ Church in Berlin. This league paralleled the already existing "German Christian Working Community." In February, guiding principles were issued, under the catchword "Evangelical National Socialists," for conducting the Church elections and for uniting forces against the anti-Nazi conservative Church leaders — the General Superintendents Otto Dibelius and Dr. Vits. Every district, every local group of the Party, and every congregation were to nominate, as quickly as possible, experts in Church matters and to send their names to a particular office of the Party. These people were not only to make preparations for the elections but to be on the watch for expressions of views opposed to National Socialism. Religious questions played virtually no part in the election campaign; it was predominantly political. The Nazi slogans were carried into the Church: repudiation of the liberal spirit, of Jewish Marxism, internationalism, and pacifism.

Meanwhile a ministerial councillor, named Konopath, and Pastor Hossenfelder negotiated with the " German Christian " League, the " Christian Germans," and the " Thüringian ' German Christians ' " to form a united Church party. Hitler ordered that the name " Evangelical National Socialists " be dropped, since it did not lend itself to his pretended neutrality. At the suggestion of Gregor Strasser, then in charge of the national organization of the Party, the name " German Christians " was taken over from the Thüringian group. This new name had the added advantage of attracting people who were not National Socialists. The leadership of the " German Christians " lay in the hands of Hossenfelder, who had been a member of the Nazi Party since 1929. On May 23, 1932, Hossenfelder was officially appointed by Strasser to have charge of the conduct of the election campaigns in all the regional evangelical Churches. Thus the " Faith Movement of the ' German Christians ' " was sanctioned by the Party for the whole Reich and was no longer restricted to the Church in Prussia. With the publication of the Guiding Principles (*Richtlinien*) on June 6, the Movement was officially born.[18] The principles were intended to indicate the way in which " all believing Germans " could achieve a reformation of the Church. They announced that the Movement was fighting for a union of the twenty-nine regional Churches into a State Church. Claiming to take their stand on " positive Christianity " and on " heroic piety " in the " German spirit of Luther," they castigated godless Marxism, the Center Party, a mission to the Jews, intermarriage between Jews and Germans, pacifism, internationalism, and Free Masonry. All this was based upon the belief that " race, nationality, and the nation [are] orders of life granted and entrusted to us by God, for whose preservation God's law requires us to strive." The campaign carried on by the " German Christians " was not unsuccessful: in the elections in the Old Prussian Union they won a third of all the seats.

That the election campaign of the " German Christians " was not even more successful is due to the theological revival that took place " between the times " and which was reviewed in the preceding chapter. As a sign that the theological awakening had taken effect, and as a sign of hope for the Church, a group of twenty-one pastors at Altona issued on January 11, 1933 — a few weeks before Hitler assumed power — " A Word and Confession to the Need and Confusion in Public Life." [19] The leader of this group was Pastor Hans Asmussen, who was later to play such a prominent role in the Synod of Barmen and the Church Struggle. The declaration noted that many people were asking about the nature of the Church. Some expected material help from the Church. Others looked for its support in a political struggle. The Church could not satisfy these demands because its task was to sharpen the conscience and to proclaim the gospel. Then in five articles dealing with the Church, the limits of man, the State and its tasks, and the commandments of God, the Altona Statement addressed itself to the needs of the hour. The Church, it said, is a host called into existence by God's contemporaneous Word, in which Christ is truly present. It is concerned with the actual world and everyday affairs of birth and death, marriage and the family, calling and profession, states and political parties. God's Word reveals that we are not able to live as we should, yet his power is magnified in Christ's members in spite of their weakness. Church members are not better than others. Their difference consists in their recognition of God's judgment upon their unrighteousness and their trust in his forgiveness.

Because the living Christ is present in his Church, he is its strength. Hence, the nature of the Church may not be determined by anything else, neither by the State or a party nor by science or a *Weltanschauung*. It must be free to proclaim the Word. In principle, the Church is not an organization, yet an organization is necessary if it is to do God's will. The organization, however, should always be changed to meet the demands of the time without surrendering anything of its preaching. It is not restricted to any social class, for the Church exists for all. The Church is misused when it is made the stage for military, political, and party celebrations, or when it is expected to approve any particular economic system or political party, military service, or pacifism, or to declare that a hero's death for the Fatherland is itself a blessed death.

God has created man to have dominion over the earth. We may respect man's achievements in the field of technical and economic skill. But in spite of these achievements in war and peace, great miseries have come upon us by reason of our sin. Therefore we reject dreams of a future earthly kingdom of perfect righteousness, peace, and universal well-being. A political party that holds on to the prospect of such a national utopia becomes a religion. These things belong to the new world which God will give through Jesus Christ. Until then the noblest human effort stands under the cross that Christ has borne.

The State is a creation of God made necessary to order human society because of sin. There is no one true form of the State. Men are to seek that form which will best serve God's will in the light of the existing situation. We are called to be obedient to rulers. But when rulers do not seek the welfare of the State, each individual must decide when he must obey God rather than men. The deification of the State is to be rejected; a State becomes anti-Christian when it purports to be lord of the conscience. We condemn the fact that parties have largely become political confessions of faith, thereby endangering not only faith in God but the existence of the State.

Every nation must have a religion, even if it be the religion of godlessness and the cult of Lenin. By God's providence we Germans have been led to Christianity. This fact should not be overlooked by civil authorities in all their undertakings. To be sure, faith is not innate, it is a miracle of God's grace. But our people should not be robbed of the opportunity to honor God. We believe that the government is to rule in a fatherly way, taking upon itself the needs of the people. Since God is the creator of life, human life should be respected and protected, not because of the value of the individual and the nation, but out of respect to the Creator who has created it. It is to be condemned as sin when citizens are exploited or when the prevailing unemployment is taken lightly. The gospel is, therefore, the only help and perfect salvation even for our earthly fatherland.

The substance of the Altona declaration has been given at some length because of its historical importance as the first of the Confessions of Faith which were to be a characteristic feature of the struggle and because it exercised a profound influence and determined the line the Church was to follow.[20] Unhappily the Church had to go through very deep waters before something in the spirit of the Altona pronouncement could become the Confession of the Evangelical Church in Germany.

When Hitler became Chancellor on January 30, 1933, the "German Christians" were already well organized. Bernhard Rust was appointed Minister of Education for Prussia and he in turn named Hossenfelder as his adviser in Church affairs. Hitler's policy at this stage was still to persuade the Christian populace that his Party was Christian and that he himself was neutral with respect to the various denominations. Accordingly in his speech before the first meeting of the Reichstag on March 23, 1933, he declared:

> The national Government sees in the two Christian Confessions the most important factors for the preservation of our nationality. It will respect the agreements that have been drawn up between them and the provincial states. Their rights are not to be infringed. It expects, however, and hopes that conversely the work upon the national and moral renewal of our nation, which the Government has assumed as its task, will receive the same appreciation. All other denominations will be treated with the same impartial justice.
>
> The national Government will provide and guarantee to the Christian Confessions the influence due them in the schools and education. It is concerned for genuine harmony between Church and State. The struggle against materialism and for the establishment of a true community in the nation serves just as much the interests of the German nation as it does those of our Christian faith.
>
> The Reich Government, seeing in Christianity the unshakable foundation of the moral and ethical life of our people, attaches utmost importance to the cultivation and shaping of the friendliest relations with the Holy See.
>
> The rights of the churches will not be curtailed; their position in relation to the State will not be changed.

These sentences appeared, at first glance, to be quite conservative. At any rate, they served to quicken false hopes and illusions, as if Hitler, as General Superintendent Wilhelm Zöllner expressed it, "had again laid down the *magna charta* of the independence of Church life." [21] Actually these words said no more than Point 24 of the Party program and what Hitler had written in *Mein Kampf*. They say nothing in favor of Christianity and betray a woeful misunderstanding of the Church when they look upon it as a means of stabilizing the social and political order. Moreover, it is significant that the sentence about guaranteeing the Church's influence in the schools was dropped from the "official text" of the speech issued by the Eher Publishing House the following year and is missing in almost all the official publications of the Party.[22] Thus, these words had for Hitler a temporary tactical value of placating the Churches while he was consolidating his political position. He never really wanted to grant independence to the Church — not even to a " German Christian " Church. His feigned tolerance and indifference toward Christianity was changed into, or rather exposed as, hatred and enmity when the Church refused to let itself be merely an instrument in his administration of the State and when the church itself demonstrated its spiritual independence. The Church leaders were well aware that the " German Christians " would not miss the favorable chance to form a State Church, and they had no intention of surrendering the Church to their revolutionary goals. In a proclamation of the German Evangelical Church Committee, the executive organ of the Church, issued March 3, it declared that the Church is called " to serve the whole nation and not particular groups in the nation and independently of the political situation." [23] General Superintendent Otto Dibelius wrote in a confidential pastoral letter to his ministers that " the gospel does not recognize the self-sufficient man but the justified sinner," that it preaches love rather than hatred, and that " the theme of evangelical proclamation is the Kingdom of God and not nationalism." " The gospel is opposed to every human ideology, be it National Socialist or socialist, liberal, or conservative, and it does not confirm man in his selfish desires, but judges him. The nation and State can be built up only when men first bow beneath the gospel. Only then will tradition and freedom and all other human affairs acquire their Christian right." [24]

Naturally these statements by the Church leaders did not sit well with the " German Christians " and when they held their first national convention in Berlin on April 3–5, Wilhelm Kube, as leader of the Prussian Landtag faction of the Nazi Party, declared in his opening words of welcome that his faction would use all means at its command to make allowance for the transformation in the nation even in the area of Church politics. " Therefore, I reject the unheard-of attack made by Dr. Dibelius upon our movement." He assured those present that they would see in the 211 men of the Prussian faction their defense and their champions " in the effort to carry on in the twentieth century the German revolution in the spirit of Martin Luther." Among the members of the honorary committee for the convention were Hermann Göring and Wilhelm Frick, high-ranking Government officials, whose presence belied the supposed neutrality of the State in Church affairs. The convention met under the slogan: "The State of Adolf Hitler appeals to the Church and the Church has to hear his call." Dr. Friedrich Werner, later president of the Evangelical Church government office, declared that the basis of the Church's constitution had to be the *Führerprinzip*. Only then could the unification of Church and State produce the necessary increase of power needed by the nation. The convention closed by passing a resolution that called for the creation of a Reich Church and the right of believers to revolt.

"God has created me a German. Germanism is a gift of God. God wants me to fight for my Germany. Military service is in no sense a violation of Christian conscience, but is obedience to God. The believer possesses the right of revolution against a State that furthers the powers of darkness. He also has this right in the face of a Church board that does not unreservedly acknowledge the exaltation of the nation. For a German the Church is the fellowship of believers who are obligated to fight for a Christian Germany. The goal of the "Faith Movement of 'German Christians'" is an evangelical German Reich Church." [25]

The first direct interference by the State in Church matters took place in Mecklenburg. On April 18, an article appeared in the Nazi newspaper, *Niederdeutschen Beobachter,* bearing the inflammatory title: "Farmers, conquer the Church!" The article stated that evangelical Christians were threatened by a priestly hierarchy in the evangelical Church. With few praiseworthy exceptions, the preachers have failed us in the struggle for the way of the German people to God. Therefore, farmers, take over the government of the Church yourselves and all administrative functions. The upshot of this rather romantic and revolutionary appeal was that the author, a certain Walther Bohm, was named State Commissioner for the Evangelical Church in Mecklenburg by Walter Granzow, the president of the government of Mecklenburg. This use of political force shocked Church circles throughout Germany. The Church leaders responded by sending telegrams and letters to Reich President Hindenburg, to Hitler, and to the Minister for Internal Affairs. Thereupon Hitler called on Frick to settle the matter. The latter immediately summoned Bishop Rendtorff, Granzow, and Bohm to Berlin. Granzow was persuaded to withdraw the Commissioner, and Hitler personally assured the bishop that he stood by his statement of March 23 and would guarantee the independence of the Church. Perfectly satisfied, the naïve bishop then publicly announced that he had joined the National Socialist Party.[26]

Granzow's act of State inference was in line with the ambitions of the radical wing of the " German Christians," but it did not coincide with Hitler's policy in 1933. Before he had gained power he was willing to make use of all revolutionary forces. Once in the saddle he was anxious to avoid any unnecessary unrest. Just as he curbed the revolutionary goals of the Brown Shirts within his Party, so he sought to curb the radical elements in the Faith Movement. In April it looked as if the Churches were prepared to submit to him. The Catholic bishops retracted their prohibitions against the Nazi Party and von Papen was successfully negotiating a concordat with the Vatican. Evangelical churchmen were manifesting a desire to cooperate and were working on a new Church constitution in tune with the new political situation. Hossenfelder liked to describe his Faith Movement as the " Storm Troop of Jesus Christ." But as Hitler abandoned his Chief of Staff, Ernst Röhm, and turned to the Army generals, so he turned from the revolutionary Hossenfelder to the Army chaplain Ludwig Müller.

Müller was born on June 23, 1883, at Gütersloh, in Westphalia. He was ordained in 1909 and called to a Naval chaplaincy in 1914. After the war he served as chaplain at Cuxhaven and Wilhelmshaven. In 1926 he became an army chaplain in Königsberg, when he met Hitler. The two men had much in common because of their military background and became intimate friends. Müller is said to have made himself useful to Hitler in various ways. Duncan-Jones relates in his book that when he met Müller in Berlin in July, 1933, he got " the impression of a man who, though undoubtedly sincerely religious, was without any theological acumen." [27] In 1932, Müller became the leader of the " German Christians " in East Prussia. He was a prominent figure at the convention held in April, 1933, even though he himself was essentially moderate in his views. What he wanted was a national Church somewhat similar to the Church of England. This was better suited to Hitler's immediate purposes. On April 17, Hitler had had a lengthy and exhaustive discussion with Müller on the problems of a united German evangelical Church. Eight days later Hitler appointed him his confidential adviser and deputy in Church affairs and charged him with the responsibility of creating a Reich Church. Upon his appointment Müller explained: " I am to see to it that the struggle for the future of the evangelical Church will not be conducted like the political struggle. Adolf Hitler does not want to cause any religious crisis." [28] And the next day Müller issued a statement that was calculated to pacify all parties. " The confidence of the Reich Chancellor has laid upon me an important and arduous task. With trust in God and with a consciousness of my responsibility to him I set to work. The goal is the fulfillment of the longing of evangelical Germans since the time of the Reformation. The situation at the moment is as follows: the ' German Christians ' want an evangelical German Reich Church. They have stirred up the Church people. The Church administrations also want a great ' evangelical Church of the German nation.' This Church is now to be built. The Reformation Confessions of our fathers will point us the way. . . . In the name of the Reich Chancellor, I call upon all concerned to engage in honest co-operation. May the Lord of the Church grant us the Spirit of unanimity, that together we may set to work with complete confidence." [29] At the same time, Müller retained his position as leader of the " German Christians " in East Prussia, and remained on good terms with Hossenfelder, who was appointed an adviser in the Prussian Ministry of Education. Hossenfelder realized that he could not now achieve the goals of his Faith Movement by revolutionary tactics and resorted to other methods, namely, a demand for new Church elections, since the elections of November, 1932, had been based upon an outmoded electoral law. Through direct and secret elections, which had never been used in the Church, together with the appropriate propaganda, he wanted to use the uncritical masses of baptized Christians for his purposes.

IV

The Formation
of the German Evangelical Church
and Its Constitution

ON THE SAME DAY on which Hitler interviewed Müller, he
granted an audience to Hermann Kapler, president of the
German Evangelical Church Federation, and assured him also that
he would stand by his statement concerning the relation of Church
and State. A special meeting of the executive committee of the Federation was held in Berlin on April 25, at which the need for a new
Church constitution on the basis of existing Confessions of Faith was
acknowledged, and Kapler was authorized to take the necessary steps.
To assist him Kapler called upon a leading Lutheran, Bishop August
Marahrens, of Hanover, and the Reformed minister, Dr. Hermann
Albert Hesse, of Elberfeld. (Kapler belonged to the United Church.)
This was the famous Committee of Three, which was charged with
formulating a new constitution for the Church in Germany. Thus
were initiated the steps that were to lead to the publication of the
constitution of the German Evangelical Church and its acceptance
by State law on July 14, 1933. The law was signed by Reich Chancellor Hitler and by the Minister for Internal Affairs, Wilhelm Frick. It
was also signed by the leaders of all Evangelical Churches.[1] The articles of the constitution, and especially the first article, were of im-
mense importance for the origin of the Barmen Declaration. The
Confessing Church took its stand upon the first article and repeatedly
appealed to it throughout the Church Struggle.[2] It is now our task
to trace the stormy events between May 5 and July 14 amidst which
the new Church arose.

The Committee of Three called upon certain experts to assist them
in their heavy task, notably the Church lawyer Prof. Theodor Heckel,
of Bonn. When they convened on May 5 certain " German Chris-

tian " leaders were invited to attend and to submit recommendations for the new constitution. These were Prof. Karl Fezer, of Tübingen, Dr. Friedrich Werner, and Pastor Otto Weber, the Director of the Reformed Theological School in Elberfeld.[3] Werner submitted ten articles which *inter alia* declared that they favored an evangelical Reich Church of a Lutheran character in which Reformed congregations would be incorporated in such a way that justice would be done to their uniqueness. " We do not want a State Church; neither do we want a Church that is a State within the State, but an evangelical Reich Church which in faith acknowledges the sovereignty of the National Socialist State and proclaims the gospel in the Third Reich." The document further declared that it should be " the Church of ' German Christians,' that is, of Christians of the Aryan race." It will not be a bulwark of reaction or the mouthpiece of democratic parliamentarianism, but have a Reich bishop at its head. He should be a Lutheran, with a Reformed vicar at his side.[4] Although there was agreement concerning the Church's ministry to the nation and in affirming the National Socialist State, the " German Christians " provoked a heated discussion. The meeting adjourned, to resume again on May 16.

On that date Müller, in agreement with Hossenfelder and with Hitler's approval, decided to take over the office of " protectorate " for the " German Christians " in order to ensure a unified line in the struggle for a reorganization of the German Evangelical Church.[5] Thus Müller became no longer a mere liaison between Hitler and the Church but a representative of a party in the Church. Moreover, on the same date — May 16 — the new Guiding Principles (*Richtlinien*) of the " German Christians " were published. They were drawn up by Professor Fezer and signed by Müller, Hossenfelder, and Missionary Inspector Ludwig Weichert.[6] They were to serve as a basis for discussions by the Committee of Three, which were scheduled for the next day in the cloister at Loccum. Hesse has related [7] that on the evening of the sixteenth they stayed in a hotel in Hanover, where they conferred with Professor Heckel. In another hotel Müller was with the " German Christian " theology professors Hirsch, Fezer, and Goeters and presented them with the new principles of the Faith Movement. Müller composed a nationalistic introduction that was enthusiastically received by the professors. The whole document was laid before the Committee of Three, which retired for " quiet meditation " at the invitation of Bishop Marahrens to a cloister in Loccum for the days of May 17–19.[8] It was moderate in tone and represented the greatest possible approach between the " German Christians " and the groups in the Church who were interested in a new constitution. It bore only slight resemblance to the radical principles drawn up in June of 1932. The word " race " appears but once and then in an innocuous context. Many who had opposed the radical views of the Faith Movement were relieved, only to learn later that the leaders of the Movement never had any idea of replacing the older statement with the new one. In fact, toward the end of May, Hossenfelder wrote that the original principles of the Movement were still in force, and that the new document was simply a further interpretation of them.[9] The truth is that at this particular time the " German Christians " were evidently hoping that they would gain control of the Church by getting their men into the chief offices — notably that of the Reich bishop — and were temporarily seeking to ingratiate themselves.

The office of a Reich bishop was one of the most fiercely debated issues with which the Committee of Three had to deal. On April 13, the Lutheran Superintendent Wilhelm Zöllner had publicly declared: " We need bishops at the head and not an ecclesiastical parliament. . . . The false adaptation to the democratic principle of the Weimar State must go." We have already noted that this too was the demand of the " German Christians." Hesse later admitted that he was deeply ashamed that he had not uncompromisingly resisted the efforts to establish Lutheran episcopacy as long as the necessary safeguards were secured for the Reformed Church. As it was, Hesse had his misgivings. Marahrens' explanation that in the Lutheran view " the bishop is the man who most directly receives the initiative from the Word of God " seemed to Hesse to be worse than the Roman doctrine of papal infallibility.[10] The Reformed churchmen back in the twin cities of Wuppertal-Barmen and Elberfeld had repudiated the idea that a bishop is a spiritual leader and teacher of the Church, but they too were not prepared to object to a bishop as an administrative head of the Church. It was not surprising, therefore, that the trio in Loccum were able to issue a manifesto which declared that the great stirring of the German people was the work of God and called for a united German Church in which the forces of the various *Landes-kirchen* would render welcome assistance and that "at its head should be a Lutheran Reich bishop," supported by a Spiritual Ministry, which would share with him the direction of the Church. There should also be a national synod composed of men elected and called from among those prominent in the life of the Church.[11]

While it was possible to secure agreement about a Reich bishop in theory, a violent conflict broke out when the question was raised of who he should be. When the Committee of Three took the position that the nomination and election of the bishops should be exclusively the business of the Church, Müller demurred. He contended that the Reich Government should concur in the selection. The representatives of the Churches emphatically rejected this idea and appealed to Article 137 of the constitution of the Reich, whereby Church bodies were granted the right to choose their own officers. Moreover, the political clauses in the agreements or contracts made with certain states within the Reich were not valid since no contract existed for the Federation of Evangelical Churches as a whole. Müller was obliged to concede the force of these arguments. It was then agreed that the Committee of Three should be empowered to put the new constitution into force at an appointed time, after which agreement should be sought concerning who should be bishop. Finally the Committee sought an audience with Hitler to report to him the results of their deliberations and the nomination for the election of a bishop. After this method of procedure had been decided upon, Müller announced that the Chancellor wanted to receive the three-man committee *before* agreement had been reached concerning the person of the future bishop. Since Müller assured them it was merely a matter of etiquette and that Hitler would make no recommendations, the churchmen agreed. The audience was set for the first of the following week but was postponed because Hitler was occupied with foreign affairs.[12]

On the evening of May 22 the Committee of Three was again in Berlin. At that meeting Hesse was in favor of either Hans Meiser, bishop of Bavaria, or Marahrens for Reich bishop, but the Lutherans were backing Dr. Friedrich von Bodelschwingh, who was the director of the Bethel Institute near Bielefeld, which consisted of a theological school and a sanatorium for orphans and epileptics. Von Bodelschwingh, a man of deep piety, stood above all ecclesiastical and political parties and was universally respected as a man of high Christian character.[13] In order to determine whether he would be willing to accept the position, it was decided to invite him to come to Berlin. At first von Bodelschwingh wanted to refuse the office but offered to postpone his decision until after representatives of all the *Landeskirchen* had met at a conference in Eisenach on May 26.[14]

Meanwhile several things occurred that were calculated to influence the work of the Committee. On May 12, the Young Reformation Movement was founded and published twelve articles concerning the formation of the Church. This Movement was the forerunner of the Confessing Church and was composed of younger ministers and theologians. Among its members were Dr. Hans Lilje, then secretary of the Christian Student Movement and editor of *Junge Kirche,* and the theologians Professor Schreiner, of Rostock, Professor Karl Heim, in Tübingen, Walther Künneth, of Berlin, Ritter, Staehlin, Brunstäd, and Lütgert. They stood behind the appeal of the Committee of Three and demanded that decisions be taken solely on the ground of the nature of the Church. They urged that the Reich bishop be named as quickly as possible, and that the spiritual Church administration be set up which would include the co-operation of the congregation. They categorically rejected the exclusion of non-Aryans from the Church. The Church had to give an answer to questions about race, nation, and State on the basis of the existing Confession of Faith. The Movement also demanded that the State afford the Church the influence it needed in press and radio for the spiritual upbuilding of the people and freedom from all political pressures to carry out its God-given task. A week later the Movement issued a statement containing sixteen theses that were an expansion of the original twelve articles.[15] It declared: " The appointment of the first Reich bishop must not result from a popular election along democratic lines or from his being named by the Government, but solely by the Church itself. We repeat our demand that the Reich bishop be appointed immediately. . . . He should be a minister who enjoys the confidence of active, worshiping congregations. We are thinking of a man like Friedrich von Bodelschwingh." Unfortunately the variety of theological schools represented in its membership, some of whom went over to the " German Christians," made it impossible for the Young Reformation Movement to make a united attack upon the root of the " German Christian " heresy. It imagined, for instance, that it could join forces with the " German Christians " in their repudiation of the nationalist or racial religion of the *Tannenberg-bund,* and the Nordic or Aryan paganism as set forth in the writings of Alfred Rosenberg, Herrmann Wirth, Ernst Bergmann, Jakob Hauer, and others. Actually there was little difference between these theses and the conservative principles of the " German Christian " Faith Movement issued on May 5. This explains why the Young Reformation Movement failed to play any significant role in the recovery of the Church's faith. Its leaders were too much under the spell of " the historical hour " of January 30, that is, of Hitler's coming to power, which was interpreted as a positive sign of the ways of God. What remained of the Movement was the publication *Junge Kirche,* which appeared first as an information sheet and then as a fortnightly periodical for Reformation Christianity until it was banned in 1941.

While the Committee of Three were waiting to hear when they could be received by Hitler, a district meeting of the " German Christians " was held on May 23 at which Müller was unanimously nominated as a candidate for the office of bishop. The next morning Hossenfelder communicated this action to President Kapler " out of loyalty," as he put it, before it was announced in the public press. Kapler replied that the Churches were already agreed upon a name for the office and expressed surprise that the " German Christians " should have taken this action since Müller himself had desired that no name be put forward before the audience with Hitler. Müller explained that it was merely a matter of a party in the Church expressing its preference and assured Kapler that no word about it would appear in the papers. Kapler doubted whether this was possible, and the Committee decided to announce in the press that the Churches were agreed upon a candidate without disclosing his name. On Wednesday afternoon, however, the papers carried the news that Müller had been nominated and had even been approved by the Church leaders. To correct these false reports the Committee had to announce the name of its candidate — von Bodelschwingh.

On May 26, a conference of delegates from all the regional Churches was held at Eisenach. First, the steps taken by the Kapler committee were approved and the Loccum Manifesto was endorsed. When the matter of the election of the Reich bishop came up, Bishop Rendtorff, of Mecklenburg, nominated Müller. Eleven Churches voted for him, and thirteen against. Another vote was held in which eleven Churches sided with von Bodelschwingh and eight opposed. The final vote was taken on May 27 and von Bodelschwingh was elected with a large majority. Only three *Landeskirchen* voted against him: Württemberg, Mecklenburg, and Hamburg.[16] In accepting the high office, von Bodelschwingh declared:

> I have not desired the office of bishop for myself, but I am taking the path of obedience. When the responsible men in the Church have chosen one who comes from a ministry to the poor and the sick, it shows the way I have to go further. It is the way of the diaconate. If I had my way, I would rather be called Reich deacon than Reich bishop. But the name is not important. An office acquires its name from a will to serve rather than to rule.
>
> We thank God that he has given us a government which with a reverence for history strengthens the will to work mightily for a better future, which wishes to lead us back again to the discipline, faithfulness, and integrity of our fathers, and which honors work. In a joyful spontaneity we Christians want to place ourselves heart and soul at its disposal in this service to the nation.[17]

It is worth-while to quote von Bodelschwingh's statement of acceptance in full, for the discerning reader will not fail to detect in it the real misery and confusion of the Church at that time. Here was a man of deep piety and humanitarian instincts, a man who embodied the rugged virtues of the Victorian era, tinged with warm nationalistic sentiments, a man of peace and good will who wanted to remain above and outside the warring ecclesiastical parties and theological schools. Yet he was a man who was blind to the theological issue of the day. That issue was whether the norm for the reformation of the Church was to be " a reverence for history " and political changes, or Jesus Christ alone as attested in Holy Scripture. Von Bodelschwingh was still under the spell of what the theologian Paul Althaus called " The German Hour of the Church " — the title of a book in which he wrote: " Our evangelical Churches have welcomed the turning point of 1933 in Germany as a gift and miracle of God." [18] Von Bodelschwingh also allowed himself to be used by men who up to that time imagined that the "German Christians" could be defeated by diplomacy and Church politics. Thus he consented to accept the office of Reich bishop *before* the Church had made any decisions in matters of faith. As is so frequently the case, the Church was attaching greater weight to organization and administration to achieve unity than to the purity of its proclamation. Fortunately a new note was soon to be sounded.

This note was sounded — significantly on the day von Bodelschwingh took office — in the so-called Düsseldorf Theses, a statement issued by Reformed Church theologians in the Rhineland on the form of the Church. Among the signatories were Karl Barth, Wilhelm Goeters, Hermann Hesse, Wilhelm Niesel, Alfred de Quervain. The Düsseldorf Theses are important because they were the first distinctly theological statement with a confessional ring to it, with the possible exception of the Altona Statement of January 11, 1933. The first article was a literal adoption of the first of the Ten Theses of Berne of 1528: " The holy, Christian Church, whose only head is Christ, is born of the Word of God, abides in the same, and hears not the voice of a stranger " — a striking testimony to the belief that the times of the Reformation had returned in which the great Confessions had appeared to combat the heresies then threatening the unity and faith of the Church. The Düsseldorf Theses are important not only because they were addressed to the then burning question of the Reich bishop but because they set forth principles concerning the nature and form of the Church, which were later embodied in the Barmen Declaration.[19] Moreover, since reference was made to the Düsseldorf Theses in a resolution adopted by the Second Free Reformed Synod in Siegen, March 26–28, 1938, and were later included in the *Bekenntnisschriften und Kirchenordnungen der nach Gottes Wort reformierten Kirche* published by the Reformed Alliance in Germany, 1938, these articles have lost their initial private character and must be reckoned among the official Confessions of the Reformed Church.

Once von Bodelschwingh had been elected and Müller defeated for the office of Reich bishop the feigned spirit of co-operation by the "German Christians" disappeared and turned into open hostility.

Müller lined up with the " German Christians " who announced that they still wanted him to be bishop. The moderate principles of the Movement were dropped in favor of the earlier radical articles. On June 1, it launched a political propaganda campaign in the style that had carried the Nazis into power. Members of congregations and of local organizations of the SA and the SS were urged to send telegrams to Kapler, Müller, Reich President Hindenburg, and to Hitler protesting the naming of von Bodelschwingh because (1) he is not the confidant of Hitler, (2) he is not from the ranks of the " German Christians," and (3) the Church people have been ignored in his election. A wave of public meetings were organized, the press and radio daily carried stories and editorial comments favoring the cause, and " German Christian " groups were set up in as many congregations as possible. Müller himself pursued a milder course of action by calling in question the legality of the election of the Reich bishop before the constitution had been drawn up. There would have been some plausibility to this stand if Müller himself had taken it *before* the election and if for that reason he had not permitted his own name to stand for election. The Church leaders replied that in order to avoid irretrievable damage, the Church Committee was authorized to take measures that were to be ratified at the next assembly of the Kirchentag. Failing to unseat von Bodelschwingh on supposed legal grounds, Müller resorted to pressure from the side of the State. He informed the Committee of Three in a letter dated June 15 that the Reich Chancellor deeply regretted that work on the reorganization of the Church had " taken such a thoroughly disagreeable turn " and that he [Hitler] had refused his request to grant an audience to the Committee or to von Bodelschwingh. Müller reiterated his contention that the office of Reich bishop did not exist and would not exist until the constitution had been upheld by a vote of the Church constituency.[20] Further political pressure was exerted when Frick, the Minister for Internal Affairs, advised von Bodelschwingh of the difficulties that his election had produced.

Outright invasion of the Church by the State occurred when on June 24 the Prussian Minister of Education, Bernhard Rust, doubtless with Hitler's permission, appointed a State commissar, Dr. August Jäger, for the Evangelical Church of Prussia. Jäger was a " German Christian," one of those lawyers in the Nazi State who serves a dictator's purpose by lending to his actions the color of legality. For

Jäger, all spheres of public life were but functions of a supreme will to which they were subordinated. He had no understanding for the nature of religion, let alone for the Christian Church.[21] It will be recalled that a commissar had been imposed upon the Church of Mecklenburg-Schwerin. This time the whole of the largest of the Evangelical Churches, that of Prussia, was involved and wrought such devastation as the Church had not hitherto experienced. The circumstances surrounding Jäger's appointment were as follows: Kapler tendered his resignation as president of the Old Prussian Union Church on June 21 because of ill-health. (Since June 1, he had been unable to attend the meetings of the Committee of Three, and they had been presided over by von Bodelschwingh.[22]) According to a " political clause " in the contract existing between the Prussian Church and the State, no one could be named chairman of the Church's board of administration without having been first certified as politically unobjectionable. To circumvent this proviso the board decided to empower the General Superintendent, Ernst Stoltenhoff, to carry on the administration without appointing anyone officially as president. The Prussian Government immediately declared this action illegal and that the contract had been broken. Rust, the Prussian Minister of Education, seized the opportunity to discharge Dr. Trendelenburg, who was director of Church affairs in the Ministry of Education, and to appoint Jäger director and also commissar for the whole Church.[23] Rust explained that the situation in the nation, State, and Church required that the prevailing confusion and unrest be ended and that the State's action was an emergency measure which had to do simply with " the earthly organization of the Church and its relation to the State. . . . The Church's faith and Confession are in no way affected."

Jäger's first step was to discharge all Church-elected officers and to appoint " German Christians " in their places. Almost all the members of the Church's administrative boards were dismissed. These measures were backed up by ominous threats. " Since the State in the interest of itself, the nation, and the Church cannot tolerate opposition of any kind, any effort to resist will be regarded as treason. I demand that strict care be taken that my decrees and those whom I have publicly authorized be not sabotaged. Any such attempt would be rebellion against the authority of the State and would be immediately suppressed." [24]

The immediate consequence of Dr. Jäger's appointment was von Bodelschwingh's resignation as bishop. To the Committee meeting in Eisenach on June 23–24, he explained: " By the appointment of a State commissar for the whole of the Evangelical Churches of Prussia, I have been deprived of the possibility of carrying out the task entrusted to me." [25] Walther Trittelvitz in a brief but rather effusive sketch of von Bodelschwingh's life speaks of him as the " secret bishop " who continued to exercise an influence through private contacts with leaders in Church and State.[26] It is fortunate, however, that there were others who spoke out boldly. Otto Dibelius, the General Superintendent of Kurmark, a district of Brandenburg, who was one of the first pastors to be dismissed, replied that he would refrain from all administrative business until the legality of Dr. Jäger's action was determined. But he refused to allow his functions as bishop and priest to be taken from him by any State commissar. They had been conferred upon him by the Church and could be withdrawn only by the Church. " They remain my duties as before. I must and shall fulfill them — especially at this time when true spiritual guidance is needed more than ever by the Church." The suspended General Superintendents of the Prussian Church and the officers of the Church consistory registered a vigorous protest. They issued an appeal for a special day of penitence and prayer to be held on July 2. Hossenfelder, whom Jäger had appointed vice-president of the Evangelical Church Council, countered with the announcement that July 2 would be observed as a day of thanksgiving and intercession and ordered that a message be read from all pulpits in Prussia. The message read in part: " All who are concerned for the welfare of the Church . . . must be deeply grateful that the State has assumed the great burden of the reorganization of the Church. Until that great hour when the evangelical Church of the whole Reich has its new constitution, actions against the good intentions of the State are acts of disobedience. . . . We call upon the congregations to co-operate joyfully, prayerfully, and gratefully in this great work of reorganization. In this work we are putting our trust in Almighty God. He will bless those who truly love and desire his Church."

Meanwhile Ludwig Müller had taken possession of the buildings of the Church Federation with brown-shirted SA troops on June 28 and had issued the following Decree for the Removal of the Critical

State in Church and Nation: "The German Evangelical Churches have fallen into a critical state. The unconditionally necessary unity of the nation and the Church are in peril. The emergency demands extraordinary measures. In agreement with the State Commissar for the Evangelical Church of Prussia I am therefore taking over with the authorization of the Reich Chancellor and for the sake of the Church and its gospel the administration of the Church Federation. In particular I am assuming the chairmanship of the Council of the Federation and taking charge of the Kirchentag, the Committee of the Church, and its subcommittees. With trust in God, and conscious of my responsibility to God and our people, I set to work in obedience to the truth of the pure gospel of Jesus Christ." [27]

One of the encouraging signs at that time was the way in which the ministers promptly and boldly registered their protests and took a stand behind their regularly called and ordained leaders. The very next day Westphalian ministers of the Synod of Bielefeld drew up a Confession of Faith containing seven articles.[28]

> In view of the naming of a State Commissar for the Evangelical Church of Prussia, we raise our voices in protest as called preachers of God's word and as leaders of our congregations. . . .
>
> We protest against our official General Superintendents' being prevented from speaking to their congregations according to their conscience. We are determined to follow our Church leaders.
>
> We regard the appointment of a State Commissar as an intolerable violation of the freedom of the Evangelical Church. . . . Because of our obligation to the Confessions of our Church, we enter a vigorous protest against the appointment of Church leaders and ecclesiastical bodies by the Commissar. Not only because we desire equal status with the Roman Catholic Church but for reasons of justice and fairness we demand freedom for the Evangelical Church, freedom from the State Commissar, freedom to preach, also in the press and on the radio, freedom for the Church to rebuild itself and to reinstate the Church leaders dismissed by the Commissar.

This Bielefeld Confession was signed by fifty persons, and later several hundred others joined in. As Wilhelm Niemöller, himself one of the signatories, has observed, the men who made this statement were well aware of the character of the State to which it was addressed. But they also knew that they were bound by their ordination vows. Their " Confession " was destined to give direction to the action of the Church in the long years ahead.

But true and necessary as the Bielefeld Confession was, it did not get at the real issue facing the Church. It stopped at the point of insisting upon the Church's independence from the power of the State. It did not go beyond the question of Church organization. It remained to Karl Barth to lay bare the theological issue. This he did in the famous pamphlet *Theological Existence Today* — written on the very day on which von Bodelschwingh resigned as Reich bishop.[29] Within the first half year after its publication thirty thousand copies were sold. By a " theological existence " Barth meant that in the midst of our life in other respects, as, say parents, citizens, and Germans, the Word of God may be what it simply is and only can be for us. " The mighty temptation of our age," he wrote, " is that we no longer appreciate the intensity and exclusiveness of the demand of the divine Word . . . so that in our anxiety in face of existing dangers we no longer put our whole trust in the authority of God's Word, but we think we ought to come to its aid with all sorts of contrivances, and we thus throw aside our confidence in the Word's power to triumph. . . . And this means that we seek for God elsewhere than in his Word, and seek his Word somewhere else than in Jesus Christ, and seek Jesus Christ elsewhere than in the Holy Scriptures of the Old and New Testaments." From this standpoint Barth then discussed recent happenings in the Church.

Barth first drew attention to the then current cries for Church reform which, he insisted, had not proceeded from the Word of God alone but from the desire to assimilate Church and State. The demand for Church reform was coupled with the demand for a Reich bishop. Yet it was obvious that the desired bishop was to be after the Hitler pattern, that the leadership principle in the State was to be transferred to the Church. Barth bluntly characterized the principle of leadership talked about as " sheer nonsense." He noted that the Reformed Church had declared its stand on the question of a bishop, but that the Lutherans had not explained their understanding of the office. Hence it was a " colossal blunder " to appoint or elect a Reich bishop until his powers had been defined. The Church has not comported itself as a Church which *possesses* its Leader during these re-

, cent months. Yet *He* possesses it. " When it is recognized that He, and He alone, is the Leader, there is the possibility of theological existence. And then, in all deference, even if one be but an ever-so-insignificant theologian, or an obscure village pastor, or even not a pastor or theologian at all but ' merely' somebody like a lay elder, then one is *himself* the genuine Bishop."

Turning to the doctrines of the " German Christians," Barth uttered an absolute and unreserved No! He maintained that the Evangelical Church would cease to exist if these teachings ever came to have sole sway within its borders and that the Church ought to choose to be thinned down to a tiny group and go into the catacombs than make a compact, even covertly, with this doctrine. But " however bad they may be, it seems to me [Barth wrote] that far worse has been the attitude till now that the Evangelical Church has adopted by entering into engagements with them." Here Barth upbraided the Committee of Three for permitting Ludwig Müller to work with them and for the theologically intolerable Confession they issued from Loccum. The Young Reformation Movement also came in for sharp criticism because of its flabby, compromising attitude to the " German Christians " and because of its enthusiasm for the new office of Reich bishop. Barth saw in the Young Reformers a greater peril than in the " German Christians." For under the mask of contending for the independence of the Church, they were perpetuating the old compromises of creation *and* redemption, nature *and* grace, nationalism *and* gospel. Barth perceived that the real issue was not the freedom of the Church from political pressure or from the oppression of the " German Christian " party, but the freedom of the Word of God in preaching and theology — a freedom that had been generally threatened long before the rise of Hitler and the " German Christians." Once this freedom was grasped, " there would then be no talk about all being favorable if Church politics won, or of all being lost if it were defeated." Thus did Barth exhort the Church " to carry on theology, and only theology, now as previously as if nothing had happened." The telling effect that Barth's pamphlet had upon many may be illustrated in the case of Dr. Hermann Hesse, the Reformed Church member of the Committee of Three. Dr. Hesse's own account is as follows: " In my utter helplessness I telephoned Karl Barth and asked him to go with me to Berlin. It was July 3, 1933. We met in the train at Hamm. Barth put into my hand a pamphlet and said: 'Read that!' . . . It was entitled *Theological Existence Today*. I read and read while the professor paced up and down the train. It was an attack upon us three men, upon the 'German Christians,' and the Young Reformation Movement. All of us were accused because of our natural theology. As I read, the scales fell from my eyes. Here lay my mistake since my early days under Schlatter! Besides Holy Scripture, another side of revelation had been authoritative for me, namely, nature. When I had finished reading, I was deeply moved. I could only give the professor my hand and say: 'You are right! I am grateful to you for everything!' Then began for me through God's great grace a whole new era. For me the deepest meaning of Barth's pamphlet lay in the fact that according to Rom. 2:4, I am grateful for the riches of God's kindness and forbearance and patience by which he is able to lead a man to repentance."

Although Barth's rallying call to a " theological existence " was to find an increasingly favorable response, political maneuvering persisted. Von Bodelschwingh enlisted the support of the aging President Hindenburg, who in an interview with Hitler on June 29 and in a follow-up letter written the next day warned that if the situation in the Church persisted, it could result only in serious harm to the nation. " Before God and my conscience," Hindenburg wrote, " I feel bound to do all I can to avoid such a calamity." Unfortunately the influence of the eighty-six-year-old president was on the wane. Hitler did promise to settle the conflict and made Frick, the Minister for Internal Affairs, responsible. Frick, however, refrained from taking any action on the ground that under Müller's administration, work on the new constitution for the Church was progressing and would soon be finished. Müller, however, had already dissolved the committee that had been working on the constitution and had appointed a new one composed of four Lutheran bishops, four representatives of the " German Christians," a representative of the Old Prussian Union and one from the Young Reformation Movement, and Dr. Jäger. Affiliated with this committee were the members of the former Committee of Three — Marahrens, Hesse, and Seetzen. Bishop Meiser and Prof. Karl Fezer were co-opted. On July 10, the draft of the constitution was ready, which the Committee of Three had prepared in co-operation with Professors Fezer and Heckel. The next day the representatives of the regional Churches met in the offices of the Minister for Internal Affairs and unanimously adopted the constitution laid before them by Bishop Marahrens.

With the publication of the constitution, hopes were kindled on all sides that the conflict in the Church had been settled and peace had been restored. On July 12, Hitler sent the following telegram to President Hindenburg: "Following the conclusion of the work on the constitution of the German Evangelical Church yesterday, negotiations have been concluded today on the settlement of the Prussian Church conflict in a way equally satisfactory to the State and the Church. The internal freedom of the Church, for which I am specially concerned, will doubtless be assured by the withdrawal of the Commissars and Assistant Commissars of the State. The internal reorganization of the regional Churches will be brought to an early completion by a free election of the evangelical Church people in accordance with Church law." Two days later the constitution was confirmed by State law and was published. At the same time, the Church elections were announced and set for July 26. The State Commissar was retired and the Church officers removed by him were reinstated.[30] These steps were actually initiated by Hitler and were directed first of all against the " German Christians " and the power politics of Jäger.[31] Hitler was quite willing to sacrifice the Faith Movement just as he had sacrificed the SA in favor of the Army, if thereby he could consolidate the nation behind his government. Moreover, Hitler, who had no understanding for religion, much less for Christianity, looked upon the Church as an entity that could be " functionally " integrated into the State, as an organization to cultivate the religious life. He thought the Church's Confession could be separated from its " external order." The State was to guarantee the external order of the Church as a corporation, and the Church was to be left free to develop its own inner spiritual life. But the Church was to learn that its order grows out of and must conform to its Confession. This insight which the Church was gradually to recover was to prove the reef upon which Hitler's policies with respect to the Church would be shipwrecked. The peace that many thought had been achieved by the formulation of a constitution was soon to be exposed as a spurious peace. For as Wilhelm Niemöller has observed: " The constitution was a contradiction in itself. On the one hand, it spoke about the gospel being the inviolable foundation of the Church, and on the other hand the Church's order was regulated in a highly unevangelical manner." [32]

V

The Pastors' Emergency League
and the Disintegration
of the "German Christians"

THE HOPED-FOR PEACE failed to materialize. For the Church, elections were prescribed by State law and the date set by the Government. From Hitler and his personal representative, Rudolf Hess, down to the members of the SA, and even the police, all political officials actively campaigned on behalf of the "German Christians." Using the vast organization of the State and the mass means of communication, the "German Christians" carried on an unscrupulous agitation. They called for "a new Church of Christ in the new State of Adolf Hitler." Hossenfelder proclaimed that "the 'German Christians' are the SA of Jesus Christ in the struggle to do away with bodily, social, and spiritual distress." The Young Reformation Movement announced that it was fighting for a "confessing Church," for a "free Church" independent of political pressures. It recommended that voting lists be drawn up under the head of "Evangelical Church." But on July 17, officials of the State Secret Police (Gestapo) appeared in the Movement's national offices and confiscated there and at the printers' more than 620,000 pieces of election literature. Complaints were made to the Ministry for Internal Affairs, with the result that the literature was released but the name under which the Young Reformation Movement was running was changed from "Evangelical Church" to "Gospel and Church" by action of the State. It is true that the Ministry for Internal Affairs did issue orders to secure a free election in which no votes would be intimidated. But the Ministry was powerless to implement its orders. The National Socialist newspaper, *Völkischer Beobachter,* published a statement to the effect that it is the obvious duty of every evangelical member of the Nazi Party to cast his vote in favor of the "German

Christians." On the eve of the election, Hitler delivered a speech over a nationwide radio network in which he explained that a State that is prepared to guarantee the internal freedom of religious life has the right to hope that " those forces in the Churches will be heard which are determined to support the freedom of the nation." This will be achieved, however, only by " the forces of a living movement. I see these forces marshaled in that section of the evangelical population which has taken its stand in the ' German Christian ' Movement on the ground of the National Socialist State." [1]

As a result of this propaganda campaign carried on by State officials, thousands of people voted who for years had never darkened the door of a church. It came as no great surprise, therefore, when on July 23, the " German Christians " won an overwhelming victory. The voting in some provinces was two to four times as heavy as it had been in any previous election. As Professor Kupisch has pointed out, the election was a classic example of the opportunities a dictatorial power possesses to misuse the democratic right to vote.[2] On August 4, the Church senate of the Prussian Church elected Ludwig Müller president of the consistory, with the title of bishop. The General Synod of that Church convened on September 4 and 5, one day after the Reich Party congress was held in Nuremberg under the slogan " Triumph of Faith." A leading " German Christian " declared that the synod was " spiritually characterized by the Faith Movement, outwardly by honorary brown uniforms of the Hitler movement." It passed a law establishing the office of bishop and bishoprics. It abolished the office of General Superintendent and the place of the superintendents was taken by ten bishops, with their sees set up in various cities. Hossenfelder, for example, was elected bishop of Brandenburg and in this capacity was Müller's representative and vice-president of the consistory. The synod passed a further law concerning the legal status of ministers and Church officials. It provided for the discharge of those who " on the basis of their previous activity do not guarantee that they will at all times unreservedly support the national State and the German Evangelical Church." Another law was passed whereby ministers and officials of non-Aryan descent or " married to a person of non-Aryan descent " were retired. Exceptions were permitted when it could be shown that the person in question had rendered signal service in the " upbuilding of the

Church in the German spirit." [3] With the passage of these laws, the assimilation of the largest of the *Landeskirchen* to the State was accomplished. President Karl Koch, of Bad-Oeynhausen, chairman of the " Gospel and Church " minority group in the synod, was shouted down as he tried to read a statement in which he protested that secular principles and methods had been introduced into the Church, making further co-operation impossible. Unable to continue speaking, Koch and his friends left the meeting.

At the very time when God's judgment lay heaviest upon his Church, when the " German Christians " were celebrating their victory and to the Church " belonged confusion of face," there — where the darkness was deepest — the light of God's mercy began to dawn. " God's judgments were the veil of his ever-present grace " (Kupisch). For the events at the Prussian General Synod were the occasion for Martin Niemöller to organize the Pastors' Emergency League (*Pfarrernotbund*). [4] On September 21 he sent a circular letter to all German pastors inviting them to join the League. " Because of this need we have formed an ' Emergency League ' of ministers who have given written assurance to one another that in their preaching they will be bound only by Holy Scripture and the Confessions of the Reformation and to the best of their ability will succor those brethren who in doing so have to suffer." The response exceeded all expectations. Immediately 1,300 signed up. By the end of September the number mounted to 2,300, and by January 15, 1934, there were 7,036 members. In spite of heavy losses [5] and in spite of the imprisonment of its founder on July 1, 1937, the League was never dissolved or banned, and it rendered service until as late as Christmas, 1944. It not only was the root from which the Confessing Church sprang, it remained its conscience throughout the Church Struggle. At the same time, it never wanted to take the place of the Church. It sought no positions of power in either Church or State. Rather, it quickly ranged itself within the Confessing Church. The opponents of the League looked upon it as an illegal, unconstitutional organization, yet its pronouncements were made publicly and on its own authority. The pledge, formulated by Niemöller in October, 1933, and subscribed to by every member, reflects the purpose of the League. It read as follows:

1. I engage to execute my office as minister of the Word, holding myself bound solely to Holy Scripture and to the Confessions of the Reformation as the true exposition of Holy Scripture.

2. I engage to protest, regardless of the cost, against every violation of this confessional stand.

3. I hold myself responsible to the utmost of my ability for those who are persecuted on account of this confessional stand.

4. In making this pledge, I testify that the application of the Aryan paragraph within the Church of Christ has violated the confessional stand.

This vow, reminiscent of the Scottish covenants in the sixteenth century, while in no sense a Confession of Faith, laid bare the basic issue, namely, anti-Semitism, particularly as it related to the nature of the Church.

Six days after Niemöller had circulated his letter — September 27 — the National Synod of the German Evangelical Church met in Wittenberg. It provided the Pastors' Emergency League with its first opportunity to raise its voice in protest. Twenty-two Berlin ministers — among them Dietrich Bonhoeffer — sent a statement to the synod in the name of their two thousand brethren. (The statement had been drafted by Martin Niemöller and Friedrich Müller.) Dr. Karl Koch, president of the Westphalian Church, handed it to the newly elected Reich bishop Ludwig Müller. Niemöller himself distributed copies of it to the delegates, and nailed other copies to the trees and telegraph posts in Wittenberg, not far from the church where four hundred years before another Martin had nailed his famous theses. The declaration vowed: "We will not cease to combat everything that is destructive to the nature of the Church." [6]

The founder of the Pastors' Emergency League, Martin Niemöller,[7] then virtually unknown to the general public, was destined to become a symbol for the Confessing Church and Germany's most famous churchman throughout the world. Born in Lippstadt, Westphalia, January 14, 1892, a son of the manse, he embarked upon a career in the German Imperial Navy from 1910–1920, serving as a U-boat commander during World War I. Upon leaving the service, he studied theology at the University of Münster from 1920–1923. In

1931, he was called to be minister of the Lutheran Berlin-Dahlem congregation. As a result of his work in the Emergency League, it was natural that he should play a prominent part in the Synod of Barmen. Although he did not participate directly in drawing up the Theological Declaration, he had more to do with its reception and proclamation than anyone else. " When I think of Martin Niemöller," Barth wrote, " I think of him as the embodiment of ' Barmen.' . . . It is no accident that the names ' Barmen ' and ' Dahlem ' later became inseparable. . . . Pastor Niemöller in the Dahlem congregation was and is exemplary for the ' Church Struggle.' " Accordingly, Niemöller was appointed to the Council of the Old Prussian Church and of the German Evangelical Church. On July 1, 1937, he was arrested. Although he was acquitted, at his release he was seized by the Gestapo and placed in solitary confinement in the Concentration Camp in Sachsenhausen as Hitler's personal prisoner; from 1941 until the end of the war he was in Dachau Concentration Camp. At the conference of Church leaders in Treysa, Niemöller stressed the guilt not of the National Socialists and the German people but of the Church, especially the Confessing Church. From this attitude emerged the " Stuttgart Confession of Guilt " of October, 1945, which, though highly offensive to many in Germany, was the solid ground for immediate resumption of fraternal relations with Churches in enemy lands. Because his name had become famous throughout the world, he was enabled to make many trips to foreign countries. He did far more than any other man to heal the painful wounds left by the war, and the harvest of good will and material relief he reaped for his devastated country was incalculable. Since the war Niemöller has served on the Executive Committee of the World Council of Churches, from 1945 to 1956 on the Council of the German Evangelical Church, and since 1947 has held the post of Church President of the Evangelical Church in Hesse and Nassau. During these latter years he has persisted in his ministry of reconciliation — between a divided Germany and between East and West power blocs. His prophetic voice has been raised on behalf of world peace, and therefore against military service and the rearmament of Germany, especially with atomic weapons: " It has taken many years of my life," he has confided, " to realize that God is not the enemy of my enemy. . . . He is never the enemy of his enemies." Therefore a Christian is prevented from taking part in the formation of a "Christian" front against an "anti-Christian" one. Such is the man whom God raised up in September, 1933, to be the outstanding leader of the Confessing Church, and to become one of Germany's most illustrious sons since the days of Martin Luther.

At the National Synod held in Wittenberg on September 27, Ludwig Müller was elected Reich bishop. He in turn formed a Spiritual Ministry composed of Hossenfelder for the United Church, Simon Schöffel for the Lutherans, and Otto Weber for the Reformed Church. Friedrich Werner, a lawyer, was the fourth member. In his address the new bishop announced: "The old has passed away. The new has emerged. The Church's political struggle is past. Now begins the struggle for the soul of the people."[8] Though Müller doubtless believed his words, they were an illusion. The Church Struggle was actually just beginning. Opposition was rising not only from the side of orthodox Christians but from the radical element in the Faith Movement. It wanted to get rid of a "bishop's Church" and contended for a "second revolution" in the Church. It claimed to be the movement that was identified with the ideals and objectives of the Nazi Party and acted as if one could not be a true National Socialist without being a "German Christian." Such a claim was contrary to the interests of the Party, which was intent upon gaining the support of all Church groups for its domestic and foreign policies. Rosenberg, as the spokesman for the Party, publicly stated that the power of the State or of the Party no longer backed any particular group or denomination.[9] Thus on October 11, Müller was forced to issue a public statement to the effect that no member of the Church would be discriminated against because he was not a "German Christian." Doubtless thereby Müller sought to pacify the Church, yet it is likely that he was more anxious to pacify Hitler, whose personal representative, Rudolf Hess, issued a decree two days later that no National Socialist would be discriminated against because of his membership in any particular religious association.[10]

The fanatical "German Christians" were not to be held in check by meager concessions and grandiose promises. Their representative, a Dr. Reinhold Krause, succeeded in arranging a monster demonstration for the "German Christians" in the Berlin Sport Palace on November 13, at which he delivered the major address. The purpose was to " rekindle the fighting spirit of the Movement and to place again in the forefront the old goals of the ' German Christians.' " [11] Krause wanted the mass demonstration to be held on October 26, but it had to be postponed because the leaders of the Nazi Party were opposed to having such a dangerous meeting held prior to the Reichstag election and a plebiscite on Germany's withdrawal from the League of Nations, which were to be held on November 12. Krause's conclave was set for the thirteenth. Twenty thousand gathered in the Sport Palace, among them Hossenfelder and his followers. The demonstration opened with a procession of flags. A choir sang " Now Thank We All Our God," and a chorus of trumpets blared out the strains of " A Mighty Fortress Is Our God." Johann Schmiedchen, a friend of Krause's, chaired the meeting and set the tone in his opening remarks. He declared that the Faith Movement had only apparently achieved its goals and that the defeated enemy had to be pursued until he fled in disarray. Hossenfelder reported that he had given instructions for carrying out the Aryan paragraph in the Churches. It was Krause, however, who created a sensation with his speech. He declared that the German Reformation begun by Luther would be completed in the Third Reich by the formation of a new Church — " not a Lutheran, not a Reformed, not a United, not a synodical or consistorial Church, not an episcopal or a Church with General Superintendents, but one, mighty, new all-embracing German national Church." It would not be a clerical Church bound to Confessions, but a people's Church. The first step in the creation of an indigenous Church must be to get rid of " the Old Testament with its Jewish morality of rewards, and its stories of cattle dealers and panders." The New Testament had to be expurgated of all perverted and superstitious passages, and the whole scapegoat and inferiority complex theology of the Rabbi Paul had to be renounced. Even an exaggerated portrayal of the Crucified had to be guarded against. Krause's speech was interrupted frequently by loud and enthusiastic applause, and he was accorded a tremendous ovation at its conclusion. Then followed the dedication of sixty new flags of the Faith Movement. Finally a resolution was passed, with but one dissenting voice, which expressed the special demands made by Krause and his friends — the discharge of ministers who are not willing to co-operate in the completion of the Reformation in accordance with the spirit of National Socialism; swift execution of the Aryan paragraph without any weakening of it; the placing of all Christians with alien blood in a Jewish Christian Church; removal of anything un-Germanic from the Church service and the Confession, especially the Old Testament; freeing the gospel of its Oriental distortions and the presentation of a heroic picture of Jesus as the basis for a Christianity in which the proud man who as a child of God is conscious of the divine in himself and in his people takes the place of broken servile souls; a single true Church service that is a service to one's fellow countrymen and which completes the German Reformation of Martin Luther and alone does justice to the totalitarian claims of the National Socialist State.

The Sport Palace demonstration provoked a storm of indignation. The first to protest were three leaders of the Pastors' Emergency League: the brothers Martin and Wilhelm Niemöller and Pastor Jacobi. The next afternoon they saw Reich bishop Müller and declared that they could not recognize a Church in which such a meeting was tolerated as an evangelical Church. They demanded that Müller immediately dissociate himself from the Faith Movement and discharge those Church officers who were responsible for the meeting or had not protested against it. On the following Sunday — November 19 — some thirty thousand members of the League read from their pulpits a denunciation of the Church government because it had failed in its duty. They had not defended the faith against attacks made upon it in the Sport Palace, yet they still held office. Paganism was invading the Church, and its leaders were silent. " We preachers of the gospel," they said, " refuse to earn the reproach of the prophet of being dumb dogs but owe it to our congregations and our people to oppose this falsification of the gospel. We emphatically recognize the Holy Scripture of the Old and New Testaments as the only standard and rule of our faith and life, and the Confessions of the fathers as its Reformation interpretation." Protest meetings were held in many cities, as for example in Augsburg and Dortmund, where over ten thousand persons attended. A number of presbyteries demanded the resignation of the Church leaders who had participated in the Sport Palace demonstration. The upshot was that Müller notified Krause on November 15 that he had been relieved of all his Church offices. On the same day the Reich bishop issued a statement sharply condemning Krause's attacks upon the Bible, and ordered that all Church organizations were bound to the Bible and Confession and could act only in service to the congregations and the Church. At the same time he supported Hossenfelder, who in turn appointed a Pastor Friedrich Tausch, an avowed " German Christian," to take Krause's post as a district supervisor. " The impression grew that Ludwig Müller's word could not be trusted. It was then that he began to receive the nickname ' Lügen Müller ' [lying Müller]." [12] Müller's vacillation was due in part to the wave of protests from the Emergency League and other Church groups, and in part to pressure from the National Socialists. The latter had no objection to attacks upon the Bible, but they could not tolerate a man who demanded " a mighty, new, all-embracing national Church " and particularly when he did this in the name of National Socialism. The Party was blamed for the religious unrest in the nation. Consequently the press bureau of the Party issued an official statement in which it voiced its annoyance. It insisted upon the Party's strict neutrality in religious disputes. The Faith Movement was recognized as a movement that had done much to interest Church circles in the tasks of the State. " But a preference for this or that theological position is out of the question since such questions lie outside the political sphere. The task of the German people today is to struggle for its economic reconstruction and to contend for its honor in the eyes of the world and not to wear itself out in splits over religious disputes." [13] Three days later — November 30 — Dr. Frick, the Minister for Internal Affairs, issued a regulation to the effect that the Chancellor had decided that, since the current disputes within the Evangelical Church were a purely ecclesiastical affair, no interference would be countenanced, and that Church officers were not authorized to induce political bodies to intervene. [14] Finally, Wilhelm Kube, leader of the Nazi faction in the Prussian Landtag and one of the founders of the " German Christians," now professed a sharp separation of ecclesiastical and political matters, and declared that differences of opinion in religious questions may not be carried over into politics and that no one has the right to appeal to the National Socialist Movement when he blesses or curses in Church matters. [15]

Thus the collapse of the Faith Movement of " German Christians " was prepared by the Nazi State and by evangelical Church groups led by the Pastors' Emergency League — but for entirely different reasons. Following the Sport Palace fiasco, the majority of " German Christian " groups in the *Landeskirchen* separated from Hossenfelder and acknowledged the authority of the Reich bishop alone. Already in September, one hundred and fifty " German Christian " pastors in Württemberg had left the Movement to join the Emergency League. In Saxony under the " German Christian " Bishop Friedrich Coch the name of the Movement was changed to " The People's Missionary Movement (German Christian) " and the " Twenty-eight Theses " were substituted for the original guiding principles.[16] These theses were drawn up by a Dr. Walther Grundmann. He espoused the idea that since Christianity had already experienced a Hellenizing of the gospel without damage to its substance, it could also undergo a " Germanizing " process. The Twenty-eight Theses represented the creed of the moderate " German Christians," yet the basic tenets were retained: Church leaders must enjoy the confidence of the Government, application of the Aryan paragraph to Church officials, recognition of the totalitarian claim of the Nazi State as God's call to family, people, and State.

Hossenfelder's position was further weakened when many professors publicly resigned from the Movement, among them Fezer, Bornkamm, Gerhard and Helmut Kittel, Gogarten, and Beyer. A leadership conference in Weimar was called by Hossenfelder for November 23–24 for the purpose of rallying the dissident forces behind his administration. It was a disappointment for him. The Bavarian " German Christians," instead of professing " unconditional obedience " to Hossenfelder, declared their loyalty to their bishop, Hans Meiser. The " Thüringian ' German Christians ' " also withdrew their support. Following the Weimar conference, Hossenfelder and fifty of his loyal henchmen traveled to Berlin and were received by Reich bishop Müller on the evening of November 24. Although on the same day a number of non " German Christian " Church leaders had declared that Hossenfelder was no longer acceptable as Church minister, Müller signified his intention to retire Schöffel instead of Hossenfelder. Thereupon followed renewed protests from the Church leaders. They demanded that the Spiritual Ministry be reorganized, that the use of political pressure and force be renounced, and that Müller, in the interest of his independence as Reich bishop, abandon his role as the patron of the "German Christians." This time the Church leaders were successful, and on November 29 the Spiritual Ministry was retired. A new Ministry was appointed, in which Hossenfelder was not a member, and which passed a law whereby all officials of the Reich Church government were forbidden to be members of any Church party. In line with this law, Müller then resigned his position as "protector" or "patron" of the Faith Movement. Hossenfelder endeavored to circumvent this law by issuing an order that "German Christians" were no longer a political party in the Church but strictly a faith *movement*. "As of today [December 6], I am withdrawing the Movement from the political struggle within the Church." [17] On December 19 a number of Lutheran bishops, and on December 20 the Pastors' Emergency League, again voiced their distrust of Müller's new Spiritual Ministry, with the result that the next day Hossenfelder was relieved of all his offices, that is, bishop of Brandenburg, vice-bishop of Prussia, and vice-president in the consistory of the Prussian Church. On the same day, Hossenfelder was also forced to hand over his leadership of the Faith Movement to a Dr. Christian Kinder. Kinder was a well-meaning man of the middle wing of the "German Christians." He was responsible for reorganizing the Movement under the new name of "Reich Movement" and for the adoption of the Twenty-eight Theses of the Saxony "German Christians" as its basis. These theses, as we have seen, differed little from the earlier directives of the Movement, and surpassed earlier pronouncements with its muddled thinking. Kinder strove to neutralize the "German Christians" theologically, so that they would no longer appear to be a Christian form of National Socialist ideology and so that the Nazi Party would not be directly identified with any particular religious group. On the other hand, he strove to make the Movement acceptable to the Church leaders as a respectable partner in discussions of Church matters. In other words, Kinder endeavored to placate the two sides from which the "German Christians" had been attacked: the Nazi State and the Church leaders. Thus he encouraged the illusion that Christian faith and Nazism were reconcilable, or at least that they could be confined to separate compartments. As the year 1933 drew to a close, the situation in the Church had by no means been clarified by the establishment of Müller's new Church Ministry, the retirement of Hossenfelder, and the defeat of the radical "German Christians." [18]

Before the record of the turbulent events of 1933 is concluded, mention must be made of Müller's most traitorous act of incorporating the Evangelical Youth of Germany in the Hitler Youth on December 21 — an action that was to have the direst consequences not only for the Church and for Germany but for the rest of the world. For Hitler knew that if he were to recruit a generation of fanatical youth who would fight and die in his wars of conquest, they had to be educated in the ideology of the *Herrenrasse*. Accordingly in June of 1933, Baldur von Schirach was appointed Youth Leader of the Reich. He began cautiously by assuring Erich Stange, head of the Evangelical Youth, that the different organizations would retain their independence. At that time the Evangelical Youth had more than seven hundred thousand members. As late as October 22, both Müller and Hossenfelder gave assurances that there was no thought of dissolving the young people's societies, although they were expected to " dedicate themselves to the great task of missionizing the people." However, when on November 17 the whole of the Evangelical Youth was placed under the direction of the Reich bishop it was evident which way the wind was blowing.[19] Von Schirach delivered a speech in Braunschweig in which he said: " We claim that all other youth organizations in Germany no longer have any right to exist. These organizations have to disappear in favor of the Hitler Youth. I would like solemnly to stress that we do not wish to accomplish this by force but by the magnitude of our efforts. For us it is an intolerable situation that under the pretext of certain special Church interests youth organizations are set up and still stand aloof." The protests of Stange and other Church leaders were of no avail. On December 20, Müller personally signed an agreement with von Schirach, without any authorization whatever; the Evangelical Youth was incorporated into the Hitler Youth, with the provision that unless a youth under eighteen years was a member of the Hitler Youth, he could not belong to the Evangelical Youth. All athletic and political education was to be in the hands of the Hitler Youth. On two afternoons in the week and on two Sundays in the month young people would be free to take part in purely Church activities. In an appeal to parents, Müller explained that " the incorporation had been for him a difficult decision to make, over which he had wrestled with God in prayer." He had been forced to this decision " by the responsibility laid upon him in virtue of his office for the gospel and the education of the German people in the gospel." Stange was discharged by Müller as leader of the Evangelical Youth and by von Schirach from the Reich Youth Council. Thus a hundred years' of youth work in the Church was destroyed and Christian education among the young was virtually stifled. Subsequent protests were unavailing. Hitler had gained a tremendous victory in his campaign to control the minds as well as the bodies of the German people. Sad to relate, he had won his victory with the co-operation of traitors inside the Church!

While the stormy events of the latter half of 1933 were taking place, theological work continued unabated. Reference was made in the previous chapter to the publication of Barth's trumpet call for a *Theological Existence Today*. This proved to be the beginning of a new series of pamphlets published by Barth and his close friend, Eduard Thurneysen, under that general title. It continued publication until 1941. At first Barth himself was a regular contributor until the State police banned articles written by him. In the forewords Barth frequently commented on the current situation in the Church; indeed, the forewords written during the second half of the year afford us a critical commentary on the events recorded in this chapter. While many Church leaders, even within the Pastors' Emergency League, were rejoicing over the disintegration of the " German Christians " and were prepared to make capital out of the Sport Palace " scandal " and the resultant dismissal of Hossenfelder, Krause, and others, Barth was not at all happy. He wrote:

> My great concern is that the [Church] opposition in this situation could be as little a match for the extraordinary peril of the present moment as it was last summer, and precisely when it is satisfied with all sorts of partial successes! The Reich Church government and even the administrative board of the " German Christians " reacted promptly enough to that scandal in such a way that those who were most guilty among them were banished to the wilderness while they themselves now suddenly posed as the protectors of " Bible and Confession." . . .

Will the opposition understand that by this the crisis in which we find ourselves is not altered in the slightest? There really was no sense in suddenly attacking the " German Christians " on November 15 as if right then the mystery of evil had been manifested in the extravagances of Herr Krause. It was obvious that the Reich Church government and the supposedly better ones among the " German Christians " *could* and had to shake off these people and even silently ignore the " resolution " that had been solemnly passed at that meeting in the Sport Palace. It was obvious that under the pressure of the embarrassing situation that arose they could and had to make those other concessions as well. . . . They could do it because the substance of the " German Christian " faith was not affected one bit. For this reason it is senseless to conclude from the concessions made that a serious change has taken place in the nature, attitude, and character of the " German Christians " or of the " German Christian " Church governments. As long as the false tendency of their doctrine (recently expressed again in the third and fourth articles [20]) that clearly prevails in all their literature (including the speeches of the Reich bishop himself), and as long as the injustice by which they acquired power in the Church on June 24 and July 23 and perpetuated after they possessed it, is not categorically and openly called in question, it would do no good even if the day after tomorrow the wretched Aryan paragraph were completely to disappear from sight. . . . A hundred per cent victory by the opposition in the field of Church politics would also be of no help if the opposition did not still know how to get at the root of the virulent disease of our Church which has finally broken out in the " German Christians " though not first or only in them. Even the creation of a Free Church without a clarification of the basic issues could be of no help to us. . . . The resistance has to go farther and be directed against the ecclesiastical-theological system of modern Protestantism which in no way is embodied in the " German Christians " alone if everything is not to have been in vain.

The above quotation is from the foreword to the pamphlet entitled *Lutherfeier 1933*. Besides two articles on Luther, it contained Barth's *Counter Theses* to the Rengsdorf Theses and a brief memorandum consisting of six articles which Barth laid before the board of the Pastors' Emergency League that met in Berlin on November 15.

Both these documents are enormously important as forerunners of the Barmen Declaration and are therefore reproduced here in full.

The Rengsdorf Theses were "worked out in a deep, earnest, and unanimous discussion" at a "conference of ten ministers and laymen" called by Dr. Oberheid, newly appointed "German Christian" bishop of Cologne-Aachen, and sent to all ministers' homes in the Rhineland.[21] We give each thesis, followed by Barth's reply.

* 1. The "*Deus dixit*" (God has spoken) is only a formal and hence not an appropriate expression for God's revelation. It leads theology astray into "existential thinking," which does not conform to reality. The revelation of God is enclosed in *Deus creavit, salvavit, sanctificavit* (God has created, saved, sanctified). God is Creator and Redeemer, who gives the Holy Spirit to the world.

1. The term "*Deus dixit*" refers to the fact that God's revelation in Jesus Christ has *occurred* once and for all and has been *attested* once and for all in Holy Scripture. We do not know what creation, redemption, sanctification are; we have to let God's Word tell us.

Whoever opposes this term today as being "only formal" replaces the free Word of God by an arbitrary statement of human reason and places himself outside the evangelical Church.

2. There is not a "universal Christianity." Christianity as such is an unreal abstraction. For a German there can be only a Christianity rooted in the German nationality.

2. The genuine particularity and concreteness of "Christianity" on the ground of German nationality is not to be derived from what we know about this ground, but it is to be accepted as that form in which the one commandment and the one comfort of the Word is revealed to us upon this ground according to its own wisdom and will.

Whoever preaches today "a Christianity rooted in German nationality" binds God's Word to an arbitrarily conceived *Weltanschauung,* thereby invalidating it, and places himself outside the evangelical Church.

* 3. There is no contradiction between an unreserved position in favor of the gospel on the one hand and an equally unreserved position in favor of German nationality (National Socialist State) on the other.

3. The Christian Confession of Faith is the only "unreserved" position that is required of us and permitted to us. Hence all other positions (including those in regard to German nationality and the National Socialist State) are subject to reservations.

Whoever today talks about two "unreserved" positions imagines he is able to serve Yahweh and Baal, God and Mammon, and places himself outside the evangelical Church.

4. The gospel has been brought into close contact with us Germans through a Reformation corresponding to the character of the German people. History confirms that this proclamation of the gospel is adapted to the Germanic race.

4. The Reformation as the Church's renewal from God's Word has not come into "close contact" with the Germans in keeping with their character but in accordance with the wisdom and will of divine providence. It was and is as much adapted and unadapted to the Germanic race as it is to every other race.

Whoever today treats the Reformation as a specifically German affair interprets it in terms of profane history and places himself outside the evangelical Church.

5. The National Socialist revolution has stamped upon the German a uniform attitude which in the same way does justice to faith and nationality.

5. A human "attitude" that does justice to faith is the mystery of a man's new birth by God's Word and Spirit. It can neither be "stamped" by the National Socialist revolution nor be directly or indirectly identical with the "attitude" that has been stamped upon the nation by the National Socialist revolution.

Whoever today proclaims a stamping of faith by events such as the National Socialist revolution makes faith itself to be a transitory human work, and places himself outside the evangelical Church.

6. The nation is founded upon the good things for which a German gives his life. These are a healthy family life, blood and soil, loyalty to nation and State, and in all obedience toward God.

6. For obedience toward God, Jesus Christ alone has given his life as a substitution for the disobedience of us all. Discipleship of Jesus Christ can indeed mean that we give our life for

the blessings we have received from God, but it can also mean
that we surrender them.

Whoever today uncritically mentions in the same breath the
giving of one's life in obedience to God and for the good things
of the German people denies the fact of sin, reconciliation
through Christ, and the freedom of the divine commandment,
and places himself outside the evangelical Church.

7. State and Church are orders both willed by God. Consequently they cannot prove to be in conflict. If, however, this
should happen, then an encroachment from one side or the
other has occurred. The Church owes obedience to the State in
all temporal matters. The State has to guarantee to the Church
scope to carry out its commission.

7. Not divine orders but the human realities of Church and
State must and will always find themselves in conflict in history dominated by sin. *Wherein* the obedience in temporal matters which the Church owes the State consists, and *what* scope
the State has to guarantee to the Church for carrying out its
commission, are questions that have to be asked ever again by
both sides giving heed to God's Word.

Whoever today thinks he is finally able to settle the relationship between Church and State on the basis of general considerations apart from listening to the living Word is already actually thinking of an authoritarian State instead of from the
promise given to the Church (for Church and State!) and
places himself outside the evangelical Church.

Conclusion: The "theology" of the Rengsdorf Theses is
clearly not a theology but a specimen of a gnosis that operates
with Christian concepts but which neither understands nor
deals with the first, second, or third articles (of the Creed) as
a Confession of God's Word but treats all three as explications
of human reason (with the current emphasis upon the national
factor). In addition, it has put itself in possession of outward
Church authority by an act of usurpation. For both reasons it
is not a philosophy to be discussed but to be entirely rejected
and opposed just for the sake of Christian love.

The Memorandum which Barth presented to the leaders of the
Pastors' Emergency League illustrates how he endeavored to firm up
the Church's opposition late in 1933. Barth grasped that the " German Christians " were but a manifestation of a much deeper heresy

threatening the Church not only in Germany but perhaps also in other lands, and this is what makes this history have continued significance for us.

CHURCH OPPOSITION 1933

Fundamentals

1. The protest is directed against the teaching of the " German Christians " advocated by the German Church government because it is a heresy and because it has become the prevailing doctrine in the Church through usurpation.

2. Because the teaching and conduct of the " German Christians " is nothing else than an especially striking consequence of the whole development of modern Protestantism since 1700, the protest is directed against an existing and spreading corruption of the whole evangelical Church.

3. The protest against the heresy of the " German Christians " cannot begin with the Aryan paragraph, the rejection of the Old Testament, the Aryanism of the " German Christian " Christology, the naturalism and Pelagianism of their doctrine of justification and sanctification, or with the deification of the State in " German Christian " ethics. It has to be directed fundamentally against the source of all single errors, namely, that the " German Christians " assert German nationality, its history and its political present, as a second source of revelation *beside* Holy Scripture as the only source of revelation, and thereby show themselves to be believers in " another God."

4. The protest against the " German Christian " usurpation in the Church cannot begin with the suspensions and similar particular infringements by the " German Christian " Church governments. In view of the events of June 24, the Church elections of July 23, and the constituting and decisions of the synods in August and September, it has to deny the legality of these Church governments as such.

5. In every single action the protest has to have in view the *essence* and totality of the sickness of the Church. Individually and together a meaningful, serious, and effective protest can be raised only where there is a clear agreement about the essence and totality of this sickness, and therefore where there is a will to combat it in its essence and as a whole.

6. Whoever holds " another opinion " in one of these five

points belongs to the " German Christians " himself, and should no longer be permitted to trouble a serious Church opposition.

In the foreword to the next issue of *Theologische Existenz heute,* under date of December 11, Barth reviewed the events of the previous two months that had led to the breakup of the " German Christians." He attached no great importance to it, however. " Their spears were and are hollow and sooner or later could come to no good end. . . . But it is not a question of the ' German Christians.' It is that all this could take place within the bosom of our evangelical Church and in such a way that all of us, whether we belong or have belonged to the ' German Christians ' or to the opposition, have reason to be ashamed before the face of God and the angels that it was possible. . . . In view of past events, we certainly have no cause to rejoice or be reassured. They have brought no relief. They have shown us — and for this I hold myself also responsible after what I have done in this Church the last twelve years — how little vital faith, love, and hope there is among us. . . . Nothing is achieved by a deuteronomic reformation of the temple. We need a conversion. Otherwise what is coming could be worse than what has been."

Alongside Barth's theses and articles, mention must be made of the Eight Articles of Evangelical Doctrine drawn up by Heinrich Vogel, then pastor in Dobbrickow bei Luckenwalde and now Professor of Theology in Berlin, " because of present-day heresy to serve as instruction for the erring, as consolation for the afflicted, on the basis of Holy Scripture." [22] They were first published in November, 1933. In these articles the Scriptures of the Old and New Testaments are acknowledged as God's Word, which is to be heard only in faith through the Holy Spirit. The attempt to rend the unity of the Old and New Testaments, or to do away with them or to abbreviate them, is condemned. Thereafter Scripture is confessed " as the only source of revelation," and the " acceptance of other sources of revelation in nature and history " is rejected. " We hear God's voice not in the voice of the people who today cry ' Hosanna ' and tomorrow ' Crucify' but in the Word of Scripture." The sermon is dealt with as " the present proclamation of God's Word subordinate to Holy Scripture, whose true preacher and hearer is the Holy Spirit alone." The second article deals with the sacraments. The third affirms the

Triune God and rejects nature deities, and the idols of culture, race, class, folk, and humanity. Next, the nature of God's law is defined and distinguished from civil law and from social customs. Sin is " disobedience, unbelief, and enmity to God's Word," which is known only " through the cross of our Savior and Lord, Jesus Christ, in which it is judged and forgiven." Then follows an article on grace in which it is asserted that we are redeemed through the blood of Christ and not by our own blood and natures. As to the Church it is said: " We confess the Church as the congregation of Jesus Christ which the Holy Spirit creates and preserves by God's Word and the sacraments. The Church is not the expression of all the religious forces of our nation; it is the body of Jesus Christ, of which we are members only through baptism in faith." The banning of Jewish Christians in the Church is condemned. The Church owes the gospel to the world. But it also owes a protest against heresies that destroy or adulterate the gospel. With regard to order in the Church, ecclesiastical authorities are an earthly order of an earthly Church, to which obedience is due in ecclesiastical affairs, unless its directions be against God's Word. They are not to be obeyed because of any religious leadership principle, but because of, and so far as it is demanded by, the Word of Holy Scripture. So an episcopal office that is founded on the leadership principle with teaching authority, as well as one equipped with power to appoint and to depose, is condemned. The last article dealt with the orders of creation. They are not to be discerned from visible nature but through God's Word. " The State has its dignity and power neither by a social contract nor by the will of the nation, but by the authority of the grace of God, for the purpose of resisting evil and of making possible and maintaining the life of men in society, as members of their people, in marriage and family. Therefore we owe the civil authorities obedience unless they order us to act in opposition to the Word of God." Concerning the relationship between Church and State, it is explained: " Church and State have their distinct authority by the same Word of the authority of God's grace, that same Word which is the Creator, Judge, and Lord of all human authority. Therefore State and Church have to recognize in each other the distinct authority given to them and also to keep it within the limits set for them. But a co-ordination of Church and State ignores and confuses the nature and task of the

State to which is given the sword and the Church to which the Word of God is commanded and promised. Therefore we condemn the deification of the State as much as the secularization of the Church, and making the State into a Church or the Church into a State." [23]

These articles, being merely the views of an individual theologian or even of a group of theologians, were far from being a Church Confession of Faith. Nevertheless they were the seed from which a Confession was to grow. Such seed was also sown by Walther Bach's and Joachim Beckmann's replies to the Rengsdorf Theses, by Martin Niemöller's propositions concerning the Aryan question in the Church, by a Confession drawn up by a group of Westphalian pastors, and by the "Tecklenburg Confession." [24] The last named was a lengthy and wordy document that was presented to the Synod of Westphalia for adoption, but "in the whirl of events received little attention." [25]

Theologians like Ernst Wolf, Heinrich Vogel, Hans Asmussen, Peter Barth, Edmund Schlink, Heinrich Schlier, Max Lackmann, and Alfred de Quervain contributed to the series *Theologische Existenz heute*. About the same time, another series with the title *Bekennende Kirche* and edited by Theodore Ellwein and Christian Stoll appeared. It stressed the Lutheran standpoint. Among its contributors were Georg Merz, Hans Lilje, and Hermann Sasse. Later in April of 1934, *Evangelische Theologie* appeared as a monthly periodical to take the place of *Zwischen den Zeiten*. It was edited by Ernst Wolf in co-operation with Wilhelm Niesel, Paul Schempp, and Wolfgang Trillhaas. It rendered yeoman service to the cause of the Confessing Church until it was banned the end of 1938.

In concluding this survey of the theological work that accompanied the political actions in the Church in the latter half of 1933, mention must be made of the stands taken by various theological faculties. On September 11, the ministers and laymen assembled at the Kirchentag for the Electorate of Hessen requested the theological faculties of Marburg and Erlangen universities to give their judgment upon the law passed by the General Synod of the Old Prussian Union Church concerning conditions of employment of ministers and Church officials. The Marburg faculty declared that the regulation requiring "unreserved" support of the national State, as well as the Aryan paragraph, were irreconcilable with the nature of the

Church and the gospel. The first threatened the independence of ministers in their preaching and officials in their administrative duties in subjection to God's Word. The Aryan paragraph reduces Church members of non-Aryan origin to a second-class status, whereas it is indisputable that the message of Jesus Christ is delivered to all races and that all who believe and are baptized belong to the Church of Jesus Christ.[26] In view of the subsequent fate of six million Jews in Germany, it is painful to relate the equivocal reply given by the Erlangen faculty on September 25. Proceeding from the principle that the external order of the Church " according to Reformation teaching has to correspond not only to the universality of the gospel but also to the historic-national organization of Christian mankind," it has to be asked whether Jews domiciled in Germany belong in a full sense to the German people or to their own nationality and thus are an alien people. On this question the Church as such cannot decide. " Here the answer can be given only by our people in view of their special biological-historical situation. Since today our people regard the Jews in their midst more than ever as a foreign nationality, and the Church in the present situation is called to reflect anew upon its task of being a national Church for Germans, the holding of offices in the Church by those of Jewish stock would be a heavy charge and restriction. Consequently the Church has to demand that its Jewish Christians be restrained from holding offices. Their full membership in the German Evangelical Church will not thereby be disputed or curtailed any more than other members of our Church who somehow do not fulfill the requirements for admission to Church offices." [27] Perhaps even more dreadful than its deliverance about Jewish Christians holding office in the Church was the Erlangen statement about the positions of Jews in the State. " In the struggle for the renewal of our people the new State excludes men of Jewish or half-Jewish origin from leading offices. *The Church has to acknowledge the basic right of the State to take such legislative measures*" (italics added). This shameful document was composed by the theology professors Paul Althaus and Werner Elert, at the behest of the faculty after it had had a " thorough discussion which resulted in complete agreement in the essential demands "!

Fortunately about the same time (September 23) twenty-one New Testament professors and lecturers — among them Bultmann, Deismann, Jeremias, Jülicher, Lietzmann, Lohmeyer, K. L. Schmidt, Schniewind, von Soden, and Windisch — issued a statement on the Jewish question on the basis of the evidence of the New Testament.[28] They came to the conclusion that "Jews and Gentiles are qualified to be Church office-bearers in basically the same way. They are called to a Church office by the Church and only by it solely in accordance with their faith, walk, and personal aptitude. . . . This position is based upon the fact that according to the New Testament the Church owes its existence in the world to the Holy Spirit alone. . . . It is therefore our opinion that a Christian Church may not surrender this standpoint in its teaching and action." When one considers that in 1933 there were only thirty-seven Jewish Christian ministers in the Church, of whom eight had been retired, it will be seen that for the Church it was a matter of principle, a question of its own nature, which it dared not evade.

In response to a request from fifteen superintendents of the Evangelical Lutheran Church, the Leipzig faculty gave its considered judgment upon the Twenty-eight Theses of the "German Christians."[29] It came to the conclusion that "the Twenty-eight Theses contradicted in important points not only the letter but the spirit of the Confessions." In marked contrast was the stand taken by the Berlin faculty. It commissioned its seventy-five-year-old Emeritus Professor of the History of Dogma, Reinhold Seeberg, to draw up an evaluation of the theses. He characterized them as "positively Christian"; their authors had "tried to formulate basic Christian truths as the requirements of the National Socialist movement demanded." He defended the Aryan paragraph on the ground that it was not in the slightest derogatory to non-Aryan Christianity but was intended to point out the ineffectiveness of non-Aryans in the light of present-day views.[30]

VI

The Synodical Movement:
The Way to Barmen

ON JANUARY 4, 1934, Reich bishop Müller issued " a decree concerning the restoration of order in the German Evangelical Church." This decree, which became generally known as the " Muzzling Order," forbade ministers to introduce into their sermons any subject matter dealing with the Church controversy. The Church is to serve exclusively " the preaching of the pure gospel." The use of Church buildings for demonstrations and rallies was forbidden. Any public criticism of the Church government or its measures by Church officials would be punished by immediate suspension and cut in salary, leading to eventual dismissal after disciplinary proceedings had been taken. At the same time, Müller revoked a law of November 16 that had postponed the application of the Aryan paragraph in the provincial Churches until such time as the question should be settled for the whole Reich.[1] In effect the Aryan paragraph was reimposed in the Churches that had adopted it, notably the Church in Prussia of which Müller himself was bishop, and the decree was issued on the same day that Müller had telegraphed a conference of provincial Church leaders in Halle that he was seriously ill and could not attend but would shortly be ready to take important steps. He urged them to await his decisions. Thus the Church leaders were induced to delay action while the perfidious bishop had already taken action that would " legally " prevent them from doing anything in the future.

A storm broke loose against this episcopal dictatorship. The Pastors' Emergency League, which now numbered over four thousand members, drew up a protest that was read from the pulpits of their churches the following Sunday. It deplored the unrest and dissension

129

that had continued in the Church ever since the Church elections of the previous summer had ushered in a new administration. It complained that the Reich bishop had still not yet appointed a Spiritual Ministry. Although there was a strong movement to introduce into the Church pagan religious ideas that would threaten its Biblical foundations, a large number of ministers and Church members were demanding that the Church's doctrine, life, and administration be in accord with the Confessions of Faith. The bishop's decree amounted to a declaration of war against those who sought to establish the peace of the Church on Scriptural grounds alone. In spite of threats of violence, these could not remain silent about the present misery of the Church. The protest also complained that the bishop had revived a law (the Aryan paragraph) which he himself had abolished for the sake of the peace of the Church. Consequently he had lost the confidence his office should enjoy. "When we oppose his decree, we do so in agreement with the Augsburg Confession, which in the article concerning the power of bishops declares the following: 'When bishops teach or ordain anything contrary to the gospel, we have God's command not to obey them in such a case. Even properly elected bishops are not to be followed when they err.' We too must act in relation to the Reich bishop according to the text: 'We must obey God rather than men.'" [2]

The reading of this protest from nearly four thousand pulpits was outright rebellion against the authority of the Reich bishop. At the same time, Müller was under fire from his banished "German Christian" supporters. At the moment, therefore, when the would-be ecclesiastical dictator was discredited, the secular dictator intervened on his behalf. Hitler summoned the leaders of the Churches to the conference in the Reich Chancellery for January 25.[3] About forty attended, among them prominent "German Christian" leaders, the bishops Wurm, Meiser, Marahrens, and Schoffel, Karl Koch, president of the Synod of Westphalia, and Martin Niemöller, head of the Pastors' Emergency League. It was the first and last meeting between Hitler and Niemöller.

The clergy were ushered into Hitler's study, where he was seated at his desk. Behind him stood Reich bishop Müller. Also in attendance were Hermann Göring and Wilhelm Frick, the Minister for Internal Affairs. The latter introduced the visitors to the Chancellor.

Hitler began to read a prepared statement concerning the purpose of the conference. He had hardly uttered more than a few sentences when Göring rushed into the room and requested permission to read a transcript of a telephone conversation between Niemöller and Walther Künneth, then one of the co-chairmen of the Young Reformation Movement, that had taken place scarcely an hour before, and which Göring's police had listened in on. Künneth had called to inquire about information concerning the impending meeting. Niemöller replied that he understood that Frick was anxious to secure a peaceful solution because of Müller's precarious position and had solicited the support of the aged President Hindenburg. At that point Niemöller's secretary is said to have jokingly called into the telephone something about Hindenburg administering extreme unction to Hitler. Göring seized upon this silly remark to exclaim: " These people are trying to drive a wedge between yourself and the Reich President! " Hitler exploded in anger. During his outburst Niemöller moved forward so as to be able to speak when Hitler ceased ranting. He tried to explain that the remark about extreme unction was meant as a joke and should not be taken seriously. He concluded by saying that the Confessing Church was concerned only for the Church, the nation, and the State. To this Hitler replied: " You leave the care of the Third Reich to me, and you look after the Church." Again Göring threw oil on the fire when he claimed that he had proof that the Emergency League had " foreign connections." As the clergymen were taking their leave, Niemöller took the opportunity to say a few words to Hitler. " You have said that I should leave the care of the German people to you. I am bound to declare that neither you nor any power in the world is in a position to take from us Christians and the Church the responsibility God has laid upon us for our people." Hitler never forgot and never forgave the Dahlem pastor. It was the reason Niemöller was later dealt with as the " personal prisoner of the Führer."

That same evening Niemöller's home was searched by the Gestapo for incriminating material. A few days later a homemade bomb exploded in the hall. Although no one had called the police, they were on hand in a matter of minutes. Fortunately no one was hurt and the damage was slight. Though alarming enough, these tokens of official displeasure, as Dietmar Schmidt has observed, were easier to bear

than the reproach of Niemöller's colleagues. His intemperate words
to Hitler were blamed for the failure of the conference. Among the
churchmen who attended, President Koch was the only one who did
not leave him in the lurch. In the negotiations with the Reich bishop
that were held on January 26–27, the Lutheran bishops capitulated
and declared: " Under the impact of the great hour in which the
Church leaders of the German Evangelical Church met with the
Reich Chancellor, they unanimously affirm their unconditional loyalty to the Third Reich and its Führer. They sharply condemn all
insidious criticism of the State, nation, and (Nazi) Movement that
is apt to endanger the Third Reich. In particular they condemn the
practice of using the foreign press to misrepresent the Church conflict as a fight against the State. The assembled Church leaders close
their ranks behind the Reich bishop and are willing to carry out his
measures and orders in the sense desired by him, to prevent opposition
to them within the Church, and to strengthen the authority of the
Reich bishop with all the constitutional means at their disposal." [4]

Almost at once the bishops began to suffer pangs of conscience.
They realized that they had gone too far in their servile surrender
to Müller, but they made Niemöller and his unfortunate telephone
conversation the scapegoat.[5] The next day — the twenty-eighth —
Bishop Meiser recanted to the extent of writing to the Reich bishop
that the declaration of submission to his authority was not an acknowledgment of the legality of his " Muzzling Order " of January 4. On the contrary, " I take my stand on the side of the ministers
of the Emergency League and the seventy-three professors of theology in so far as they have declared it to be contrary to the Church's
Confession of Faith." However, the damage had already been done.
The day following the audience with Hitler, Müller issued an unconstitutional " order to secure the unified management of the Evangelical Church of the Old Prussia Union." [6] Niemöller was given
leave of absence by the bishop on January 27 and, without a trial, was
superannuated February 10, effective March 1.[7] Indeed, the first three
months of 1934 were marked by dictatorial acts by Müller. Over two
hundred ministers were subjected to disciplinary measures, suspensions, and dismissals. These, of course, failed to silence the Emergency
League. On January 31, it sent a message to the Church leaders de-
ploring their capitulation, and another to the Reich bishop protesting
that his administration represented a violation of the gospel and the

Confession of Faith. Naturally the League also vigorously protested against the forced retirement of Niemöller.[8]

However, it was becoming increasingly clear that protests as such were not enough and that further negotiations with Müller's administration offered no prospect of success. There remained for Christ's flock the one thing possible — the one thing the Church can do when all other possibilities have been exhausted, namely, a common Confession of Christ in the face of a heresy that threatens the life of the Church as the true bride of Christ. Thus in the early months of 1934, a new movement appeared on the scene, in which the laity played as important a part as the clergy. A. S. Duncan-Jones has called this the " synodical movement, because it took the form of local synods of clergy and laity who expressed their mind on the dangers that threatened the Church." [9] It arose in the Rhineland, where the Reformed Church was strongest. On January 3 and 4, the First Free Reformed Synod met in Barmen-Gemarke. The 320 elders and ministers representing 167 congregations in Germany adopted a " Declaration Concerning the Right Understanding of the Reformation Confessions of Faith in the German Evangelical Church of the Present," which had been drawn up by Karl Barth.[10] Following in the line of the Altona Statement of January 11, and the Düsseldorf Theses of May 27, 1933, this Declaration is unquestionably the most important forerunner of the Barmen Declaration made by the whole evangelical Church at the end of May. In the first place, it marked an advance to a Confession *by the Church,* and not by an individual theologian or group of theologians. In this connection it is significant that in the introductory remarks which Barth made to his " explanation," he said he could not accept responsibility for presenting a Confession; that he did not know whether the situation was ripe for a Confession; that confessing could be only the act of the Church; and that therefore the " explanation " he was presenting to the delegates was in the nature of a question that they have to answer as the representatives of their congregations. " In this way and only in this way does a genuine Confession of Faith arise." They answered the question by unanimously declaring that Barth's " explanation " " bears witness to the truth of Holy Scripture, and that they gratefully assume responsibility for it." Thus precisely as an explanation of historic Confessions adopted by the Church, it became itself a Confession! It is important, secondly, because, although it was a declaration by a Reformed Church synod, it strove to speak on behalf of the *one* evangelical Church of Jesus Christ in the face of a common error. When this synod declared that " the congregations which have been united in the one German evangelical Church are called upon to recognize anew, in spite of their Lutheran, Reformed, or United origins and responsibilities, the majesty of the one Lord of the one Church," and rejected the view that special denominational interests could take precedence over the need for common, evangelical confessing, it was, in fact, a cry for a confession by the *whole* Church. Thirdly, the Declaration is important because in its articles on the Church in the Present, the Church Under Holy Scripture, the Church in the World, the Message of the Church, and the Form of the Church, it anticipated much of the doctrinal material found in the later Barmen Declaration. Humanly speaking, the Barmen Declaration of May would have been impossible without the Reformed Church Declaration of January.

The Reformed Synod in Barmen was followed by a Reformed Synod in Pomerania on February 4, which adopted the Barmen Declaration. Then on February 18 and 19, a Free Evangelical Synod was held in Barmen. It was composed of ministers and elders from Reformed, Lutheran, and United congregations representing thirty of the thirty-three local synods in the Rhineland. It too adopted the Reformed Barmen Declaration. This synod demonstrated what had hitherto only been declared, namely, that Lutheran, Reformed, and United Church differences were not an obstacle to a common confession at that time, and thus it represented another significant step toward a Confession by the whole evangelical Church in Germany.[11] However, the belief that Lutheran, Reformed, and United churchmen could utter a common word at that time without doing violence to their respective confessional origins and differences did not go unchallenged. It was contested by Hermann Sasse, Erlangen Professor of Church History, in an article that appeared in the March 10 issue of *Junge Kirche* entitled " Union and Confession." In the foreword to the seventh number of *Theologische Existenz heute,* dated January 26, Barth had written:

> Today Lutheran and Reformed churchmen cannot and may not confess against one another, but they can and must con-

fess with one another as *evangelical* Lutheran and *evangelical* Reformed. I have never been a friend of the so-called " union " of the nineteenth century, nor am I today. Unless we are entirely mistaken, it was not born of a common confession but of an acute lack of insight and confession then shared by both the Lutheran and Reformed Churches. . . . The error that has broken out in the theology and Church politics of the " German Christians " does not have its origin in the school of either Luther or Calvin, but it is — Schleiermacher, R. Rothe, and W. Beyschlag may be numbered among its special fathers — the typical error of the final stage of just that " union " of the nineteenth century. It does harm to both the Lutheran and Reformed Confessions. Consequently Lutheran and Reformed churchmen — whatever special way they may have come or will go — are today summoned to an agreement of faith. . . .

Today the conflict in the Church is not over the Lord's Supper but over the First Commandment, and we have to " confess." In the face of this our need and task, that of the Fathers must recede; that is, there must still be a serious opposition between theological schools, but it must no longer be divisive and schismatic.

To this, Sasse replied that it was an error to say that the German Evangelical Church (which was not a Church in a theological sense) had been formed of congregations of Lutheran, Reformed, and United " origin " and " responsibility." It had been formed of *Landeskirchen* in which the Augsburg Confession had been authoritative. " Our bishops made the great sacrifice of subscribing to the new Church constitution for the sake of the nation and the State only on the basis of a solemn assurance laid down in the constitution that the confessional stand would be safeguarded." The German Evangelical Church would be a true Church, some argued, only when it had been brought to a common Confession of Faith in which agreement had been achieved concerning such matters as the Lord's supper. " We [Lutherans] have no other outward bond of unity, which at the same time gives expression to the *consensus de doctrina evangelii,* than our Confession. We, the Lutheran Churches of the world, stand on the basis of this Confession, in spite of all differences in polity and liturgy. . . . Our Confession would no longer be in force the moment we declared that the opposition between the Lutheran

and Reformed Churches is no longer a schismatic opposition but
only an opposition between theological schools within the same
Church. We would then be admitting that all Lutheran Confessions
from the Augustana to the Formula of Concord had erred in all essential points and that the whole development of our Church's doctrine had been false. . . . To say that the question of the real presence of the body and blood of Christ in the Sacrament of the Altar
should no longer be schismatic but only a difference between theological schools, just because a Herr Hossenfelder has appeared on the
scene in Berlin, is as impossible for us as it would be for our fellow
Lutherans in America if a new prophet were to appear in San Fran-
cisco." Consequently Sasse concluded that " for the time being there
is nothing else but for us to stand side by side as good Lutheran and
good Reformed churchmen, and to confess the faith of the fathers
in common where we *can* and divided where we *must*." Moreover,
Sasse contended that only a properly constituted Lutheran body had
the authority to make doctrinal pronouncements for the Lutheran
Church. In other words, the Free Evangelical Synod in the Rhineland, though composed in part by Lutherans, could not speak for the
Lutheran Church. Thus some months prior to the meetings of the
Synod of Barmen at the end of May, the seed was being sown that
was to yield the bitter fruit of strife and dissension between the Confessing Church and the Lutheran Confessionalists at Barmen and
throughout the Church Struggle.

Nevertheless the movement toward a common Confession by
Lutheran, Reformed, and United churchmen within the German
Evangelical Church continued to make progress. It was helped along
when the Council of Brethren of the Pastors' Emergency League met
in Hanover on February 20 and unanimously decided to ask the
Council of Brethren of the Evangelical Synod in the Rhineland to
receive them into the synod. At the same time it stated that it would
ask the members of the League and their congregations to join the
Free Evangelical Synod. " We hope in this way to achieve with our
brethren and their congregations in the Rhineland through further
organization a Free Evangelical Synod for the whole German Evangelical Church." [12] On March 7, delegates from congregations in
and near Berlin (two ministers and four laymen from each church,
four hundred men and forty women altogether) assembled in

Dahlem for a Free Evangelical Synod for Berlin and Brandenburg. It, too, unanimously affirmed the Barmen articles as well as Heinrich Vogel's " Evangelical Answer to the Present Heresy," which corresponded to his " Eight Articles " already referred to.[13] On March 16, the First Westphalian Confessional Synod was constituted in Dortmund the same day the Secret Police dissolved the regularly called Synod of Westphalia. The new synod elected Dr. Karl Koch its president, elected a Council of Brethren to carry on its business, and " associated its witness and confession in fraternal unity of faith with that of the Free Evangelical Synod in the Rhineland." [14] This paved the way for a joint meeting of these two synods in Dortmund, April 29. Here the authority of the existing Church government was repudiated and Church authority in Westphalia and the Rhineland claimed for the synod itself. Thus a precedent was established for similar action by the Synod of Barmen for the whole evangelical Church in Germany.

Before a synod representative of the whole Church in Germany could be convened, the synodical movement had to spread to the southern provincial churches of Bavaria and Württemberg. Fortunately the seriousness of the situation was being recognized by those Churches which had not yet come under the direct rule of Ludwig Müller. They perceived that Müller's ambition was to extend his power over those Churches which had not succumbed to a " German Christian " administration. Moreover, the Pastors' Emergency League was acquiring more and more members in these *Landeskirchen,* and Confessional Societies were formed with the express purpose of combating " German Christian " inroads. Perhaps, as Karl Kupisch has suggested,[15] under the impression that the Reich bishop had not reciprocated in kind to the pledge of loyalty the bishops had given him on January 27, the Bavarian Church issued a lengthy document over the signature of Bishop Meiser on March 17. This pronouncement reflects a conservative Lutheran confessional attitude rather than a fighting spirit. Nevertheless, by its appeal to the Lutheran Confessions it left no doubt as to the stand it would take in the event that illegal steps were taken to bring it into line. It insisted that a hierarchical understanding of the office of bishop is irreconcilable with the Lutheran Confession, and raised the question as to whether the leadership principle in the Church would not end in a new papacy where a single man decrees about the Church's doctrine and order.[16]

The fears of the Bavarian Church were soon shown to be justified. On April 12, the notorious Dr. August Jäger, who the previous year had wrought such havoc as State Commissar in the Prussian Church, was appointed the "Legal Administrator" (*Rechtswalter*) in the new Spiritual Ministry of the German Church. His appointment was marked by messages of peace for the Church signed by himself and by the Reich bishop. The past was to be erased, and the disciplinary measures taken against officeholders were rescinded.[17] It was all so much camouflage. Three days after Jäger's appointment both he and Müller interfered in the affairs of the Württemberg Church. Jäger believed he could immediately embark upon a program of "incorporation" of single provincial Churches into the German Evangelical Church by taking advantage of a conflict that had arisen within the Württemberg Church between its bishop, Theophil Wurm, and the "German Christians" in the Standing Committee of the Church Council.[18] The evening radio newscast of April 14 carried a report which stated that Bishop Wurm had lost the confidence of the Committee and that his congregations were protesting that he had fostered unrest among the people by his attitude. In particular, his connections with the Pastors' Emergency League were not understood. Bishop Wurm was no longer acceptable as a public official in the new Reich. Because of the emergency that had arisen in the Church, the Reich governor felt obliged to summon the Reich bishop to settle the issue. The next morning Bishop Wurm explained to his congregation in the course of the regular church service that the Standing Committee had never met to pass a want-of-confidence vote in him; that he could be deposed from office only by a two-thirds majority of the Council; that in recent days he had received abundant evidence of the support of congregations; and that he had frequently demonstrated his positive attitude toward the Third Reich. Later it was pointed out that the bishop could not have had connections with the Emergency League, since it had been dissolved on January 31. The same afternoon, Jäger, with the Reich bishop's authorization, demanded that Wurm cancel the meeting of the Council that was scheduled for the next day — the sixteenth. Wurm replied that he could do it only if the false radio report of the previous evening was publicly retracted. Jäger said that he was neither willing nor in a position to do this, and then extracted from his brief case a previously drawn up decree, signed by the Reich bishop and himself, to regulate the situation in the Württemberg Church. It declared that the calling of the Council henceforth required the consent of the Reich bishop, and that the meeting set for April 16 had been postponed until June 11.

This highhanded action was all that was necessary to induce Bishops Meiser and Wurm of Bavaria and Württemberg to join hands with their brethren in Northern Germany at the Ulm Conference of April 22. It was the most representative gathering of "Confessionals" that had been held, bringing together delegates from the Bavarian and Württemberg Churches, the Free Synods in the Rhineland, Westphalia, and Brandenburg, as well as many "confessing" congregations throughout Germany. The Ulm Declaration was signed by President Koch, of Westphalia, Dr. Hans Asmussen, of Altona, Martin Niemöller, of Berlin, Heinrich Vogel, of Dobbrikow, Bishops Meiser and Wurm, and others. It maintained that the actions of Reich bishop Müller belied his protestations of peace and instead had the effect of destroying one of the last bulwarks of a Confessional Church in Germany. Moreover, for a long time the action of the Reich Church government had had no legal basis. However, the most striking feature of the Ulm Declaration was the statement with which it began. "We, the assembled representatives of the Württemberg and Bavarian provincial Churches, of the Free Synods in the Rhineland, Westphalia, and Brandenburg, as well as of many confessing congregations and Christians throughout Germany, make this declaration before this congregation and the whole of Christendom as *the constitutional evangelical Church of Germany*." This was a new note. The opposition had ceased to be merely a theological school or movement *within* the Church; it was daring to claim that it was the true evangelical Church — with the implicit excommunication of the "German Christians" and the Reich Church government.[19]

Jäger's policy of "incorporation" was a dismal failure in Bavaria and Württemberg, but it succeeded in Nassau-Hesse, Saxony, Schleswig-Holstein, Thüringia, and Hanover.[20] Indeed, Jäger and Müller were congratulating themselves upon their enforced, organizational unity of the Reich Church. But it was soon to prove a hollow unity in the face of a Church unity grounded in a Confession of the one Lord of the one, holy, catholic, and apostolic Church at Barmen.

VII

The First Confessional Synod
of the German Evangelical Church

1. Preparation for the Synod of Barmen

IN ORDER TO MEET the interference in Church affairs by the "German Christians," the Confessing Church had already, in March of 1934, formed itself into a "Confessional Fellowship of the German Evangelical Church." It was led by the Council of Brethren, which was the executive body. Besides the already existing Free Confessional Synods, it was composed of the provincial Churches of Württemberg and Bavaria. A forerunner of the Reich Council of Brethren was the Council of Brethren, which the Pastors' Emergency League (*Pfarrernotbund*) elected when it was constituted on October 20, 1933. It was reponsible for the formation of the Confessional Fellowship. Representatives of the two executive councils met in the seminary of Nuremberg, April 11, and founded the Nuremberg Committee, from which the Reich Council of Brethren emerged. It was on April 12, 1934, that August Jäger was appointed to the Reich Church government as a so-called "legal administrator." He immediately instituted his policy of assimilation by incorporating the Church of Württemberg. Thereupon representatives of the whole Confessing Church in Germany met in Ulm on April 22, as we have described above, to register their first public protest. Here, calling themselves "the constitutional evangelical Church of Germany," the confessing Churches struck a new note. The opposition was ceasing to be merely an opposition party within the Church; it was declaring itself to be the true evangelical Church. The declaration went on to say that actions taken by the Reich Church government are in contradiction to its protestations of desiring peace. " This ' desire for peace ' is obviously not born of God's Word and Spirit. . . . They declared: The Confession of the German Evangelical Church is in danger. The ministry is robbed of its authority by the ' German Christians ' and their toleration by the leading Church officials. For a long time now the Reich Church government has had no legal basis." [1] At Ulm the need became apparent for a strong organization of the Confessing Church. Consequently the Nuremberg Committee decided to call a " Free German National Synod in Barmen." The Nuremberg Committee, which later was officially known as the " Council of Brethren," of the Confessional Synod of the German Evangelical Church (commonly called the " Reich Council of Brethren "), held its second meeting on May 2, 1934, in the Hospiz St. Michael in Berlin. Those present were: Koch, Meiser, Wurm, Niemöller, Beckmann, Link, Bosse, Immer, Fiedler, Horn, and Jacobi. These men initiated the first action of the " Confessional Church." It took the form of a communication to the Reich Secretary of the Interior containing the following statement:

I. The conflict which for a long time has shaken the German Evangelical Church is harmful to the nation. The Church law to relieve the Church situation, issued April 13, 1934, has increased rather than lessened the tension.

II. A compromise between the differences of the " German Christians " and the Confessional Church is *impossible*. On the one hand, there is a movement of power politics which is unecclesiastical in its ideas and actions; on the other, there is the will to renew the Church according to its own nature.

III. The present Church government prevents peace by its action in that (1) it is based upon power and not upon trust; (2) it replaces law by arbitrary rule; (3) the Confession of Faith is injured rather than defended; (4) it opposes the Confessing Church rather than the enemies of the Church.

IV. In order to bring about peace, it is necessary that (1) the constitution of the German Evangelical Church be restored. Resistance should not be made to the further development of the constitution along legal lines; (2) the orders and laws of the Reich bishop and the Reich Church government, which have been established as illegal, must be retracted; (3) compensation must be made for all disciplinary actions taken. The State has to decide whether it should instigate legal proceedings; (4) the firm resolve must be carried out that the State and the party do not interfere in the dissension within the Church.[2]

Of greater consequence than this statement was the decision, suggested by Pastor Karl Immer, to form a Theological Committee, which should undertake the theological preparation for the planned meeting of the Confessional Synod. It was decided that Karl Barth, Hans Asmussen, and Thomas Breit should be the committee. President Koch desired that it be a subcommitte of the Nuremberg Committee, and so it was decided that "this committee of three should perform the preliminary work for the Theological Nuremberg Committee and work out a draft for the German Confessional Synod."

The third meeting of the Nuremberg Committee was held in the Hotel Schirmer in Kassel on May 7. This time the Confessional Fellowship turned its attention to the congregations and their members, and in six articles formulated the Kassel Declaration concerning the situation in the Church.

> 1. We have repeatedly demanded that the present Church government desist from its unconfessional and unconstitutional ways. It has paid no attention to the warnings we have made because of an earnest concern for Church and nation. On the contrary, it has completely destroyed the basis upon which the constitutional unification of the German Evangelical Provincial Churches was made, and thus it has undermined its own authority. We are, therefore, obliged to deny to the present Reich Church government the character of a truly evangelical Church administration.
>
> 2. We desire one German evangelical Church with a spiritual leadership that is clearly and firmly rooted in a Confession of the gospel, obedient to the Lord of the Church, and therefore faithful in its ministry to the nation and to the State.
>
> 3. We refuse to submit to (a) an illegal government by force which is founded upon arbitrariness rather than the sworn constitution; (b) to an unspiritual leadership that adheres to human standards rather than to God's Word; (c) an unevangelical oppression of conscience which tries to prevent the free proclamation of the word.
>
> 4. We hold ourselves responsible for guarding the Confession of our Fathers and for defending the constitution of the

German Evangelical Church. We know that we are upheld by the hope and trust of all whose deepest concern is the existence, purity, and authority of the German Evangelical Church. We will not and may not abandon the Church of the Reformation to those who have changed it in its inner nature.

5. We solemnly declare that we will not obey regulations that are contrary to the Confession and the constitution. As the legitimate German Evangelical Church, we cannot give up this position until there is the assurance that the affairs of the German Evangelical Church will be conducted exclusively upon the ground of the constitution and truly in the spirit of an evangelical Confession.

6. We appeal to all evangelical congregations and Christians to stand behind us with their prayers and by their actions. We ask and exhort all who are willing to go along with us to form local Confessional Fellowships within their Churches. When it seems propitious, we will call for a common demonstration of a confessing . . . [Church]. May God bless the work we have undertaken solely for the sake of his honor.[3]

The significant thing in this Declaration, like that of Ulm, is that the undersigned characterize themselves as " the legitimate German Evangelical Church." In Kassel, questions concerning the convening of the Confessional Synod, the most propitious time in view of the situation in the Church, and a Confession of Faith, were thoroughly discussed. Koch suggested that the synod meet the week after Whitsunday (May 20). Niemöller thought that a week later would be better. Koch agreed, and it was decided to hold the synod on Tuesday, Wednesday, and Thursday, May 29–31, in Barmen. Pastor Karl Immer was charged with the responsibility of making local arrangements. The " German Christians " had planned a series of mass meetings for the week following Whitsunday to culminate in a great national congress. Meinzolt thought that if the synod met at a later date it would have the advantage of having the last word. At the same time he emphasized that the synod had to be a genuine synod and not a *concursus hominum*.

When the question of the legality of the synod was debated, Niemöller took the position that the synod had to be constituted in accordance with the Reich Church constitution. Bishop Meiser was of the same opinion: " The Confessing Church has to be projected into the Reich Church." Fiedler expressed the view: " Legality and continuity have to be preserved. The constitution of the Reich Church should remain in force." In this regard Gerhard Niemöller has observed in his book that these leaders were still optimistic. Their hopes were not to be fulfilled.[4]

Much more difficult for the committee was the question of a Confession of Faith. Meiser doubted whether it was wise to tackle the problem at all. It would be disastrous to produce a common Confession. They would be lending a hand toward the formation of an unwanted union. Representatives of Lutheran and Reformed Churches could meet together, but a Confession would have to be dealt with separately. He was opposed to a " minimal Confession." A consensus could be reached concerning urgent questions of the moment: Church officers, the authority of a Church administration, the conception of a leader in the Church, and complaints against the " German Christians." Koch also thought that it would be untimely to deal with the question of a Confession. Jacobi was of the opinion that the differences between the Reformed and Lutheran Churches could be quietly deferred. Others felt that to open up the confessional question on the floor of the synod would be improper. Beckmann was in favor of " compact resolutions," since no one wanted a new Confession. Wurm alluded to the fact that the Württemberg Church wanted to be a Biblical but not a confessional Church. Accordingly, he stressed the common element in the Confessions. Late in the afternoon Koch suggested that the points raised by Meiser be left to the theological committee of three to work out. When Meiser moved that Sasse be added to that committee, it was agreed.

At the end of the meeting, Koch recommended that the following be members of the Legal Committee for the synod: Fiedler, Flor, Meinzolt, Lücking, Kotte, Müller (of Dahlem), and Graeber (of Anhausen). These seven men were elected. At Koch's request, Harder was added to the committee. It was commissioned to work out a plan for the organization of the Confessional Synod before the next meeting of the Nuremberg Committee. For the Legal Committee, Flor, Fiedler, and a third Church lawyer from Saxony, probably Kotte, were to investigate thoroughly all the legal questions that might arise out of the meeting of the synod. Fiedler prepared six " Rules for the Meeting of a German Confessional Synod." These also contained

" rules of order " in which rules were laid down for the calling and convening of the synod, rules of debate, passing of resolutions, the election of a chairman, and the formation of committees. In addition a plan to defray the cost of the synod was drawn up, with an estimated budget and regulations for the disbursement of funds.[5]

Fiedler's Rules were presented at the next meeting of the Nuremberg Committee in Saalfeld on May 18. After some discussion, it was agreed that the number of delegates should not exceed 120. With respect to the agenda it was decided that the committee itself should be responsible for determining the order of business. Koch was nominated to be the chairman, Meiser and Pressel as first and second vice-chairmen respectively. In case they would be needed, a theological committee and a legal committee were appointed to meet during the synod. Three groups of reports were to be given at the synod: (1) a confessional message; (2) the constitution; (3) practical tasks. Three legal reports were assigned to Flor, Fiedler, and Meinzolt. It was further proposed that a Council of Brethren, consisting of at most eleven members, be formed as a standing committee. Half the members were to be laymen, half ministers. In regard to finances, Meinzolt had no hesitation in suggesting that the provincial Churches should share in the expenses of the Confessional Fellowship. The assessment scale could be reckoned from the number of ministers. Extra expenses would have to be covered by local receipts. Flor was of the opinion that the Reich Secretary for the Interior should be immediately informed of the forthcoming meeting of the synod. When Meinzolt and Müller demurred, Niesel suggested that it simply be reported to the local police authorities. Finally the agenda for the synod was settled as follows: (*a*) opening address by the president; (*b*) report of the Theological Committee; (*c*) reports on the situation in the member provincial Churches; (*d*) three reports from the Committee on Legal Matters; (*e*) three reports from the Committee for Practical Work.

Fourteen days before the synod met in Barmen the Theological Commission, which had been set up in Berlin, met in the Basler Hof in Frankfurt am Main, May 15–16. An account of their deliberations will be reserved for the section in this chapter on the history of the development of the text of the Declarations.

Meanwhile the Committee on Legal Matters held a second meeting in Leipzig, May 22. There recommendations drawn up by Fiedler were somewhat altered and expanded. The "recommendations" were multigraphed and distributed later to the members of the synod.[6]

The Committee for Practical Work was also active. It prepared a concise statement for the meeting in Leipzig which bore the title "The Practical Tasks of the Confessional Synod of the German Evangelical Church." This was worked over and expanded with an introduction.

At this point the attitude which the State took toward the forthcoming meeting of the synod should be recorded. In the file of the presidium, "NSDP, Partei, Staat, Kirche," there is to be found a letter with the heading "Herrn Pfarrer Röhricht für Niemöller" from which we learn that a friend of the author worked in the office of von Detten, who was the director of the Office for Cultural Peace. This friend learned that on Monday afternoon, the day before the synod convened, von Detten had personally urged upon Heinrich Himmler, Chief of German Police, that under no circumstances should the synod be disturbed. He argued that there was a chance of an internal split and police action would only have the effect of unifying the synod. Himmler followed this advice. Yet there can be no doubt that originally the State had planned to suppress or to disturb the synod meetings.

2. SITE AND COMPOSITION OF THE SYNOD

Barmen is a link in a chain of cities in the winding valley of the Wupper river in North Rhine-Westphalia. It lies about fifteen miles east of Düsseldorf, adjoining Solingen to the southwest and Remscheid to the south. In 1929, Barmen and its twin city Elberfeld, together with Beyenburg, Cronenberg, Ronsdorf, and Vohwinkel, were incorporated as the city of Wuppertal. Before that time, indeed as early as 1903, these cities were linked by the famous interurban suspension tramway over the Wupper river. With a population of over four hundred thousand before the war, Wuppertal was one of the chief industrial centers of Germany, noted for its textiles, iron and steel milling, chemicals, dyes, and pharmaceuticals. Although 50 per cent of Barmen and Elberfeld was destroyed by a series of air raids in which a half million incendiary bombs and fifty thousand phosphorous bombs turned them into a modern Sodom and Gomorrah, Wuppertal has made an astonishing recovery. Its three hundred and twenty-five thousand inhabitants in 1946 have now risen to the original high figure. Once again it is not only a flourishing industrial city, but a center of culture, learning, and piety, with its theater, opera house, zoological garden, libraries, schools, churches, seminaries, and theological colleges (*Hochschule*).

One cannot in justice describe Wuppertal as a beautiful city. Yet it offers a happy blending of beauty and utility in its landscape and architecture which makes for a sense of solidity and well-being. Its citizens fit into their environment with the sturdy virtues of honesty, industry, and thrift. Above all, a curious combination of a strict Calvinist orthodoxy and a fervent evangelical pietism has left an indelible mark. The pietistic strain goes back to the Reformed mystic and hymn writer Gerhard Tersteegen (1697–1769), whose influence was also felt by the Wesleys and whose most familiar hymn is:

> God himself is with us:
> Let us now adore him,
> And with awe appear before him.

The mixture of rigid orthodoxy and experientialism was continued in the Krummacher brothers — Friedrich Adolf (1767–1845), professor, preacher, and poet; and Gottfried Daniel (1774–1837). The latter was minister in Elberfeld from 1816 till his death. His appearance there just at the time of the religious awakening produced a revival that was felt throughout the whole country. Friedrich Wilhelm Krummacher (1796–1868), elder son of Friedrich Adolf, succeeded to his uncle's pulpit in Elberfeld. A vigorous opponent of the rationalism of the day, a colorful personality and a pulpit orator, the younger Krummacher became the most famous of the three. His sermons attained an enormous vogue in both German and English. Among the best known were " The Suffering Savior," " Elijah the Tishbite," and " Elisha."

The Krummachers were the forerunners, and, in part, the contemporaries of Hermann Friedrich Kohlbrügge (1803–1875), whose work and influence have already been discussed in Chapter II. They welcomed Kohlbrügge with open arms when he came to Elberfeld in 1833. But since Kohlbrügge was really the rediscoverer of the Reformation message of salvation through grace alone, he was to find himself in opposition to both rationalism and pietism. Although he and Daniel Krummacher remained fast friends, he became estranged from the more pietistic F. W. Krummacher. For a number of years Kohlbrügge was forced to live in retirement in Utrecht. Then in 1847 he was recalled to Elberfeld to become minister of the independent Dutch Reformed congregation, which he served till his death in 1875. He lies buried in the church's simple, unadorned graveyard — his grave, like all the others, marked by a flat, stone slab, eloquent of the faith that in life as in death men are nothing in themselves, since Christ is all their boast!

Whatever may be the justification for the theological criticism that Kohlbrügge made of pietism, and whatever may be the justification for criticisms that may be made today of the witness of missionaries in the nineteenth century, the fact remains that the missionary and evangelistic movements were outgrowths of pietism. The light of the gospel that burned so brightly in the valley of the Wupper was carried to distant parts of the world through the founding of a society for the propagation of Christianity in 1799 — " the legitimate child of pietism." From this grew the undenominational Rhineland Missionary Society with its Mission House in Barmen, where for well over a hundred years missionaries have been trained and sent out to Africa and Indonesia.

With such a long tradition of deeply evangelical piety, it was not surprising that Barmen should be chosen as the site of the First Confessional Synod of the German Evangelical Church. Moreover, it was no accident that the Barmen-Gemarke Church was the meeting place of the synod. For as we have already seen, here the first Free Reformed Synod and the first Free Evangelical Synod in the Rhineland were held, setting the pattern for all future confessional synods. From the very first, all its ministers — Karl Immer, Erich Schmidt, Paul Humburg, Harmannus Obendiek, Paul Kuhlmann, and Adolf Lauffs — took a firm stand against attempts by the " German Christians " to take over control of the congregation.[7] Thus the synod could count upon the fullest co-operation and progress of the congregation. The meetings of the synod were front-page news in the *Barmer Zeitung* and local printing companies printed large editions of the official reports.

The Synod of Barmen was composed of 139 delegates drawn from eighteen provincial Churches and from the most varied geographical, denominational, and theological backgrounds.[8] Members of Lutheran, Reformed, and United Churches, and of various free synods found themselves united in a common devotion to Jesus Christ. Of the 139 delegates, 53 were laymen. Among the clergymen there were Bishop Hans Meiser, of Bavaria, Bishop Theophil Wurm, of Württemberg, President Karl Koch, of Westphalia, and Dr. Hermann Hesse, moderator of the Alliance of Reformed Churches in Germany. Six university professors were in attendance: Karl Barth, then at Bonn University, Gerhard Ritter, of Freiburg, Otto Schmitz, of Münster, Hans von Soden, of Marburg,[9] Friedrich Delekat, of Leipzig, Hermann Sasse, of Erlangen, and Rudolf Hermann, of Greifswald.

The synod was an extraordinarily youthful one, the average age being not more than forty. Many of its commissioners later assumed prominent positions in the Church or became professors of theology. Heinrich Vogel, the author of the "Eight Articles of Evangelical Doctrine," later was appointed professor of theology in Berlin. His chief publications have been *Christologie* and *Gott in Christo*. Georg Merz, formerly co-editor with Barth of *Zwischen den Zeiten,* became professor of theology in Neuendettelsau. Heinrich Held was subsequently elected president of the Evangelical Church in the Rhineland. Upon his death in 1958 he was succeeded by Dr. Joachim Beckmann, who had published the *Kirchliches Jahrbuch 1933–1944* and was a lecturer in the Theologische Hochschule in Barmen. Martin Niemöller became president of the Church of Hesse-Nassau; Hugo Hahn, bishop of the Evangelical Lutheran Church in the Free State of Saxony; Gerhard Jacobi, bishop in Oldenburg; Ludolf Müller, bishop of Saxony; Hans Asmussen, director of the Kirchliche Hochschule in Berlin and later provost in Kiel; Karl Lücking, vice-president of the Synod of Westphalia; Kurt Scharf, president of the Brandenburg Confessional Synod; and Paul Humburg,[10] president of the Confessional Synod of the Rhineland. Also present as a delegate to the synod was Wilhelm Niemöller, brother of Martin, the founder of the Pastors' Emergency League, who was destined to become the foremost authority on the history of the Church in Germany from 1933 to 1945. Dr. Friedrich von Bodelschwingh, the director of the famous Bethel sanatorium for epileptics near Bielefeld, who had served as Reich bishop for a brief period, was appointed a special member of the synod by its Working Committee.

Certain personalities who were particularly active either in preparations for the synod or in its conduct deserve special mention. Foremost among these was, of course, the Reformed Church theologian Karl Barth. Indeed, so far as human judgment can discern, there would not have been a Synod of Barmen without the work of Karl Barth, not simply because he was the author of the original draft of the Theological Declaration and was an active member of the synod's Theological Commission which whipped the Declaration into final shape, and not simply because of the dominant role he played at the Free Reformed Synod of Barmen in January which paved the way for a synod of the whole evangelical Church, but because of the way in which he had shaped and molded theological thought in Germany during the years " between the times " — 1917–1934. Barth and Barmen are inextricably bound together. Yet at the plenary sessions of the synod, Barth never spoke at all. Indeed, it was almost forgotten to invite him, but two days before the synod convened he received a telegram from President Koch inviting him to attend. Barth's work for the synod was accomplished in committee, and he could safely leave to Hans Asmussen the task of guiding the Declaration through the synod. Perhaps Barth decided to keep silent in the public meetings to avoid any resentment or offense his name and person might occasion.

Asmussen fully justified Barth's confidence in him. He had worked with Barth on the committee that drew up the Declaration and on the synod's Theological Commission. But it was on the floor of synod that Asmussen showed his true greatness. His address, which introduced the Theological Declaration to the delegates, was in fact a commentary on the six articles. Inasmuch as the address was adopted by the synod along with the Declaration, it bears the character of synodical authority. A translation of the address is given in the appendix of this book. Born August 21, 1898, Asmussen was ordained a Lutheran minister. While serving in Altona, he was the chief author of the Altona Confession of January 11, 1933, which was the first confessional statement addressed to the confused situation. He was suspended from the ministry by his Church authorities on February 15, 1934, and later served in Bad-Oeynhausen as theological adviser to President Koch. A member of the Church's Council of Brethren, he was one of the most eloquent and courageous leaders in the Confessing Church. In addition to many articles and pamphlets dealing with the Church Struggle, Asmussen was the author of several widely read theological works, chief among them being *Die Offenbarung und das Amt, Die Seelsorge,* and a commentary on the epistle to the Galatians.[11]

Although Martin Niemöller did not play a prominent part in the proceedings of the synod, he must be reckoned among its most illustrious members. As one of the leaders of the Young Reformation Movement and as the founder of the Pastors' Emergency League, he was one of those principally responsible for the calling of the synod. Another man, much less known, matched Niemöller's organizing and administrative genius. He was Pastor Karl Immer, one of the ministers of the Barmen-Gemarke congregation.[12] More than any other man, he was responsible for the emergence of the free synods. He desired that the Church should come to speak through responsible synods. Obendiek relates that " at that time none of us knew what a free synod might be as distinguished from an ecclesiastically and legally accredited synod, and none of us knew what the outcome of the experiment would be. But the free synods . . . were a bold venture not only in view of the State but of the development of the provincial Churches in Germany." Without Immer's vision, initiative, and energy these synods would never have been held. Moreover, no one appreciated more highly or worked more tirelessly to publicize the work of the Confessing Church. In spite of Government prohibitions, he published the reports of the important synods of the Church. He published the Church paper *Unter dem Wort* (Under the Word), and he managed to find ways and means of distributing literature by trucks, cars, and special carriers. No wonder the Gestapo arrested this " dangerous man " in August, 1937, and confined him to the prison on Alexanderplatz in Berlin! Six days later he suffered a stroke and was released by the police. Half crippled and in poor health, Immer was spared for seven years, during which time he devoted his frail strength to warning and encouraging his brethren. He died on June 6, 1944.

The synod was presided over by Karl Koch, of Bad-Oeynhausen. Since 1927 he had served as president of the Synod of Westphalia, enjoying the confidence and deep respect of the whole Church. When the synod was arbitrarily dissolved on March 16, 1934, Koch was the leader of the opposition, and with the majority of the old synod, founded the Westphalia Confessional Synod. It was natural that by way of the joint meeting with the Synod of the Rhineland he should become president of the national synod and titular head of the Confessing Church. " He presided over the Synod of Barmen as a prudent father, energetically and impartially. In awkward situations he was able to help out with a kindly gesture and now and then to inject a little humor in the midst of strenuous work." [13]

In addition to Karl Barth and Hans Asmussen, the other members of the Theological Commission that prepared the first draft of the Barmen Declaration were Joachim Beckmann, Georg Merz, Wilhelm Niesel, Harmannus Obendiek, Eduard Putz, and Hermann Sasse. Brief biographical notes about these men are in order.

Beckmann (b. 1901) was at that time a Lutheran minister in Düsseldorf. On February 19, 1934, he was elected to the Council of Brethren of the Free Evangelical Synod of the Rhineland, was one of the signers of the Kassel Declaration of May 7, and, following Barmen, was a member of the Council of Brethren of the German Evangelical Church, for a time serving as its chairman. Today he is president of the Evangelical Church in the Rhineland.

Georg Merz (b. 1892) came from the Lutheran Church in Bavaria. In 1930, he was appointed a lecturer at the Theological School in Bethel, and in this way he came to be a delegate from Westphalia to the Barmen Synod. He, with Barth, was one of the editors of the periodical *Zwischen den Zeiten.*

Wilhelm Niesel (b. 1903) was a Reformed Church minister who even prior to the Church Struggle was also a lecturer in the Theological School in Elberfeld. Niesel is one of the foremost living authorities on Calvin. His book, *The Theology of Calvin,* written in 1938, was translated into English in 1956. He is a co-editor of a new edition of Calvin's works and editor of the *Bekenntnisschriften und Kirchenordnungen* of the Reformed Church (1938). Niesel is at present Moderator of the Reformed Alliance in Germany.

Harmannus Obendiek (b. 1894) was also a Reformed minister who shared with Paul Humburg and Karl Immer the care of the Barmen-Gemarke congregation, where the synod met. Like Beckmann, he was a member of the Council of Brethren of the Free Evangelical Synod of the Rhineland. He was active in the Alliance of the Reformed Churches and was largely instrumental in lining the Alliance up with the Confessing Church instead of letting it take a separate course as was done by the Lutheran Council. When Dr. Hermann Hesse, then moderator of the Alliance, was banished with his son Helmut to the Dachau Concentration Camp, the management of the Alliance was placed in the hands of a committee of three, with the result that Obendiek virtually served as the interim moderator. After the war his friends wanted him to let his name stand for election, but he declined on the ground that he had enough to do as a pastor of the Gemarke Church and as a lecturer in practical theology in the Theological School. In theology the two chief problems to engage his attention were demonology and confessionalism. Of his many publications the most important is his study of the devil in the writings of Martin Luther. In 1954, Obendiek attended the meetings of the Presbyterian World Alliance in Princeton, New Jersey, and of the World Council of Churches in Evanston. While on a preaching and lecturing tour through the states of the Northwest, he was killed in an automobile accident in South Dakota, September 14, 1954.[14]

Eduard Putz (b. 1907) was a young Bavarian minister who began as one of the " old soldiers " of the Nazi Party and became a soldier of Jesus Christ in the Confessing Church, famous as a preacher and lecturer.

Prof. Hermann Sasse (b. 1895) was minister in Oranienburg and Berlin from 1921 to 1933, and then became professor of Church history in Erlangen. He worked with the World Conference on Faith and Order and became known for his writings on the ecumenical movement. An avowed Lutheran confessionalist, he was the only delegate to the Barmen Synod to dissent from its action. He later became a bitter opponent of the Confessing Church.

Ludwig Steil and possibly Friedrich Müller were the only delegates to the synod who sealed their confession of Christ with their lives. One authority claims that Müller was murdered by poisoned food,[15] but Martin Niemöller disputes it: " Already legends about his death have begun to arise. . . . But Fritz Müller needs no other martyr's crown than the one he bore during his lifetime." [16] Niemöller avers that Müller died from a heart attack on the battlefield before the gates of Leningrad on September 20, 1942. As co-founder of the Pastors' Emergency League and a member of the Council of Brethren throughout the Church Struggle, he took part in every important decision. Niemöller may be forgiven an understandable exaggeration when he described his Dahlem colleague as "the one churchman of stature to appear in those critical years."

Ludwig Steil was born October 29, 1900. He was minister in Holsterhausen, a member of the Westphalian Council of Brethren, and President Koch's representative in the Church administration in Münster. His fearless, outspoken witness to Christ made him a marked man in the State. At length he was arrested, September 11, 1944. Two days before Christmas he was placed in the dreaded Dachau Concentration Camp, where he died on January 17, 1945.[17]

This account of outstanding members of the Synod of Barmen would by no means be complete without mention of those laymen who played a prominent part. Deserving of special mention were the lawyers Eberhard Fiedler, Wilhelm Flor, and Hans Meinzolt. Fiedler, born in 1898, was a lawyer in Leipzig and an elder in the Nicolai congregation in that city. From 1933 on, he represented the Pastors' Emergency League in legal matters. He was elected to the Council of Brethren at Barmen and served as legal adviser in the office of the presidency of the Confessional Synod in Bad-Oeynhausen. Later he served on the first provisional Church board. He died on November 29, 1947. Flor first attracted attention by an article that appeared in *Junge Kirche,* October 19, 1933, "The Church Conflict Judged in the Light of a Legal Standpoint." Together with Pastor Müller, of Dahlem, he is the father of the "ecclesiastical emergency polity." The Confessing Church in Saxony elected him to be its president in February, 1937. He died November 19, 1938. Hans Meinzolt, born 1887, was a prominent Bavarian lawyer who from 1933 to 1945 was vice-president of the Church Council in Munich. In October, 1934, he was relieved of his Church offices. He published a series of articles dealing chiefly with legal questions affecting the Church. He took part in numerous negotiations and meetings of the Confessing Church and participated in all the Confessional Synods of the German Church. Other prominent lawyers were Ludwig Metzger, of Darmstadt, who, after the war, became a member of the Federal Diet in Bonn, and Gustav Heinemann, of Essen, who was a member of Adenauer's cabinet until he resigned in protest against the latter's policy of rearmament and remilitarization.

Finally, we should mention Dr. Reinold von Thadden-Trieglaff. Born in 1891, the son of a noble family, he succeeded Georg Michaelis, former German Chancellor, as National Chairman of the German Student Christian Movement in 1928. In April, 1934, he was elected president of the Confessional Synod of Pomerania and chairman of its Council of Brethren. Later he was appointed to the Council of the German Evangelical Churches and was one of the signatories of the famous Memorandum sent to Hitler in July, 1936. Following the war, he became the founder and president of the Kirchentag — a mighty congress of evangelical Christians, which at first was held yearly and now every other year in the major cities of East and West Germany.

3. PROCEEDINGS OF THE SYNOD [18]

The Synod of Barmen was constituted with a church service on the evening of Tuesday, May 29, in the Gemarke Church, which was filled to overflowing. After the opening hymn, Superintendent Hahn, of Dresden, read the Scripture lesson from the first chapter of the book of Revelation. Following the customary hymn before the sermon, he preached from the first seven verses of the second chapter. In the course of his sermon he declared that the Church in Germany, including the Confessing Church, had " abandoned the love you had at first." Christ demanded complete surrender, but the Church had lapsed into a Christianity of custom and tradition. The result had been that contrary to the will of the Lord of the Church, the Church had allowed itself to be used for worldly purposes. It is true that the Confessing Church had been granted the gift to perceive the spirit of error — to " hate the works of the Nicolaitans " — for which Christ alone should be given the glory, lest one fall prey to the spirit of a self-righteous judge. Moreover, the hatred mentioned in the text must be directed against evil itself and never against persons. The sermon concluded with a call to repentance. In the intercessory prayer, mention was made of the Reich President (Hindenburg) and the Chancellor (Hitler). Following the Lord's Prayer, the service ended with the hymn.

After the church service a short meeting was held to attend to

business matters and to announce the agenda agreed upon at the
fifth meeting of the Nuremberg Committee in Barmen that day.
The calling of the roll revealed that 139 delegates from eighteen
regional Churches had arrived, among them the bishops of Bavaria
and Württemberg, as well as the representatives of all free synods.

Fifty-three of the delegates were laymen. President Koch, as the
chairman of the committee to make preparations for the synod on
behalf of the Confessional Fellowship, had sent out the official invita-
tions about the middle of May. A scheme had been devised whereby
the Churches, synods, and Confessional Fellowships were required
to send a certain number of delegates of which half should be ministers. They had until May 25 to report the names of their delegates
to the office in Bad-Oeynhausen. The delegates were certified upon
their arrival and received instructions concerning their billets and
places of meeting. In regard to the choice of delegates, it was urged:
"We request that only those men be sent who enjoy the full confidence of the confessing congregations within their Church districts.
Only those who refuse to submit to or to co-operate with a heretical
and violent Church government will be recognized. The Council of
Brethren must reserve to itself the right to refuse delegates who in
its opinion do not meet these requirements."

President Karl Koch, of Bad-Oeynhausen, the chairman, opened
the first business session of the synod shortly after nine o'clock,
Wednesday morning. The assembly stood to sing the first three
stanzas of a hymn.[19] Bishop Marahrens, of Hanover, although not an
official delegate, was called upon to conduct the opening devotions.
He delivered a brief meditation on Ezek. 3:22-23a.[20] This was followed by prayer and the singing of another hymn. The business of
the synod got under way with the calling of the names of those delegates who had arrived after the meeting of the previous evening.
Then the chairman announced that contrary to the original order of
business Pastor Asmussen would deliver his report for the Theological Commission, following which the Lutheran, Reformed, and
United Church Conventions should retire to discuss Asmussen's Report and the Theological Declaration. It will therefore be noted that
while the synod was constituted and acted as a whole, it also acted in
its several denominational branches.

A brief opening address was delivered by President Koch.[21] At the outset he referred explicitly to the daring involved in the claim that they had gathered here as the " Confessional Synod of the German Evangelical Church." He saw this daring not so much in the fact that it would be displeasing to the present Church government in Berlin, but rather in the grave responsibilities involved in this tremendous claim. He admitted to some that it might seem to be audacious presumption. Actually " we feel driven by an obligation from which we cannot escape." A *status confessionis* has existed for almost a year and compels us to act. Koch declared that they were gathered together in an awareness of their solidarity with all Germans and fellow citizens in a fateful period. In spite of charges leveled against them, he insisted that they were not indifferent to the fate of the nation. Yet Koch was not dismayed by the tribulations the Church was encountering. Quoting the text, " You meant evil against me, but God meant it for good," he asked whether the course followed by the Reich Church government in order to achieve a united German Church and which we firmly believe to be a false course might not nevertheless be the means of leading the evangelical Church into a deeper unity. " It may well be that the hardships which 1933 and 1934 have brought upon us will help to bring about the one German Evangelical Church."

Following President Koch's address, Pastor Asmussen delivered his lecture on " The Theological Declaration Concerning the Present Situation in the German Evangelical Church." [22]

At the conclusion of the report, the delegates, standing, sang four stanzas of a hymn. President Koch described Asmussen's address as " an extraordinarily valuable ' solida declaratio.' " He reminded the synod that no provision had been made for a discussion of the Declaration at this time. Instead he recommended that first the different groups should have an opportunity to give their opinion. Pfarrer Friedrich Gräber, from Essen, thought that they should first see how the provincial Churches reacted to this vote before they (the delegates) should engage in separate confessional discussions. Dr. Meinzolt was the next speaker and he urged that the explanations given by Asmussen be more clearly worked into the theses. For this purpose he suggested that after the meeting a few delegates deliberate as to whether this was desirable. The chairman agreed with Dr. Meinzolt. Then Dr. Fiedler, the lawyer from Leipzig, associated himself with Gräber's suggestion, namely, that the individual provincial Churches should meet and report their views to a committee to be named, in order to avoid the impression that the Barmen Declaration was the product of a small group and that no opportunity had been given the provincial Churches to express themselves. Pfarrer Edward Putz and Dr. Joachim Beckmann argued that the theses should be checked against the teaching of Holy Scripture and the Reformation Confessions. Beckmann had previously introduced this proposal in a written form and now repeated it orally as the spokesman for a group that had worked until four o'clock in the morning over the theses and had prepared certain recommendations. Pfarrer Karl Ritter, from Marburg, argued that the synod should act according to its constitution, namely, that it should act now through the different confessional groups gathered in the synod, registering their opinions. Otherwise many of them would not have a good conscience as to the constitutionality of the synod. At this point the chairman adjourned the discussion and suggested that the different conventions — the Lutheran and the Reformed — should meet to deliberate at the close of the session. The chairman announced that the synod would reconvene at four o'clock that afternoon. Following prayer, the morning session recessed at 12:12.

The Lutheran and Reformed Conventions met separately immediately after the adjournment of the morning session of the synod at 12:12. The Lutherans met in the Hotel Vereinshaus; the Reformed, in the parish hall. They began their work of examining and proving the Theological Declaration and Asmussen's exposition of it and continued until 5 P.M. Then Bishop Meiser and another Lutheran got in touch with members of the Reformed party to form the final deliberating commission. This theological commission, consisting of Asmussen, Barth, Beckmann, Merz, Niesel, Obendiek, Putz, and Sasse, conferred from five o'clock until one o'clock the next morning and gave the Theological Declaration its second draft or wording.

Due to certain difficulties that arose in connection with the business of the conventions, the synod itself did not reconvene until 4:52 P.M. In the absence of the chairman, Pastor Friedrich Gräber filled in with a brief talk. When President Koch appeared, he distributed two leaflets to the delegates and to guests who had registered: *The Up-*

building of the Confessing Church of the Old Prussian Union and
*The Legal Status of the Evangelical Church of the Old Prussian
Union.*[23] It should be explained that the Synod of the Old Prussian
Union Church met in Barmen on May 29 — the day on which the
Synod of Barmen convened for the whole German Evangelical
Church. The Union was the largest and most influential of those
regional Churches whose administration had been destroyed by the
Reich Church government. The Council of Brethren of the Prussian
Union was composed of men like Koch, Beckmann, Immer, Jacobi,
and Martin Niemöller, all of whom exerted a great influence
throughout the whole German Church. The circulation of the two
statements issued by the Synod of the Old Prussian Union on the
floor of the Synod of Barmen indicates that the delegates to both
synods were fully informed about their respective actions. It is too
much to say that the Synod of the Prussian Union directly influenced
the Synod of Barmen. However, it is safe to surmise that if the Prussian Union had been weak in its stand or if it had embarked upon a
separatist course, it would have seriously handicapped the work of
the larger, more inclusive, Synod of the German Church. Actually it
declared that it was " prepared, while fully maintaining its own existence, to stand together with the other independent Churches in the
German Evangelical Church and to act jointly with them." [24]

The sederunt actually got under way with the singing of two
stanzas of a hymn. Prayer was offered after the reading of a Scripture verse and then the last stanza of the same hymn was sung.
Dr. Fiedler, a lawyer, then delivered his address on the subject " Confessional Fellowship and the Constitution of the Reich Church."
When the Declaration of the Legal Committee concerning the Legal
Status of the Confessional Synod of the German Evangelical Church
was mentioned by Dr. Fiedler in the course of his speech, Pastor
Immer interrupted him in order to distribute copies of the Declaration to those who did not have them.[25] After Dr. Fiedler concluded his address and the chairman warmly thanked him, Dr. Flor,
a lawyer from Leipzig, followed with his paper on " A Study of
Recent Church Legislation." [26]

After the chairman conveyed various greetings that had been
received, the debate on the " Declaration Concerning the Legal Status
of the German Evangelical Church " was opened.[27] Since there was

no desire for a general discussion of the document, the delegates proceeded to consider the five points seriatim. The first four points were passed without discussion, except that in reference to the second point Pastor Niemöller stressed that here the Confessional Synod is charged not only with the task of representing the various Confessions, but of assembling the Confessing Congregation, and that is something more. He had missed this emphasis in Dr. Fiedler's presentation. The fifth point, however, gave rise to considerable discussion.

Prof. Gerhard Ritter, of the University of Freiburg, objected to the statement that " the congregation is the bearer of the proclamation of the word " on the ground that " according to Reformation teaching the office stands over against the congregation with a peculiar independence." According to Lutheran doctrine, at least, the office and the congregation in a vital polarity constitute the Church as a whole so that it is impossible to think of the congregation without the office or the office without the congregation. Yet it is not correct to treat the office as the mere expression or representative of the congregation. In support of his contention, Professor Ritter referred to the words of absolution and to the role of the bishop in Luther's teaching. Actually the third, fourth, and sixth articles of the Theological Declaration teach that the commission to proclaim the gospel of the free grace of God had been committed not to certain offices but to the whole Church. Professor Ritter had exposed a point at which considerable disagreement might have arisen between some Lutheran and the Reformed churchmen in the synod. However, the five speakers who followed Professor Ritter were not inclined to enter into a discussion of the " polar " relation of the preaching office and the congregation. It was the general feeling that in the present situation the rights of the congregation had to be secured. Pastor Niemöller rose to a point of order and asked that the delegates vote to retain the sentence as it stands or refer it to a committee. He saw no point of a general discussion of office and congregation in the synod itself. When the vote was taken by a show of hands, the majority was in favor of the article as it stood. Dr. Horst Michael, of Berlin, contended that the Declaration had passed only its first reading, since the previous day it had been agreed that the legal declarations would be adopted only after the Theological Dec-

laration had been accepted by the synod. The chairman replied
that if it was so desired, the synod could come back to it on the
morrow, but it now stood adopted. Evidently there was no strong
move to revive the point, as the Declaration was not brough up
again.

President Koch announced that several proposals had been received, five from the Free Evangelical Synod of Berlin-Brandenburg
and one signed by Heinrich Vogel, Dr. Berger, Gloege, Hinz, and
Wilhelm Gross.[28] He suggested that they be referred to the Council
of Brethren, and it was agreed. After Pastor Immer had distributed
to all delegates and guests lists of the members of the synod, Pfarrer
Dürr announced that on the following day representatives of the
Church of Baden wished to present a motion in writing to the effect
that " the synod extend an official invitation to the administrative
board of our regional Church to associate itself with the Confessional
Synod and to refuse to negotiate with the present ' German Christian' Church office." The chairman took cognizance of this notice
of motion, and then called attention to a typographical error in a
printed copy of *The Legal Status of the Evangelical Church of the
Old Prussian Union* that had been distributed to the delegates that
morning. As the session drew to a close, Pastor Immer invited the
delegates to supper in his parish hall and announced that in the
evening a public meeting would be held at which reports would be
given concerning the difficulties under which many ministers were
laboring in various parts of Germany. With the singing of a hymn,
and with prayer, the synod recessed at 7:20 P.M.

The evening in the Klingelholl parish hall provided a welcome
relaxation from the afternoon session. The common meal gave the
delegates an opportunity to become better acquainted and to exchange views. The reports offered a bird's-eye view of the struggle
the Church was undergoing in many areas. The gravity of the situation was impressed upon all and gave rise to fervent intercession. At
the same time a note of joy, even of humor, was not missing as the
speakers related amusing incidents.[29] Conditions in East Prussia,
Bremen, Hanover, the Saar, Saxony, and Württemberg were described. Perhaps most significant was the singing of the " hymns of
the Confessing Congregation." Hymns that had emerged from periods in the history of the Church's persecution acquired new and

vital meaning. Their singing underscored, as it were, the vivid reports and constituted a confession and prayer of its own.

At 9:15 A.M. on Thursday, May 31, the synod reconvened. Devotions were conducted by Pastor Dr. Friedrich von Bodelschwingh. Following the singing of three stanzas of a hymn, he preached from Matt. 11:29: " Take my yoke and learn from me." [30] He developed three points. With the new paths along which the Church had embarked there were linked a common bearing of a new yoke, a new learning, and a new suffering. His sermon made a deep impression and, as Karl Immer reported, sounded " like a mother comforting and exhorting her children vexed by all sorts of fears and anxieties." Following the prayer after the sermon, the last two stanzas of a hymn were sung.

The chairman recalled the motion made the previous day by delegates from the Church of Baden, and suggested that they get in touch with other delegates who had expressed an interest in it and that perhaps the motion could be expanded. After Pastor Immer had made one or two announcements, Dr. Meinzolt delivered his address on " Our View of a Proper Constitution for the German Evangelical Church." [31] His address took the form of a commentary on a series of leading propositions and subpropositions. The synod waived a general discussion of the paper and took it up section by section. Most of the discussion revolved around the best way to guarantee the rights of the local congregations within the regional and national Church and how to take advantage of the vital forces in congregations. The chairman eventually suggested that the present propositions be adopted by way of a first reading. He thought that when the matter was brought up again at the afternoon session, a better wording might possibly be found. This was agreed to. Meanwhile a motion by Michael, Niemöller, and Hesse had been handed to the chairman: " that it be resolved that the present Reich Church does not have the right to put a constitution in operation or even to bring about its reform. The synod and the Churches represented by it refuse to co-operate with the present Church government in any reform of the constitution." Debate on this motion was also deferred till the afternoon session.

At this point Pastor von Bodelschwingh rose to make a personal explanation concerning an article in the *Basler Nachrichten* to the

effect that the Reich Church government had made personal over-
tures to him to act with others on its legal committee. He admitted
that he and another man had been approached,[32] but they had of
course immediately declared that they could not accept a position unless the South German Churches concurred, and that they could not
think of co-operating unless the South German Churches were given
the assurance that the work would be done in perfect freedom and
with equal rights. No promise of any kind had been made which —
as it might appear — would initiate a split in the Ulm group. (The
Ulm group were the representatives of Württemberg and Bavarian
regional Churches, and of the Free Synods of the Rhineland, Westphalia, and Brandenburg, as well as many confessing Christians and
congregations throughout Germany, who issued the Ulm Declaration on April 22, 1934, as " the legitimate evangelical Church of Germany.") Pastor von Bodelschwingh then stated that he doubted
whether it was advisable to bind the South German Church leaders
by a resolution of the synod. He preferred that this suggestion (the
motion by Michael, Niemöller, and Hesse) be transmitted in proper
form to the synod's committee.

   This little episode might well be lost upon the casual reader of the
minutes of the synod unless he were aware that the State Church
government was trying at that very time to subvert the authority of
the Confessing Church and its synod. The idea was to appoint a
legal committee composed of outstanding Church leaders like von
Bodelschwingh and Bishop Marahrens. The motion made by Michael, Niemöller, and Hesse amounted to a declaration by the synod
that it would not even contemplate negotiating with any Reich
Church officials. The Confessional Synod, standing on the Confession
of Faith, was to be the sole authority for any changes in the Church's
constitution. In the face of the motion, von Bodelschwingh felt
obliged to assure the synod that he and presumably his brother would
have nothing to do with the invitation from the side of Reich Church
authorities. At the same time, von Bodelschwingh's stand was somewhat weakened by his recommendation that the leaders of the
South German Churches be permitted to act independently of a decision by a synod of the whole evangelical Church in Germany. It
was this sort of independent action which later seriously weakened
the ranks of the Confessing Church.

President Koch requested that copies of the *Second Reading of the Declaration of the Theological Committee* be distributed and then declared that the synod stood adjourned for a fifteen-minute recess. When it resumed at 11:43 A.M., he announced that the motion by Michael, Niemöller, and Hesse had been withdrawn, and that it would be reworded during the noon hour and presented at the afternoon meeting. After the singing of a stanza of a hymn, the chairman drew attention to several typographical errors in the printing of the second proposed reading of the Declaration, and then called upon Pastor Asmussen to explain the reasons for the changes made in the text since its first reading and how they came about.[33] Asmussen reported that the committee of the Lutheran Convention had met the previous afternoon until 5 P.M., at which time it reported to the convention on those points in which a change had seemed advisable.[34] Thereupon Bishop Meiser and another Lutheran had conferred with the Reformed brethren concerning the formation of the final deliberative commission. This theological committee consisted of Asmussen, Barth, Beckmann, Merz, Niesel, Obendiek, Putz, and Sasse. It conferred from 5 P.M. until 1 A.M. in the Evangelical Parish House. It was also known as the " Inter-Confessional Committee." Asmussen said:

> If I have the honor to report on the changes, I would like to emphasize that the draft now in your hands is presented in the name of these four men after mature deliberation.[35] During these last days we have experienced that the preparation for a discussion of these theses has been at times quite passionate. In another connection I stated that I would not have approved if these theses and my address had been adopted en bloc in the form of a proclamation. . . . To me it seems to be to the credit of the First Confessional Synod of the German Evangelical Church that in it there has been room for all sorts of scruples — those born of passion, those of misunderstanding, those prompted by serious ideological and confessional considerations, as well as those of legal considerations.
>
> Two stages may be distinguished in the preparation [of this Declaration]. The first was marked by the fact — it could not have been otherwise — that the various delegates had come here with special interests and with a definite picture in their minds of their fellow delegates: those from the north had their opinion of those from the south and vice versa, the Reformed of the

Lutheran, the Lutheran of the Reformed. Consequently in these conversations all the widely diverse interests converged. No one wants to decide what passions were spiritual and what were carnal. I do not presume to do so. I do not regard it as a sign of special spirituality if a man appears to be devoid of passion. Nor do I think that the opposite is a mark of special spirituality. And one may indeed say that the second phase of the preliminary proceedings, in spite of restrained passions involved in them, was marked more by sober reflection. The brethren who worked here yesterday afternoon until one o'clock in the morning probably did not find their work burdensome. They will agree with me when I am bound to say that this work will be counted among the most pleasant intellectual and spiritual recollections of my life.

It can now be said that in the preparation [of this document] almost all objections were at least discussed. Further than that, the objections raised were dealt with very great care, and that the wording, the word order, and the meaning of the words were weighed to the last detail — perhaps too much so for the laymen. At this point I am obliged to say that we theologians need to pursue such a work with the greatest possible exactness. Venerable brothers and sisters: we have gathered here in the consciousness that the word which we want to utter in common has to stand as a sign. Could anything be more understandable than that all delegates were animated with the desire to see this sign set up as quickly as possible? Now these have been days of discussion and debate. I say that it is good that they have been, and that it is good that they are now past. It would not have been a good thing if, under the color of making a Confession, we had repeated what was proclaimed in the course of a rally, like the adoption of the famous twenty-eight points.[36] We cannot settle it as easily or as fast as that. When a woodworker makes a piece of furniture, when a locksmith matches a piece of metal to a hundredth of a millimeter, when a lawyer carefully weighs the issues in a brief or in a judgment, then it is obvious that theologians should also uphold the honor of their calling and not neglect to work in an orderly and neat fashion. It is perhaps — no, it is certainly — a good thing that in this evangelical synod, laymen and theologians have sat together, in order that the *élan* be not lost through theological scrupulousness and that through theological refinement the *élan* be kept on the right track.

At this point in his report, Asmussen dealt candidly with the matter of Hermann Sasse's defection.

> In order to avoid any misunderstanding, I would like to state now publicly that Professor Sasse has taken a special position which requires clarification in order that the bond which binds him to us be not broken through misunderstanding. We know our brother Sasse as one who has . . . for the sake of the Confession and for conscience sake from the beginning of the German Evangelical Church.[37] We know him as one of the very few university professors who have supported us by word and deed in the Church Struggle and at the risk of their lives. (*Applause.*) We would not be true to ourselves, brothers and sisters, if we asked anyone to say Yes when he was unable to do so. However, from our work together last night we gathered the impression that this theological position in regard to the articles is not such as should . . . here.[38] I do not think that the dissent will go so far as to result in a split.[39]

Following these introductory remarks, Asmussen proceeded to give explanations for the changes in the text of the Theological Declaration. Some of this material will be found in the footnotes to the official text given in Appendix VII. Asmussen concluded his report with these words:

> I believe, and it is my hope and my impression that, since in the meetings of the commission the matters have been really examined from every angle, it will not be necessary to repeat at length and so vehemently everything (*loud applause*) that was discussed yesterday. We will gladly let anyone speak who has anything on his heart. But we have faithfully performed our work in a fellowship in which no one had to say what the other said. So let us now bear witness to the world — such is my earnest prayer — that we are a synod that really believes that God has given us a common word to utter. (*Applause.*)

President Koch then observed that " seldom has a document been produced in which every word had been weighed. . . . This is not ordinary coinage but a polished casting." He invited several to voice their attitude to the Declaration. First to speak was Pfarrer Julius Schieder, from Nürnberg. He referred to the initial misgivings entertained by the Bavarians and to the cross of confessional divisions.

Since, however, the passages offensive to the Bavarians had been changed, he declared in their name: "We have the faith and the courage to stand by this Declaration." Professor Ritter, from Freiburg, was the next to register his concurrence. He too admitted the apprehension he had had in regard to the text as first presented. The work of the commission had relieved his conscience. He was glad that the first draft had not been adopted in a "frenzy of enthusiasm." If such had been the case, he would have left Barmen with the feeling that in the end one no longer took theological work seriously. Now he could leave with the feeling that he could wholeheartedly advocate it sentence for sentence to all his friends. "It is not so that here each one stands alone. On the contrary, we must first answer to God for what we do here. Then we can answer to the members who look to us because they believe that we are willing and determined to represent their convictions, their needs, and their hopes in this assembly. He referred to the fact that he had described Asmussen's speech of the previous day as "a good Lutheran commentary to a good Reformed document." "Now I am obliged to say that it is neither Lutheran nor Reformed. Here truly resounds the voice of the Confessing Church in which we hear and recognize that we are again united." Professor Ritter referred to the fact that the laymen found it difficult to understand the confessionalism that emerged in the discussions. He explained that the truth is never composed of pieces of the truth, so that one could say that such and such a percentage of the truth was held in common, and the rest lay in doctrinal differences. "The truth is always a *totum,* a living whole." In Barmen no compromise has been made; rather, we have been granted a common word. "Now we can wholeheartedly join in."

Dr. Eberhard Baumann, from Stettin, was the next speaker. "In the name of my Reformed friends I can state that we unanimously agree with this changed version of the Theological Declaration. We do so greatly rejoicing that we can appear before our congregations with this result. They will share it with us as a precious gift of God in a grave hour. It is also a joy that we have found ourselves marching shoulder to shoulder, the Lutherans and the Reformed, in the struggle for the Church's life." With reference to the cross of confessional divisions which Pfarrer Schieder mentioned, Dr. Baumann said: "When this cross that weighs upon us in evangelical Germany presses us deep down into Holy Scripture, and when under its burden this cross lets us look to the Lord of the Church in utter earnestness, then it will be a blessing now as before."

Very moving was the brief address given by a layman, Dr. von Thadden, on behalf of the Lutheran laity. The laymen, he said, had come to the synod in the hope that the synod would profess a fighting fellowship within evangelical Christendom, but also with the fear that the Evangelical Church in Germany would collapse if it failed to reach a common Confession.[40] They were all the more grateful for the result they found in these theses. He conceded that laymen are not able to judge the value of particular theological points. But they did know that the congregations are being challenged today by the Lord of the Church to make a Confession of Faith. In conclusion Dr. von Thadden alluded to the extraordinary importance that the Reformation Confessions had acquired anew. " In this struggle many of us laymen realized for the first time what we possess in the heritage of our fathers. . . . We are willing to receive this heritage from God's hands and to use it as property entrusted to us." He related that Prof. Traugott Hahn had said to him shortly before he had been martyred: "' In the moment when the hour of persecution and martyrdom strike for the Church of Jesus Christ, that will be the moment when the members and the confessions of the German Reformation will stand closer together than before.' " [41]

It was most fitting that the next speaker should be the brother of Traugott Hahn, Superintendent Hugo Hahn, of Dresden. Speaking on behalf of the Evangelical Lutheran Confessional Society in Saxony and Hanover he said: " We too have regarded it as a gift of God that in a time of need confessing Christians of different Reformation Confessions have been forged together under one yoke, and we are certain that it is the yoke of Christ. . . . We are completely united with our brother Asmussen in profound gratitude that this word has been taken so earnestly; that it has been so carefully considered, even if our beloved laymen have not always been able to understand why we have made it so difficult for ourselves; and above all, that the consciousness of being responsible for the Confession entrusted to us has come alive in us through God's grace. At the same time all of us here are fully aware that if we had not arrived at a common word, it would have been not only a great misfortune but also disobedience to the will of Jesus Christ for us in this hour. Then we would have broken loose from the common yoke of Jesus Christ."

In the name of the delegates from the Old Prussian Union and the rest of the Church present, President Koch expressed thanks to those who had worked on the Declaration. "We are in hearty agreement with these articles which, if God wills, one day will have considerable importance for the future German Evangelical Church. Permit me as your chairman to add another word. I would like to express an especially warm word of thanks to the commission, which worked from yesterday afternoon until late into the night, composed of the synodical delegates Asmussen, Barth, Beckmann, Merz, Putz, and the two co-opted members Obendiek and Niesel. I would also like to thank Dr. Sasse for the part he willingly played in the theological formulations in the committee. Now I suggest to the synod that all open discussion cease [agreed], and that we refrain from a discussion of details [agreed]. In responsibility to God and to the Church we can now settle the issue. A final motion has been presented:

1. *That the synod acknowledge the Theological Declaration Concerning the Present Situation of the German Evangelical Church, together with the address by Pastor Asmussen, to be a Christian, Biblical, and Reformation witness, and accepts responsibility for it.*

2. *That the synod transmit this Declaration to the confessional conventions to work out a responsible interpretation from the standpoint of their respective Confessions."*

The chairman called for the vote and asked the delegates to stand. He announced that there was an overwhelming majority in favor of the motion. He suggested that perhaps it would be desirable to take the negative vote, and requested that those standing take their seats. "Opposed, please stand. Only delegates are permitted to vote. Are there any opposed? No. Have any refrained from voting? No. Then this Declaration has been unanimously adopted." The assembly rose and sang the last stanza of "Now Thank We All Our God":

All praise and thanks to God
The Father now be given,
The Son, and Him who reigns
With them in highest heaven,

The one eternal God,
Whom earth and heaven adore;
For thus it was, is now,
And shall be evermore.

Since it was nearly 1 P.M., the chairman suggested that the synod recess and deal with the report of the Committee on Practical Work at the afternoon session.[42] Pastor Asmussen rose to remind the delegates: " The text of the Declaration may not be published before the authentic text has been given out by the business committee of this synod." (*Spirited agreement.*)

The meeting recessed at 1:10. It reconvened at 4:22 P.M., with the singing of two stanzas of a hymn. President Koch drew attention to the fact that the morning session had forgotten to vote upon the second part of the motion, namely, to transmit to the Confessional Conventions the Theological Declaration for their study and interpretation. He said that he would like to rectify this omission in order that the synod might act in a constitutional manner and all conditions be satisfied. " Unless there is any objection, I would like to rule that the synod has also adopted this second point, and that this Theological Declaration has been transmitted to the Confessional Conventions."

President Koch then announced that the Confessional Conventions would meet as soon as the Executive Council of the synod was notified by this or that confessional group. However, the Executive Council itself would not call the conventions but would hand the notice on to Bishop Meiser for the Lutherans and to one of the leaders of the Reformed Church. Professor Ritter asked whether it would not be better if the conventions were to meet immediately at the close of the synod to appoint committees to deal with practical matters and to prepare for meetings of the different conventions at a later date. The chairman admitted that this would be a practical arrangement, but feared that there would not be enough time, since the synod still had considerable business to attend to. Thereupon Dr. Ritter urged that the executive boards of the different conventions keep in mind the necessity of appointing such committees. In retrospect we can now say that this time a chairman's natural zeal to save time and to forego a meeting of the conventions at the close of the synod was a grave mistake. For the conventions never did meet, and no committees were appointed. It seems that Bishop

Meiser and the Lutherans were not anxious to draw the implications of Barmen for their ecclesiastical decisions. The Reformed church-men, on the other hand, felt no need to meet, since they were in complete agreement with Barmen from the start. The two attitudes to-ward Barmen — that of the Lutherans and of the Reformers — were based upon their respective views of a Confession of Faith. The Lutherans tended to absolutize their Confessions as timeless expressions of Biblical truth, whereas the Reformed Church looks upon its Confessions as historically conditioned and valid only until such time as they should be superseded by a newer and perhaps better Confession. The fact that the conventions never met is to be deplored because it meant that the reformation of the Church's faith and order was not pursued further.

The business in connection with the Theological Declaration having been concluded, the chairman recalled that the morning's discussion of the paper " Our View of a Proper Constitution for the German Evangelical Church " had given rise to a motion that was subsequently withdrawn. It was now to be replaced by a statement that also bore upon the paper. He called upon Dr. Meinzolt to read it:

> We declare that it is the unanimous mind of the synod that we deny that the present Church administration of the German Evangelical Church has any authority or right to undertake a reform of the constitution; on the contrary, we expressly demand that the existing constitution be respected.
>
> We declare that as long as the present Church administration exists, the Confessing Church categorically refuses to negotiate with it in regard to constitutional matters.
>
> Under these circumstances the Confessional Synod dispenses with passing a resolution concerning the overture presented by the Legal Committee, " Our View of a Proper Constitution for the German Evangelical Church," and transmits it to the Council of Brethren as material for " future work."

This statement was adopted by the synod and was of far-reaching significance. It provided synodical justification for the uncompromising stand taken later by the Council of Brethren in all its dealings with the " German Christians " and the Reich Church government.

The next item of business was the report by Pfarrer Georg Schulz, of Barmen, for the Committee on Practical Work.[43] In the discussion that followed, Pfarrer Ludwig Steil, a member of the committee who died on January 17, 1945, in the Dachau Concentration Camp, was the first speaker. He said that the committee realized that there should be another section in the report entitled " The Closed Door," inasmuch as there were areas from which the Church was excluded, such as the Youth Work Camps and the Brown Corps. Dr. von Thadden, a layman, felt that the office of preaching was confined too much to the clergy. Does not a proclamation of the word take place in a given actual moment when something is said from God's Word? Cannot therefore the laity do much to go through " the closed doors "? Dr. Walther Thieme, director of the City Mission, Berlin, took strong exception to Point 3 in which the Home and Foreign Missionary Societies were required to decide in favor of the Confessional Synod. He feared that there was an attempt to dissolve the societies and to let the congregations inherit their work. He urged the synod to recognize the tension that must exist between organized congregations and a Home Missionary Society. When the speaker launched into theology and into the history of the missionary movement, he was interrupted by the chairman's gong. Actually, of course, the synod had no desire to dissolve the societies or to interfere with their independent activities. It simply wished to insist that they could not work with or within a confessing Church and remain neutral or indifferent to the error of the " German Christians," as Pastors Niemöller and Dr. von Rabenau, of Berlin, pointed out. Several others spoke, not to oppose the committee's recommendations but to stress points they felt were particularly important. For instance, several laymen emphasized the part to be played by the local congregations and individual Church members. This note was sounded again and again throughout the synod. As the hour was drawing late, the chairman strove manfully to terminate the discussion. Finally he suggested that the first two recommendations be adopted by the synod and the last two be referred to the Council of Brethren for interpretation. Then a motion was passed naming the members of a permanent Council of Brethren and outlining its powers.

The Working Committee presented a motion that had originated with Pfarrer Gerhard Jacobi to the effect that " the Confessional Synod protest against all external and internal pressure brought upon assistant ministers and candidates by the ' German Church ' administration, and that it charge the Council of Brethren of the Confessional Synod with the spiritual care and the personal welfare of young theologians." It was adopted unanimously. The chairman then declared that the following statement also pertained to the previous motion:

> The synod directs the Councils of Brethren of the provincial synods entrusted with the care of candidates for the ministry to take a special interest in non-Aryan theological students. Those who have already been prevented from taking examinations or employment through the enforcement of the law concerning Church officials, as for example in Old Prussia, must have access to a spiritual office within the Confessing Church. The same care must be afforded the non-Aryan brethren for whom the possibility of studying theology is now closed.

The chairman suggested that this be referred to the Council of Brethren to consider in what way this concern could best be met. It was agreed. Then Lücking, Fiedler, and Held presented a resolution in regard to the silencing of the Church press, which was adopted. Delegates from Baden, Kurhessen, and Lippe moved that the synod commission its Council of Brethren to decide in what way the administrative bodies of all the German regional Churches that had not yet submitted to the Reich Church government could be required to join the fellowship of the German Evangelical Church in the interest of Church unity in Germany and the restoration of a constitutionally legal status. Niemöller remarked that we do not have the right to require Churches and individuals to join us. We ought not to resort to pressure; otherwise we won't have a solid front.

Two delegates moved that a proclamation be published and read to the congregations. President Koch informed them that a message to the congregations had already been drafted. Before he called upon Pastor Asmussen to read it, he ruled that a motion by Dr. Thieme be handed to the Council of Brethren as a suggestion, namely, that two representatives of the Home Missionary Society be added to the Committee on Practical Questions. Asmussen explained that the " Appeal to Evangelical Congregations and Christians in Germany " [44] was

conceived as a preface to the theological, legal, and practical pronouncements. He requested that the Council of Brethren be permitted to change the wording in places. The message was greeted
with enthusiastic applause and was ordered to be sent out after it had
been edited. Actually, the " Appeal " is of considerable theological
importance, since it reflects the way in which the synod desired its
declarations to be received.

The chairman said he had forgotten that there was a motion that
requested the Council of Brethren to present a case in regard to the
desecration of Sunday by all kinds of unnecessary work. The motion
was approved, though the minutes do not give its exact wording or
its authors. It serves to prove that Barmen was not altogether unlike
most Church assemblies in which important and unimportant matters are rushed through in the last minutes. Nevertheless, the pressure of time did not prevent the synod from adjourning in reverent
praise and thanksgiving to Almighty God. It stood to sing the first
and third stanzas of the hymn " Wunderanfang, herrlich Ende " —
Wonderful beginning, a glorious end! Bishop Meiser, of Munich, delivered a brief meditation on Ps. 102:13-14.[45] He alluded to the fre-
quency with which mention had been made about the " great
responsibility laid upon us. And in truth it is impossible for us to ex-
aggerate this responsibility. It finds expression when we refer to ourselves as ' the Confessing Church.' " " Are we not in danger of presumption when we apply this word to ourselves? " the bishop asked.
The recognition of our responsibility drives us to prayer. We can begin and conclude all our deliberations only in the presence of God —
in gratitude for the blessings of health, of Christian fellowship and
unity, for permission to meet unmolested, for the clarity of insight
granted us, for a deeper understanding of God's Word and the Confession of Faith. But in the great task of building God's house it is
ever necessary to turn to God's Word. " O Lord, thou wilt arise and
have pity on Zion." If we had not known it before, then we have
learned in the past months of the Church Struggle that nothing is
accomplished by our deliberations, strategy, and planned action when
God does not build his house among us. Ever again we need to im-
plore God's help. " Our prayer can be only one of humility that
acknowledges the justice of God's ways and that does not prescribe
for him either the day or the hour, the way or the means."

After a prayer the synod sang the fourth and fifth stanzas of the hymn it had begun.

The chairman adjourned the synod with these words:

> We stand at the close of the first meeting of the Confessional Synod of the German Evangelical Church.
>
> Honored Delegates, greet all those who belong to us, near and far, who would like to have been with us but were unable to do so. And now, my beloved brethren, I commend you to God and to the Word of his grace. Amen.
>
> The meeting of the Confessional Synod of the German Evangelical Church is concluded.

The time was 7:20, Thursday, May 31, 1934.

4. THE HISTORY OF THE DEVELOPMENT OF THE TEXT OF THE BARMEN THEOLOGICAL DECLARATION

This section will deal with the history of the origin and development of the Declaration from its initial draft till its final form. It will also give an account of the various drafts and copies of the text still extant.

As already noted, the Nuremberg Committee, which was afterward called the Council of Brethren of the Confessional Synod of the DEK and was commonly known as the Reich Council of Brethren (*Bruderrat*), appointed a committee of three — Asmussen, Barth, and Breit — at its meeting in Berlin on May 2, 1934, and commissioned them "to work out a draft for the German Confessional Synod."[46] They met in the Basler Hof in Frankfurt am Main, May 15–16, two weeks before the opening of the synod in Barmen. Hermann Sasse, Professor of Church History at the University of Erlangen, was added to the committee when the Nuremberg Committee met in the Hotel Schirmer in Kassel, May 7, but for some reason he did not attend.[47] The committee deliberated a whole day. Thomas Breit acted as chairman and opened the meeting with a brief meditation, which was followed by some preliminary remarks by Hans Asmussen. Then Barth enumerated the three main requirements: (1) We have to proceed from Articles 1 and 4 of the constitution of the DEK. The presupposition of all discussions is the fact that this legal basis of the constitution has been broken. (2) It is necessary to take a position at the start in regard to questions about the source of revelation, justification, and sanctification. (3) The problem of the structure of the Evangelical Church is a question of the Confession of Faith. Asmussen added that a theological statement has to be the basis for a solution of the task laid upon them. Breit, on the other hand, felt that it ought not to be a confessional declaration, since they were starting from the constitution and in the Reich Church no particular Confession had existed. Barth replied: " It is not a matter of a new Confession. The Barmen Declaration (of January, 1934, by the Reformed Churches) was not even that. It is a question of an exposition, an interpretation of the Confession of Faith. Such had also been the case earlier." When Breit then characterized the reference to the Church's constitution as questionable, Asmussen said that they had to start not only with the constitution but with the regional Churches (*Landeskirchen*). This point was cleared up when Barth insisted that a theological declaration had to have a legal basis, and alluded to Article 2, according to which the DEK is an alliance or federation of Churches. Breit then argued that they should abide by the decisions of the Reformation lest it be suspected that the Lutheran Churches had abandoned their Confession. Barth answered that no one will prevent the Lutherans or us from giving an answer to the questions that confront us today, while the old Confessions remain in force. Thus we detect even in this committee of three at least the ingredients of the dispute over confessionalism, which later was to break out into the open and grievously weaken the cause of the Confessing Church. However, the three were agreed that their purpose was not to achieve a Church union. " We do not want a union," Barth said. It was simply to be a matter of the three Churches — Lutheran, Reformed, and United — confessing their faith on the basis of their ancient Confessions in face of existing concrete errors.

We may safely assume that this general discussion took place during the forenoon, since Asmussen's minutes of the meeting give no account of a discussion of the theses drawn up. Barth composed the original draft himself, following the noon meal.[48] He wrote it in his own handwriting. He had brought no preliminary manuscript or notes along. He explained [49] that since the meeting of the Reformed

Free Synod in January of that year and because of the constant discussions of the time, he knew pretty well what ought to be declared by the synod. Nevertheless, when one considers carefully the unity and consistency of the various theses, not to mention the depth of theological insight, one must acknowledge that this original draft was a particularly inspired piece of extemporaneous writing. Breit and Asmussen immediately agreed to the propositions drawn up by Barth. Asmussen stressed again that all the propositions had to be governed by the first thesis, and Barth added that they had to bear the character of a *conditio sine qua non*. Thus emerged on May 16, 1934, what Barth called the " Frankfurt Accord." [50]

To date, no one appears to know the whereabouts of this original handwritten manuscript. Professor Barth and his secretary, Fräulein von Kirschbaum, are of the opinion that it had been sent with the rest of his papers concerning Barmen to Prof. Ernst Wolf in Göttingen. The latter, however, has no knowledge of it. Barth is also of the impression that the Declaration was typed up *after* he returned to Bonn. However, it would appear that his memory has failed him here, for on May 17 — the day after the meeting in Frankfurt — Asmussen sent to President Koch a copy of the Theological Declaration. In an accompanying letter from Altona, dated May 17, he wrote: " We thought that the Declaration should be kept as brief as possible. This was practical because we did not want to discuss publicly any more than necessary the relationship of Lutheran and Reformed theology within our front." Later, Asmussen delivered the original draft signed by the three to Koch in person. Thus it would seem that Barth's handwritten draft was typed up in Frankfurt — probably by his secretary, Fräulein von Kirschbaum. This earliest typewritten manuscript is to be found in the Bielefeld Archive. It is typed on lined paper. Corrections and additions are written in — some with green pencil and some in ink. It originally contained only five theses; Asmussen wrote in the sixth in shorthand and pencil.

The second extant draft of the Declaration is a single-spaced typewritten manuscript containing numerous notes written in by Asmussen in green and black pencil. A list of fifteen names is given in green pencil at the end of the document. Unfortunately it is no longer known where and when this particular draft was written and what significance is to be attached to the list of names. Noteworthy is that it is very much like the "Frankfurter Konkordie."

The so-called "Frankfurt Concord" is typed in purple ink on ordinary white typewriter paper. Asmussen's copy is in the Bielefeld Archive and Professor Wolf has Barth's copy. Although there are a few very minor changes written into the text, there is no doubt that they represent the same stage in the development of the Declaration. But when and where this third (?) draft was written is no longer known.

The next official draft marks the fourth revision. Barth's copy bears the note: "Second Draft of the Committee," whereas Asmussen's copy has the note: "Leipzig Draft (May 22, 1934)," written in red pencil. (Professor Wolf has Barth's copy in his possession. Asmussen's is in the Bielefeld Archive.) Both copies are typewritten on yellow paper. Gerhard Niemöller comments that this draft manifests a marked Lutheran confessionalistic ring. It appears to have been drawn up at the meeting of the Council of Brethren in Leipzig on May 22.

Sometime between the Leipzig meeting and the convening of the Synod of Barmen on May 29 a fifth draft was typed up, probably by Asmussen. It nullified the changes made at Leipzig and is almost identical with the Frankfurt Concord. It is entitled "Proposal of the Theological Committee for the Confessional Synod of the DEK." It was prepared by the Theological Commission of the Synod of Barmen and distributed to the delegates. Several copies of it are in the Bielefeld Archive. Two of them were Asmussen's and one contains emendations made by the Commission, which he had written in in his own handwriting. The other has the corrections made with a red pencil and has a list of the members of the Commission appended. Professor Wolf also has two copies of this draft, on one of which Barth had written in the emendations.

The final draft is, of course, the one adopted by the synod. The copy that was prepared for the printers and bears the signatures of Asmussen, Barth, Beckmann, Putz, and Obendiek is in the Bielefeld Archive.

In addition to the above-mentioned drafts and revisions, the Bielefeld Archive also has a draft of a statement on which Asmussen wrote in red pencil "Erlangen Entwurf." It appears to be the same lined paper on which the original Frankfurt draft was typed. But two different typewriters were used. Although this Erlangen statement, like Barmen, contains six theses and the anathemas, the text is quite different. Was this Asmussen's personal paper which he took to Erlangen? Who wrote it? Where did the author acquire the number six? Why did nothing come of it? These are questions that will doubtless never be answered.[51]

Still another draft exists. It is entitled " Message Concerning the Situation in the Church." It appears to have been written by Christian Stoll and to have been conceived as a pronouncement to be made by the synod. In six theses and antitheses it deals with the ground of the Church, its standards and tasks, its office and polity, with strong affinities to the Lutheran symbols and in relation to the administration of the German Evangelical Church. Nothing came of this document either.

When the Committee of Three met in Frankfurt — May 16 — it was agreed that Asmussen should prepare a paper on the articles of the Declaration to be delivered at the synod. Asmussen submitted his paper to Barth and Breit and they gave it their full approval. In his letter of May 23, Barth wrote: " The paper is the product of a single mold. As a whole and in detail I recognize it to be an exact replica of what I had in mind when I made the proposals for the text of the Declaration. The Declaration and the text [of Asmussen's paper] fit together like a top to a kettle, so that later someone might wonder whether something like the miracle of the Septuagint had not taken place."

An account of the way the Theological Declaration fared in the plenary sessions of the synod and the changes made in the text by the synod's Theological Commission have already been given in this chapter in the section on the proceedings of the synod. Since the Theological Declaration was adopted by the synod in conjunction with Pastor Hans Asmussen's address, a translation of his address is appended. It represents, as it were, the official commentary on the Declaration. However, it probably would not be in keeping with the mind of the synod to accord equal authority to Pastor Asmussen's address, inasmuch as the six articles of the Declaration were the basis for his exposition. The Declarations concerning the legal status of the Church and the Church's practical work expressly recognized that they had to be based upon the Church's Confession, and so they

too should not be thought of as possessing the same importance. It is
true that the synod actually devoted much more time to a consideration of legal and practical matters, but it never lost sight of the fact
that polity and practical theology may never be divorced from the
Church's Confession of Faith. For this reason it was quite proper
when later it became customary to quote only the Theological Declaration without reference to Pastor Asmussen's commentary or to
the declarations on legal and practical matters. Here too is the justification for our concentrating upon the text of the Theological Declaration.

The translation has been diligently compared with previous translations and has been submitted to Professor Karl Barth for his approval. Explanations have been given in footnotes for the manner in
which difficult German words and constructions have been rendered.
No effort has been spared to make this translation authentic and
" official." See Appendix VII.

VIII

The Nature of a Confession of Faith, Illustrated from the Theology and History of Barmen

THE BARMEN THEOLOGICAL DECLARATION was born May 31, 1934. Hitherto we have followed the period of its pregnancy, when it lay hidden in the womb of the theology, declarations, and pronouncements that preceded it, and we have witnessed the travail and pain in which it was delivered while evil powers stood ready to devour it. The life of a man properly begins at his birth and, if his life merits recording, a biographer portrays his tender years and then relates his impact upon his environment — first upon his immediate family and then upon the world at large. So it is with a Confession of Faith. It is not to be thought of as a dead document but in personal categories as a living, acting word. It acts upon its environment and the environment reacts to it. It affects the lives of all who come in contact with it. The Barmen Declaration is such a document. It invited and secured decisions from the Church and the nation. It evoked love and hate, joy and grief, praise and blame, obedience and disobedience.

The history of the Church Struggle in Germany is essentially the history of the Church's response to Barmen in its faith and order, preaching and action, and in its relations with the Third Reich, the "German Christians," the Lutheran and Reformed Churches, and the Ecumenical Church. Barmen was the pivotal point around which discussions and decisions turned in regard to the whole life and work of the Church. It was the point of departure for subsequent synods held in Dahlem (1934), Augsburg (1935), and Bad-Oeynhausen (1936). Its decisions were binding upon the Council of Brethren and the administrative boards of the Confessing Church in their conduct of the Church's practical affairs and in their dealings with

181

the Reich Church government and the Hitler State. Sad to relate, the history of Barmen is also the account of the Church's failure always to measure up to the insights granted it.

As already indicated in the foreword to this book, the full account of the history of the Barmen Declaration from May 31, 1934, till the end of hostilities May 7, 1945, would require several volumes, and even then the tale would not be complete. There would still need to be a presentation of the role that Barmen has played in postwar Germany. Indeed, Barmen has taken its place among the great historic Confessions of the Church, and there is no telling what its influence will be in the future. In this concluding chapter we will be content to touch upon some of the highlights of the Church Struggle in order to illustrate the nature of a Confession of Faith. What have the theology and history of the Barmen Declaration to teach us concerning the marks of a genuine Confession? What is the relation of a Confession of Faith to Jesus Christ, Holy Scripture, and Church proclamation? What is its significance for the Church and for Church union? What is the dogmatic and ethical character of a Confession? What is the nature of its authority and freedom? These are some of the questions for which we will seek answers in this last chapter.

1. The Barmen Declaration teaches first and foremost that a Confession of Faith is a written document drawn up by the Church which *confesses Jesus Christ*. While the Church confesses certain doctrines and dogmas and supplies answers to specific questions, it does so only in order to bear witness to Christ. It confesses a living Person who is the Lord and thus calls for a personal relationship of trust and obedience to him — not to the Confession as such or to the doctrines contained in it. Accordingly, in its preamble Barmen declares: " We are bound together by the confession of the one Lord." Jesus Christ is directly spoken about in the first three articles and indirectly in the other three. A Confession is therefore not the publication of the opinions, convictions, ideals, and value judgments of men. It does not set forth a program or system of theology or ethics. It is not a set of principles or constitution for a fraternal order, social service club, or a religious society. It is not a political or ethical, religious platform. It does not bear witness to certain events, powers, figures, and truths in nature and history that may be championed by certain groups in society. It confesses Jesus Christ as the one Lord, the one

justification and sanctification of men, the one revelation, and the one Word of God which we have to hear, trust, and obey in life and in death.

It is not surprising that the Barmen Declaration encountered its fiercest opposition at just this fundamental point concerning the exclusiveness of the confession of Jesus Christ. What is surprising is that the initial attack came not from the " German Christians " but from within the evangelical Church itself, thereby illustrating that a Confession's foes will be those of its own household. On June 11, a group of professors and ministers issued the " Ansbach Counsel." [1] A covering letter opened with this sentence: " We offer these articles in the conviction that at last the authentic voice of Lutheranism has to be heard in theological and ecclesiastical discussions." Prof. Werner Elert drafted the eight articles and Prof. Paul Althaus signed the Counsel after it had been twice revised. In opposition to Barmen the Ansbach Counsel declared that " the unchangeable will of God meets us in the total reality of our life as it is illumined by God's revelation. It binds everyone . . . to the natural orders to which we are subject, such as family, nation, race. . . . In this knowledge we thank God the Lord that he has given to our people in its need a Leader [Hitler] as a ' pious and faithful sovereign.' " Later, in an article, Elert denounced the first article of the Barmen Declaration as a " provocative reiteration of the antinomian heresy of the Reformation period. . . . The statement that apart from Christ no truth is to be acknowledged as God's revelation is a rejection of the authority of the divine law *beside* that of the gospel." [2]

The " German Christians " greeted the Ansbach Counsel with glee. It was printed in full in *Evangelium im Dritten Reich* (No. 26, July 1) under the headline " Leading Theologians Refute Barmen." It editorialized that here theologians of world-wide fame had refuted once and for all the pretentious decrees of the Synod of Barmen. " What they say coincides to a large degree with the standpoint which we ' German Christians ' have continually taken. Fully aware of what we are doing, we publish the theological statement of these men before we utter our final and conclusive word to the Barmen articles." This word was never uttered. The " German Christians " never attempted to answer Barmen theologically. The only mention of the events at Barmen appeared in the June 3 issue of *Evan-*

gelium im Dritten Reich among a number of brief news reports. It was headed "Lutherans Remain Lutherans," and read as follows: "According to information we have received, attempts have been made by circles in the Ulm front to produce a new Confession. However, the results have been sharply rejected in most Lutheran circles against the leadership of the Barthians in the confessional fellowships."

A month later Althaus published an article entitled "Scruples Concerning the 'Theological Declaration' of the Barmen Confessional Synod."[3] With reference to the first article he regretted the omission of any mention of the law of God and of a *revelatio generalis* and argued that prior to the saving revelation there is a primal revelation, a "self-witness of God in the reality of the world and ourselves" and a *justitia civilis* that corresponds to God's will even if it does not justify a man before him." Prof. Gerhard Kittel added his criticism on the same score in his "Public Questions Addressed to the men of the Council of Brethren of the 'Confessional Synod of the German Evangelical Church,'" which was followed by a sharp exchange of letters between him and Karl Barth.[4] Describing himself as a National Socialist theologian, Kittel professed his adherence to the "Twelve Articles" drawn up by a group of Nazi theologians and ministers in Tübingen, which perceived in the National Socialist Movement a "call of God" and expressed gratitude that God had given to our people in Adolf Hitler a leader and deliverer to whom we are united and obligated with our bodies and our lives.

These attacks upon the cardinal thesis of the Declaration did not go unanswered by theologians within the camp of the Confessing Church. Nevertheless, they had the effect of sowing seeds of disunity. The refusal to accept the confession of Jesus Christ as the one revelation and the one justification and sanctification of men was the root cause of the defection of the Lutheran confessionalists about whom we shall hear more presently.

2. According to Barmen, a Confession of Faith confesses Jesus Christ *as he is attested for us in Holy Scripture*. It does not confess a mystical Christ who may be apprehended in the general religious consciousness, in world history, or in reason and experience, but the Christ whom the Church hears in the witness of the Old and New Testaments. Not just the New Testament but also the Old — the Old

Testament that tells *what* Jesus Christ is, as Wilhelm Vischer once put it, and the New Testament that tells *who* he is. A Confession of Faith acknowledges Jesus Christ to be the unity of the Bible. Moreover, a Confession is a commentary on Holy Scripture. This is true of all Creeds and Confessions, but Barmen has the special merit of making it explicit by introducing a text of Scripture before each article. Scripture is not appended in footnotes, as if the Confession wishes to prove its statements by the proof-text method. On the contrary, a Confession looks upon itself as subordinate to Scripture, as a fallible, provisional exegesis of Scripture. The question of whether its exegesis is good exegesis must always be asked. Thus in its appeal to congregations and Christians in Germany, the Synod of Barmen said: " Try the spirits, whether they are of God! Prove also the words of the Confessional Synod of the German Evangelical Church to see whether they agree with Holy Scripture and with the Confessions of the fathers. If you find that we are speaking contrary to Scripture, then do not listen to us! But if you find that we are taking our stand upon Scripture, then let no fear or temptation keep you from treading with us the path of faith and obedience to the Word of God."

3. A Confession of Faith is a confession of *the one, holy, catholic, and apostolic Church*. It is not the Confession of an individual theologian, of a party within the Church, or even of a particular denomination or group of denominations. It speaks for the whole Church to the whole Church. This, of course, is not to be understood in a sociological, legal, or statistical sense. From this standpoint no Confession, not even the so-called ecumenical Creeds, were ever produced by the whole Church for the whole Church. The ecumenicity of a Confession is grounded in the fact that it undertakes to confess the one Lord and the one faith attested in Holy Scripture and given to the whole Church.[5] The Synod of Barmen made this claim when it dared to speak in the name of the German Evangelical Church and not merely in the name of an orthodox party opposing the " German Christians " and when it declared that " we are bound together by the Confession of the one, holy, catholic, and apostolic Church." This one Christian Church, Article 3 states, is " the congregation of the brethren in which Jesus Christ acts presently as the Lord in word and sacrament through the Holy Spirit." Moreover, the synod dared to speak in the name of the one Church in spite of

the fact, or rather just because of the fact, that it was composed of "the representatives of Lutheran, Reformed, and United Churches, of free synods, Church assemblies, and parish organizations." The existence of many denominations and schools of theology is not an insuperable barrier to a Confession speaking in the name of the one, holy, catholic Church. A Confession that did not assume the awful daring and risk involved in such a claim would prove only that it was not a genuine Confession. Consequently, a Confession does not confess the "Reformed point of view," or Calvinism, Lutheranism, Methodism, or Barthianism. It will not even wish to represent "evangelicalism" or "Protestantism," for that would be to confess an ecclesiastical tradition rather than Christ.

The Church confesses, we said, not an individual theologian or group or society. Of course, it will usually be the case that a Confession will be written by one man or a small committee. (We have seen that Barth wrote the original draft of Barmen as a member of a committee of three.) But it becomes a deliverance of the Church when it has been deliberated and acted upon by a plurality of the Church through the representatives of congregations in something like a synod or council. The Lutheran, Reformed, and United Churches, and all the *Landeskirchen,* were represented at Barmen.[6] The synod subjected the text of the Declaration to the closest possible scrutiny before it passed the following resolution: "The synod acknowledges the Theological Declaration Concerning the Present Situation of the German Evangelical Church together with Pastor Asmussen's address to be a Biblical, Reformation testimony, and assumes responsibility for it." Then the synod prefaced its Declaration with the words: "We publicly declare before all evangelical Churches in Germany . . ." and closed by inviting "all who are able to accept its declaration to be mindful of these theological principles in their decisions in Church politics. It entreats all whom it concerns to return to the unity of faith, love, and hope."

4. A Confession of Faith is an act in which *the Church is born or reborn.* In and with its Confession of Faith, the Church's outward unity becomes visible. Of course, the Church exists prior to its Confession but in such a way that its unity and faith are scarcely manifest. Hence the Declaration speaks of its common confession and unity being "grievously imperiled" and "threatened," about its the-

ological basis having been " continually and systematically thwarted and rendered ineffective by alien principles." " When these principles are held to be valid . . . the Church ceases to be the Church." The Church is " devastated " and its unity " broken up." Thus with its Confession, the Church emerges where it had been scarcely recognizable.

On the other hand, the Confessing Church that was born with the Barmen Declaration was not and was never intended to be a union Confession, that is, a Confession in which the Lutheran and Reformed Confessions would be completely unified. In the Appeal to the Congregations and Christians in Germany, the synod declared that it was not its " intention to found a new Church or to form a union." It believed that " we have been given a common message to utter in a time of common need and temptation." At the same time, the synod declared: " We commend to God what this may mean for the interrelations of the Confessional Churches." Barmen spoke of itself as a " federation of German Confessional Churches," and with Barmen arose the Confessing Church. Unfortunately it was not generally recognized that while not seeking to " found a Church or to form a union," the Church had in fact been granted by God a *partial* union at Barmen. In this partial union the one, holy, catholic, and apostolic Church was manifest. This partial union did of course raise, in an acute fashion, the question of the further unification of the various Confessions that grew out of the Reformation. When the synod commended to God what this may mean for the interrelations of the Confessional Churches (Lutheran, Reformed, and United), the meaning was not that it was shoving off on God something it was unwilling to tackle itself. On the contrary, the synod passed a motion transmitting the Theological Declaration to the Lutheran and Reformed Conventions " for the purpose of working out an interpretation of it on the basis of their Confessions." The responsibility for convening the Lutheran convention was left with Bishop Meiser. Unhappily he never called it. Had he done so, it might have prevented, or at least narrowed, the breach that developed between the Confessing Church and the Lutheran confessionalists.

5. A Confession of Faith, as the voice of the one, holy, catholic Church, *reflects its unity and continuity with the Church of the fathers.* Consequently the Declaration states: " Precisely because we

want to be and to remain faithful to our various Confessions, we may not keep silent." The Appeal to the congregations reads: " In fidelity to their Confession of Faith, members of Lutheran, Reformed, and United Churches sought a common message for the need and temptation of the Church in our day. . . . Nothing was further from their minds than the abolition of the confessional status of our Churches." There can be no thought of doing away with the ancient Creeds and Confessions. Here the watchword is, " Remove not the ancient landmark which thy fathers have set " (Prov. 22:8; cf. 23:10; Deut. 19:14). The Confessions of the fathers ought not to be tampered with. Even amendments to them tend to obscure the boundary lines that define our spiritual inheritance. They must stand just as they are, as landmarks of God's Spirit upon his Church and what it means to be a confessing Church. The old Confession will remain the point of departure for a new Confession. For in spite of their imperfection and fallibility, yes, their doctrinal crudities, they have been, and still are, first, a mighty signpost directing us to Jesus Christ in Scripture, and secondly, an invitation and challenge to confess Christ in our day.

A new Confession does not seek to replace the older Confessions but to clarify and to explain them in the face of new questions. Thus Barmen, with exemplary reserve, speaks of itself as a " theological explanation." (The German word *Erklärung* may be translated by " declaration " or " explanation.") This does not mean, however, that such an " explanation " is *merely* an " explanation " and not itself a genuine Confession. The Lutheran confessionalists in Germany both during the Church Struggle and since 1945 have argued that Barmen is not a genuine Confession on the ground that it was merely an explanation to combat the errors of that time, whereas the Lutheran symbols of the sixteenth century bear the character of " sufficiency " and " completeness " as doctrinal standards. This view of a Confession dates from the nineteenth century and was fathered by Wilhelm Loehe (1808–1872), who taught that the Reformation is " completed in its *doctrine;* it is incomplete in the *consequences* of the doctrine." But it can be shown that the Reformation Confessions understood themselves as " explanations " of the early Creeds called forth to combat heresy in their own day. For instance, the Formula of Concord explains that " because directly after the times of the

apostles, and even while they were still living, false teachers and here-
tics arose, and symbols, i.e., brief, succinct confessions, were composed against them in the Early Church, which were regarded as the
unanimous, universal Christian faith and confession of the orthodox
and true Church, namely, the Apostles' Creed, the Nicene Creed,
and the Athanasian Creed, we pledge ourselves to them." Moreover,
its pledge to the ancient Creeds did not prevent the Formula from
recognizing the Augsburg Confession, the Apology, and the Articles of Smalcald as "the unanimous consensus and declaration of
our Christian faith and confession, especially against the papacy and
. . . other sects *as the symbol of our time.*" And the Formula of
Concord was itself a "repetition and explanation of certain articles
of the Augsburg Confession." Similarly Barmen is a genuine Confession in that it clarified the meaning of the Reformation Confessions in a new situation, confessed the old faith in a new way, and
gave a more precise definition of the old. In order to counteract the
errors of that time, Barmen had to speak more clearly than the Reformers had done, especially in regard to revelation and the Word
of God. It was faithful to the Reformers by going farther in the direction to which they pointed. Attention is drawn to three examples of the way in which Barmen went beyond the teaching of the
Reformation.

a. The first thesis of the Declaration contains four propositions:
the Word of God is Jesus Christ; the Word of God is attested in
Holy Scripture; the Word of God is one Word; and the Word of
God is the only revelation of God, or, rather, the only revelation
which the Church could acknowledge as a source of its proclamation.
A comparison of this thesis with the Confessions of the Reformed
Church reveals that no Reformed Confession teaches that Jesus
Christ is God's Word. They state that God's Word is the eternal Son
or the Scriptures. No Reformed Confession teaches that God's Word
is testified to in Holy Scripture. Usually they explain that God committed his word to writing. Furthermore, no Reformed Confession
asserts that God's Word is one. The Reformers dealt with the three
forms of God's Word — revealed, written, and preached — but they
did not concern themselves with the problem of their unity. Finally, no Reformed Confession teaches that God's Word is the only
revelation and the only source of Church proclamation. Instead,

they teach that there is a judging knowledge of God which can be acquired from a divine revelation in nature, history, and in man himself. The general revelation does not yield a saving knowledge of God's truth and will; it serves to render man without excuse and denounces him as being *de facto* ignorant of God. Barmen sharpened an insight implicit in the Reformers. For when one considers their over-all doctrine of *solus Christus, sola gratia,* and *sola scriptura,* one will not be able to claim that Barmen was unfaithful to their basic intent.

b. The Synod of Barmen had no intention of settling an ancient quarrel between the Lutheran and Reformed Churches concerning the doctrine of the law, or of producing a new doctrine. It simply wanted to withstand the errors of the "German Christians." Yet in doing so, it succeeded in throwing new light upon the problem. In the first thesis, we hear: "Jesus Christ . . . is the one Word of God which we have to hear." According to the second thesis, we have to hear this one Word as a twofold word: first as gospel, and then as law, but both together — as "God's assurance of the forgiveness of all our sins" and "with the same seriousness" as "God's mighty claim upon our whole life." These two — assurance and claim, gospel and law — are one Word because Jesus Christ himself is God's assurance and claim, and because "through *him* befalls us a joyful deliverance *from* the godless fetters of this world *for* a free, grateful service to his creatures." It is not a matter of forgiveness as such, or of a demand as such, but of Jesus Christ himself. With a beautiful consistency throughout the six articles, the priority of the gospel to the law is set forth and both are presented in an inseparable connection. We have in mind the phrases: "trust and obey"; "could and would have to"; "justification and sanctification"; "Word and sacrament"; "with its faith as with its obedience, with its message as with its order"; "from his comfort and from his direction"; "the ministry entrusted to and enjoined upon"; "in gratitude and reverence"; "trusts and obeys"; "his own Word and work through sermon and sacrament." One will not find this sequence and unity of the gospel and law in either a Lutheran or a Reformed Confession. The Reformation sequence "law-gospel" is familiar. The Reformers, to be sure, were not ignorant of God's holy, just, and good law — God's liberating and saving law. Calvin liked to speak of "Christ as the soul of the law." But usually this aspect of the doctrine was a sort of afterthought. The gospel was not the ground and criterion, the content and liberating character of the law.

The Reformation sequence " law-gospel " was not wrong in itself. It has its legitimate place in the doctrine as a whole. However, it needs to be made clear that the law which judges us and drives us to the gospel is God's gracious law and not a bare law divorced from Christ. There were historical reasons why the Reformers spoke first and often abstractly about the law. Nevertheless, it was a weakness or at least a one-sidedness. The Synod of Barmen was faced with a situation in which God's law was confused with moral, religious, political, and even biological laws. For the National Socialists, German blood and soil were divine laws. The Erlangen school, headed by Werner Elert and the signatories of the Ansbach Counsel, asserted: " God's word speaks to us as law and gospel. . . . The law . . . encounters us in the total reality of our life . . . and binds us to the natural orders to which we are subject, such as family, folk, and race (i.e., blood relationship)." In an article, Elert wrote: " What Holy Scripture, especially the New Testament, describes as ' law ' can in no sense be called a testimony to Christ. The proposition that apart from Christ no truth is to be acknowledged as God's revelation is a rejection of the divine authority of the divine law *beside* that of the gospel." [7] In order to combat this abstract conception of the law, which had the effect of ascribing divine authority to the Nazi ideology, Barmen had to proclaim the gospel as the ground of the law and to present both in their togetherness. In doing so, they superseded Reformation teaching. However, if it is true that historically the Lutherans have stressed the gospel and the Reformers the law, then Barmen has unintentionally brought both closer together.

c. No unbiased scholar would dare to assert that the teaching of Barmen concerning the relation of Church and State in the third and fifth theses is either Lutheran or Reformed. Here, too, Barmen was not literally faithful to the Confessions. If it had been, the Confessing Church would have had to admit that Hitler had the right to reform the Church, to appoint a Reich Minister for Church Affairs, to name a Reich bishop and Reich Church committees, as Barth observed in his exposition of John Knox's Confession of 1560.[8] Actually, this part of Reformation teaching was a severe handicap to the Confessing

Church in its fight against the Reich Church committees. The Lutheran bishops and the Lutheran Council, which favored the committees, could plausibly appeal to the Reformation symbols. Consequently it had to be established that the State could not fulfill the Church's vocation, and that the Church does not " trust and obey " the State as an ordinance of God but " the power of the word by which God upholds all things." In his book on *Barmen,* Prof. Ernst Wolf has pointed out that Barmen, in contrast to Catholic thought, to the political theories of the nineteenth century, and partly to the teaching of the Reformation, does not speak of the State as a divine order and hence about the being and nature of the State but of the *task* the State has by divine appointment. " It says nothing about the *origin* of the State or of its *structure,* but it speaks of its place, namely, in a world not yet redeemed, and of its divinely appointed task." For this reason the Church does not keep silent about political questions but " calls to mind the Kingdom of God, God's commandment and righteousness, and thereby the responsibility of both rulers and ruled." This responsibility is to " provide for justice and peace."

6. In and with its Confession of Faith the Church *claims to be the one, true Church*. Outside this Church, there is no salvation for one who willfully and knowingly separates himself from it. Of course, the *extra ecclesiam nulla salus* does not imply that the one, true Church in which salvation may be found has not existed in other times and places. Nor does it mean that the Church is the indispensable mediatrix of salvation or a " redemptive society." It means that outside the Church that confesses Jesus Christ there is no revelation, no faith, and no knowledge of salvation. However, where Christ and his salvation are present in the Church's confession of him, and where a man has encountered Christ in it and then has deliberately and consciously separated himself from that Church, for that man there is no salvation. For him there remains the threat of damnation.

The daring of a Confessing Church lies in its claim to be the true Church. The genuineness of a Confession is reflected in the willingness of its confessors to venture and to stand by this stupendous claim. Throughout the Church Struggle the Confessing Church did not take its stand upon the Reformation Confessions but upon the Barmen Declaration as the only legitimate interpretation of the Reformation symbols. For this reason it claimed to be the true evangelical Church in Germany. It repeatedly asserted that an individual could not be faithful to the Lutheran and Reformed Confessions without being faithful to Barmen. Naturally this claim did not go unchallenged. Both the "German Christians" and the Lutheran confessionalists professed their loyalty to the old standards. Either a person completely repudiated the claim of the Synod of Barmen or took the position that one could be faithful to the Reformation without subscribing to Barmen. The history of the Confessing Church demonstrates, however, that when one tried to be true to the Reformation without Barmen the resistance to the Reich Church government and the Hitler State was weakened and sabotaged.

The claim of the Confessing Church to be the one, true evangelical Church of Germany was contested on two fronts: by the Reich Church government and by the Lutheran confessionalists. The latter, led by men like Hermann Sasse, Werner Elert, Paul Althaus, and Bishop August Marahrens, took the position that Barmen had no "authority in matters of doctrine for Lutherans . . . since the Lutheran Confessions do not recognize an evangelical Church that is above the Confessions or the teaching office of such a Church." [9] Sasse went to the length of referring to the Confessing Church as a "sect, and indeed the worst that has appeared on the soil of German Protestantism." [10] On the other side we have Dietrich Bonhoeffer taking the position that "whoever knowingly separates himself from the Confessing Church in Germany separates himself from salvation" [11] because in the Barmen Declaration "the Word of the Lord of the Church is heard in all its human weakness and differences of opinion." [12] "Either the Barmen Declaration is a true confession to the Lord Jesus which has been wrought by the Holy Spirit," Bonhoeffer wrote, "in which case it has the capacity to build or split the Church, or it is the expression of the opinions of certain theologians binding on no one." [13]

Hermann Sasse, then Professor of Church History at the University of Erlangen, has the dubious distinction of being the first to raise the confessionalist issue and to challenge the authority of the Synod of Barmen in doctrinal matters. Sasse's position, which he consistently maintained in his writings from 1934 to 1936, is most instructive for the relation of a contemporary Confession to the ancient Creeds and Confessions and therefore deserves to be dealt with in some detail. Before he left the synod on the night of May 31, Sasse handed President Karl Koch the following statement:

> As a member of the synod, I make the following statement concerning the text presented by the Theological Committee and adopted by the synod:
>
> 1. I agree with the Biblical truths presented in Articles 1 to 6 and with the rejection of the false doctrines, although it is my opinion that here and there the text can be interpreted in a different way by Lutheran theologians than by theologians of the Reformed Confession of Faith. These articles could have been accepted by the synod as a theological opinion and as a basis for further work by conventions of theologians which would determine what errors are to be rejected today in the evangelical Churches of Lutheran and Reformed Confessions.
>
> 2. Under no circumstances, however, should these articles be adopted by the synod as a whole because by such adoption the synod assumes to itself a teaching office over Lutheran and Reformed congregations. It is true that a free synod can say what is pure doctrine and what is error when the constitutionally appointed agencies fail in their duty. But only a Lutheran synod can speak for Lutherans, and a Reformed synod for Reformers. When the synod avoided the *itio in partes* required in the passing of a resolution concerning questions dealing with a Confession of Faith, and instead adopted as a body a doctrinal statement, it actually declared that it had authority in matters of doctrine for Lutherans and Reformers. As such, it can never be acknowledged by the Church of the Augsburg Confession, since the Lutheran Confessions do not recognize an evangelical Church that is above the Confessions or the teaching office of such a Church. Consequently the resolutions passed in the synod in regard to doctrine can never claim to have binding authority, regardless of whether they are objectively correct or not.
>
> 3. The six articles are preceded by a preamble in which not only is the "German Evangelical Church" acknowledged to be an existing legal body, but regulations with respect to its constitution were also adopted, without a protest, which are contrary to the Lutheran Confession and constitutionally invalid. Article 1 of the constitution is quoted as follows: "The inviolable foundation of the German Evangelical Church is the

gospel of Jesus Christ as it is attested for us in Holy Scripture and brought to light again in the Confessions of the Reformation." This article has meaning only when it is assumed that the differences in the understanding of the gospel which arose at the time of the Reformation are no longer differences which should divide the Churches; that today there is a common understanding of the gospel over and above the Confessions; that the rejection of the errors of Zwingli and Calvin in the symbols of the evangelical Lutheran Church is unwarranted; and that the teaching of Article 7 of the Augustana concerning the unity of the Church is false. To accept these views without protest signifies the sacrifice of the evangelical Church in favor of the union. It means to subordinate questions of truth to questions of expediency.

Consequently I am obliged solemnly to protest against the resolutions of the Free Synod of Barmen as a violation of the evangelical Lutheran Church. I am no longer able to see in the so-called Confessional front a real and effective representative of the Confession of the Lutheran and Reformed Churches. I deeply regret that the great hour of a confederation of true Confessional Churches in Germany has been missed and that thereby steps have been taken toward a new union which will efface and dissolve the Confession of the Reformation. — Barmen, May 31, 1934.

Hans Asmussen prepared an official reply to Sasse's statement on behalf of the Theological Department of the office of the president in Bad-Oeynhausen. He argued that a free synod has " the right to judge between true and false doctrine when the proper agencies falter in their duty." However, the six articles were discussed and found to be true by the Lutheran and Reformed delegations separately before they were presented to the plenary session of the synod. " This fact immediately refutes the charge that questions of truth had been sacrificed to expediency." Moreover, the articles adopted at Barmen were not intended to give expression to all doctrines in a common formulation but " simply as a defense of evangelical Christianity against a concrete enemy in a particular situation. . . . The rejection of the teachings of Zwingli and Calvin in the symbols, and thus the authority of the symbols themselves, is not abrogated."

Unfortunately Sasse's polemic in the debate that ensued between him and Asmussen took on an offensive tone that made an objective discussion of the issues all but impossible.[14] Nevertheless, he maintained a fairly consistent stand. Yet his attitude to a Confession was literalistic and legalistic, wooden and unimaginative. He rightly perceived that the Church union movements of the nineteenth century under the influence of the liberalism of the period had resulted in a confessionlessness which weakened the faith. He referred specifically to the union of 1817 in Germany and to the union movements in Canada, China, and in North and South India. The Church union in Canada in 1925 was cited as a classic example of the dissolution of the Confession, the watering down of the faith, and the achievement of just another denomination instead of a genuine union. He concluded: "Union is confessionlessness. That is the lesson of nineteenth-century Church history."[15] Sasse, however, was not alone in exposing the theological shallowness of the union movements of that period; Barth also drew attention to it in an article in which he explored the possibility of a Confessional Union.[16] At the same time, Sasse's diagnosis was too simple. His equation of union and confessionlessness blinded him to the fact that even those Churches which refused to enter into unions, presumably for the sake of their Confessions, were also not immune to the virus of natural theology. A merely formal or romantic attachment to a Confession is no sure guarantee against heresy. Secondly, it blinded him to the concrete and urgent questions of the hour. Instead of joining forces with those who had united in fighting the common enemy, the "German Christians" and the Reich Church government, he spent his energies combating the supporters of the Barmen Declaration. Thus indirectly and doubtless unintentionally he aided and abetted the "enemy" and weakened the ranks of the Confessing Church. He saw no difference between the union of 1817 and the common action taken by Lutherans and Reformers at Barmen. Both spelled for him the end of the Lutheran Church. Depressing to record is the fact that at a time when the "house was on fire," when the very existence of the evangelical Church was at stake, many Lutherans were intent upon preserving institutional Lutheranism.[17]

The views expressed by Sasse, Elert, and Althaus virtually became the basis of the policy of the official bodies of the Lutheran Church, namely, the Lutheran Council and the Lutheran bishops. As early as

April 18, 1933, the Martin Luther League " gratefully and joyfully professed the goals for which the leaders of the German nation were striving," and urged that the Evangelical Church of Germany become a Lutheran Confessional Church. " Only in this way will German Lutheranism be able to fulfill its unique task within the framework of ecumenical Lutheranism." At the very first meeting of the Council of Brethren of the Barmen Synod on June 14, Bishop Meiser warned of the danger of the formation of a " Third Front."

The " Third Front " became a fact through the formation of the Lutheran Council, August 24–25. At first many looked upon it as an encouraging sign that Lutheranism would take its place within the camp of the Confessing Church. However, the composition of the Council raised serious doubts since many of the members had been outspoken critics of Barmen. Asmussen's name had been discussed and deliberately dropped. The Council was convened without the knowledge of President Koch and the Council of Brethren. Asmussen wrote letters to leaders of the Lutheran Church, pleading with them not to weaken the unity of the Confessing Church, but with little effect. Many Lutherans were jealous of the prominent part being played by Reformed churchmen, and Karl Barth was especially obnoxious to them. Others had refused to join the Pastors' Emergency League because they could not wholeheartedly subscribe to the article that rejected the Aryan paragraph within the Church. Still others thought they could take the oath of allegiance to Hitler required by the Reich Church government at its so-called National Synod that met in Berlin on August 9.

The Lutheran Council adopted a separatist policy when on October 5 it called for an amalgamation of Lutheran *Landeskirchen*. It issued a statement that read in part as follows: " It was hoped that the German Evangelical Church would become a Lutheran Church of Germany through the adoption of the Lutheran Confession. . . . This hope vanished when the Reich Church government adopted a policy . . . which meant nothing less than the end of the Lutheran Church in Germany. . . . A German Lutheran Church would gain world-wide authority within ecumenical Lutheranism while rendering an important service to the German nation. But a German union Church is not capable of achieving an alliance of Lutheran Churches in the world." A pronouncement by members of the theological fac-

ulty of the University of Erlangen " concerning the whole situation
of the Lutheran Church in Germany " voiced the same sentiments.

Meanwhile the claim of the Church of Barmen to be the true evangelical Church of Germany was of course being challenged by the
Reich Church government, headed by Bishop Müller. Under his direction the incorporation of the *Landeskirchen* into the Reich Church
continued apace by means of intimidation and acts of violence. The
method was to explain that an emergency situation prevailed in a
certain provincial Church which necessitated the intervention of the
Reich bishop. Ministers were dismissed or suspended from their parishes, and many were placed under " house arrest." Largely because
the people rallied round their beloved bishops, Wurm and Meiser,
such harsh tactics failed in the case of the Württemberg and Bavaria
Churches and they remained " intact." But the persecution of these
Churches had the effect of arousing the whole Confessing Church
and to the calling of the Second Confessional Synod of the Evangelical Church in Germany in Dahlem, October 24–25.[18] One hundred
and forty-three delegates assembled from all parts of the country.
Whereas at Barmen the principles for the Church's witness were
worked out, at Dahlem the principles for Church polity were laid
down. Dahlem declared that the Reich Church government had been
shattered, summoned the Council of Brethren to assume the leadership of the Church, selected from it a council to administer the
Church's affairs, and called upon congregations, pastors, and elders
to refuse instructions from the Reich Church government and to
stand by the synod and its organs. This declaration was forwarded
to the Reich Church government, bidding it to take cognizance of
the step taken and to acknowledge that " in Church matters, its doctrine and order, the Church alone is called to judge and decide without prejudice to the State's right of supervision." The Council of
Brethren vigorously set to work to implement the Dahlem pronouncement in regard to finance, education, and examination of
candidates for the ministry, and the ordination and induction of
ministers. As Wilhelm Niemöller has observed, " if the whole Confessing Church had actually acted in accordance with the Dahlem
resolutions, Church and nation would have been spared much trouble. Unfortunately it has to be recorded that . . . all too often many
brethren could point to a cheaper, simpler, and easier way." [19]

The Reich Administrator for Church Affairs, Dr. August Jäger, resigned his office on October 28 on the pretext that he had completed his task. In spite of demands from the Council of Brethren, the Lutheran Council, and other Church groups that Müller resign, he stubbornly clung to his pseudo-episcopal office. Actually it did not matter much. He was bishop in name only — virtually without a Church. The "German Christians" had sunk to a low ebb, and Hitler had assured Bishops Marahrens, Wurm, and Meiser in a two-hour audience on October 30 that he no longer had any interest in the dispute and would leave the Church to settle its own affairs. It appeared as if the Confessing Church had gained a striking victory and would have peace to put its house in order. The respite, however, only gave freer rein to the confessionalist struggle.

The rupture of the unity of Barmen and Dahlem came to a head at a meeting of the Council of Brethren in Dahlem on November 9. At this time, Bishop Meiser disputed the sole authority of the Council, which hitherto he had so strongly stressed, on the ground that Churches with legal constitutions had arisen since Barmen, and therefore the Council could no longer speak for the whole Church. President Koch reported that a number of professors had recommended the formation of a temporary executive board which would embrace a wider circle than the Confessional Synod. Martin Niemöller contended that there could not be two emergency administrations and that the administration set up at Dahlem was the only legitimate one. The Confessional Synod is the true German Evangelical Church. The argument waxed back and forth. Some insisted that Barmen and Dahlem were the legal synods of the Church and were opposed to any extension or weakening of the front; others claimed that the synods were not unconditionally binding and that the front had to be widened to save the national Church. To make a long story short, the first Provisional Board of Administration was set up with Bishop August Marahrens at its head as *primus inter pares*. Karl Immer, Hermann Hesse, and Martin Niemöller resigned from the Council of Brethren in protest. They believed that Barmen and Dahlem had been forsaken and that the "Third Front" had been victorious; and they feared that a compromising, mediating course would be followed under the leadership of Marahrens.

In order to preserve the continuity of our account of the Confessing Church's struggle to maintain itself as the one, true Church in fidelity to its Confession, we must pass lightly over the distressing events of 1935. While the Reich bishop faded into the background, the new Provisional Board was confronted more definitely by the naked power of the State. It had to contend against the alarming growth of paganism in the press, radio, theater, and schools, and against the secularization of public life. The State reacted by placing hundreds of pastors in jail or under house arrest and by curtailing the financial support of the Church. Professors were dismissed from their chairs, notably scholars like Otto Schmitz, K. D. Schmidt, Günther Dehn, Dietrich Bonhoeffer, Hans Iwand, Edmund Schlink, and Karl Barth. The persecution had the effect of unifying the Church, and this unity found expression in the Third Confessional Synod, held at Augsburg on June 4–6. Such was the harmony that prevailed that Immer, Hesse, and Niemöller resumed their positions in the Council of Brethren.

The peace of Augsburg was short-lived. On June 26, a law was published whereby all legal questions touching the Evangelical Church would be decided not by the law courts but by a special bureau set up by the Ministry of the Interior. The effect was to deprive ministers of the legal protection of the courts they had hitherto enjoyed against the arbitrary discipline of the Reich bishop. The new law virtually placed them under police control. A. S. Duncan-Jones was certainly right when he described this law as " the most significant event in the whole process whereby the State attempted to crush religious freedom, so far as the Protestant Church is concerned." [20] Then followed the " dictatorship " of Hans Kerrl, whom Hitler appointed on July 16 as Reich Minister for Church Affairs with absolute powers to restore " peace " in the Church. (Hitler had forgotten his promise to the three bishops not to interfere in Church matters — that is, if he had ever intended to keep it.) Kerrl's first edict was the appointment of a Reich Church Committee empowered to administer the internal affairs of the Church. The nomination of Wilhelm Zöllner as chairman was calculated to inspire confidence, since he enjoyed widespread respect. The Church Committees (a Committee was also appointed for each *Landeskirche*) were warmly greeted by the Lutheran confessionalists. Yet the appeal that the Reich Committee issued immediately after it had been appointed embraced the very errors of the " German Christians " condemned at Barmen. It took its stand on the first article of the Church's constitution, namely, that " the inviolable foundation of the German Evangelical Church is the gospel of Jesus Christ . . . ," and then went on to say: " Bound by this faith we admonish and request that evangelical congregations stand by the nation, the Reich, and the Führer in prayer, loyalty, and obedience. We affirm the rise and growth of the National Socialist nation on the basis of race, blood, and soil. We affirm the will to freedom, national dignity, and socialist readiness for sacrifice, even of one's life in devotion to the common good of the nation. Herein we recognize the God-given reality for our German people." The task of providing a theological apology for the work of the committee was assigned to a subcommittee composed of Zöllner, Althaus, Elert, Gogarten, and others. They obliged with the argument that it was consistent with the principles of the Reformation for the State to render legal assistance whenever an emergency existed in the Church. Of course, the emergency had been created by the State itself. Moreover, this argument was a patent contradiction of the stand taken at the Synod of Dahlem. Even granting that a genuine emergency prevailed and that the State had the right to restore civil order even within the Church, on Reformation principles the State never had the right to intervene in such a way that peace was established by imposing its ideology upon the Church and by taking sides with one party to the dispute, in this instance with that of the " German Christians."

Meanwhile, as the debate continued concerning the legitimacy of the Reich Church Committees, an eight-page pamphlet bearing the title *The State Church Is Here!* was being secretly and widely circulated. Its anonymous author was Otto Dibelius. It cut through to the heart of the matter, describing how the State had laid its hand upon the Church's finances and had taken over the administration of the Church. It showed how its administration worked hand in hand with the dread Gestapo — all with the purpose of subjecting the Church to its own *Weltanschauung*. The pamphlet was never discussed publicly, since no one was allowed to possess a copy. Yet it warmed the hearts of many, strengthened their resolve, and clarified the situation. The Council of Brethren came to see ever more clearly that in the face of a ruthless, totalitarian State vacillation, compromise, and expediency could no longer be tolerated within the ranks of the Church. It took drastic action in regard to the authority of the Reich Church Committee.

At its meeting in Berlin, January 3, 1936, the following resolution was passed by a vote of 17 to 11.[21]

1. The Provisional Board of Administration of the German Evangelical Church is the organ for the direction and administration of the Church. (Resolution of the Augsburg Confessional Synod, III, 3.) It is responsible to the Confessing Church, whose course has been determined by Holy Scripture as attested in the Reformation Confessions of Faith and clearly set forth in the resolutions of its Confessional Synods.

2. The Provisional Board of Administration is unable to operate, because all its members do not acknowledge that the principal resolutions of the synods are binding upon them.

3. At the present time, the Confessing Church needs more than ever an administration that stands solidly upon the decisions of the Church. Therefore it has to be asserted that whoever cannot affirm, in allegiance to the resolutions of the Confessional Synods, the following propositions is not in a position to speak or to act on behalf of, or in the name of, the Confessional Synod:

a. The Church has to separate itself from false doctrines in the sense of the Barmen Declaration;

b. The Word of God attested in the Reformation Confessions is the only rule and standard of the polity of the Church;

c. As a consequence of a fundamental confessional continuity, the Confessing Church is the legitimate Church and its organs its legitimate representative and administration;

d. Allegiance to the resolutions of the Synod of Barmen excludes any recognition of the Church Committees as an administrative body of the Church.

4. The Reich Council of Brethren, inasmuch as it is based upon the Confessional Synod and is therefore solely qualified to represent it, will undertake a new administration of the Confessing Church until a Confessional Synod is convened.

5. Whether, and in what form, co-operation is possible with brethren who think they are bound to take another course can be decided only after this rearrangement has taken firmer shape.

This decision is the outcome of a conviction that has long prevailed within the Council of Brethren. Henceforth there can be no doubt about the fact that no one can be a member of State Church Committees acting in the name or on behalf of the Confessing Church, as long as they reject the Barmen Declaration and at the same time claim to be the administrative board of the Church.

In the very near future President Koch will call a Confessional Synod of the German Evangelical Church in order that it may homologate the step that has been taken. Meanwhile we have appointed Albertz, Asmussen, Kloppenburg, Lücking, Müller, Niemöller, and von Thadden a committee to make preparations for the meeting of the Synod.

On the same day on which the majority of the Council of Brethren took this daring step — for their only authority was the fact that they took their stand with Barmen — the Provisional Board of Administration met and deliberated the unprecedented action. They came to the conclusion that they could not admit the legality of the action taken, but also expressed a desire for the calling of a synod as soon as possible. Of course, it was to be expected that the Bavarian Lutheran Church Council and other Lutheran leaders would capitalize on the fact that a substantial minority within the Council of Brethren itself had opposed the forthright repudiation of the State's appointed committees.

It was therefore a good thing when at last the Fourth Confessional Synod met in Bad-Oeynhausen, February 17, 1936.[22] It lasted six days and even then failed to conclude its business. The 154 delegates, representing 20 provincial Churches (*Landeskirchen*), numbered 109 ministers and theologians and 45 laymen. The outstanding feature of the synod was the fact that the Confessing Church did not fall apart but held together. A motion by Martin Niemöller passed — with but three dissenting votes and two abstaining — by which the synod declared itself to be " the legitimate synodical organ of the German Evangelical Church." Perhaps the most important and far-reaching step taken was the reorganization of the Council of Brethren with powers to elect a new Provisional Board of Administration. With respect to Church administration the synod declared: " Church administration is an office of the Church. Therefore it can be called and installed only by the Church. Its office-bearers must be obligated to be obedient to God's Word in keeping with the Church's Confession. Church members may not form a Church administration simply because they themselves profess their loyalty to the Scriptures and the Confession. The Church that is bound to God's Word is called to judge and decide in matters of doctrine and order. The civil government oversteps its own office when it sets itself up as an administration of the Church." For these reasons the synod expressly rejected the right of the Reich Church Committee to decide in matters of faith and doctrine. Unfortunately it failed to draw the implications of these principles. It did not categorically repudiate the Reich Committees. Nevertheless it elected a new Council of Brethren, which in turn elected the second Provisional Board of Administration. Unlike the previous Board, this group was made of iron. In all its pronouncements it displayed an exemplary fearlessness and reflected the spirit and letter of Barmen.

On July 16, the new Board addressed itself directly to the problem of confessionalism within the German Evangelical Church. It declared:

> The Barmen Theological Declaration possesses binding authority upon the Church. We are conscious that as members of Lutheran, United, and Reformed Churches we are bound together today in the German Evangelical Church. Whoever wishes truly to confess the Confession of his Church today, whether Lutheran or Reformed, cannot bypass the doctrinal decisions made at Barmen. Whoever does not acknowledge those decisions actually surrenders the Reformation Confessions. . . . The "Council of the Evangelical-Lutheran Church of Germany," which was organized at the same time as the present Provisional Board immediately after the Synod of Bad-Oeynhausen in March of this year, has to date neglected to take an unequivocal stand in regard to Barmen. So far as we are able to see, this Council was formed not on the basis of the Lutheran Confession but because of a political attitude to the Church Committees. It becomes increasingly apparent that the Council of the Lutheran Church of Germany is not primarily concerned about those obligations which should accrue today from the Lutheran Confessions in the German Evangelical Church but about the desire to preserve if possible the outward

existence of the Lutheran Churches in Germany. Consequently
the Council has not united in itself all Lutheran Churches in
Germany but only those which think that a tactical co-operation with the Church Committees is important and necessary
in opposition to the judgments and decisions of the Confessional Synod of Bad-Oeynhausen. At the moment, the Provisional Board of Administration is engaged in conversations with
representatives of the Council. The meaning and purpose of
these conversations can only be to unify the forces of the Confessing Church. The Board appeals for a genuine alliance of all
Lutheran and Reformed Churches within the Confessing
Church. The way in which such an alliance can be achieved is,
first of all, through the Lutheran and Reformed conventions.
The conventions were assigned the task, first in Barmen and
again in Bad-Oeynhausen, of giving an authoritative interpretation of the doctrinal decisions taken at Barmen. It is urgent
that the conventions assume this task now.

Thus the Confessing Church reiterated its claim to be the one, true
Church and repudiated the pretensions of the confessionalists. The
Lutheran Council continued to pursue its divisive policy — but outside the administration of the Confessing Church. The Reich Church
Committee dragged on until it abjectly tendered its resignation on
February 12, 1937, explaining that Kerrl had made it impossible for
it to carry on its work. The course of events had demonstrated that
the Council of Brethren, and not the Lutheran Council, had been
right from the start when it had opposed first the Reich bishop, then
Dr. Jäger, and lastly Kerrl and the Church Committees, and had insisted upon the Church abiding by the Barmen Declaration.

7. We resume our discussion of the nature of a genuine Confession
of Faith with the observation that *it occurs when the Church is convinced that its faith and unity are " grievously imperiled " by a heresy
that has ripened and come to a head*. This is the *dogmatic* character
of a Confession. For the Synod of Barmen it was the heresy of the
" German Christians," who taught that in addition to God's revelation in Christ attested by Scripture there is a natural revelation in nature and history: in German blood, race, and soil, and in the event of
the National Socialist revolution and the rebirth of the German soul.
They also sought to introduce a *Führerprinzip* into Church polity.
As Hans Asmussen explained, it was not merely a question of innu-

merable acts of violence, injustice, and maladministration but of
theological principles that struck at the very heart of the Church's
faith. Moreover, the synod saw in the false doctrines of the " German
Christians" the culmination of the errors of the theology of the
eighteenth and nineteenth centuries. To quote Asmussen again:
"We are raising a protest against the same phenomenon that has
been slowly preparing the way for the devastation of the Church for
more than two hundred years. For it is only a relative difference
whether, beside Holy Scripture, in the Church historical events, or
reason, culture, aesthetic feelings, progress, or other powers and figures are said to be binding claims upon the Church." In brief, a Confession of Faith unequivocally raises the question of long-standing
heresy. It is a militant action of the Church by which it withstands
and purges itself of error.

8. A Confession of Faith not only is relevant for the Church's own
doctrine and life but *bears definite implications for concrete social
and political issues*. This is the *ethical* character of a Confession. It
possesses both ecclesiastical and secular significance. It is a witness to
Christ before the Church and the world. It does not shrink from
dealing with concrete issues such as racialism, anti-Semitism, nationalism, Fascism and Communism, militarism and economic exploita-
tion. In short, it is relevant for social and political justice, freedom,
and peace. A Confession which lacked this dimension would not be
a true Confession; a Church that neglected to draw the implications
of its Confession for the social and political order and that was concerned only about the purity of its own teaching and piety would certainly not be a Confessing Church — not the one, holy, catholic
Church of Christ. For then it would have denied that Christ died
for the world, and that it has been elected and called to serve the
world with its message of God's grace for all peoples.

The Confessing Church has often been blamed in just this regard.
It has been charged with being primarily concerned for its own spiritual and physical existence and with being woefully weak in its
witness against the horrible crimes committed by the Hitler State.
We have no wish to minimize the force of the accusation. In the famous " Stuttgart Confession" made by the leaders of the Confessing
Church immediately following the war, they acknowledged their
share in the guilt for the miseries which National Socialist Germany

had brought upon the peoples of the world. The Christian Church —
Protestant and Roman Catholic — cannot deny culpability for the
atrocities inflicted upon the Jews, for the rape of defenseless peoples, and for the destruction of all human rights. At the same time it
has to be recognized that this is not the whole truth about the Protestant and Roman Catholic Churches. We recall the judgment of
Albert Einstein reported in the first chapter of this book. The press,
the universities, legal profession, artists, trade-unions, and political
parties all capitulated to Hitler. " Only the Church stood squarely
across the path of Hitler's campaign for suppressing the truth. . . .
The Church alone has had the courage to stand for intellectual and
moral freedom."

To the extent to which the Confessing Church failed to present a
united, forthright witness against the Hitler State, it failed to remain
faithful to the insights of the Barmen Declaration. When the Declaration stated that Jesus Christ is the one Word of God that we have to
trust and obey, it implied that Hitler's policies and acts of violence
had to be condemned as contrary to God's Word. When it asserted
in the second article that Jesus Christ is " God's mighty claim upon
our whole life " and that there are no " areas in which we would
not need justification and sanctification through him," it was clear
that politics is not an area exempt from the Lordship of Christ. The
doctrine of the separation of the two kingdoms, the spiritual and the
temporal, was tacitly rejected. Article 5 taught that " the State has by
divine appointment the task of providing for justice and peace " and
that the Church " calls to mind the Kingdom of God, God's commandment and righteousness, and thereby the responsibility both of
rulers and of the ruled." It rejected the false doctrine that " the State
. . . should or could become the single and totalitarian order of
human life." The Confessing Church failed in the degree to which it
failed to spell out that justice and peace which the State has been appointed to provide, and in the degree to which it failed to make explicit God's commandment and the responsibility of rulers and ruled.

Nevertheless the Confessing Church was by no means entirely
silent! Without going into all its pronouncements on social and
political questions, we will cite one memorable document. On June 4,
1936, the Provisional Board and Council of the Confessing Church
sent a lengthy Memorandum to Hitler. It not only called attention to

the anti-Christian and pagan character of the Nazi State but openly condemned anti-Semitism, racialism, concentration camps, secret police methods, violation of the ballot, oaths of allegiance contrary to God's Word, the destruction of justice in the civil law courts, and corruption of public morals.[23] " No action taken by the Confessing Church in the twelve years of the conflict between Church and State is of comparable significance. Ten leading men of the Confessing Church here opposed a totalitarian State with utter frankness and without any personal security. They spoke of God's testimonies before kings and were not ashamed (Ps. 119:46). They had to put up with being forsaken, disavowed, and maligned even by those who like them bore the name of Christian. They had to be prepared for that, and they were prepared. But the testimony that God is God stood firm. And the evangelical Church may be glad and thankful that in the midst of its confused and often grievous history this testimony was made — to the honor of God and the blessing of men." [24] The Memorandum was a living, actual exposition of the second, fifth, and sixth articles of the Barmen Declaration, and was delivered in the consciousness of responsibility to the synods of the Church. The Memorandum was a faithful commentary on Barmen. We venture the conviction that without it the true *ethical* character of the Theological Declaration might easily be missed and overlooked. A translation of the full text is therefore given in Appendix VIII to this book. It merits careful reading.

From the Memorandum one gains the impression that its authors were not so much concerned with " influencing the government " or " changing public opinion " as with confessing Jesus Christ no matter what the cost or how useless it might seem. Gone was all thought of expediency, strategy, and so-called " public relations." The authors made no attempt to salve their consciences by writing to lower functionaries; they addressed their protest to the highest authority — Hitler himself! The final draft was prepared by Dr. Wilhelm Jannasch, and after the Council of Brethren had adopted it at its meeting in Berlin on May 28, he personally delivered it to the chancellery on June 4. Only three copies of the original Memorandum existed: the one sent to Hitler; one given to Pastor Birger Forell, a minister of the Swedish legation, for safekeeping; and a third held by Dr. Friedrich Weissler for the Provisional Board.

Much to the amazement of the Board and contrary to its wishes, the Memorandum first appeared in the foreign press before it was known about in Germany. Naturally the National Socialist and " German Christian " newspapers labeled the publishing of it in foreign countries as " traitorous." But the Board was not dismayed. It calmly explained that the publishing had occurred " without its knowledge or agency " and then declared: " We are now compelled publicly to stand by this message. We must now bear witness before the congregations concerning those matters which agitate us with respect to our nation and the Church." At a joint meeting of the Board and the Council of Brethren in Kassel, July 29, it was decided to adopt in principle a draft of a message to the congregations, prepared by General Superintendent Dibelius. The substance of the communication, read from the pulpits of about three quarters of the ministers of the Confessing Church and of which about a million copies were distributed, is essentially the same as the Memorandum sent to Hitler and need not be reproduced here. Although it was received with gratitude by thousands of ministers and congregations, the sad fact is that many ministers and Church bodies failed in their duty, with the result that whole areas never heard the message of the Provisional Board at all. In Hanover no mention was made of it. In Württemberg the bishop declared: " The Württemberg Church administration has not thought it proper to read the message issued by the Provisional Board at this time and has advised its ministers to this effect; consequently a prohibition [from the Reich Church government] is superfluous." Most distressing was the way in which the Lutheran Council dissociated itself from the action of the Board at a time when they were sorely pressed.[25]

Two points may be touched upon in concluding this brief account of the momentous document. Wilhelm Niemöller has cleared up the mystery of how it got into the hands of the foreign press. Werner Koch and Ernst Tillich were in touch with foreign correspondents to whom they gave reports on Church life and work in Germany. Tillich borrowed the copy of the Memorandum from Dr. Weissler for a night in order to read it. He copied it out in full. While Koch and Weissler intended to disclose only the existence of the document and its essential contents, Tillich felt constrained by the stubborn silence of the Government to " lend the Memorandum its full weight " by the publication of the entire text. No doubt the three men were motivated by a desire to further the cause of the Confessing Church, even if they acted contrary to the will of the Board. Tillich and Weissler were arrested on October 6, 1936, and Koch on November 13. All three were placed in concentration camps. Koch was released in December of 1938 and Tillich a year later, whereas Weissler died in Sachsenhausen on February 19, 1937, as the result of dreadful and prolonged mistreatment. He was the first martyr of the Confessing Church.

Of considerably less importance is the question of whether Hitler ever actually received the Memorandum and read it. Niemöller has weighed the slim evidence available. He comes to the conclusion that there is no reliable information about how it was handled at the highest levels. The important thing is that the Government and Party leaders were fully apprised of its contents. The Memorandum accomplished its purpose. The silence had been broken, and the Lordship of Christ over Church, State, and society had been proclaimed.

9. A genuine Confession of Faith *invariably provokes opposition from the false Church and from the world precisely because in its witness to God's free grace for all peoples it constitutes a radical attack upon the false Church and the world*. As a fighting action of the Church it runs against the stream. According to Matt., ch. 10, the confessors will be hated by all men. A man's foes will be those of his own household, and he will be dragged before governors and kings for Christ's sake. In the light of the opposition of the Hitler State, of the " German Christians," and of the Lutheran confessionalists to the Confessing Church already reviewed, the point need not be labored. However, opposition to a Confession does not always take the form of physical violence. The devil resorts to murder only when he has failed as the tempter. Lies and half-truths by which the Confession is ridiculed, discredited, assimilated, and nullified are more subtle weapons in his arsenal. The Confession may be slandered because of its uncharitableness, the faults and failing of its advocates, its anti-intellectualism and reactionary spirit, its onesidedness. A wily method is to label it, as for example, Communist, anti-American, liberal, or neo-orthodox. More cunning still is the method of explaining the Confession and explaining it away on the basis of

the historical and sociological circumstances in which it was produced, or of subsuming it under some universal philosophical principle and then accepting it as " an interesting point of view." " Then the tolerance of the world becomes the most terrible weapon of its intolerance " (Barth). Or, as we have seen in the case of the Lutheran confessionalists, the force of a Confession can be blunted by a pious appeal to ancient symbols. The genuineness of a Confession will be seen, however, in the willingness of its confessors to resist the temptation to abandon the Confession, in their willingness to suffer false accusations, ridicule, hatred, persecution, and martyrdom. On the other hand, we need to beware of idealizing and romanticizing a confessing Church. The men who remained faithful to Barmen were not heroes, not even good, courageous men. They were sinful, fallible, and fearful men who nevertheless were free to believe, obey, and suffer. According to Barmen, the Church is " the Church of pardoned sinners " and through Christ it receives " the joyful deliverance from the godless fetters of this world to a free, grateful service to his creatures."

A genuine Confession, therefore, will not merely confess, declare, and teach; implicitly or explicitly, it will also condemn, reject, and anathematize the opposing error. Accordingly, the second paragraph of each article of the Barmen Declaration begins with the words: " We reject the false doctrine. . . ." Naturally this condemnation, this *damnamus,* does not make pleasant reading, especially for the champions of the errors condemned. This feature of a Confession has often been lamented and denounced on the ground of its intolerance and lovelessness. The truth is that the negative exists for the sake of the positive, for the sake of definiteness and clarity. Hitler had no objections to Christians who confessed that Jesus is Lord; but he was enraged when they confessed that Jesus is Lord and Hitler is not. Moreover, the *damnamus,* like the woes Jesus pronounced upon the Pharisees, has to be uttered just for the sake of a genuine love for the erring brethren. To spare them the anathema would be neither loving nor truthful. Obviously the anathema ought not to be exercised rashly or self-righteously. But if we do not have the confidence to say, " We condemn," if we still want to indulge in innocuous, sweet-sounding affirmations that can neither give offense nor engender strong loyalties, then it is a sure sign that we are not ready to confess at all. Then we are still satisfied with registering our opinions, convictions, and sentiments. And he who wished to escape to some Hegelian synthesis above the dialectic of thesis and antithesis, of truth and error, faith and heresy, would be a spectator — unfit for the " either-or " decision involved in a Confession.

10. Finally, a Confession of Faith *possesses a relative and subordinate authority and freedom*. They are founded upon and limited by the absolute and unique authority and freedom of God's word in Holy Scripture. When the Church confesses Jesus Christ as attested in Holy Scripture in the name of the one, holy, catholic, and apostolic Church and in continuity with the Fathers, when its Confession fulfills both the dogmatic and ethical requirements of a Confession, and when it comes forth with an unequivocal Yes and a No, such a Confession exercises authority. We describe here not a possibility or postulate but a fact, a reality. Such a Confession possesses a binding and imperative character. The authority of a Confession is not to be understood in a legalistic or constitutional sense. The authority of a Confession is *spiritual*. It is a self-attesting authority based upon its witness to Christ in Scripture. Its authority, therefore, does not depend upon its being ratified by Church law. The authority of the Creeds and Confessions is not due to the fact that they have been adopted in the constitutions of certain Churches. Conversely, the authority of a Confession is not abolished or lessened by the fact that certain Churches have refused to recognize their validity in Church law. Who will deny that the ecumenical Creeds and the Confessions of the Reformation still exercise authority even in so-called confessionless Churches? It would therefore be a mistake to repudiate the authority of the Barmen Declaration on the ground that it had been drawn up by the German Evangelical Church and had not been formally recognized by our Churches.

The authority of a Confession, we said, is relative and subordinate to Holy Scripture. It binds us not to itself but to Scripture, or rather to Christ in Scripture. We are commanded to *obey* God alone but to *honor* our fathers and mothers in the faith. The Confession, we said, is a commentary on Scripture. It therefore cannot replace Scripture and it cannot dispense with our own exposition and application of Scripture. Moreover, the Confession is not the only commentary we have to read. But as a decision of the Church, it deserves the highest

honor and respect. There are Biblicists who argue that we can go to
the Bible directly without any dogmas or any commentaries at all.
But they fail to see that " no one has ever read the Bible with his own
eyes and no one ever should. The only question is what interpreters
we allow and in what order we let them speak " (Barth). A Confession, far from being a handicap to the understanding of Scripture,
will be a stimulus and guide to a better exegesis. Consequently a
proper respect for the authority of a Confession involves a criticism
of *all* its statements, subjecting them to the ruthless judgment of the
Word of God. Does not the Synod of Barmen challenge us to see
whether it agrees with Scripture, and bid us not to listen to it if we
find that it does not take its stand upon Scripture? Whenever a Confession is elevated to the status of revelation or is made the law or
content of the Church's preaching, the Roman Catholic error of
equating revelation and tradition is revived, and the proper spiritual
authority of a Confession is undermined.

The *freedom* of a Confession consists in the God-given freedom
in which it occurs, in which it ever again asserts itself, and in the
freedom it creates in those who hear it. A Confession occurs in the
freedom of the Holy Spirit. The primary condition of a Confession,
the possibility of a Confession, is not that men decide to confess
Christ for a variety of reasons — say, for the sake of a Church union
— but that Christ for no reason at all, that is, in his sovereign freedom, has decided to confess himself to us. A Confession is Christological not only in the fact that its articles are related to Christ but in the
sense that he is *the* confessor. The Church confesses only *in him!* The
Confession occurs not when we think we have discovered the truth,
but when the truth has found us. Consequently, " with gratitude to
God " the Synod of Barmen declared: " We may not keep silent,
since we believe that we have been *given* a common message to utter." " There are things which one may and can do only when one
must do them. To these things belongs a Christian Confession of
Faith. Not enthusiasm, not good intentions, not practical brotherly
love, nor a concern for Church politics, can take the place of this
' must,' this recognition of the inevitability of the Creed in despair.
One first says, ' *Credo*,' when all other possibilities have been exhausted, when one is utterly confounded and when one says nothing
more than just, ' *Credo*.' Every other Creed is a humbug of the

devil, even if it were literally the Apostles' Creed." [26] One cannot postulate, plan, or will to draw up a Confession. True Confession never takes place for the sake of preserving *our* Christianity. It occurs when men feel constrained to say Yes to Christ without any ulterior motives and without any regard for the consequences. When the Church loses its life for the sake of its confession, it finds it. In a joyous freedom from questions of co-called practicality and expediency — a freedom that reflects the freedom of the gospel itself — the Church confesses. True Confession is recognized by this carefree attitude in contrast to the anxious questions: What will come of it? What will be achieved by it? How many will be with us? Who will agree with us? "We believe, and therefore we speak" (II Cor. 4:13) is the mark of a Confession.

Creeds and Confessions may be abolished by Churches for the sake of "intellectual freedom." They may be misunderstood, ignored, and forgotten over long periods of the Church's history and in large sections of the Church. This can be due to that opposition which a Confession invariably provokes and which we discussed earlier in this chapter. Yet it is extraordinary how, in the freedom of the Holy Spirit, especially in times of crisis for the Church, the ancient Confessions can come alive and speak mightily, overcoming the long-standing indifference and opposition to them. It is astonishing how the answer to the first question of the Heidelberg Catechism — "I belong not to myself but to my faithful Lord and Savior" — or that of the Westminster Shorter Catechism — "Man's chief end is to glorify God, and to enjoy him forever" — can acquire profound meaning and power in a new situation.

Lastly, a Confession of Faith creates freedom in those who hear it — the freedom to choose, to decide, to act, to obey. As a witness to God's word and as a reflection of its authority and freedom, it emancipates men. It bestows upon them a freedom they did not have and could not have of themselves. A Confession does not tyrannize or coerce. It does not force itself upon men. It does not extort subscription. It grants men the freedom to prove its words and then to respond in obedience.

"If you find that we are speaking contrary to Scripture, then do not listen to us! But if you find that we are taking our stand upon Scripture, then let no fear or temptation keep you from treading with us the path of faith and obedience to the Word of God, in order that God's people be of one mind upon earth and that we in faith experience what he himself has said: 'I will never leave you, nor forsake you.' Therefore, 'Fear not, little flock, for it is your Father's good pleasure to give you the Kingdom.'"

A study of the nature and history of the Barmen Theological Declaration naturally prompts questions in the mind of the student. What is the likelihood of something like Barmen happening in other countries? One would be foolish to prophesy. It will occur, we heard, in the freedom of the Holy Spirit. Are there any signs of a bounteous outpouring of the Spirit upon our Churches? Are we living "between the times"? Were those twelve terrible yet blessed years of the Church under Hitler a foreshadowing of the destiny of the Church in other lands in this atomic age? Were they prophetic of a return for us too to a pre-Constantinian, New Testament time of the Church? Are we on the threshold of a day when the Church knows that its only weapon and defense will be its Confession of Faith? Are we conscious of some great heresy by which our Churches are "grievously imperiled" and of some great truth by which we are possessed? Are we prepared to make dogmatic and, much more important, ethical decisions as a Church, and for the sake of them to lose our life in order to find it? Are we really ready for the fearful "either-or" decision involved in a Confession of Faith?

These are questions which for the time being must remain questions, that is, until they become intolerable to bear. Meanwhile, we must remain dissatisfied with any Church document — say, a plan for the reunion of Churches — that falls short of any of the ten marks of a genuine Confession that have been gleaned from the study of the theology and history of Barmen. (A study of the early ecumenical Creeds and the Reformation Confessions would reveal the same trenchant characteristics!) Such dissatisfaction could be a sign of our repentance and of a humble waiting for the coming of the Spirit. Meanwhile we may also recognize that no Confession of Faith has ever arisen that was not preceded by long, arduous, and intense theological activity. The road to Barmen was paved by a Luther and Calvin renaissance, by the translation of Kierkegaard into German, and, above all, by the work of the Dialectical School of theology. Are the revival of Biblical theology within the last twenty years, the republication of the Church fathers and the works of Luther, Calvin, and Wesley, and the translations of Kierkegaard, Barth, and Bonhoeffer signs that something like Barmen is in the offing? We do not know. At any rate, we are charged with that earnest theological labor without which no Confession is possible.

APPENDIXES

APPENDIX I

THE PROGRAM OF THE NATIONAL SOCIALIST GERMAN WORKERS' PARTY

The program of the German Workers' Party is a program for the times. The leaders have no intention, once the aims announced in it have been achieved, of setting up new ones merely in order to ensure the continued existence of the party through artificially stimulated discontent of the masses.

1. We demand the union of all Germans to form a Great Germany on the basis of the right of self-determination of nations.

2. We demand the equality of Germany with other nations, and the abolition of the Peace Treaties of Versailles and Saint-Germain.

3. We demand land and territory [colonies] for the sustenance of our people and for settling our superfluous population.

•4. None but members of the nationality may be citizens of the State. None but those of German blood, irrespective of religion, may be members of the nationality. No Jew, therefore, is a member of the nationality.

5. Anyone who is not a citizen of the State may live in Germany only as a guest and must be subject to the law for aliens.

6. The right to determine the leadership and laws of the State is to be enjoyed only by citizens of the State. We demand, therefore, that all public offices, of whatever kind, whether in the Reich, in the States, or in the municipalities, shall be filled only by citizens of the State. We oppose the corrupt parliamentary system of filling posts merely with a view to party considerations and without reference to character or ability.

7. We demand that the State shall make it its first duty to promote the industry and the livelihood of the citizens of the State. If it is not possible to maintain the entire population of the State, then the members of foreign nations (noncitizens) must be expelled from the Reich.

8. All further immigration of non-Germans must be prevented. We demand that all non-Germans who entered Germany subsequent to August 2, 1914, shall be forced to leave the Reich forthwith.

9. All citizens shall enjoy equal rights and duties.

10. The primary duty of every citizen is to work either intellectually or physically. The activities of the individual must not clash with the interests of the community but must be realized within the frame of the whole. *We therefore demand:*

11. Abolition of incomes unearned by either work or effort.

Breaking of the Bonds of Interest Slavery

12. In view of the enormous sacrifices of property and life demanded of a people in every war, personal enrichment through war must be regarded as a crime against the nation. We demand, therefore, ruthless confiscation of all war profits.

13. We demand nationalization of all trusts.

14. We demand profit sharing in large concerns.

15. We demand the extensive development of old-age pensions.

16. We demand the creation and maintenance of a healthy middle class, immediate communalization of department stores and their lease at cheap rates to small merchants, and extreme consideration for all small merchants in purchases by the Federal Government, states, and municipalities.

17. We demand land reform adapted to our national needs, the enactment of a law for confiscation without compensation of land for public purposes, abolition of land interest, and prevention of all speculation in land.*

18. We demand a most ruthless struggle against those whose activities are injurious to the public interest. Base crimes against the nation, usurers, profiteers, etc., irrespective of creed or race, must be punished with death.

19. We demand the substitution of a German common law for the materialistic cosmopolitan Roman law.

20. In order to make it possible for every talented and diligent German to acquire a higher education and thus be able to occupy leading positions, the State must carry out a thorough reconstruction of our entire educational system. The curriculums of all educational institutions must be adapted to the needs of practical life. The comprehension of political ideas, from the beginning of a child's understanding, must be the goal of the school (through civic education). We demand the education of intellectually gifted children of poor parents without regard to class or occupation, and at the expense of the State.

21. The State must take care of improvement in public health through protection of mothers and children, through prohibiting child labor,

---

* The following statement is necessary to clear up the false interpretations given by our opponents to point 17 of the program of the NSDAP: In view of the fact that the NSDAP holds to the view of private property, it is self-evident that the phrase "confiscation without compensation" refers only to the creation of legal means whereby land which was acquired in illegal ways or which is not being administered to the best interests of the nation's welfare might be expropriated if necessary. This is directed primarily against Jewish land-speculation companies.

Munich, April 13, 1928   [Signed] ADOLF HITLER through increasing physical development by obligatory gymnastics and sports laid down by law, and by the extensive support of all organizations concerned with the physical development of young people.

22. We demand the abolition of mercenary troops, and the formation of a national army.

23. We demand a legal battle against deliberate political lies and their dissemination by the press. In order to make possible the creation of a German press we demand:

a. All editors and contributors of newspapers appearing in the German language must be members of the German nationality.

b. Non-German newspapers must require express permission of the State before they appear. They must not be printed in the German language.

c. Non-Germans must be forbidden by law to participate financially in German newspapers or to influence them. As punishment for violation of this law we demand that such a newspaper be immediately suppressed and the non-German participating in it be immediately expelled from the country. Newspapers that give offense to the national welfare must be suppressed. We demand legal battle against any tendency in art and literature that exercises a disintegrating influence on our national life. Institutions that violate the above-mentioned demands must be shut down.

24. We demand liberty for all religious confessions in the State, in so far as they do not in any way endanger its existence or do not offend the moral sentiment and the customs of the Germanic race. The party as such represents the standpoint of "positive Christianity" without binding itself confessionally to a particular faith. It opposes the Jewish materialistic spirit within and without and is convinced that permanent recovery of our people is possible only from within and on the basis of the principle of:

General Welfare Before Individual Welfare

25. In order to carry out all these demands we call for the creation of a strong central authority in the Reich with unconditional authority by the political central parliament over the entire Reich and all its organizations, and the formation of chambers of classes and occupations to carry out the laws promulgated by the Reich in the various individual States of the federation. The leaders of the party promise that they will fight for the realization of the above-mentioned points and if necessary even sacrifice their lives.

Munich, February 24, 1920

After due consideration, the general membership of the party decided on May 22, 1926, that "This program is never to be changed."

The Guiding Principles of the Faith Movement of the "German Christians," June 6, 1932

1. These guiding principles seek to show to all believing Germans the ways and the goals leading to a reorganization of the Church. They are not intended to be or to take the place of a Confession of Faith, or to disturb the confessional basis of the evangelical Church. They are a living Confession.

2. We are fighting for a union of the twenty-nine Churches included in the "German Evangelical Federation of Churches" into one evangelical State Church. We march under the banner: "Outwardly united and in the might of the spirit gathered around Christ and his Word, inwardly rich and varied, each a Christian according to his own character and calling!"

3. The "German Christian" ticket is not intended to be a political party in the Church in the ordinary sense. It pertains to all evangelical Christians of German stock. The time of parliamentarianism has outlived itself even in the Church. Ecclesiastical parties have no religious sanction to represent Church people and are opposed to the lofty purpose of becoming a national Church. We want a vital national Church that will express all the spiritual forces of our people.

4. We take our stand upon the ground of positive Christianity. We profess an affirmative and typical faith in Christ, corresponding to the German spirit of Luther and to a heroic piety.

5. We want the reawakened German sense of vitality respected in our Church. We want to make our Church a vital force. In the fateful struggle for the freedom and future of Germany the Church in its administration has proven weak. Hitherto the Church has not called for an all-out fight against atheistic Marxism and the reactionary Center Party. Instead it has made an ecclesiastical pact with the political parties of these powers. We want our Church to be in the forefront of the crucial battle for the existence of our people. It may not stand aside or even turn its back upon those fighting for liberty.

6. We demand that the Church pact [political clause] be amended and that a fight be waged against a Marxism which is the enemy of religion and the nation and against its Christian social fellow travelers of every shade. In this Church pact we miss a confident daring for God and for the mission of the Church. The way into the Kingdom of God is through struggle, cross, and sacrifice, not through a false peace.

7. We see in race, folk, and nation, orders of existence granted and en-

trusted to us by God. God's law for us is that we look to the preservation of these orders. Consequently miscegenation is to be opposed. For a long time German Foreign Missions, on the basis of its experience, has been calling to the German people: "Keep your race pure," and tells us that faith in Christ does not destroy one's race but deepens and sanctifies it.

8. In home missions, properly understood, we see a vital Christianity based on deeds which in our opinion, however, is not rooted in mere pity but in obedience to God's will and in gratitude for Christ's death on the cross. Mere pity is charity and becomes presumptuous, coupled with a bad conscience, and makes people soft. We know something about Christian duty and Christian love toward those who are helpless, but we also demand that the nation be protected against the unfit and inferior. In no event may home missions contribute to the degeneration of our people. Furthermore, it has to keep away from economic adventures and not become mercenary.

9. In the mission to the Jews we perceive a grave danger to our nationality. It is an entrance gate for alien blood into our body politic. It has no justification for existence beside foreign missions. As long as the Jews possess the right to citizenship and there is thereby the danger of racial camouflage and bastardization, we repudiate a mission to the Jews in Germany. Holy Scripture is also able to speak about a holy wrath and a refusal of love. In particular, marriage between Germans and Jews is to be forbidden.

10. We want an evangelical Church that is rooted in our nationhood. We repudiate the spirit of a Christian world-citizenship. We want the degenerating manifestations of this spirit, such as pacifism, internationalism, Free Masonry, etc., overcome by a faith in our national mission that God has committed to us. Membership in a Masonic Lodge by an evangelical minister is not permissible.

APPENDIX III

THE CONSTITUTION OF THE GERMAN EVANGELICAL CHURCH, JULY 14, 1933

At this time when Almighty God is letting our German people pass through a new historical era, the German Evangelical Churches unite in carrying on and perfecting the unity brought about by the German Evangelical Church Federation and forming with one accord one GERMAN EVANGELICAL CHURCH.

It unites the Confessions arising out of the Reformation and co-existing with equal rights in a solemn league and bears thereby testimony: one body and one Spirit, one Lord, one faith, one baptism, one God and Father of us all, who is above all, and through all, and in all.

The German Evangelical Church has enacted the following Constitution:

Paragraph I
Article 1

The inviolable foundation of the German Evangelical Church is the gospel of Jesus Christ as it is attested for us in Holy Scripture and brought to light again in the Confessions of the Reformation. The full powers that the Church needs for its mission are thereby determined and limited.

Paragraph II
Article 2

(1) The German Evangelical Church is divided into member Churches (*Landeskirchen*).

(2) Christian communities of similar confession may be admitted. The mode of their admission will be determined by law.

(3) The *Landeskirchen* remain independent in confession and worship.

(4) The German Evangelical Church may give to the *Landeskirchen* direction for their constitutions, in so far as these are not bound by confession. It has to promote and guarantee legal unity among the *Landeskirchen* in the domain of administration and jurisprudence.

(5) Leading officeholders of the *Landeskirchen* are appointed after consultation with the German Evangelical Church.

(6) All ecclesiastical officeholders shall, on entering office, be called upon to pledge themselves to the constitution of the German Evangelical Church.

Paragraph III
Article 3

(1) The German Evangelical Church regulates the whole of German ecclesiastical legal status.

(2) It arranges its relationship to the State.

(3) It determines its attitude toward outside religious bodies.

Article 4

(1) The German Evangelical Church will equip and employ German Evangelical Christendom, united in her, for the fulfillment of the divine mission of the Church. It has therefore to endeavor, on the basis of the Holy Scriptures and the Confessions of the Reformation, to maintain a harmonious attitude in the Church and to give Church work aim and direction.

(2) The special care of the Church is to be devoted to the inner mind of the German people, above all, to the youth.

(3) It takes under its care and protection voluntary Church work of importance for the entire Church, especially in the domain of home and foreign missions.

(4) It has to maintain and strengthen the connection with Evangelical Germans abroad.

(5) It cultivates the relations with the sister Churches abroad.

Paragraph IV
Article 5

(1) The head of the Church is the Lutheran Reich bishop.

(2) The Reich bishop is assisted by a Spiritual Council.

(3) A German Evangelical National Synod co-operates in the appointment of the Church's officials and in legislation.

(4) Advisory Chambers guarantee to the living forces inherent in the German Evangelical soul free creative co-operation in the service of the Church.

Article 6

(1) The Reich bishop represents the German Evangelical Church. He is called upon to give visible expression to the coherent Church life in the *Landeskirchen* and to guarantee a homogeneous leadership for the work of the German Evangelical Church. He takes all necessary measures for the safeguarding of the constitution.

(2) The Reich bishop installs the members of the Spiritual Council in their office. He meets the leading officeholders of the *Landeskirchen* regu-

larly for discussion and consultation. He nominates and dismisses the officials of the German Evangelical Church.

(3) The Reich bishop installs the members to the Spiritual functions, especially to preach, to issue proclamations in the name of the German Evangelical Church, and to order extraordinary penitential and festive services.

In so far as this applies to the preservation and care of a Confession other than his own, his power to act will be taken over by the appropriate member of the Spiritual Council.

(4) The Reich bishop shall receive his own diocese. For the discharge of the affairs of Church administration he has his official residence in Berlin.

(5) The Reich bishop is proposed to the National Synod by the official leaders of the *Landeskirchen* together with the Spiritual Council and appointed to the bishropric by the National Synod.

(6) Further details will be decreed by law.

Article 7

(1) The Spiritual Council is called upon under the leadership of the Reich bishop to govern the German Evangelical Church and to legislate.

(2) It consists of three theologians and one jurist member. In appointing the theologians, attention shall be paid to the confessional character inherent in the German Evangelical Church. The number of members can, in case of need, be increased. The members are independent in the administration of their office. They are responsible to the Reich bishop for the unity of the Church.

(3) It is the especial task of the theological members to strengthen the spiritual bond of the *Landeskirchen* with the German Evangelical Church, likewise the fellowship among members of the same confession and their confidence in the other members of the German Evangelical Church.

(4) The members of the Spiritual Council are appointed by the Reich bishop. The theological members are proposed to the Reich bishop by the official leaders of the *Landeskirchen*. The office of the jurist member is united with the position of the leading jurist member in the administration of the Evangelical Church of the Old Prussian Union. This position is filled only with the consent of the Reich bishop. The holder of the position must possess the qualifications necessary for the office of a judge or of the higher civil service.

(5) The jurist member is the substitute of the Reich bishop in legal matters. He administers the German Evangelical Church chancery as the supreme ecclesiastical administrative board.

(6) Further details will be decreed by law.

Article 8

(1) The German Evangelical National Synod consists of sixty members. Two thirds are sent by the German Evangelical *Landeskirchen* out of their synods and governments. One third is chosen by the German Evangelical Church from persons who have done prominent service in the Church.

(2) The appointment of the members of the National Synod will be regulated by law. Their term of office is six years.

Special attention must be paid in admitting new members when the election of a new synod is taking place.

(3) The National Synod is convened by the Reich bishop at least once a year. The Reich bishop shall, moreover, comply with a request of the National Synod for a meeting. Place and time of the session is fixed by the Reich bishop. He opens the synod with divine service and presides over the first session until the chairman has been elected. The synod establishes its own rules of procedure.

Article 9

(1) Advisory Chambers will be called upon by the Spiritual Council to perform permanent responsible work and have the right to give consultative opinion.

(2) The members are nominated by the Reich bishop in agreement with the Spiritual Council.

Paragraph V
Article 10

The laws of the German Evangelical Church are decreed by the National Synod in co-operation with the Spiritual Council or by the latter alone. They are drawn up by the Reich bishop and published in the Official Gazette of the German Evangelical Church. They come into force on the fourteenth day after the publication of the Official Gazette unless something to the contrary is stated.

Paragraph VI
Article 11

(1) All receipts and expenses are entered every year in a budget which will be fixed by law before the beginning of the financial year.

(2) Resolutions about the granting of loans or the taking over of financial responsibilities debited to the account of the German Evangelical Church require sanction by law.

(3) Account of the budget management must be rendered every year

to a Budget Committee chosen by the National Synod. This committee will grant the discharge.

(4) The German Evangelical Church raises its financial requirement through assessment from the *Landeskirchen*.

Paragraph VII
Article 12

(1) The constitution may be altered by law in so far as provisions relating to confession or worship are not involved. This law requires the consent of two thirds of the existing members of the National Synod or the unanimous approval of the Spiritual Council.

(2) Any alteration of the constitution that affects the structure of the executive bodies of the German Evangelical Church can be made law only by the co-operation of the National Synod.

[Signed by the leaders
of all German Evangelical *Landeskirchen*]

Berlin, the 11th of July, 1933

APPENDIX IV

THE DÜSSELDORF THESES, MAY, 1933

God's providence has led us to an hour in which we are again faced with the question: What is the evangelical Church?

1. The holy, Christian Church, whose only head is Christ, is born of the Word of God, abides in the same, and hears not the voice of a stranger.

2. The Word of God is spoken to us through the Holy Scriptures of the Old and New Testaments.

3. The Word of God spoken to us is our Lord Jesus Christ.

4. Jesus Christ is the Savior of the world and the only Lord of an elect Church that he has called to eternal life out of all nations.

5. The Church lives solely from the fact that each new day it is called and borne, comforted and governed, by its Lord.

6. The Church in all its members lives through carrying out the ministry of preachers, teachers, elders, and deacons instituted and ordered by Jesus Christ.

7. The ministry of preachers consists chiefly in the proclamation of God's Word to the Church and the world through the exposition of Scripture, Baptism, and the Lord's Supper.

8. The ministry of teachers consists in the instruction of youth, in the education of future preachers, and in an investigation and examination of the purity and soundness of Church proclamation that is to be carried on ever again, and all upon the basis of Holy Scripture.

9. The ministry of elders consists in a special, common supervision of the order, doctrine, and life of the Church.

10. The ministry of deacons consists in the care of the needy, sick, and forsaken, no matter who they may be.

11. The authority and power of this ministry is founded solely upon the free grace of the Lord of the Church.

12. Jesus Christ is the only " spiritual leader " of the Church. He is its heavenly King who lives on earth through his Spirit in every one who is obedient to his commission in serving him in the Church.

13. The offices of preacher, teacher, elder, and deacon together serve the edification of the Church. In all the variety of ministries and gifts, each has its promise and authority directly from the Lord of the Church.

14. The dominion of a single congregation over others or the dominion of an episcopal office over other offices does not correspond to the Lordship of the heavenly Lord over single congregations but rather the service that congregations mutually owe one another and which they seek to render to one another in the form of synods composed of servants appointed thereto.

APPENDIX V

The 320 Reformed elders and ministers who have assembled from 167 evangelical congregations in Germany at a free Reformed synod declare that the explanation concerning the right understanding of the Reformation Confessions in the German Evangelical Church of the present, which was composed by Herr Professor Dr. Barth, and which they have heard, *bears witness to the truth of Holy Scripture, and gratefully assume responsibility for it.*

I. *The Church in the Present*

1. In view of the ecclesiastical events of the year 1933 the Word of God leads us to repentance and conversion. For in these events an error has become ripe and visible, which has had a devastating effect upon the Evangelical Church for centuries. It consists in the opinion that beside God's revelation, God's grace, and God's glory, a justifiable human arbitrariness also has to determine the message and form of the Church, that is to say, the temporal way to eternal salvation.

The view is thereby rejected that the development of the Church since the Reformation has been a normal one, and that in the need of our Church today it is only a matter of a passing disturbance, upon the removal of which that development might proceed normally.

2. This error is the same as the error of the Church, of the pope, and of the fanatics, against which the Reformation Confession of Faith is directed. If the Evangelical Church succumbs to it, it has ceased to be an evangelical Church. This error must be recognized and combated even in its subtlest and purest forms; and the old Confession must be opposed to the old error with a new joyfulness and explicitness.

The view is thereby rejected that the error of human arbitrariness in matters of the message and form of the Church is an opinion among others which could now have, as previously, at least in its more lofty forms, a right within the Evangelical Church.

3. In view of the unanimity with which this error manifests itself today, the congregations that have been united in the one German Evangelical Church are called upon to recognize anew, in spite of their Lutheran, Reformed, or United origins and responsibilities, the majesty of the one

Lord of the one Church and therefore the essential unity of their faith, their love, and their hope, their proclamation by preaching and sacrament, their Confession of Faith and their task.

The view is thereby rejected that the legitimate representation of Lutheran, Reformed, or United "interests" might or should still take precedence over the need for a common, evangelical confessing and action against error and on behalf of truth.

II. *The Church Under Holy Scripture*

1. The Church has its origin and its existence exclusively from the revelation, the authority, the comfort, and the guidance of the Word of God, which the eternal Father uttered once for all when the time was fulfilled through Jesus Christ, his eternal Son, in the power of the Holy Spirit.

The view is thereby rejected that the Church could or should be based upon, or should appeal to, a divine revelation in nature and history accessible to man in spite of the Fall other than the revelation of the Triune God.

2. The Church hears that Word of God which has been spoken once and for all through the free grace of the Holy Spirit in the twofold yet single witness of the Old and New Testaments, which in both of its constituent parts is mutually qualified, that is to say, in the witness of Moses and the prophets to the coming of Jesus Christ, and in the witness of the Evangelists and apostles to Jesus Christ who has come.

The view is thereby rejected that the Biblical writings are to be understood as witnesses from the history of human piety; that the New Testament is preponderantly or exclusively the standard for Christian piety; that therefore the Old Testament could or should be depreciated, repressed, or eliminated altogether in favor of the New.

3. The Church lives by the free grace of the Holy Spirit in that, while accepting in faith the witness of Holy Scripture and obediently handing it on, it recognizes and proclaims the severity and the mercy, the honor and the loving-kindness of the Triune God.

The view is thereby rejected that the Church could and should still recognize and proclaim God's activity in the current events at a given time in addition to his action in Jesus Christ testified to by Holy Scripture.

III. *The Church in the World*

1. The Church is in the world. Emulating the incarnate Word of God, it identifies itself unreservedly with the whole need of man, who was created good by God but who fell into sin and stands under the divine curse.

It trusts and obeys alone the mercy that befalls this man in Jesus Christ. In keeping with God's promise, it waits for a new heaven and a new earth in which righteousness dwells.

The view is thereby rejected that the Church could or should repose its *unreserved* trust in a quality of this world knowable to man apart from the mercy of God in Christ, and could or should render *unreserved* obedience to the inner laws of this world knowable to man.

2. In keeping with the instruction of God's word, the Church gratefully acknowledge that changes in the history of mankind and of nations, the political, philosophical, and cultural experiments of men, are subject to the disposition (*Anordnung*) of the divine command and the divine patience. It therefore follows such experiments with its prayers of intercession in a sober recognition of their temporal, finite, and limited justice, and also recalling God's Kingdom, law, and judgment, setting its hope in Him who guides all things in order to make all things new.

The view is thereby rejected that the Church could or should discern in the actual fact of this or that human experiment not so much a proof of divine patience as, rather, an approximation to the restoration of the divine order of creation.

3. The Church exists in the world under Holy Scripture. It serves men and people, State and culture, when it is concerned about being obedient to the Word of God prescribed for it and to his Holy Spirit with respect to its message and its form.

The view is thereby rejected that the Church has to serve men by accommodating its message and form to their momentary convictions, wishes, and purposes or by placing them at their disposal — thereby obeying men rather than God.

IV. *The Message of the Church*

1. The Church's commission consists in delivering in Christ's stead and therefore in the service of his own Word and work the message of the Kingdom of God that is at hand. It does this through sermon and sacrament in the exposition of and in accordance with the prophetic-apostolic witness. God the Creator has adopted his creatures; God the Reconciler, sinners; and God the Redeemer, his beloved children in free grace.

The view is thereby rejected that the Church could or should utter the Word of God the Creator, Reconciler, and Redeemer as its own word instead of serving the Word, and therefore, instead of proclaiming free grace, could or should act " dynamically."

2. The free grace in which God adopts us is the promise fulfilled in the

power of the Holy Spirit of the presence of Jesus Christ as the Lord who for us became a servant in order to mortify our old life and to bring our new one to light.

The view is thereby rejected that the grace of God consists in moral or religious perfections of which man could boast not only with respect to him who justifies the ungodly but also with respect to some endowment of his own.

3. The gift of grace is our membership in Jesus Christ: in him we are justified by the miracle of faith which ever again accepts the forgiveness of sins, which has taken place in him. And in him we are sanctified by the miracle of obedience that ever again submits itself to the judgment and direction of the commandment, which comes from him.

The view is thereby rejected that (a) the " gospel " and the " law," our justication and our sanctification, are not the revelation and the work of the *one grace of Jesus Christ;* that (b) our justification as sinners is accomplished by our suddenly or gradually becoming better men; that (c) the gift of free grace is not also our being claimed for obedience to God's commandment or that this sanctification of ours is something else than a gift of free grace.

4. Our life, which is grounded in Jesus Christ through the Holy Spirit and for which we must beg him new each day, waits in faith and obedience for its redemption through the coming Lord: in the resurrection of the dead, through judgment and unto eternal life.

The view is thereby rejected that a life in faith and obedience could in any respect be a self-contained, self-sufficient life withdrawn from a waiting upon the coming Lord, and therefore from hoping in him and fearing him.

V. *The Form of the Church*

1. The Church of Jesus Christ is the visibly and temporally structured reality of the congregation which is called, assembled and upheld, comforted and ruled, by the Lord himself through the ministry of proclamation. It is the likewise visibly and temporally structured reality of the *unity* of such congregations.

The view is thereby rejected that the Church receives its temporal and visible form at its own discretion or in virtue of external necessities, like a religious society whose purpose could be realized just as well in one form as in another.

2. The form of the Church is determined by the fact that its outward order as well as its inward life stand under the promise and under the

command of Jesus Christ as the sole Lord of the Church. Individually and together the congregations are responsible to him for seeing that persons called from among them are found for the ministries of preaching and oversight, and of teaching and charitable work, which accompany preaching, and that these services are properly carried out by them.

The view is thereby rejected that the congregations could or should be relieved of responsibility for the appointment and administration of the ministries of the Church by a special office of a "leader" in the Church.

3. The Church of Jesus Christ, as far as its message and form are concerned, is one and the same in different times, races, peoples, states, and cultures. The justification for differences in Churches in this or that place depends upon whether they are consistent with the unity of the Church's message and form.

The view is thereby rejected that (a) the justification for temporal, national, and local differences in Church forms is to be derived from special revelations of God in history; that (b) it is consistent with the unity of the message and form of the Church to limit membership and qualification for service in the Church to those who belong to a particular race.

4. On the basis of the instruction of God's Word, the Church sees in the State an ordinance (*Anordnung*) of the divine command and divine patience, in virtue of which man may and should strive, within the limits of his understanding of reason and history and in responsibility to the Lord of lords, to discover justice and to administer and maintain it by force. The Church cannot deprive the State of this its special office. At the same time, however, it cannot allow the State to deprive it of its own office; it cannot permit its message and its form to be determined by the State. Bound to its commission, it is in principle a free Church in a State which in principle is likewise free in being bound to its commission.

The view is thereby rejected that the State is the highest or even the only ("totalitarian") form of a historical reality visibly and temporally fashioned to which therefore the Church with its message and form also has to submit and conform and into which it has to be integrated.

APPENDIX VI

THE ULM DECLARATION, APRIL 22, 1934

In the Name of the Father, the Son, and the Holy Ghost!

We, the assembled representatives of the Württemberg and Bavarian provincial Churches, of the Free Synods in the Rhineland, Westphalia, and Brandenburg, as well as of many confessing congregations and Christians throughout Germany, make this declaration before this congregation and the whole of Christendom as the constitutional evangelical Church of Germany:

We are burdened by a great concern for the German Evangelical Church. The Reich Church government, it is true, has talked about peace in its recent decrees and laws, but its deeds contradict its protestations. They reveal that this "will for peace" is not born of God's Word and Spirit.

It is not possible to preach peace and then immediately do violence to a Church that is bound to a Confession of Faith such as the Württemberg Church. But this has happened by the Church law laid down by the Reich bishop which, contrary to the constitution of the German Evangelical Church, prevented the meeting of the Württemberg Church Council.

Because of a constant endangering of the Church and its Confession and also in the interest of the truth, we exhibit, before Christendom and all who are willing to hear, a unity in which we intend, with the help of God's strength, to remain faithful to the Confession, even though we have to expect that in doing so we will incur much trouble. However, we assembled Church leaders, representatives of Free Synods and delegates from many congregations and districts in Germany, are comforted by God's Word and rejoice to take upon ourselves what God lays upon us — come what may — in order that the cross of Christ may really govern the life of the Church. Nor will we let ourselves be prevented in this even if the German public should be misled in the way they have been, concerning the situation of the Church in Württemberg. As against the picture presented by the Reich Church government, we declare that it is impossible to speak of a serious rift in the Württemberg Church. Nor does what has been reported about the Reich bishop's visit in Württemberg correspond to the facts. The Reich bishop neither saw nor spoke to the Württemberg bishop. With God's help we intend to set God's Word and the Confession of our Church in word and deed over against the application of force and slander, fully confident that God will not forsake his cause.

235

The unexpressed intention of the Reich Church government to restore peace in the Church in Württemberg by its decree manifestly did not achieve true peace within the Reich Church. Rather, it was a violent destruction of one of the last bulwarks of the Confessional Church in Germany. We testify that the German Evangelical Church would lose God's blessing if it gave way to such falsehood. It would lapse into disorder if in this way the highest Church administrative body undermined the dignity and authority of the leader of a provincial Church, and the congregations spiritually and legally were deprived of their rights.

Therefore we challenge all congregations, elders, sessions, Church managers, and ministers to stand together with us against this peril to the Church. In spite of all attempts to veil the truth, we bear witness that the Confession of Faith is in danger in the German Evangelical Church! The ministry is robbed of authority by the "German Christians" and by the fact that they are tolerated by the highest Church authorities. For a long time the action of the Reich Church government has not had any legal basis. There is violence and injustice against which all true Christians must pray and bear witness to the Word. As a fellowship of determined fighters obedient to the Lord Jesus Christ, we pray Almighty God to open the eyes of all Christians to the danger that threatens our beloved Church. May he not let us waver in remaining faithful to his honor and in his service. May we also do all that he requires of us in loyalty and service to our nation and State. Ministers and congregations of the Württemberg Church, rally round your bishop! You Christians who speak the German tongue, stand together with us all, firmly grounded upon God's Word, constant in prayer, joyful in faith and love! Then this day will bring a blessing upon our whole Church and our whole nation!

God grant it!

APPENDIX VII

THE DECLARATIONS, RESOLUTIONS, AND MOTIONS ADOPTED BY THE
SYNOD OF BARMEN, MAY 29–31, 1934

I. *An Appeal to the Evangelical Congregations and Christians in Germany*

The Confessional Synod of the German Evangelical Church met in Barmen, May 29–31, 1934. Here representatives from all the German Confessional Churches met with one accord in a confession of the one Lord of the one, holy, apostolic Church. In fidelity to their Confession of Faith, members of Lutheran, Reformed, and United Churches sought a common message for the need and temptation of the Church in our day. With gratitude to God they are convinced that they have been given a common word to utter. It was not their intention to found a new Church or to form a union. For nothing was farther from their minds than the abolition of the confessional status of our Churches. Their intention was, rather, to withstand in faith and unanimity the destruction of the Confession of Faith, and thus of the Evangelical Church in Germany. In opposition to attempts to establish the unity of the German Evangelical Church by means of false doctrine, by the use of force and insincere practices, the Confessional Synod insists that the unity of the Evangelical Churches in Germany can come only from the Word of God in faith through the Holy Spirit. Thus alone is the Church renewed.

Therefore the Confessional Synod calls upon the congregations to range themselves behind it in prayer, and steadfastly to gather around those pastors and teachers who are loyal to the Confessions.

Be not deceived by loose talk, as if we meant to oppose the unity of the German nation! Do not listen to the seducers who pervert our intentions, as if we wanted to break up the unity of the German Evangelical Church or to forsake the Confessions of the Fathers!

Try the spirits whether they are of God! Prove also the words of the Confessional Synod of the German Evangelical Church to see whether they agree with Holy Scripture and with the Confessions of the Fathers. If you find that we are speaking contrary to Scripture, then do not listen to us! But if you find that we are taking our stand upon Scripture, then let no fear or temptation keep you from treading with us the path of faith and obedience to the Word of God, in order that God's people be of one mind upon earth and that we in faith experience what he himself has said: "I will never leave you, nor forsake you." Therefore, "Fear not, little flock, for it is your Father's good pleasure to give you the kingdom."

237

II. *Theological Declaration Concerning the Present Situation of the German Evangelical Church*

According to the opening words of its constitution of July 11, 1933, the German Evangelical Church is a federation of Confessional Churches that grew out of the Reformation and that enjoy equal rights. The theological basis for the unification of these Churches is laid down in Article 1 and Article 2(1) of the constitution of the German Evangelical Church that was recognized by the Reich Government on July 14, 1933:

> Article 1. The inviolable foundation of the German Evangelical Church is the gospel of Jesus Christ as it is attested for us in Holy Scripture and brought to light again in the Confessions of the Reformation. The full powers that the Church needs for its mission are hereby determined and limited.
> Article 2 (1). The German Evangelical Church is divided into member Churches (*Landeskirchen*).

We, the representatives of Lutheran, Reformed, and United Churches, of free synods, Church assemblies, and parish organizations united in the Confessional Synod of the German Evangelical Church, declare that we stand together on the ground of the German Evangelical Church as a federation of German Confessional Churches. We are bound together by the confession of the one Lord of the one, holy, catholic, and apostolic Church.

We publicly declare before all evangelical Churches in Germany that what they hold in common in this Confession is grievously imperiled, and with it the unity of the German Evangelical Church. It is threatened by the teaching methods and actions of the ruling Church party of the " German Christians " and of the Church administration carried on by them. These have become more and more apparent during the first year of the existence of the German Evangelical Church. This threat consists in the fact that the theological basis, in which the German Evangelical Church is united, has been continually and systematically thwarted and rendered ineffective by alien principles, on the part of the leaders and spokesmen of the " German Christians " as well as on the part of the Church administration. When these principles are held to be valid, then, according to all the Confessions in force among us, the Church ceases to be the Church, and the German Evangelical Church, as a federation of Confessional Churches, becomes intrinsically impossible.

As members of Lutheran, Reformed, and United Churches we may and must speak with one voice in this matter today. Precisely because we want to be and to remain faithful to our various Confessions, we may not keep silent, since we believe that we have been given a common message to utter in a time of common need and temptation. We commend to God what this may mean for the interrelations of the Confessional Churches.

In view of the errors of the " German Christians " of the present Reich Church government which are devastating the Church and are also thereby breaking up the unity of the German Evangelical Church, we confess the following evangelical truths:

1. *" I am the way, and the truth, and the life; no one comes to the Father, but by me."* (John 14:6.) *" Truly, truly, I say to you, he who does not enter the sheepfold by the door but climbs in by another way, that man is a thief and a robber. . . . I am the door; if anyone enters by me, he will be saved."* (John 10:1, 9.)[1]

Jesus Christ, as he is attested for us in Holy Scripture, is the one Word of God which we have to hear and which we have to trust and obey in life and in death.

We reject the false doctrine, as though the Church could and would have to acknowledge as a source of its proclamation, apart from and besides this one Word of God, still other events and powers, figures and truths, as God's revelation.[2]

2. *" Christ Jesus, whom God made our wisdom, our righteousness and sanctification and redemption."* (I Cor. 1:30.)

---

[1] The translation of the texts from the Bible is that of the Revised Standard Version and therefore not always an accurate rendition of the German.

[2] The reader who wishes to pursue a study of all alterations made to the text of the Declaration through its several drafts is referred to Gerhard Niemöller's work on Barmen. Only the more important changes will be noted here. The phrase " as a source of its proclamation " was not in the original draft; it was added at Barmen. The original wording indicates, moreover, that Jesus Christ *is* the revelation and not merely " acknowledged " to be God's revelation. Attention is drawn to the translation of the German construction *" als könne und müsse die Kirche . . . anerkennen,"* which is usually translated, " We reject the false doctrine that the Church can and must . . ." After consultation with several German scholars, and with Professor Barth himself, I decided to employ the more literal and admittedly more awkward construction above. Involved here is a characteristic point in Barth's theology and in the Barmen Declaration, namely, that sin and evil do not have a positive existence as that which is created and willed by God. They exist as that which God hates and negates, as an impossible possibility. Therefore it is not possible for the Church to acknowledge other truths, etc., as God's revelation. This is the lie propounded in false doctrine. *" Gestalten "* has been rendered as " figures." The German word conveys the historical structure that lies behind a person and the history made by that person. It indicates a person who influences the course of events and attracts a following. The implied contrast is doubtless between Jesus and Hitler.

As Jesus Christ is God's assurance of the forgiveness of all our sins, so in the same way and with the same seriousness he is also God's mighty claim upon our whole life. Through him befalls us a joyful deliverance from the godless fetters of this world for a free, grateful service to his creatures.[3]

We reject the false doctrine, as though there were areas of our life in which we would not belong to Jesus Christ, but to other lords — areas in which we would not need justification and sanctification through him.

3. "*Rather, speaking the truth in love, we are to grow up in every way into him who is the head, into Christ, from whom the whole body [is] joined and knit together.*" (Eph. 4:15–16.)

The Christian Church is the congregation of the brethren in which Jesus Christ acts presently as the Lord in Word and sacrament through the Holy Spirit. As the Church of pardoned sinners, it has to testify in the midst of a sinful world, with its faith as with its obedience, with its message as with its order, that it is solely his property, and that it lives and wants to live solely from his comfort and from his direction in the expectation of his appearance.[4]

We reject the false doctrine, as though the Church were permitted to

---

[3] "*Zuspruch*" has been translated "assurance." But here it also implies a judicial verdict made by God in Jesus Christ. It could therefore also be translated "adjudgment." Likewise, "claim" ("*Anspruch*") is something God has done in Christ. Men are "claimed" by God *in him* before they come to hear and know about it. It is a pity that in English the play on words in "*Zuspruch*" and "*Anspruch*" cannot be brought out.

[4] This paragraph originally read: "The Christian Church is the congregation of brethren in which Jesus Christ is proclaimed as the Lord. It has to testify with its faith as with its obedience, with its message as with its order, in the midst of a sinful world and itself as the Church of sinners, that it is solely his property, and that it wants to live solely from his comfort and from his direction." In Barmen the article was given its present complicated form when Hermann Sasse insisted upon mentioning the sacrament. Thereupon the Reformed theologians on the Theological Commission — Barth, Obendiek, and Niesel — requested that the Holy Spirit be mentioned. In a letter to Wilhelm Niemöller, dated Schoeller, January 11, 1954, Wilhelm Niesel stated that he had suggested the phrase: "Through the Holy Spirit." Concerning this point, Barth recalled in a letter to Niemöller, dated Basel, October 17, 1953: "In the deliberations of the Commission during the synod the first paragraph of Thesis 3 acquired its present complicated form when Sasse and Althaus insisted upon having the 'sacrament' mentioned. Thereupon I could do nothing but insist upon mentioning the Holy Spirit! This is how the paragraph became so 'Calvinist,' as it was afterward lamented." Actually Althaus was not a member of the Commission. When Barth linked his name with Sasse's, it is possible that Sasse had conferred with Althaus, or that Barth's memory had slipped. The point is of considerable interest in view of Barth's later teaching concerning the "sacraments." In his report to the synod, Asmussen said: "If you read this sentence slowly, you will see that every word has been weighed with the greatest exactness."

abandon the form of its message and order to its own pleasure or to changes in prevailing ideological and political convictions.

4. "*You know that the rulers of the Gentiles lord it over them, and their great men exercise authority over them. It shall not be so among you; but whoever would be great among you must be your servant.*" (Matt. 20: 25–26.)

The various offices in the Church do not establish a dominion of some over the others; on the contrary, they are for the exercise of the ministry entrusted to and enjoined upon the whole congregation.

We reject the false doctrine, as though the Church, apart from this ministry, could and were permitted to give to itself, or allow to be given to it, special leaders vested with ruling powers.

5. "*Fear God. Honor the emperor.*" (I Peter 2:17.)

Scripture tells us that, in the as yet unredeemed world in which the Church also exists, the State has by divine appointment the task of providing for justice and peace. [It fulfills this task] by means of the threat and exercise of force, according to the measure of human judgment and human ability. The Church acknowledges the benefit of this divine appointment in gratitude and reverence before him. It calls to mind the Kingdom of God, God's commandment and righteousness, and thereby the responsibility both of rulers and of the ruled. It trusts and obeys the power of the Word by which God upholds all things.

We reject the false doctrine, as though the State, over and beyond its special commission, should and could become the single and totalitarian order of human life, thus fulfilling the Church's vocation as well.

We reject the false doctrine, as though the Church, over and beyond its special commission, should and could appropriate the characteristics, the tasks, and the dignity of the State, thus itself becoming an organ of the State.[5]

---

[5] These two paragraphs on false doctrines of State and Church were originally one, and read as follows: "We reject the error, as though the State were the only and totalitarian order of human life. We reject the error, as though the Church had to conform to a particular form of the State in its message and form." Merz contended that the *damnatio* had to be completely altered in view of the fact that the synod was opposed not to the State but to the "German Christians." For a time it appeared that an agreement could not be reached. However, during a recess Barth reworded this section and his new version was accepted. Attention is drawn to the fact that the fifth thesis does not speak of the State as an "order" or "ordinance" (*Ordnung*) of God, but as having a specific task by or according to God's "appointment" or "ordering." Barth himself informed me that the German word *Anordnung* (here translated "appointment") is to be understood in the sense of *ordinatio* instead of *ordo*. In keeping with the obvious intention of the framers of the Barmen Declaration to get away from the idea of "orders," with which the doctrine of the State has been burdened, I have used the word "appointment."

6. " *Lo, I am with you always, to the close of the age.*" (Matt. 28:20.)
" *The word of God is not fettered.*" (II Tim. 2:9.)

The Church's commission, upon which its freedom is founded, consists in delivering the message of the free grace of God to all people in Christ's stead, and therefore in the ministry of his own Word and work through sermon and sacrament.

We reject the false doctrine, as though the Church in human arrogance could place the Word and work of the Lord in the service of any arbitrarily chosen desires, purposes, and plans.

The Confessional Synod of the German Evangelical Church declares that it sees in the acknowledgment of these truths and in the rejection of these errors the indispensable theological basis of the German Evangelical Church as a federation of Confessional Churches. It invites all who are able to accept its declaration to be mindful of these theological principles in their decisions in Church politics. It entreats all whom it concerns to return to the unity of faith, love, and hope.

Verbum Dei Manet in Aeternum

III. Resolution of the Confessional Synod of the German Evangelical Church

1. The synod acknowledges the Theological Declaration Concerning the Present Situation of the German Evangelical Church together with Pastor Asmussen's address to be a Biblical, Reformation testimony, and assumes responsibility for it.

2. The synod hands this Declaration over to the Confessional conventions for the purpose of working out an interpretation of it on the basis of their Confessions.

IV. Declaration Concerning the Legal Status of the German Evangelical Church

1. The unimpeachable basis of the German Evangelical Church is the gospel of Jesus Christ as it is testified to in Holy Scripture and brought to light again in the Confessions of the Reformation. The present Reich Church administration has abandoned this unimpeachable basis and has been guilty of numerous violations of the law and the constitution. It has thereby forfeited the claim to be the legitimate administration of the German Evangelical Church.

Only those who are called and who desire to hold fast to Holy Scripture and to the Church's Confession of Faith as its inexpugnable foundation, and who desire to make both the authoritative standard of the German Evangelical Church again, may legitimately speak and act in the name of the German Evangelical Church.

The congregations and Churches agreed in such a Confession are the legitimate German Evangelical Church; they are assembled as the Confessional Synod of the German Evangelical Church.

2. In the present Church emergency, the Confessional Synod has the task of assembling the confessional congregations in the German Evangelical Church and of representing them, of caring for their fellowship and common tasks, and of working to the end that the German Evangelical Church be led according to the gospel and the Confession of Faith, and that thereby its constitution and law be safeguarded.

3. It is impossible to divorce the Church's outward order from the Confession of Faith. Accordingly, the division of the German Evangelical Church into regional Churches, as provided in the constitution, has its basis in the Confessions. Regional Churches bound to a Confession may not be robbed of their independence through membership in the German Evangelical Church by means of an administration or by external compulsion, since the Church's outward order always has to justify itself to its Confession. The incorporations which hitherto have been made by the Reich Church government lack legal force.

4. The unity of the German Evangelical Church is also not achieved by recklessly setting up a central authority that is based upon a worldly *Führerprinzip* foreign to the Church. A hierarchical structure of the Church is contrary to the Reformation Confession of Faith.

5. The German Evangelical Church can achieve a genuine Church unity only by (*a*) protecting the Reformation Confessions and by requiring an organic federation of the regional Churches and congregations on the basis of their confessional stand; (*b*) by giving to the congregation as the bearer of the proclamation of the Word the place due to it. It must be its earnest desire that the Spirit of the Lord Christ and not the spirit of temporal rule be decisive in the Church of our fathers.

In obedience to the Lord of the Church there is such a strong unifying power that in spite of the differences in the Reformation Confessions we can stand together in a unity of purpose and action in the German Evangelical Church.

V. *Declaration Concerning the Practical Work of the Confessional Synod of the German Evangelical Church*

The sixth point of the common witness of the Confessional Synod of the German Evangelical Church states: "Lo, I am with you always, to the close of the age " (Matt. 28:20). "The word of God is not fettered." (II Tim. 2:9.) The commission of the Church, upon which its freedom is founded, consists in delivering the message of the free grace of God to all people in Christ's stead, and therefore in the ministry of his own Word and work through sermon and sacrament."

The Confessing Church of Germany is thereby summoned to a work of service. God has granted us confessing congregations. Through the resuscitation of many Church members and pastors, a new sanctified will to service has been awakened. When the Confessional Synod of the German Evangelical Church takes over the administration of German evangelical Christendom, it assumes a great responsibility for the new gifts and powers given by God. Consequently the following is recommended as urgent work for the Confessional Synod of the German Evangelical Church:

I. Ministering to the Spiritual Renewal of Ministers

If the minister is to perform in the Spirit of the Word of God the new tasks given to him by God for the edification of the congregation, he needs the permanent discipline and guidance of the Holy Spirit.

1. The spiritual ministry of the brethren among one another.
   a. The ministers must unite and regularly meet in the various synods for mutual service, for common work under God's Word, and for prayer. From time to time ministers' wives must also take part in such meetings.
   b. We also need in our Church men who exercise the office of exhortation and comforting, and who will be free from time to time to strengthen and admonish the brethren in different places, especially those who are isolated.
   c. Special retreats of several days' duration away from the large cities; if possible also for ministers' wives.
   d. Spiritual fellowship held at regular intervals.
2. Serious theological training in order to attain an extensive agreement in questions of doctrine in conferences constituted according to the Confession of Faith.
3. Systematic education for the pastoral ministry. This education, which hitherto has been more or less left to chance, demands serious training in the preaching, instruction, and pastoral work of the minister.
4. The care of theological students:
   a. By meetings at the universities and during vacations.
   b. In suitable assistantships.
   c. In seminaries for preachers.

    d. In theological schools.

    e. Retreats.

II. Edification of the Confessing Congregation

The relation of the minister and the congregation is of the most intimate nature. The pastor takes his place in the congregation and the congregation stands behind its pastor. Although a confessing congregation may be willing to serve, it nevertheless has to be equipped for that purpose. No Church order for confessing congregations is to be prescribed here. But we would like to draw attention to the resolution passed by the Prussian Confessional Synod: " The Upbuilding of the Confessing Church in the Old Prussian Union." [6] Here reference to ways in which service may be rendered in congregations is made only in connection with the witness of the Confessional Synod.

    1. The confessing congregation as a spiritual organism.

        a. The ministry of the Word. The congregations need to learn that the Sunday Church service is the very heart of the life of the congregation. The hallowing of Sunday is to be earnestly enjoined upon the congregations. The administration of the sacraments pertains to the edification of the congregation, the meaning of which needs to be disclosed anew. Instruction, meetings of young people who have been confirmed (Christian education), Bible classes, and pastoral work all contribute to a highly necessary, personal familiarity with the Bible.

        b. Special arrangements for the training of the congregation. Men's work, retreats for elders, and evening meetings for parents to further Christian family life, and women's societies.

    2. Since voluntary societies are viable only on the basis of a confessing congregation (home missions, foreign missions, young people's societies, associations for men and women, etc.), these societies and their office-bearers are required to take a definite stand in favor of the Confessional Synod of the German Evangelical Church. Only if they make such a decision will they be entitled to have a part in the building of a confessing congregation.

III. The Mission of a Confessing Congregation

Only where brotherly aid is afforded the pastor of the congregation and the congregation lives as a spiritual organism — and that means as

---

[6] For the text, see K. D. Schmidt, *Die Bekenntnisse des Jahres 1934*, pp. 87 ff. The reference is to a resolution passed by the Prussian Synod that met in Barmen on the day the Synod of Barmen convened.

the body of Christ — is it fit for the ministry which it has to render to all people through the sermon and sacrament, namely, the ministry of the proclamation of the free grace of God in Jesus Christ. The commission is great, wide is the field and ripe for the harvest. All active members of the congregation are included in this missionary work, either as those who preach or as those who make intercession. The mark of a living congregation is that it is always a missionary congregation.

1. Special tasks within individual congregations (evangelization, distribution of literature, Bible study weeks for the deepening of the spiritual life).
2. Ministering to the alienated (freethinkers, German Faith Movement).
3. Responsibility for congregations and areas of the German Evangelical Church in special danger (compilation of a list of experienced evangelists; training of evangelists for special tasks; working out plans and programs).
4. Ministering to the Reich Army (Drill Centers, Storm Troopers, Black Corps, Hitler Youth, provision for Labor and Youth Camps).

VI. *Motions and Resolutions*

The "Declaration Concerning the Legal Status of the German Evangelical Church" was adopted unanimously.

The synod then adopted the following resolution:

"We declare that it is the unanimous mind of the synod that we deny that the present Church administration of the German Evangelical Church has any authority or right to undertake a reform of the constitution; on the contrary, we expressly demand that the existing constitution be respected.

"We declare that as long as the present Church administration exists, the Confessing Church categorically refuses to negotiate with it in regard to constitutional questions.

"Under these circumstances the Confessional Synod dispenses with passing a resolution concerning the overture presented by the Legal Committee, 'Our View of the Proper Constitution of the German Evangelical Church,' and transmits it to the Council of Brethren as material for future work."

Following the adoption of the "Declaration Concerning Practical Work," the following motions were passed:

1. That the Council of Brethren of the Confessional Synod appoint a committee to serve the spiritual renewal of the ministry.
2. That the Council of Brethren of the Confessional Synod appoint a

committee that will supply the necessary directions and principles for the work outlined in Sections II and III of the Declaration, and which is to be responsible for carrying them out. It is especially incumbent upon it to assist Churches in threatened areas.

3. That the Council of Brethren require that Home and Foreign Missionary Societies, etc., decide in favor of the Confessional Synod.

4. That the Council of Brethren issue a newssheet for the Confessing Church.

The first two motions were passed unanimously. Three and four were referred to the Council of Brethren as suggestions.

The Synod's Working Committee recommended to the synod that it appoint a permanent Council of Brethren composed of the members of the present Working Committee, namely:

President Koch, Bad-Oeynhausen
Bishop Meiser, Munich
Bishop Wurm, Stuttgart
Pastor Dr. Beckmann, Düsseldorf
Pastor Bosse, Raddesdorf (Hanover)
Dr. Fiedler, Leipzig
Pastor Dr. Hesse, Elberfeld, as moderator of the Reformed Alliance
Pastor Karl Immer, Barmen
Pastor Jacobi, Berlin
Herr Link, Düsseldorf
Pastor Niemöller, Berlin-Dahlem

and that it be authorized to carry out the tasks assigned to it, and to act for the synod in accordance with the rule that in all important matters the decision of the Confessional Synod itself must be obtained. The Council of Brethren has the power to appoint synod's committees. It is authorized to alter and enlarge its membership. (Pastor Asmussen was subsequently elected to it.) On motion this recommendation was unanimously adopted.

On motion it was unanimously adopted that the Confessional Synod of the German Evangelical Church authorize its Council of Brethren to present a case to the Reich Minister for Internal Affairs a well as to the Minister for National Enlightenment and Propaganda that the hampering of the Church press in matters of Church reform be effectively stopped.

On motion it was unanimously adopted that the Confessional Synod protest against all internal and external pressure brought upon assistant ministers and candidates by the "German Church" administration, and that it charge the Council of Brethren of the Confessional Synod with the spiritual care and the personal welfare of young theologians.

APPENDIX VIII

An Address on the Theological Declaration Concerning the Present Situation in the German Evangelical Church, by Pastor Hans Asmussen

1

According to the opening words of its constitution of July 11, 1933, the German Evangelical Church is an alliance of the Confessional Churches which grew out of the Reformation and which stand side by side enjoying equal rights. The theological basis of the unification of these Churches is laid down in Article 1 and Article 2(1), of the constitution of the German Evangelical Church that was recognized by the Reich Government on July 14, 1933:

Article 1. The inviolable foundation of the German Evangelical Church is the gospel of Jesus Christ as it is attested for us in Holy Scripture and brought to light again in the Confessions of the Reformation. The full powers that the Church needs for its mission are hereby determined and limited.

Article 2(1). The German Evangelical Church is divided into member Churches (Landeskirchen).

The Theological Declaration Concerning the Present Situation of the German Evangelical Church begins with these words. They are intended to express the following:

The Confessional Synod of the German Evangelical Church is not tantamount to the founding of a new Church. Rather, it is composed of representatives of those Confessional Churches which were united in 1933 by the constitution of the German Evangelical Church. It is, therefore, representative of the hitherto existing regional Churches in a legal suc-cession. In the union by the constitution of 1933 it was not the will of the legislator that the existing Churches should cease to be what they are: Confessional Churches. Consequently the union bore the character of an alliance (federation) in which was carried further what had been already aspired to in the German Evangelical Church Federation. Any change in the character of this union would have resulted in unforeseeable legal, and especially ecclesiastical, consequences.

The constitution gives expression to the fact that the German Evangeli-cal Church can be built only upon definite ecclesiastical and theological principles. And for this reason it must have definite theological and ecclesiastical objectives. For the German Evangelical Church these presup‹ positions and goals proceed solely from "the gospel of Jesus Christ, as it is attested for us in Holy Scripture and brought to light again in the Confessions of the Reformation." That is to say, the starting point for Church work and further desired progress is the particular basis of those Confessional Churches as determined by the character of their individual Confessions. The Reich Government legally recognized this fact on July 14, 1933.

On the basis of these theological principles and this State legislation, the Confessional Synod of the German Evangelical Church is able to define its position with a good conscience toward the Reich as follows:

> *We, the representatives of Lutheran, Reformed, and United Churches, of free synods, Church assemblies, and parish organizations united in the Confessional Synod of the German Evangelical Church, declare that we stand together on the ground of the German Evangelical Church as a federation of German Confessional Churches. We are bound together by the confession of the one Lord of the one, holy, catholic, and apostolic Church.*

With these words the Confessional Synod of the German Evangelical Church declares that it is unjust to reproach it with having abandoned its confessional, constitutional, and legal basis. We are not rebels, but for the sake of our responsibility to God and man we are bound to demand that neither we nor others be deprived of the possibility of meeting this responsibility by undermining the confessional and legal basis. We cannot in good conscience be members of a German Evangelical Church if in its words and actions it did not take seriously the fact that in its constitution it is bound to that confessional basis. It would be impossible for us to remain in it if the articles of the constitution referred to served only the purpose of a cover for gradually effecting a drastic change in the nature of the German Evangelical Church.

The question might be raised as to the extent to which we have assembled as a confessional synod of the German Evangelical Church. For we are made up of not only the lawful representatives of German Churches, but also of free synods, Church meetings, and parish groups lacking a legally acknowledged calling. But in this regard we also have a good conscience. Not rashly or precipitously have we gathered together, but as the representatives of Church bodies and associations persuaded that a confessional and legal emergency has arisen which requires the pooling of all forces, and that without any delay. The explanation and justification for our assembling in this way is the emergency in which the confessional and constitutional basis of the German Evangelical Church is critically imperiled. We have described the existing emergency in the following words:

> *We publicly declare before all evangelical Churches in Germany that what they hold in common in this Confession is grievously imperiled, and with it the unity of the German Evangelical Church. It is threatened by the teaching methods and actions of the ruling Church party of the "German Christians" and of the Church administration carried on by them. These have become more and more apparent during the first year of the existence of the German Evangelical Church. This threat consists in the fact that the theological basis, in which the German Evangelical Church is united, has been continually and systematically thwarted and rendered ineffective by alien principles, on the part of the leaders and spokesmen of the "German Christians" as well as on the part of the Church administration. When these principles are held to be valid, then, according to all the Confessions in force among us, the Church ceases to be the Church, and the German Evangelical Church, as a federation of Confessional Churches, becomes intrinsically impossible.*

Our confessional fellowship is based upon a positive and a negative factor. The common confession to the one Church of Jesus Christ unites us as representatives of this synod, and we are therefore united in the confessional and constitutional basis of the German Evangelical Church. But we are united just as much by the shocking and destructive attack made upon the basis and essence of the German Evangelical Church to which it has been exposed for more than a year. We would sin against God and we would also deny the love for our people and the Fatherland required of us if we did not publicly call attention to this fact and register the sharpest protest. For the unity of the confession to the one Church of Jesus Christ is seriously imperiled in the German Evangelical Church. As a result the Church threatens to fall apart. For only in this confession is there a German Evangelical Church.

This peril has become manifest through the teaching methods and actions of the ruling Church party of the "German Christians" as well as by the Reich Church government carried on by them. It is not a case of occasional mistakes by individuals that one finds in administrative matters and could thus be removed. On the contrary, it is a question of a false doctrine all along the line and of a conduct that not only occasionally but systematically and comprehensively opposes the gospel, the Confessions presently in force, and the constitution of the German Evangelical Church.

We would have to write thick volumes in order to enumerate the innumerable acts of violence, injustice, and breaches of the law reflected in this kind of procedure. Not unjustly do we interpret recent advances made to us by the "German Christians" as indicating that even they are beginning to realize the unforeseeable consequences that will ensue from the false doctrines they have hitherto advocated and from the hitherto unecclesiastical and illegal actions embarked upon. Moreover, anyone with any perception can see that the disastrous confusion of the legislation passed by the Reich Church government can scarcely be exaggerated. Even when now and then resistance is offered to the crudest slips in the area of doctrine we are shocked to see that this resistance is made only then when tactical considerations make it seem desirable.

The doctrinal statements opposed by us and the ensuing unchristian and illegal actions are not, however, the deepest ground of our protest. On the contrary, this protest is chiefly directed against those principles which are foreign to the nature and character of the Church and with which the Reich Church government as well as the leaders and representatives of the "German Christians" have continually and consistently nullified the theological principles of the German Evangelical Church and have made them ineffective. Our protest is therefore not an accidental or usual one; it is basic. Our protest is understood only when it is seen that it grows out of another root than that of the basic position of the "German Christians" and the Reich Church government. The threatened dissolution of the German Evangelical Church has its real source here rather than in the manifold injustices committed and in the doctrinal monstrosities so often reiterated. Because the issues at stake go so deep, so too the unity that brings us together in our synod is so deeply grounded that it could be endangered only by our members falling away from the pure gospel. May God in his grace forbid it!

If, however, someone wished to say that the unity which brings us together is a dishonest union or is a new attempt to renew the old union, we would have to protest most vehemently, if this objection were made on the ground of tactical and propaganda considerations. We define the relation of the Confessions that prevail in our fellowship as follows:

As members of Lutheran, Reformed, and United Churches we may and must speak with one voice in this matter today. Precisely because we want to be and to remain faithful to our various Confessions, we may not keep silent, since we believe that we have been given a common message to utter in a time of common need and temptation. We commend to God what this may mean for the interrelations of the Confessional Churches.

We have come together today as Lutheran, Reformed, and United churchmen. At an earlier time it was thought that the unresolved questions among us were unimportant. We regard it as a gift of God that in recent years we have learned how essential these questions are. To mention only a few of these questions: How can and is the conversation between Lutheran and Reformed churchmen, broken off more than three hundred years ago, to be resumed — concerning the Lord's Supper, the doctrine of Christ, and election? Can and may the union be described as a Confessional Church parallel to the Lutheran and Reformed Churches? Has the union a Confession at all? We are aware that these and other questions still await a uniform answer, and nothing is farther from our intention than to make light of them in any way. As pupils of the Reformers, we are concerned with resuming conversations where they were broken off in the sixteenth century and not to choose a starting point in the seventeenth century. The relation of the Confessions to one another will be very much sounder if this is respected.

We are persuaded that the knowledge of this difference is considerably clearer and more theological among us than among our opponents, and we abhor any attempt to mix up the confessional question with politics, as if the difference between Lutheranism and Calvinism could be explained by diversities of peoples. While conscious of this difference, we cannot help speaking and contending together now. For the attack upon the substance of the Christian faith on the part of the German Faith Movement and the "German Christians" lies completely outside the relation of the Confessions to one another. We are unable to understand the "German Christians" otherwise than as the forerunners — and, to be sure, for the most part unintentional — champions of the German Faith Movement itself. We do not thereby mean to say that there are not men among them who simply because of an error find themselves in the ranks of the "German Christians." However, as long as they remain there, we can see them only as standing in a common front with the extremist adversaries. The course taken recently by the "German Christians" does not alter the situation a bit, that is, as long as we are not convinced that their new emphasis upon the Lutheran Confession does not proceed from other than tactical considerations. It is up to them to show proof by manifesting through visible signs a will to repair the destruction of the rest of the evangelical Churches in Germany which they have been guilty of bringing about.

The question arises as to how we conceive of our confessional fellowship and co-operation in the future. To that question we can only answer that we do not know, and we are not so bold as to trespass upon God's

government of the world. We look upon our confessional fellowship as
something that God has brought about, and not we. Far from achieving
an approximation of the Confessions, our theology has developed, rather,
in the direction of a growing, day-by-day consciousness of our own Confessional stand. Since God has granted us this great and goodly fellowship, may he see to it what may come of it further! We trust him to bring
it to a glorious fruition.

Now that the whole world may see that God has at length granted us
a common word of faith to utter, we too now seek to give expression to
this common word:

> In view of the errors of the " German Christians " and of
> the present Reich Church government, which are devastating
> the Church, and are also thereby breaking up the unity of the
> German Evangelical Church, we confess the following evan-
> gelical truths.

The six articles that follow are not to be understood as a basis for negotiations with our opponents, as if some bargain could still be made, as if
starting from these points, we could unite with our opponents in a
common, middle line. On the contrary, they are to be understood as
conditio sine qua non. It is our very earnest concern to bear witness to this
fact. For the present struggle in the Church is certainly not a debate between parties such as has prevailed the last fourteen years; here ultimate
issues are at stake.

*1. " I am the way, and the truth, and the life; no one comes to the
Father, but by me." (John 14:6.)*

*" Truly, truly, I say to you, he who does not enter the sheepfold by
the door but climbs in by another way, that man is a thief and a robber. . . . I am the door; if anyone enters by me, he will be saved."* (John
10:1, 9.)

Each of our articles begins with a text of Scripture which in our opinion sums up a whole series of texts that confront us demanding obedience,
and which show that we are not concerned about programmatic demands
that may be open to discussion, but that we are called to life and salvation. We are standing at a place in Church history in which we believe the
attempt is being made to enter the sheepfold otherwise than through the
door. We are standing at a point in Church history at which it must have
become apparent to everyone to whom God has given faith that the issue
is the salvation and blessedness of sinners. However urgent the question
of the way in which the Church is to take its place in the Third Reich may

be, we know that for the Church it is a still much more urgent question whether its servants really enter the sheepfold through the door.

For the present time we have been given this understanding of the Biblical text:

> Jesus Christ, as he is attested for us in Holy Scripture, is the
> one Word of God which we have to hear, and which we have
> to trust and obey in life and in death.

This paragraph means that the Church's task, and indeed the only and the most urgent task, is to preach Christ. Only through an error is it possible to preach him as an idea that has been more or less realized in history. If such were the case, an interpretation of current history and the proclamation of Jesus Christ would be one and the same. The fact is, rather, that Jesus Christ is God who has come in the flesh, who has humbled himself in order to redeem us from attempts to exalt and to overreach ourselves and not a realized idea. Still today he comes to us in his Word as the One who humbled himself once and for all. For he himself is the Word, which was from the beginning, which appeared in time, and which is revealed to us in the sermon that is preached in the congregation. It follows that he alone is to be heard in the congregation. All trust and obedience performed in life and in death may be only a trust and obedience to him. When in life or in death he grants us a foundation, this foundation then is so much firmer than any others one might mention that these others are not worth mentioning at all beside him. When in life or in death he lays his claim upon us, this claim is so urgent that in the moment when he demands obedience all other ever so serious claims are invalid.

Precisely this is disputed today by those who falsely call themselves the Church as well.

> *We reject the false doctrine, as though the Church could and would*
> *have to acknowledge as a source of its proclamation, apart from and*
> *besides this one Word of God, still other events and powers, figures and*
> *truths, as God's revelation.*

For the sake of our Lord Jesus Christ we may not become weary of stressing repeatedly that it is false doctrine when other authorities are set up for the Church beside the incarnate Word in Christ and the Word proclaimed in him. That is what is happening today. The demand is constantly and everlastingly being made upon the Church and its members to acknowledge the events of the year 1933 as binding for its proclamation and exposition of Scripture, and as demanding obedience alongside Holy Scripture and over and beyond its claim. When we protest against this, we do not do so as members of our people in opposition to the recent history of the nation, not as citizens against the new State, nor as subjects against the civil magistrate. We are raising a protest against the same phenomenon that has been slowly preparing the way for the devastation of the Church for more than two hundred years. For it is only a relative difference whether beside Holy Scripture in the Church historical events or reason, culture, aesthetic feelings, progress, or other powers and figures are said to be binding claims upon the Church. All these factors cannot limit the proclamation of Christ, nor can they take a place beside Christ as subjects of proclamation. In proclamation they can have no other place than that of various marks of the one, basically unchanged world, which can find redemption in Christ and only in Christ.

2

We are conscious of being challenged to say, especially today, wherein Christ's work for, upon, and in us consists. We have to meet this challenge in order that as teachers, servants, and members of the Church we protect men, as far as possible, from confusing Christ's work with other works. Christ's work is expressed summarily in the words of Scripture:

2. " Christ Jesus, whom God made our wisdom, our righteousness and sanctification and redemption." (I Cor. 1:30.)

This text sums up the message of Holy Scripture in such a way that it becomes obvious that Christ's work is not a partial manifestation in an automatic process of redemption for men, nor is it in any sense a basis for a work to be performed by men. It is to be comprehended as his work and only as his work. It comprises everything God has done, does, and will do to remove human misery. It requires no sort of supplementing and support on the part of sinful, believing, or unbelieving men. It is all-sufficient, and therefore in no way does it suffer to be divided or split up.

We believe that today this text has to be interpreted as follows:

As Jesus Christ is God's assurance of the forgiveness of all our sins, so in the same way and with the same seriousness he is also God's mighty claim upon our whole life. Through him befalls us a joyful deliverance from the godless fetters of this world for a free, grateful service to his creatures.

We are attempting, therefore, so to express the comprehensive character of the work of Christ that he does not simply translate us from sin into a state of grace, then leave us to ourselves, but that he redeems us from godlessness and sin in order that we may belong to him and live *subject* to him, and so that his presence constantly confronts us in the life he has given us as a judging and saving claim and at the same time as our joyous deliverance from the godless fetters of this world. Thus we freely and gratefully serve him and his creatures.

The reason we reject the (false doctrine) that beside him and his Word in Holy Scripture there are still other sources of revelation is not that we think we are called upon to force through a particular theological theory of knowledge. On the contrary, our protest against other sources of revelation is made in the knowledge that the claim of such other sources is a claim to divine authority and is therefore a denial of the wisdom, righteousness, sanctification, and redemption that have befallen us in Christ.

Whoever reproaches us that our proclamation has no appreciation for the divine creation and for God's government of the world makes these reproaches from a lack of judgment or maliciously. We experience just like other people the beauty of God's creatures and their demoniacal character, the heights and depths of history that occurs under God's government of the world. But what we fear more than death is the fact that God's creatures and events in history lead us into temptation, as they have led all men into temptation in the course of history. They became heathen when they succumbed to the temptation to seek God *without Christ* from and in the creatures and events. Whenever that happens, whether under a pagan or Christian guise, there exist man's own wisdom, his self-righteousness, self-sanctification, self-redemption. Other lords than Jesus Christ, other commandments than his commandments, acquire dominion over us. They offer their services to us as saviors, but they prove to be torturers of an unredeemed world. For this reason we admonish all Christians to guard with all their might against the false doctrine that justification and sanctification may be torn asunder. We warn everyone against the misuse of the divine offer whereby one wants to have the assurance of the forgiveness of sins but rejects God's claim on the ground of the forgiveness of sins. We summarize these insights in this way:

We reject the false doctrine, as though there were areas of our life in which we would not belong to Jesus Christ, but to other lords — areas in which we would not need justication and sanctification through him.

Now we know very well that such knowledge and faith is given only to the Christian Church, and so too can be required only of it and its members, and, above all, of its ministers. Consequently we would speak and would have to speak in another tone if we were speaking to a world that attaches no value to being the Church. We are speaking, however, to a world that claims to be a Church and to Christians who have allied themselves with this world. In order to attract and to call them back, we have to oppose them in a clear-cut break with them. If we were speaking to a world that does not want to be the Church, we would oppose it by alluring it.

3

For this reason we have no more urgent exhortation for our brothers and sisters who are united with us in this confessional fellowship than that they be truly the Church and that they fight in the consciousness of being members of the Church. This Biblical exhortation is given summary expression in Eph. 4:15-16:

> 3. "*Rather, speaking the truth in love, we are to grow up in every way into him who is the head, into Christ, from whom the whole body [is] joined and knit together.*" (Eph. 4:15-16.)

When the apostle speaks in this way, he is not talking about moral honesty or of love based on blood relations. If he did that, he would be speaking about a human form of society but not about the Church. For the Church is not born of civil righteousness and a love based on blood relations but of the righteousness and love of Christ. Only in this way can it be something else than an element within human society, something else than a sociological phenomenon. Only in this way can it be a body, of which Christ is the head, joined and knit together in upright love. If we did not believe that the Church is something else than a form of human society, we would consider the whole Church struggle we are carrying on to be unjustified, yes, criminal. Thus we believe that we have to confess together this concerning the Church:

> *The Christian Church is the congregation of the brethren in which Jesus Christ acts presently as the Lord in Word and sacrament through the Holy Spirit. As the Church of pardoned sinners, it has to testify in the midst of a sinful world, with its faith as with its obedience, with its message as with its order, that it is solely his property, and that it lives and wants to live solely from his comfort and from his direction in the expectation of his appearance.*

When Jesus Christ is proclaimed as the Lord in the fellowship of brethren who are brothers not by birth but through rebirth, that is something quite different from a philosophical or cultural society making the cultivation of its convictions its business. For those gathered together in the Church become a new creation in the event of the proclamation of Jesus Christ as Lord, as Christ says: " You are clean through the Word which I have spoken unto you." Therefore it is essential that the Church testify with its Word, and, by the character of its existence, be a sign set up that it is a Church only as the property of Jesus Christ, that it can live only from his comfort and direction. It testifies that in this comfort and in this direction it has become so rich that it no longer desires to live in any other way. In this way the Church is a missionary to the world when among all forms of human society it strikes the eye as a special sign, and in its preaching explains why this is the way it is with it and not otherwise. This is true of the Church regardless of the fact that as the fellowship of brethren who have been made clean through the Word it is at the same time a fellowship of sinners with the same blood and the same origin as the children of the world. How else could it be a missionary Church if it did not show in Word and walk that precisely such imperfect, lost, and godless men as church members are, could become and be what they as Church members are: children of God who have been cleansed by the blood of Jesus Christ in the Word.

This message and this existence are rendered impossible for the Church, however, in the moment the boundary between the Church and the world is blurred. It always happens when the Church is dominated by the free will and pleasure of sinners and no longer by the unchangeable Word of God of forgiveness in Christ. We understand very well that there is a desire to introduce the wishes of our contemporaries in its upbuilding. We are aware of the desire to carry on a mission to the world by making it clear to the world that it is in its own interest to [be] Church-related and Christian. Nevertheless we must protest against just this desire. For as little as subjects can and may gain the favor of rulers by assuming the character of rulers, and as little as a teacher will be a good teacher who makes common cause with pupils, just as little will the Church be capable of being a missionary Church by placing itself on the same level with the world to which it is to go with its mission. Every man must remain true to himself if he is to be able to serve his neighbor. The Church has to remain the Church if it is to be able to carry out its mission to the world.

4

For this reason the structure of the Church also has to conform to its inner nature. Christ our Lord says:

4. "You know that the rulers of the Gentiles lord it over them, and their great men exercise authority over them. It shall not be so among you; but whoever would be great among you must be your servant." (Matt. 20:25-26.)

Christ is not opposed to princes ruling and to rulers exercising power in the sphere of the world. We too are greatly concerned that we do justice to this right of the world. But likewise we earnestly desire as teachers, ministers, and members of the Church to be distinguished just in this regard from worldly princes and rulers in accordance with the Word of the Lord: " It shall not be so among you." In this text Christ clearly and definitely shows that the Christian congregation exists only as the inversion of the world, and only then does it meet its obligations when it gives expression to this inversion of the pattern of the world. With a view to the structure of the Church, we understand the text referred to thus:

The various offices in the Church do not establish a dominion of some over the others; on the contrary, they are for the exercise of the ministry entrusted to and enjoined upon the whole congregation.

In the Church there is also an " above " and a "below," leaders and those led. Ministers and congregations are required to hand in their collections and tax certificates to their proper Church authorities at the right time, to make statistical reports, and to maintain order in the Church in connection with elections and in the worship of God. But woe to the Church when this relationship to authorities becomes the nature of the Church. That has already happened once in the history of the Christian Church in the papacy in the Middle Ages. Today it has happened a second time. For the leadership principle that has come to prevail in the Church is not restricted to reporting collections, payment of taxes, statistics, and the outward ordering of Church life, but it determines certain essential conditions without whose fulfillment, they think, there is to be neither the office of the ministry, nor a presbytery, nor a Church board, nor the voice of the whole Church in a synod. Thus out of a ministry entrusted to and commanded of the Church emerges a self-elected government that has usurped authority and wrested it to itself. The text, " It shall not be so among you," is changed to read: " It will be still worse among you."

On the basis of the message of the New Testament we acknowledge the possibility and necessity of various offices in the congregation. On the basis of the teaching of the New Testament we know that there is no final and universal order that has to be implemented concerning the number and character of the different offices. It is our opinion that in a Christian congregation there can be an episcopal and a presbyterial constitution. But we are also convinced that in a Christian congregation a devilish will to dominion can get in under an episcopal as well as under a presbyterial constitution. None of the possible constitutions guarantees Christian usage and Christian life. On the contrary, Church constitutions are to be an attempt to erect a sign that makes clear to the world what the Lord says: "It shall not be so among you." President and bishop, bishop and president, pastor and deacon, deacon and pastor, are the lowliest servants of the congregation in inverse proportion to their rank. But the decisive thing happens whenever and wherever God by his mighty hand and through his word and sacrament translates a man from death into life, from the kingdom of darkness into the Kingdom of his dear Son.

With that we have already expounded what we intend by the second paragraph that reads as follows:

We reject the false doctrine, as though the Church, apart from this ministry, could and were permitted to give to itself, or allow to be given to it, special leaders vested with ruling powers.

5

From what has been said, any honest thinking person will see how we stand in regard to the State and the people. But in order to stop the mouths of liars, let us once again hear the voice of Holy Scripture which says:

"Fear God. Honor the emperor." (I Peter 2:17.)

To this we would simply observe that when for no other reason we are absolutely concerned about being good citizens, the whole world should nevertheless know that this *one* word of Scripture binds and holds us more securely than a thousand oaths and temporal obligations could do. We have already stated often enough that it would be a crime against heaven and earth to suspect us of being rebels, obviously in the secret desire thereby to discredit us in the Church. But now once more clearly and bindingly to express our Scripturally based conviction, we summarize an exposition of the text which we have acquired from the whole of Scripture as follows:

Scripture tells us that, in the as yet unredeemed world in which the Church also exists, the State has by divine appointment the task of providing for justice and peace. [It fulfills this task] by means of the threat and exercise of force, according to the measure of human judgment and human ability. The Church acknowledges the benefit of this divine appointment in gratitude and reverence toward him. It calls to mind the Kingdom of God, God's commandment and righteousness, and thereby the responsibility both of rulers and of the ruled. It trusts and obeys the power of the Word by which God upholds all things.

It is thereby asserted that we who are members of the confessional front are kept in obedience and loyalty to the nation and the State by a divine commandment. The only reason we are being everlastingly accused of disloyalty is that Holy Scripture is not taken seriously in the way we do. Otherwise one would know and acknowledge that for us there cannot be any stronger obligation than that which with God's help already obtains among us. The everlastingly new accusations make it clear that our opponents do not respect Holy Scripture as we do, and that more is expected of the State than Scripture assigns to it for its domain.

State and Church are both bound, the latter in the realm of the gospel, the former in the realm of law. Their obligation denotes the sphere of their freedom. Any infringement of their respective obligation leads to a servitude that is alien to the nature of either Church or State. The service and tasks which each of these powers is to perform for the other result solely from the obligation peculiar to each. When the State proclaims an eternal kingdom, an eternal law, and an eternal righteousness, it corrupts itself and with it its people. When the Church preaches a political kingdom, an earthly law, and the justice of a human form of society, it goes beyond its limits and drags the State down into the mire with it.

This is our meaning when in disavowal of false doctrine we say:

> *We reject the false doctrine, as though the State, over and beyond its special commission, should and could become the single and totalitarian order of human life, thus fulfilling the Church's vocation as well.*

> *We reject the false doctrine, as though the Church, over and beyond its special commission, should and could appropriate the characteristics, the tasks, and the dignity of the State, thus itself becoming an organ of the State.*

We believe we are doing nothing but our duty before God, the only wise and just God, when in rejecting the errors of the " German Christians " we draw attention to the fact that even the political wisdom in our present form of the State, about which we do not otherwise indulge in passing any judgment, is not God's wisdom; that even the measure of justice that prevails in our public affairs is not the standard of divine righteousness. And once and for all we have to stress that we know no earthly law by which God's law could lawfully be broken. A " totalitarian State " can mean only a State that is concerned to comprise the whole life of a people *within* the limits established by God. If the " German Christians " want a comprehensiveness that goes beyond these limits, they are denying the reality and actuality of the divine commandment.

6

In conclusion we testify why the Church, in spite of its perhaps outwardly inferior appearance, is so important to us that we are continually emphasizing its unique and unsurpassable character. This testimony is contained in the words of Scripture:

> " *Lo, I am with you always, to the close of the age."* (Matt. 28:20.)
> " *The word of God is not fettered."* (II Tim. 2:9.)

There is no State, nor is there any nation, to which the text applies that Christ is with them until the end of the world. For this reason there are no politics, not even Church politics, that do not come under the Scriptural sentence: " All flesh is as grass." All political discourse is properly exposed to the forces of this world. God's Word cannot be bound because he abides with us until the end of the world. The one exists in the other.

From this alone proceeds the Church's peculiar characteristic which we have to maintain:

> *The Church's commission, upon which its freedom is founded, consists in delivering the message of the free grace of God to all people in Christ's stead, and therefore in the ministry of his own word and work through sermon and sacrament.*

When we contend for the freedom of the Church's commission, we have in mind something fundamentally different from what an earlier period intended when it spoke about human freedom. When we emphasize that the congregation cannot be reduced to silence, we are not thereby asserting a democratic principle. When we state that the only frame of reference within which the preacher may be required to stand is that of Holy Scripture in accordance with the Confession of Faith of this Church, we do not mean that the preacher enjoys a special privilege beside other citizens. On the contrary, all these concerns are nothing but an expression of our faith that in the fellowship of brethren that is called the Church, and about which we have spoken above, Christ lives, works, and rules, not simply as an idea but as the living Lord, not simply in an unattainable distance but right in our midst as Scripture says: " The word is near you, on your lips and in your heart." And another verse says: " You will all be taught of God." It is the urgent task of the Church to express through visible signs that instruction by the Holy Spirit and the presence of Christ are not desirable ideals for the Church but a starting point given to it for its action in word and deed.

In this way and only in this way is it to be understood when we reject the false doctrine as if:

> *the Church in human arrogance could place the word and work of the Lord in the service of any arbitrarily chosen desires, purposes, and plans.*

When in the course of the last year, we have repeatedly said and now reiterate that the Church's proclamation may not be placed in the service of man's self-glorification and may not be subordinated to humanly chosen desires, purposes, and plans, we do not say that these desires, purposes, and plans are not good and desirable within the limits of human reason and capacity. However, we are mindful of the fact that the judgment that they are good and desirable is a human judgment. We therefore leave to God to decide on the Day of Judgment whether in his sight these plans and desires are also desirable. For this reason we cannot tolerate it when proclamation is made to serve them. For that would imply as much that the presence of Christ and the freedom of the Word through the Holy Spirit are just as effectual in these human plans and desires as in the Word preached and in the sacrament administered in the congregation.

The judgment of the Confessional Synod of the German Evangelical Church summed up these six points as follows:

The Confessional Synod of the German Evangelical Church declares that it sees in the acknowledgment of these truths and in the rejection of these errors the indispensable theological basis of the German Evangelical Church as a federation of Confessional Churches. It invites all who are able to accept its declaration to be mindful of these theological principles in their decisions in Church politics. It entreats all whom it concerns to return to the unity of faith, love, and hope.

As already mentioned above, this means that these points do not set forth a program but are, rather, expressions of a God-given faith. Because it has been granted by God, it cannot be a matter for debate. It means that the Confessional Synod of the German Evangelical Church is so certain in this matter that it dares to involve others with it in this responsibility. In view of the " German Christians " and particularly of the tactic they have recently followed of affirming the necessity of the Lutheran Confession, it means that for the sake of the truth we are unable to regard this affirmation as making amends and hence a settlement of our grievances. Not out of pride but after serious consideration we are bound to testify that we wanted to be united with them. But the price of this unity would have to be a clearly expressed confession by the " German Christians," that they admit that their teaching and practice up till now has disrupted the Church, and an announcement of their readiness in the future to build the Church according to other principles and another order than they have tried to do in the past. For we are not free to do or not to do what we like. We prefer peace and comfort to strife and risks. But we are bound by the indestructible fact:

Verbum Dei manet in aeternum

APPENDIX IX

MEMBERS OF THE SYNOD OF BARMEN

Working Committee:
1. President Karl Koch, Bad-Oeynhausen
2. Bishop Hans Meiser, Munich
3. Bishop Theophil Wurm, Stuttgart
4. Pfarrer Martin Niemöller, Berlin-Dahlem
5. Pfarrer Lic. Dr. Joachim Beckmann, Düsseldorf
6. Pfarrer Johannes Bosse, Raddestorf
7. Pfarrer Gerhard Jacobi, Berlin
8. Pfarrer D. Hermann Albert Hesse, Wuppertal-Elberfeld
9. Pfarrer Karl Immer, Wuppertal-Barmen
10. Dr. Eberhard Fiedler, lawyer, Leipzig
11. Wilhelm Link, businessman, Düsseldorf

Appointed by the Working Committee:
12. Pastor Friedrich von Bodelschwingh, Bethel

Delegates from the Landeskirchen:

ANHALT
13. Pfarrer Martin Schmidt, Dessau
14. Albrecht Schneider, engineer, Dessau

BADEN
15. Pfarrer Karl Heinrich Dürr, Pforzheim

16. Pfarrer Hermann Weber, Freiburg
17. Prof. D. Gerhard Ritter, Freiburg
18. Friedrich Dittes, revenue officer, Kenzingen

BAVARIA
19. Thomas Breit, member of a High Consistory, Munich
20. Pfarrer Eduard Putz, Munich
21. Pfarrer Wilhelm Bogner, Augsburg
22. Dr. Julius Schieder, director of Lutheran Seminary, Nuremberg
23. Prof. D. Hermann Sasse, Erlangen
24. Dr. Hans Meinzolt, member of High Consistory, Munich
25. Theodor Christian Dörfler, director of County Court, Augsburg
26. Dr. Friedrich Lehmann, publisher, Munich
27. Dr. Wolfgang Rohde, physicist, Nuremberg
28. Fritz Memmert, businessman, Würzburg

BRUNSWICK
29. Pfarrer Heinrich Lachmund, Blankenburg
30. Dr. Karl Bode, privy councilor, Brunswick

BREMEN
31. Pfarrer Lic. Gustav Greiffen-
hagen, Bremen

DANZIG
32. Pfarrer Ernst Sperling, Danzig
33. Prof. Dr. Johannes Lührs,
Danzig-Langfuhr

HAMBURG
34. Pfarrer Wilhelm Remé, Hamburg
35. Dr. Hermann Pinckernelle,
lawyer, Hamburg

HANOVER (*Lutheran*)
36. Superintendent Wilfried Wol-
ters, Soltau
37. Pfarrer Eberhard Klügel, Ben-
ningsen
38. Friedrich Wilhelm Meyer,
farmer, Stirpe
39. Balthasor Kohlepp, laborer,
Misburg near Hanover
40. Dr. Karl Erhard, Count von
Wedel, Loga

HANOVER (*Reformed*)
41. Pfarrer Heinrich Oltmann,
Loga
42. Dr. Otto Buurmann, physician,
Loga

ELECTORATE OF HESSE
43. Pfarrer Dr. Karl Bernhard Ritter, Marburg
44. Prof. Hans von Soden, Marburg
45. August Sonnenschein, book
dealer, Marburg

LIPPE-DETMOLD
46. Pfarrer Wilhelm Böke, Wüsten
47. August Güse, farmer, Wüsten

MECKLENBURG
48. Pfarrer Henning Fahrenheim,
Schwerin i.M.
49. Pfarrer Christian Berg, Basse
i.M.

HESSEN-NASSAU
50. Pfarrer Karl Veidt, Frankfurt
a.M.
51. Pfarrer Lic. René Wallau,
Frankfurt a.M.
52. Pfarrer Karl Amborn, Horr-
weiler
53. Ludwig Metzger, lawyer,
Darmstadt
54. Hans Heinzelmann, engineer,
Frankfurt a.M.

OLDENBURG
55. Pfarrer Heinz Kloppenburg,
Wilhelmshaven-Rüstringen
56. Pfarrer Erich Ramsauer, Oldenburg
57. Lieutenant-Captain Theodor
Marcard, businessman, Varel

PRUSSIA (*Old Prussian Union*)
Berlin-Brandenburg
58. Pfarrer Dr. Eitel-Friedrich von
Rabenau, Berlin
59. Superintendent Lic. Martin
Albertz, Spandau
60. Pfarrer Kurt Scharf, Sachsenhausen
61. Pfarrer Heinrich Vogel, Dobbrikow
62. Pfarrer Friedrich Müller, Berlin-Dahlem
63. Pfarrer Eberhart Röhricht,
Berlin-Dahlem
64. Pfarrer Otto Riethmüller, Berlin

65. Pfarrer Walther Thieme, Berlin
66. Detlev von Arnim-Kröchlendorff, Kröchlendorff
67. Dr. Horst Michael, Berlin
68. Kurt Siehe, privy councilor, Berlin
69. Wilhelm von Arnim-Lützow, landowner, Berlin-Wannsee

Grenzmark
70. Pfarrer Gotthold Funke, Betsche, Kreis Meseritz
71. Friedrich Kremer, senior assistant-master, Schneidemühl

EAST PRUSSIA
72. Pfarrer Otto Glüer, Gr.-Schmückwalde, Kreis Osterode

Pomerania
73. Dr. Eberhard Baumann, consistory adviser, Stettin
74. Pfarrer Johannes Bartlett, Glowitz
75. Pfarrer Paulus Hinz, Kolberg
76. Prof. Rudolf Hermann, Greifswald
77. Dr. Reinold von Thadden-Trieglaff, landowner,
78. Frau Stephanie von Mackensen, Stettin

RHINELAND
79. Pfarrer Friedrich Graeber, Essen
80. Pfarrer Heinrich Held, Essen
81. Pfarrer D. Paul Humburg, Wuppertal-Barmen

82. Pfarrer Hermann Lutze, Cleinich
83. Pfarrer Georg Schulz, Wuppertal-Barmen
84. Pfarrer Otto Wehr, Saarbrücken
85. Pastor Alfred Viering, Missions inspector, Wuppertal-Barmen
86. Prof. Karl Barth, Bonn
87. Karl Frowein, manufacturer, Wuppertal-Barmen
88. August Mitze, textile wholesaler, Düsseldorf
89. Dr. Gustav W. Heinemann, lawyer, Essen
90. Gustav Theill, manufacturer, Remscheid

SAXONY
91. Superintendent Ludolf Müller, Heiligenstadt, z. Zt. Staats, Krs. Gardelegen.
92. Pfarrer Walther Gabriel, Halle a.d. Saale
93. Pfarrer Hans von Sauberzweig, Salzwedel
94. Bernhard Hofmann, lawyer, Magdeburg
95. Wilhelm Dose, director, Erfurt

SILESIA
96. Superintendent Lic. Alexander Warko, Hirschberg
97. Pfarrer Dr. Robert Berger, Breslau
98. Pfarrer Lic. Dr. Ulrich Bunzel, Breslau
99. Walther Beninde, lawyer, Bunzlau

100. Kurt Milde, engineer, Breslau
101. Count Adolf Seydlitz-Sandreczki, Olbersdorf

WESTPHALIA

102. Pfarrer Martin Heilmann, Gladbeck
103. Pfarrer Karl Lücking, Dortmund
104. Pfarrer Ludwig Steil, Wanne-Eickel
105. Pfarrer Wilhelm Niemöller, Bielefeld
106. Pfarrer D. Georg Merz, Bethel
107. Pfarrer Johannes Busch, Witten
108. Prof. Otto Schmitz, Münster i.W.
109. Dr. Walther Alfred Siebel, manufacturer, Freudenberg
110. Julius Brocke, patternmaker, Hagen-Haspe
111. Hermann Eickhoff, mine inspector, Dortmund
112. Wilhelm Klevinhaus, businessman, Schwelm
113. Gustav Flockenhaus, manufacturer, Gevelsberg

SAXONY (Freistaat)

114. Superintendent Hugo Hahn, Dresden
115. Pfarrer Arndt von Kirchtach, Dresden
116. Pfarrer Karl Fischer, Dresden
117. Pfarrer Lic. Walther, Leipzig
118. Pfarrer Adolf Amelung, Plauen i.V.
119. Reimer Mager, managing director, Dresden

120. Dr. Theodor Böhme, manufacturer, Dresden
121. Martin Richter, welfare worker, Dresden
122. Adalbert Küntzelmann, assistant master, Chemnitz
123. Dr. Rudolf Geizzler, lawyer, Leipzig
124. Justice Wilhelm Flor, Leipzig
125. Prof. Friedrich Delekat, Dresden

SCHLESWIG-HOLSTEIN

126. Pfarrer Ernst Hildebrand, Altona
127. Rüdolf Jager, architect, Altona-Bahrenfeld

THURINGIA

128. Pfarrer Ernst Otto, Eisenach
129. Pfarrer Gerhard Bauer, Gotha

WÜRTTEMBERG

130. Pfarrer Wilhelm Pressel, member of High Consistory, Stuttgart
131. Pfarrer Gotthilf Weber, Stuttgart
132. Pfarrer Wolfgang Zeller, Stuttgart-Zuffenhausen
133. Pfarrer Adolf Schnaufer, Schmieden
134. Pfarrer Theodor Dipper, Würtingen
135. Pfarrer Werner Schuler, Nussdorf
136. Friedrich Degeler, cooper, Heidenheim
137. Inspektor Friedrich Lutz, Stuttgart
138. Otto Seiz, auditor, Stuttgart

APPENDIX X

MEMORANDUM SUBMITTED TO CHANCELLOR HITLER, JUNE 4, 1936

The German Evangelical Church, represented by the spiritual members of its provisional administration and by the council supporting it, offers to the Führer and Chancellor respectful greeting.

The German Evangelical Church is closely associated with the Führer and his advisers through the intercession that it makes publicly and in private for the people, the State, and the Government. The provisional administration and the council of the German Evangelical Church consider, therefore, that they may undertake to give expression in the present document to the anxieties and fears cherished by many Christians in the communities, by the Councils of Brethren, and by the Church leaders in regard to the future of the Evangelical faith and of the Evangelical Church in Germany, and on which they have meditated long and earnestly.

The provisional administration of the German Evangelical Church publishes this document in obedience to the divine charge laid on it to hold forth His word and to bear witness to His commands fearlessly before all the world — even before the sovereigns and rulers of the peoples. It is confident that God accords it the wisdom to fulfill its task so clearly and so unequivocally that its solicitude concerning the Christian conscience and its love for the German people will both be unmistakably discerned.

In presenting these expositions, however, we know that we are impelled only by the one duty, as were our predecessors in office with their declaration of April 11, 1935, that unfortunately had no traceable effect, to help the suffering, confused, and imperiled members of the Evangelical Church by mediating for them. It imports us all that the Government of the Reich shall hear clearly and distinctly the voice speaking out of anxiety for the souls entrusted to the Church.

The Lord of the Church says: " For what is a man profited, if he shall gain the whole world, and lose his own soul? or what shall a man give in exchange for his soul? " These words show how great and serious is the service required by God of the Church, and they remind us at the same time of the limits set to all earthly powers and their strivings. They point out finally the danger constantly menacing unnumbered people, including members of the Church.

1. *Danger of Dechristianization*

The provisional administration appreciates what it signified in the year 1933 and in later years, that those responsible for the National Socialist revolution could declare emphatically that " in gaining our victory over Bolshevism we overcame at the same time the enemy that combated Christianity and the Christian Churches and threatened to destroy them." What we now see, however, is that the Christian Church is being combated actively and keenly by a section of the German people as it never was since 1918.

No power in the world, by whatever name it may be called, is able to destroy or to protect the Church of God against his will; this is God's concern. It is the part of the Church, however, to take up the cause of the consciences of its members that are attacked.

Many baptized Christians are menaced by the distress and confusion produced by the religious combats of the present day with temporal and eternal adversity. When even high authorities in the State and in the Party publicly assail the Christian faith (see, among others, speech by Dr. Ley), Church members who are already estranged from the Church and its message are more and more enmeshed in their unbelief, the waverers and the doubters are made completely uncertain and are driven to defection. Grave danger, as a matter of fact, exists that the Evangelical youth will be prevented from coming to Him who is the only Savior of German as well as of other boys and girls.

Against such an imperilment of members of the Churches all Church leaders conscious of their responsibility must offer strenuous resistance, and to this opposition belongs the clear question to the Führer and Chancellor whether the attempt to dechristianize the German people is to become the official policy of the Government through the further co-operation of responsible statesmen or perhaps by simply looking on, letting things take their course.

2. *" Positive Christianity "*

We sincerely hope that in order to prevent the aggravation of the religious combats in Germany the Government of the Reich will listen to what the Evangelical Church has to say. When the National Socialist Party declared in its program that it stood on the basis of a " positive Christianity " the whole Church population could not but understand and was intended to understand that the Christian faith, in conformity with the Confessions and the preaching of the Church, should be accorded freedom and protection in the Third Reich, and even help and encouragement.

Later on, however, authoritative persons in the State and in the Party have given quite an arbitrary interpretation to the words " positive Christianity." The Reich Minister for Propaganda and National Enlightenment, for example, declared positive Christianity to be merely humanitarian service, and joined to this interpretation occasionally an attack on the Christian Churches and their allegedly inadequate achievements in the domain of Christian charity, although the State itself had considerably restricted them by its prohibitions since the year 1933.

[N.B.: Speeches by Dr. Goebbels in connection with the winter relief work, and on other occasions: " If the Churches were animated by a real Christian spirit, they would never have left it to the State to assist the poor in this winter against hunger and cold. . . . I believe that Christ himself would discover more of his teaching in what we are doing than in this theological hairsplitting. . . . The people would perhaps better understand if the Church concerned itself with true Christianity."]

Then Herr Rosenberg, Reich organization leader, proclaimed his mystic doctrine of the blood to be positive Christianity, and, following his example, other notable Party leaders defamed as being negative the Christianity as confessed by believers.

[N.B.: Rosenberg: " We recognize today that the general ideas of the Roman and of the Protestant Churches are negative Christianity, and do not, therefore, accord with our soul, and we see that they stand in the way of the organized forces of the nations following Nordic-racial principles, that they have to make room for these forces, and that they must allow themselves to be transformed within the meaning of Germanic Christianity."]

[Letter from the eleventh Brigade of the SA to the administration: " No positive Christian is to be dismissed from the SA; but the negative Christians, who, being bound up with medieval dogmas, are in discord with National Socialism, may be removed. . . . The negative Christian fights for the Church, to the detriment of the people; he fights for the Church's dogmas, and in support of the lies of the priests, and thus for the devil. . . . To be an SA man and to belong to the confessional front of those who confess such a faith is absolute contradiction. . . . If we as positive Christians do not think so badly of our fellow men, we nevertheless secure ourselves against the intrusion of spies and of the elements of disintegration."]

Other members of the Reich Government have, under the cloak of positive Christianity, divested of their confessional character categorical conceptions of the Christian faith, such as belief, love, eternity, prayer, resurrection, and have given them a new, purely worldly, psychological interpretation. This has been done even by Herr Kerrl, Reich Minister for the Churches.

[*N.B.:* General Göring: " We have informed the Church that we stand on the basis of positive Christianity. We have shown the Church by our religious zeal, by the firmness of our belief, what faith really is." Reich Minister Kerrl: " That [the profession to positive Christianity] has nothing to do with dogmas, it is an independent faith, and is the love that is practical deeds, which enjoins on us to say: ' Lord, forgive them, for they do not know what they do.' The essence of National Socialism is faith, its deeds are love, and National Socialist positive Christianity is love for the neighbor."]

The harm done by such statements is all the greater as the Church is never permitted the possibility to refute with similar publicity the misrepresentations of the Christian faith proclaimed from high quarters.

3. *Destruction of the Ecclesiastical System*

The methods by means of which the German people are to be dechristianized will be understood in their full association when the statement by Herr Rosenberg, the Reich organization leader, is recalled, namely, that in the striving for a German faith " the opposing party must not be spared, it must be overcome intellectually, from the organization standpoint it must perish, and politically it must be kept impotent." (*Mythus,* page 636.) It is on this standpoint that action has been taken.

Officially, it is true, intervention in any form in the internal structure and in the religious life of the Evangelical Church is disclaimed.

[*N.B.:* Speeches by Reich Ministers Göring and Kerrl: " If in the course of the past two years there have been disturbances within the Evangelical Church, these can have been caused only by individuals, and never by the Party as such and never by the State as such." Dr. Goebbels, Reich Minister for Propaganda: " When we preach the unity of the Protestant Church we do so because we consider it to be impossible that in a time when the whole Reich is united twenty-eight national Churches can continue to exist. In this we are bringing no dogmas to bear, and we do not meddle with the interpretation of the gospel. God's command in regard to the exposition of the gospel should be placed higher than the command of human intermediaries. In the interpretation of political expediency we hold ourselves to be the instrument of God." Herr Hitler: " The Party never intended and does not intend today to combat Christianity in Germany in any way whatever. On the contrary, it has endeavored to create a great Evangelical Reich Church by uniting impossible Protestant national Churches, and without meddling in the slightest degree in confessional questions." (At the Party rally on September 11, 1935.)]

As a matter of fact, one interference has followed the other until today since the elections forced on the Church in July, 1933.

[N.B.: The most important of these interferences are: (1) The installation of the State Commissar in Prussia on June 24, 1933, and of State Commissars in Bremen, Hesse, Lippe, Mecklenburg, and Saxony. (2) Ordainment of universal Church elections by the law of the Reich, promulgated on July 15, 1933. (3) Speech by the Führer in favor of "German Christians," broadcast on July 22, 1933. (4) Prohibition to publish anything concerning Church affairs by decree (unpublished) of the Reich Minister of the Interior on November 6 and 7, 1934. (5) Establishment of the State Finance Department by the Prussian law of March, 1935. (6) Establishment of an authority over resolutions by Reich law, in June, 1935. (7) The law of September 24, 1935, to secure the German Evangelical Church, and the Church committees set up thereupon by the State.

[Against individual clergy: (1) Arrest of the Bishop of Württemberg and Bavaria in 1934. (2) Conveyance of clergy into concentration camps, especially in Saxony and in Nassau-Hessen. (3) Expulsion of clergy from their parishes, at times from their home province, especially in Prussia. (4) Arrest of seven hundred pastors (Pfarrer) in Prussia, in connection with the reading from the pulpits, ordered by the Old Prussian Synod in March, 1935, of the proclamation against modern paganism. (5) Permanent prohibition to hold Confessional Church services, clergymen and laymen forbidden to speak in public, in some cases over the whole of Germany. And others.]

The Evangelical public, who had been guaranteed freedom for the Church by the Führer just before the compulsory elections [N.B.: Telegram to the Reich President on July 12, 1933], could be informed only very inadequately concerning the progress of the Church strife.

The so-called "Work of Reconciliation," which had started with the creation of the Reich Church Ministry and the setting up of the Church committees, remedied, it is true, some abuses occasioned by state officials and members of the Party and tolerated by the State.

The Evangelical Christian who looks more closely into the matter sees, however, that by means of this conciliatory work the Church is kept in dependence on the State in regard to administration and finances, it is deprived of freedom of speech and of organization, and it is forced to tolerate the teaching of false doctrine. For him it must be a severe shock to read in the preamble to the " Reconciliation " law of September 24, 1935, that there is no truth in the statement that disquietude prevails in the German Evangelical Church, and that interferences in Church matters by the State are not really interferences, but services rendered by the State to the Church.

This course of procedure by the State lays a burden that they can hardly bear on the shoulders of the Evangelical Church members who stand by the revealed Word of God, who hold to their fathers' profession of faith, and who, because they do this, know what they, as Christians, owe to their people and its government.

4. Deconfessionalizing

A movement has been started with the watchword " deconfessionalizing," or " to overcome the confessional disunion," which is intended to render impossible the public work of the Church.

The Evangelical Church's own youth organization was long since taken away from it by an agreement between the Reich youth leader and the Reich bishop, who was in no sense entitled to enter into such an agreement. Even the full rights accorded by that arrangement are frequently not permitted to the Evangelical members of the National Socialist Youth Organization.

The chief leaders of the organized youth and, following this example, all persons holding any post of authority in the organization continually hold up their Church to the Evangelical youth as being contemptuous and suspicious, and endeavor to undermine the youth's faith in their religion. [N.B., among others: Chief district order 8-35 of the chief district of the girls' organization, dated December 5, 1935: " From this present date I forbid not only the girl and women leaders but also all girls to help in any form of confessional work " (helpers at children's services, etc.). On the signboard of the Hitler Youth at Halle on the Saale: " Where are the enemies of our Hitler Youth? They are the religious fanatics, who still today fall on their knees with wistful looks directed upward, who spend their time attending churches and praying. We, as Hitler boys, can regard only with contempt or derision young people who still today run to their ridiculous Evangelical or Catholic clubs to give themselves up to eminently superfluous religious reveries." Baldur von Schirach, the Reich Youth Leader, on November 5, 1935: " Rosenberg's way is also the way of the German youth."]

While the State holds today officially to " positive Christianity," its new organizations, such as the year on the land or the labor service, not only themselves provide no opportunity for pastoral work among the persons engaged in fulfilling that service, but they deliberately prevent any communication between the pastors of the parishes to which the young people belong. The pastors are refused permission to visit the members of their congregations, and are also forbidden to send them any Evangelical literature. [N.B., among others: Letter from the representative of the Government (Regierungs-Präsident) in Breslau, dated October 22, 1935: " In reply to your letter of October 15, to camp leaderess Schädel concerning the sending of religious literature, I inform you that the Reich and Prussian Minister for Science, for Training, and for the Education of the People emphasized in his decree that the sending of religious publications to persons who are serving their year on the land is forbidden."]

The circumstance that, for example, the Evangelical persons in a Labor Service camp were refused permission to attend a Church service on Good Friday shows how far in some cases the dechristianization has advanced. The regulations concerning the religious care of children in the year on the land speak a very clear language. The deconfessionalization of the schools is deliberately furthered by the State.

In violation of the rights of the Church the confessional schools are being abolished, and in this respect the strongest pressure is brought to bear on the conscience of the parents. The course of lessons for religious instruction that has been approved by the authorities is frequently ignored, and in many places today essential portions of Biblical instruction are simply expunged from the religious course (Old Testament), or unchristian material is put in its place (Old-German Paganism). [N.B., among others: Citation of a decree of the Ministry of State for Anhalt, against which the women of the German Evangelical Church have protested in vain.] Religious services in the schools and school prayers are neglected ever more frequently, or they are transformed to mark the dechristianization even of the outer forms of scholastic life.

The education of the coming race of theologians in the universities is entrusted more and more to professors and lecturers who have proved themselves to be teachers of false doctrine; the destruction of the theological faculties in Prussia throws a strong light on this picture. The Ministry for Science and for the Education of the People has demanded the reinstatement of teachers of false doctrine as members of the examining boards of the universities. Dechristianization is in reality the deconfessionalization of public life, which suppresses ever more and more Christian influence and Christian co-operation by means of the radio, the daily newspapers, and of public lectures.

5. *National Socialist View of Life*

The National Socialist organizations require of their Evangelical members that these shall pledge themselves without any qualification or restriction to the National Socialist view of life. [*N.B.:* Ley, Labor Front leader: " The Party claims the totality of the soul of the German people. It can and will not suffer that another party or point of view dominate in Germany. We believe that the German people can become eternal only through National Socialism, and therefore we require the last German, whether Protestant or Catholic."] This view of life is frequently presented and described as a positive substitute for Christianity that has to be vanquished.

When blood, race, nationality, and honor are thus raised to the rank of qualities that guarantee eternity, the Evangelical Christian is bound, by the First Commandment, to reject the assumption. When the " Aryan " human being is glorified, God's Word bears witness to the sinfulness of all men. When, within the compass of the National Socialist view of life, an anti-Semitism is forced on the Christian that binds him to hatred of the Jew, the Christian injunction to love one's neighbor still stands, for him, opposed to it.

The members of our Evangelical community have to submit to an especially severe conflict in their conscience when, in compliance with their duty as parents, they have to combat the penetration of these anti-Christian ideals in their children's minds.

6. *Morality and Justice*

We see with profound anxiety that a system of morality essentially foreign to Christianity is circulating among our people, and threatens to disintegrate it. We know perfectly well that in his speech on March 23, 1933, the Führer acknowledged the moral importance of the Christian Confessions for the life of the people, but the power of the new morality has up to the present been greater than that declaration.

On all sides what is of advantage to the people is regarded as being good. [*N.B.:* From the paper read before the Juridical Congress at Leipzig, 1936, by Dr. Barth, leader of the department for legal policy in the National Socialist Party: " Reich Minister Dr. Frank established the legal-political principle that ' Right is what serves the people; wrong what is detrimental to them,' and in this principle are points of discernment of the innermost connection between the vital necessities of the nation and its consciousness of justice."]

With the knowledge of Herr Derichsweiler, leader of the Reich Department, it could be declared that the expression " positive Christianity " in Article 24 of the Party program was used only in the manner in which the full truth is withheld from a person who is ill. Such an attitude places considerations of expediency above the truthfulness required in God's commandment.

This contempt of the command to be sincere and truthful, emanating from the spirit of morality based on what is advantageous to the people, will be especially evident to the Evangelical Christian from the manner in which the Church strife is officially represented (see above), from the treatment accorded to the Evangelical press and to the question of Evangelical assemblies, from the perversion of the idea of voluntariness to its opposite in connection with assemblies and with canvassing for entrance into organizations, etc.

The Evangelical Church welcomes with gratitude, in view of Christ's commands, in the Sermon on the Mount, the fact that the number of oaths in the law courts has dwindled under the dominion of the present State to a fragment. It must, however, deplore, as a fresh victory for the anti-Christian spirit, the fact that the oath is being applied to an alarming extent in swearing allegiance and as a pledge, and has thus depreciated in value to an alarming extent. Seeing that every oath in God's eyes is a declaration or assurance given under the eyes of God, even when God's name is not expressly used, the circumstance that many persons are made to swear one after the other at very short intervals must rob the oath of its dignity, and lead to the profanation and abuse of the name of God.

Evangelical parents consider it to be absolutely intolerable that pledges of the nature of an oath are taken from their children at a very early age. [N.B.: The wording of the pledge given by the Hitler Youth: " I promise solemnly to be loyal to the Führer Adolf Hitler and to serve unselfishly in the Hitler Youth. I promise solemnly to stand up at all times for the unity and comradeship of the German youth. I promise solemnly obedience to the Reich youth leader and to all leaders of the Hitler Youth. I promise solemnly by our sacred flag that I will always endeavor to be worthy of it. So help me, God."]

In the discharge of our Christian duties we hear ever more frequently of persons declaring that they did not feel bound by an oath which it would have threatened their very existence to refuse. The Evangelical Church would be able to combat more easily such a manner of thinking among its members that runs counter to the Christian requirement, if it were permitted to the Christian to give the natural explanation that no oath can cover proceedings that are contrary to God's commandments.

It has actually happened that earnest Christians, who, under God's will, were fully ready to work in obedience to their superiors, have been dismissed from their posts because they claimed the right to that explanation. It is thus very difficult for many officials to maintain an absolutely sincere attitude.

The value attached to the voting paper in the last Reichstag elections caused many Evangelical Christians pangs of conscience. That value is founded on the fact that the advantage of the people is placed above veracity. Evangelical Christians who acknowledge sincerity in their decisions were ridiculed, or even maltreated.

Evangelical Christians are convinced, on the foundation of the Holy Scriptures, that God is the protector of the right and of those without rights, and so we regard it as turning away from him when arbitrary dealing creeps into affairs of law, and things occur that " are not right before the Lord." To these things belong not only the many circumstances in the Church combat, but also what is ultimately a denial of justice by the institution and the demeanor of the Ecclesiastical Decree center. [The law of the Reich, dated June 24, 1935, concerning the procedure of the center in German Evangelical Church matters deprives Church disputes of the right to judicial decision, and substitutes for this the decision of a political functionary, who, according to an authoritative member of the decree center, sets himself the task to promote political construction. This decree center has been in existence for a year and has not yet decided one of the seventy cases that have been laid before it. The persons concerned in these cases are thus practically deprived of legal rights.]

The Evangelical conscience, which shares the responsibility for the people and the Government, is most heavily burdened by the fact that there are still concentration camps in Germany — which describes itself as a country in which justice is administered — and that the measures and actions of the secret State police are exempt from any judicial control. Evangelical Christians faithful to their Confession whose honor may be assailed are often not accorded the protection of their honor that is afforded to the other citizens.

Evangelical Christianity sees in these matters also the danger of an anti-Christian spirit gaining the ascendancy over our moral and juridical reasoning.

We have endeavored to justify publicly the great anxiety felt in widespread Evangelical circles over the circumstances that authoritative forces in this country are prosecuting the suppression of the Evangelical Church, the disintegration of its faith, and the setting aside of the Evangelical morality, in short, dechristianization on the widest scale. We cannot permit ourselves to be reassured in regard to this view of the state of affairs that we have arrived at on the basis of careful observations by the presentation of opposing statements and facts.

We beg the Government of the Reich to consider whether it can be permanently beneficial to our people that the path hitherto taken shall be followed farther. The coercion of the consciences, the persecution of Evangelical conviction, the mutual spying and eavesdropping already exert a baleful influence.

Even a great cause, if it places itself in opposition to the revealed will of God, must finally bring the people to ruin. God's Church will continue to exist, even if millions of Evangelical Christians sink under the endeavor to dechristianize the German people. The German people have, however, not been given the promise that the poison of an anti-Christian spirit shall not harm them, even if they realize only perhaps after a long time that they have been defrauded of their best inheritance by those who took Christ from them.

Our people threaten to break down the barriers set up by God; they wish to make of themselves the measure of all things. That is human arrogance, which rises up against God.

In this connection we must make known to the Führer and Chancellor our uneasiness over the fact that he is often revered in a form that is due to God alone. It is only a few years ago that the Führer himself disapproved of his picture being placed on Evangelical altars. His judgment is taken to be the standard unrestrainedly today not only in political decisions but also in regard to morality and justice in our people, and he himself is vested with the dignity of the national priest, and even of the mediator between God and the people.

[N.B.: Dr. Goebbels on April 19, 1936: "When the Führer addressed his last appeal to the people on March 28, it was as if a profound agitation went through the whole nation; one felt that Germany was transformed into one single House of God, in which its intercessor stood before the throne of the Almighty to bear witness. . . . It seemed to us that this cry to heaven of a people for freedom and peace could not die away unheard. That was religion in its profoundest and most mystical sense. A nation then acknowledged God through its spokesman, and laid its destiny and its life with full confidence in his hand." See also Göring's speeches.]

We beg, however, that our people may be free to pursue their way in the future under the sign of the cross of Christ, that our grandchildren may not one day curse the fathers for having built up a state on the earth for them and left it behind, but shut them out of the Kingdom of God.

What we have said to the Führer in this memorandum we had to say under the responsibility of our office. The Church is in the hands of the Lord.

The ecclesiastical members of the provisional administration of the German Evangelical Church. [Signed] Müller, Albertz, Böhm, Forck, Fricke.

The Council of the German Evangelical Church. [Signed] Asmussen, Lücking, Middendorff, Niemöller, von Thadden.

Notes

Foreword

1. See *Bekenntnisschriften und Kirchenordnungen der nach Gottes Wort reformierten Kirche,* ed. by Wilhelm Niesel.
2. Cf. Ernst Wolf, *Barmen. Kirche zwischen Versuchung und Gnade,* pp. 10 ff. and pp. 74–91; Heinz Brunotte, *Die Grundordnung der evangelischen Kirche in Deutschland. Ihre Entstehung und ihre Probleme.*
3. *Christusbekenntnis im Atomzeitalter?* in ThEx, new series, No. 70, pp. 15–29.
4. Wolf, *Barmen,* p. 77.
5. Chester V. Easum, *Half-Century of Conflict* (Harper & Brothers, 1951).
6. John L. Snell, ed., *The Nazi Revolution* (D. C. Heath & Company, 1959).
7. Wm. L. Shirer, *The Rise and Fall of the Third Reich.*
8. Cf., for example, Andrew L. Drummond, *German Protestantism Since Luther;* R. D. Butler, *The Roots of National Socialism 1783–1933;* Wm. W. McGovern, *From Luther to Hitler.*
9. Cf. *Evangelische Selbstprüfung,* ed. by Paul Schempp (Stuttgart, 1947), with articles by Hermann Diem, Hans Joachim Iwand, Ernst Wolf, and Herbert Wehrhahn; Walther Künneth, *Der grosse Abfall, Eine geschichtstheologische Untersuchung der Begegnung zwischen Nationalsozialismus und Christentum;* Karl Barth, *Die Deutschen und wir* and *Wie können die Deutschen gesund werden?* in *Eine Schweizer Stimme 1938–1945* (Evangelischer Verlag, Zollikon-Zurich, 1945).

Chapter I

1. See Walther Hofer, ed., *Der Nationalsozialismus. Dokumente 1935–45,* pp. 43, 51–53; Douglas Reed, *The Burning of the Reichstag;* Henri Lichtenberger, *The Third Reich,* pp. 58–61; Konrad Heiden, *A History of National Socialism,* pp. 241–253; Alan Bullock, *Hitler: A Study in Tyranny,* pp. 237–240. *Der Spiegel,* a German newsweekly, published a series of eleven articles from October 21, 1959, to January 6, 1960, on the burning of the Reichstag, based upon a manuscript by Fritz Tobias. The series sought to prove that although the Nazis used the incident to inaug-

urate a reign of terror, they were not responsible for setting fire to the building. Van der Lubbe, who wanted to protest against the Third Reich, was solely guilty of the arson. In a letter to *Der Spiegel* (Feb. 10, 1960), Walther Hofer, while acknowledging that Tobias had rendered a notable service in uncovering important documents and that his evidence was quite convincing, declared that a final judgment must wait until his investigations were presented in book form.

2. Hofer, *op. cit.,* p. 44.

3. *Ibid.,* pp. 46 f., 58–60.

4. *Ibid.,* p. 269. The outline of the history of the persecution of the Jews given here follows that given by Hofer in his book.

5. *Ibid.,* pp. 306 f.

6. *Ibid.,* pp. 276 f.

7. See Hermann Rauschning, *The Voice of Destruction.*

8. English translation of the Concordat is to be found in *The Struggle for Religious Freedom in Germany,* by A. S. Duncan-Jones, pp. 277 ff.

9. Hofer, *op. cit.,* pp. 121, 130.

10. A. S. Duncan-Jones is doubtless correct when he observes that the " mere existence of the Concordat placed a difficulty in the way of the Catholic bishops. The fact that an agreement had been made with the State prevented them from coming out in open challenge to the dominance of the State in spiritual things " (*op. cit.,* p. 165).

11. A revised edition of the encyclical was published in English by the Catholic Truth Society (London, 1939). A shorter version is given in Duncan-Jones, *op. cit.*

12. Hofer, *op. cit.,* p. 160.

13. Cited by Wilhelm Niemöller, *Kampf und Zeugnis der bekennenden Kirche,* p. 526, from *The Silent Church,* by Julius Rieger, p. 90.

14. Karl Barth, *Eine Schweizer Stimme 1938–1945,* p. 5.

15. Hofer, *op. cit.,* p. 168.

16. *Encyclopaedia Britannica* (1949), Vol. 23, p. 792.

17. Hofer, *op. cit.,* p. 172.

18. The author was standing with a Scottish friend on a balcony overlooking a street in Bonn and witnessed the arrival of long columns of gray-uniformed soldiers. That night, in company with German friends, we listened to the radio until early in the morning for word of an Allied counteraction, which never came. But at the sight of the German troops, my Scottish friend said grimly, "One day Britain will have to fight to crush this people again." It was March 7, 1936.

19. Barth, *Eine Schweizer Stimme 1938–1945,* p. 58.

20. Hofer, *op. cit.,* p. 210.

21. Bullock, *op. cit.*, p. 724.

22. H. R. Trevor-Roper, *The Last Days of Hitler*, 2d ed.

Chapter II

1. Karl Kupisch, *Zwischen Idealismus und Massendemokratie. Eine Geschichte der evangelischen Kirche in Deutschland von 1815–1945*, p. 145.

2. *Ibid.*, p. 180.

3. Ernst Bizer, *Festschrift für Günther Dehn* (Neukirchen, Kreis Moers, 1957), pp. 238 ff. In this judgment, Ernst Wolf concurs. See his book, *Barmen. Kirche zwischen Versuchung und Gnade*, pp. 33 ff.

4. Later, Wünsch modified his support on "theological grounds."

5. This fear, so incomprehensible to us in the United States and Canada, was later reflected by the Lutheran "confessionalists" in their opposition to the Confessing Church.

6. Wilhelm Niemöller, *Die evangelische Kirche im dritten Reich. Handbuch des Kirchenkampfes*, pp. 349 f.

7. Kupisch, *op. cit.*, p. 151.

8. See Karl Barth, *Die Theologie und die Kirche* (1928), pp. 76–105. This paper should be compared with two others that Barth delivered years later: *Das Bekenntnis der Reformation und unser Bekennen*, in ThEx (No. 29), and *Die Möglichkeit einer Bekenntnisunion*, in EvTh (April, 1935), pp. 26–44, and with what he wrote in *Church Dogmatics* I, 2, pp. 620–660 (Eng. tr.) concerning his definition of a Confession.

9. It has been alleged that Barth's interest in social and political problems began late in the Church Struggle with the threat and actual outbreak of the war in 1938–1939 and became more intense after the cessation of hostilities in 1945. But this particular paper reveals that he had always understood that a Church's "best dogmatics will be useless" if it does not have "the courage to pronounce a judgment upon vital problems . . . not thirty years too late, like the social manifesto of the Church conference at Bielefeld, but while the problems are still burning issues."

10. Cf. Kupisch, *op. cit.*, pp. 162 f.

11. See *Die protestantische Theologie im 19. Jahrhundert. Ihre Vorgeschichte und Geschichte*, pp. 586 f., and *Kirchliche Dogmatik* IV, 2, pp. 651–653. To the present writer it has always seemed that Kohlbrügge's most original contribution to theology was his Christological interpretation of the law of God. He taught that God's law is primarily his gracious, liberating law, which then judges and condemns us for rebelling against grace. He liked to speak of the Ten Commandments as the Ten Promises of God: You will not steal, you will not kill, etc. For his own doctrine of

the gospel and law, Barth is greatly indebted to Kohlbrügge.

12. Most of Kohlbrügge's books of sermons were destroyed by the bombings during the war, and they have not been republished. Today they are hard to secure. The present writer was fortunate in having acquired some fifty volumes of his sermons back in 1937.

13. The third edition of the first volume, *Glaube und Denken,* was translated into English under the title *God Transcendent: Foundation for a Christian Metaphysic* (James Nisbet & Co., Ltd., London, 1935). Other books by Heim in English are: *The New Divine Order* (S.C.M. Press, Ltd., London, 1930); *The Church of Christ and the Problems of the Day* (Charles Scribner's Sons, 1935); *Spirit and Truth* (Lutterworth Press, London, 1935); *The Power of God* (Lutterworth Press, London, 1937); *Christian Faith and Natural Science* (Harper & Brothers, 1953); and *Transformation of the Scientific World View* (Harper & Brothers, 1954).

14. This statement is not intended to detract from the part that Heim played in the Young Reformation Movement in its opposition to the " German Christians " or from his inspiring sermons during the Church Struggle. Cf. his book, *Deutsche Staatsreligion oder evangelische Volkskirche* (Berlin, 1933); and the volume of sermons for which he penned the foreword: *Das Wort ist deiner Kirche Schutz* (Göttingen, 1934). In English, see Heim's article in *Germany's New Religion* (Abingdon Press, 1937).

15. The sixth edition of Barth, *Epistle to the Romans,* was translated into English by Edwyn C. Hoskyns (1933).

16. Cf. the Preface to the English edition of the *Epistle to the Romans,* p. vii, and the Foreword to *Church Dogmatics* I, 1, pp. xi f. (Eng. tr.).

17. Emil Brunner, *The Word and the World* (London, 1931). Barth had entitled his original work *Christian Dogmatics in Outline* (1927) and changed it five years later to *Church Dogmatics* to indicate that " dogmatics is not a ' free' science but one bound to the sphere of the Church."

18. Cf. Bouillard's article " Dialektische Theologie " in *Lexikon für Theologie und Kirche,* Vol. 3, pp. 334 ff., and his two-volume work: *Karl Barth — Genèse et évolution de la théologie dialectique* and *Karl Barth — Parole de Dieu existence humaine* (1957).

19. See Ludwig Feuerbach, *The Essence of Christianity,* with an introductory essay by Karl Barth originally published in ZwdZ (1927), and a foreword by H. Richard Niebuhr (Harper & Brothers, 1957).

20. Cf. Paul Althaus, " Theologie und Geschichte. Zur Auseinandersetzung mit der dialektischen Theologie," in *Zeitschrift für systematische Theologie,* Vol. 1, 1923.

21. G. C. Berkouwer, *The Triumph of Grace in the Theology of Karl Barth,* Eng. tr. (Wm. B. Eerdmans Publishing Company, 1956), pp. 24–41. In the *Kirchenblatt für die reformierte Schweiz* (1940?), p. 100

(cited by Berkouwer, *op. cit.*, p. 25), Barth addressed himself to the question: " Does the theological renascence of today take its rise from the great disillusionment of the recent world war and its consequences? " and answered: " During this period it had in any case its inception. During that time we were not asleep but were taught some things by the events that took place. I neither can nor want to prove that without the world war we would be standing where we are standing today. But who can prove that we have been brought to our present positions by the world war? "

22. Berkouwer, *op. cit.*, p. 37.

23. Friedrich Gogarten, *Die religiöse Entscheidung,* p. 3.

24. Rudolf Bultmann, *Glauben und Verstehen,* Vol. I, p. 18.

25. See Parergon. "Karl Barth über sich selbst," in EvTh (1948–49), pp. 268 f., and " How My Mind Has Changed." *The Christian Century,* March 9, 1949.

26. Foreword, Eng. tr., pp. ix f.

27. "Karl Barths Dogmatik," *Theol. Rundschau* (1929), pp. 70 ff. Cf. Gogarten's "Das Problem einer theologischen Anthropologie " in ZwdZ (1929), pp. 493 ff.

28. See Barth, *Church Dogmatics* I, 1 (Eng. tr.), pp. 141–149.

29. Bultmann, *op. cit.*, Vol. I, p. 118.

30. Karl Barth, "Das erste Gebot als theologisches Axiom," in ZwdZ (1933), p. 311. This particular article is important because in it Barth specifically reproached Bultmann, Brunner, and Gogarten for acknowledging other authorities beside the revelation.

31. Emil Brunner, "Die andere Aufgabe der Theologie," in ZwdZ (1929), pp. 260 ff. Cf. *The Divine Imperative* (The Westminster Press, 1947), p. 587. Actually Brunner was not at all justified in finding in Kierkegaard a precedent for his eristics. For a discussion of this point, see my book *The Existentialists and God* (The Westminster Press, 1956), pp. 36–39, and Hermann Diem, *Die Existenzdialektik von Sören Kierkegaard,* p. 35.

32. "Die andere Aufgabe der Theologie," in ZwdZ (1929).

33. Emil Brunner, "Die Frage nach dem ʻAnknupfungspunktʼ als Problem der Theologie " in ZwdZ (1932), p. 522.

34. *Ibid.,* p. 524.

35. A full account of the "German Christians " will be given in the following chapter.

36. ZwdZ (1933), p. 539.

37. *Natural Theology.* Comprising " Nature and Grace," by Emil Brunner, and the reply " No! " by Karl Barth (The Centenary Press, London, 1946), p. 72.

38. *Deutsches Pfarrerblatt,* No. 30, p. 377.

39. See Emanuel Hirsch, *Das kirchliche Wollen der deutschen Christen* (Berlin-Charlottenburg, 1933).

40. Barth, *Natural Theology*, p. 121.

41. *Ibid.*, p. 120.

Chapter III

1. Friedrich Wieneke, *Die Glaubensbewegung deutscher Christen*.

2. Cf. Hans Buchheim, *Glaubenskrise im dritten Reich*, pp. 41 ff. It should not be inferred, however, that the ideas of the " German Christians," much less the natural theology underlying them, entirely disappeared from the German scene with the Allied military victory. What is meant is that the organization vanished with the defeat of National Socialism.

3. *Ibid.*, p. 46.

4. *Ibid.*, p. 47.

5. *Ibid.*, p. 48.

6. *Ibid.* I am indebted to this book for the following sketch of their work and the interpretation of it.

7. *Ibid.*, pp. 60 f.

8. *Ibid.*, p. 62.

9. KirchlJb 1933–44, pp. 2 f.

10. H. Schreiner, *Nationalsozialismus vor der Gottesfrage*.

11. D. H. Kremer, *Nationalsozialismus und Protestantismus*, 1931.

12. *The Church and the Third Reich: Questions and Demands of German Theologians*, Vol. I, p. 38.

13. *Ibid.*, pp. 94 f.

14. *Ibid.*, pp. 126 f.

15. *Ibid.*, p. 105.

16. See Walther Künneth, *Antwort auf den Mythus* (Berlin, 1935); Christian Stoll, *Mythus? — Offenbarung!* (Munich, 1934); Helmut Thielicke, *Christus oder Antichristus* (Wuppertal-Barmen, 1935); etc.

17. Cf. Karl Kupisch, *Zwischen Idealismus und Massendemokratie*, p. 187, and Buchheim, *op. cit.*, p. 69.

18. See Joachim Gauger, *Chronik der Kirchenwirren*, Part I, p. 67. See also Appendix II for a translation.

19. See KirchlJb 1933–44, pp. 8–12; K. D. Schmidt, *Die Bekenntnisse und Grundsätzlichen Ausserungen zur Kirchenfrage des Jahres 1933*, pp. 19–25, for the German text, and A. S. Duncan-Jones, *The Struggle for Religious Freedom in Germany*, pp. 37–39, for a résumé in English. Cf. also Wilhelm Niemöller, *Kampf und Zeugnis der Bekennenden Kirche*,

p. 29; Hans Beyer, "Das Altoner Bekenntnis vom 11. Januar 1933," in *Ostdeutsche Wissenschaft,* Band V, 1958.

20. In his collection of Confessions, K. D. Schmidt lists a proclamation that was read from all pulpits in the Reformed synodical district of Elberfeld on October 9 and 16, 1932, as the first evangelical deliverance. In spite of its excellence, it never gained widespread recognition.

21. Cited by Buchheim, *op. cit.,* p. 81.

22. *Ibid.,* p. 82, and the footnote, p. 213.

23. Gauger, *op. cit.,* Part I, p. 68.

24. *Ibid.,* p. 62.

25. *Ibid.,* p. 73. Most instructive is a reading of the history of the German Christian Movement through the eyes of its Church historian, Andreas Duhm. See his *Der Kampf um die deutsche Kirche,* Nos. 1–7. The right to rebel against the authority of the Church clearly showed, he said, "the lofty consciousness of a Reformation mission, of a divine right *against* the Church in its present attitude and form."

26. Buchheim, *op. cit.,* pp. 89 f.

27. Duncan-Jones, *op. cit.,* p. 43.

28. Gauger, *op. cit.,* Part I, p. 74.

29. *Ibid.,* p. 76.

Chapter IV

1. For the original text of the constitution, see Joachim Gauger, *Chronik der Kirchenwirren,* Part I, pp. 69–75, and KirchlJb 1933–44. For an English translation, see Appendix III to this book. The translation is taken from Adolf Keller's book, *Religion and the European Mind.* Keller acknowledged his indebtedness to Dr. Charles Macfarland for the English text. Macfarland was the author of *The New Church and the New Germany* (The Macmillan Company, 1934).

2. Gerhard Niemöller has provided the fullest account of the history of the formulation of the constitution in his book *Die erste Bekenntnissynode der deutschen evangelischen Kirche zu Barmen.* He modestly describes it as a "beginning for a detailed investigation of the emergence of the German Evangelical Church and its constitution." He gives an account of the development and changes in the text which I have omitted in this chapter.

3. *Ibid.,* p. 40.

4. Gauger, *op. cit.,* Part I, p. 77. Gauger gives the date of May 6 when the Ten Articles were published in the press.

5. Gauger, *op. cit.,* Part I, p. 78.

6. The text is given in Gauger, *op. cit.,* Part I, p. 79.

7. Hermann Hesse, *Wie ich Karl Barths Schüler, Freund und Bruder geworden bin.*

8. The document was known as The Loccum Pact or Manifesto. For the text, see K. D. Schmidt, *Die Bekenntnisse des Jahres 1933,* pp. 150 f., and RKz, June 4, 1933.

9. Wilhelm Niemöller, *Kampf und Zeugnis,* p. 42.

10. Hesse, *op. cit.*

11. The original text is to be found in K. D. Schmidt, *op. cit.,* 1933, pp. 153 f., and KirchlJb, pp. 15 f.

12. Gauger, *op. cit.,* Part I, p. 78.

13. A. S. Duncan-Jones, *The Struggle for Religious Freedom in Germany,* p. 45.

14. G. Niemöller, *op. cit.,* p. 41.

15. See K. D. Schmidt, *op. cit.,* 1933, for the German texts of both documents, pp. 145–148.

16. Gauger, *op. cit.,* Part I, p. 80.

17. *Ibid.,* p. 82.

18. Paul Althaus, *Die deutsche Stunde der Kirche,* p. 5.

19. See Appendix IV for a translation of the theses. The original text is given in *Bekenntnisschriften und Kirchenordnungen der nach Gottes Wort reformierten Kirche,* ed. by Wilhelm Niesel, pp. 325 ff.

20. Gauger, *op. cit.,* Part I, pp. 82–83. As one looks back upon the history, one is bound to admit that even if the committee had the legal right to take emergency measures before a Kirchentag was held, this surely did not justify the appointment of a Reich bishop *before* that office had been defined and sanctioned by the whole Church. The fact is the Church leaders were trying to beat the "German Christians" at their own game: politics.

21. Cf. Karl Kupisch, *Zwischen Idealismus und Massendemokratie,* p. 201.

22. G. Niemöller, *op. cit.,* p. 42.

23. Gauger, *op. cit.,* Part I, pp. 84 f.

24. *Ibid.,* p. 87.

25. *Ibid.,* p. 84.

26. Walther Trittelvitz, *Friedrich von Bodelschwingh der Sohn 1877–1946,* pp. 35 f.

27. KirchlJb 1933–44, p. 17.

28. The text of the "Bielefeld Confession" is given in K. D. Schmidt, *Die Bekenntnisse des Jahres 1933,* pp. 164 f.

29. Eng. tr. by R. Birch Hoyle. (Hodder & Stoughton, Ltd., London, 1933.)

30. Gauger, *op. cit.*, Part I, p. 92. The opening words of the constitution were as follows: " At this time when Almighty God is letting our German people pass through a new historical era the German Evangelical Churches unite in carrying on and perfecting the unity brought about by the German Evangelical Church Federation and forming with one accord one German Evangelical Church."

31. Cf. Ernst Wolf, *Barmen. Kirchen zwischen Versuchung und Gnade,* p. 55, and Hans Buchheim, *Glaubenskrise im dritten Reich,* pp. 119 f.

32. W. Niemöller, *op. cit.,* p. 54.

Chapter V

1. Joachim Gauger, *Chronik der Kirchenwirren,* Part I, p. 94.

2. Karl Kupisch, *Zwischen Idealismus und Massendemokratie,* p. 203.

3. Gauger, *op. cit.,* Part I, pp. 98–100.

4. See *Texte zur Geschichte des Pfarrernotbundes,* edited and with an introduction by Wilhelm Niemöller; Kurt Scharf, " Der Pfarrernotbund," in *Bekennende Kirche. Martin Niemöller zum 60. Geburtstag.*

5. With the capitulation of the Lutheran bishops on January 1, 1937, 1,200 Bavarian, 350 Hanoverian, and 250 Württemberg ministers dropped out without giving any reason. With the formation of a Lutheran Auxiliary Union in September 1937, 567 more members resigned. The remaining 4,689 members continued virtually unchanged throughout the Church Struggle.

6. The full text is found in *Texte zur Geschichte des Pfarrernotbundes,* ed. by Wilhelm Niemöller.

7. Cf. *Bekennende Kirche. Martin Niemöller zum 60. Geburtstag;* Wilhelm Niemöller, *Martin Niemöller. Ein Lebensbild; Macht geht vor Recht. Der Prozess Martin Niemöllers;* Franz Beyer, *Menschen Warten;* Dietmar Schmidt, *Martin Niemöller* (Eng. tr. entitled *Pastor Niemöller*); C. S. Davidson, *God's Man.*

8. Gauger, *op. cit.,* Part I, p. 104.

9. *Ibid.,* p. 98.

10. *Ibid.,* p. 106.

11. Reinhold Krause, *Der " Fall Krause" und seine Folge. Von den deutschen Christen zur deutschen Volkskirche,* p. 12.

12. A. S. Duncan-Jones, *The Struggle for Religious Freedom in Germany,* p. 58.

13. The full text is given in Gauger, *op. cit.,* Part I, pp. 114–116.

14. *Ibid.,* p. 116.

15. *Ibid.,* p. 118.

16. For the original text, see *ibid.,* pp. 121–123.

17. *Ibid.,* pp. 112–119.

18. Cf. Hans Buchheim, *Glaubenskrise im dritten Reich,* pp. 145–147.

19. A. S. Duncan-Janes (*op. cit.,* p. 64) appears to have been in error when he stated that this action had taken place in July. Müller was elected Reich bishop on September 27. Nevertheless, Duncan-Jones' chapter on the youth question is the fullest report by any scholar German or English. Cf. Gauger, *op. cit.,* Part I, pp. 124–128; JK, No. 1, 1934, pp. 18–22, 43–45; W. Niemöller, *Kampf und Zeugnis der Bekennenden Kirche,* pp. 82 f.

20. The reference is to the Rengsdorf Theses, which will be discussed below.

21. *Evangelium im dritten Reich,* No. 45.

22. For the original text, see K. D. Schmidt, *Die Bekenntnisse des Jahres 1933,* pp. 80–89. For the digest of articles given here I have drawn upon Arthur Frey's *Cross and Swastika: The Ordeal of the German Church* (S.C.M. Press, Ltd., London, 1938), pp. 145 ff. Barth later referred to Vogel's articles as proof that then Lutheran and Reformed Churches might unite in combating a common enemy. Cf. ThEx, No. 7, p. 7.

23. See K. D. Schmidt, *op. cit.,* pp. 93–98, for the German text.

24. Cf. K. D. Schmidt, *op. cit.,* pp. 93–98, 33–35, 47–66.

25. W. Niemöller, *Kampf und Zeugnis,* p. 67.

26. See JK, No. 14, 1933, for the complete original text.

27. See JK, No. 17, 1933, for complete text. Cf. the defense of the Erlangen statement by the faculty dean, Hermann Strathmann in K. D. Schmidt, *op. cit.* (1933), pp. 186–189.

28 Cf. JK, No. 15, 1933, for complete text.

29. Cf. JK, No. 2, 1934.

30. Cf. Kupisch, *Zwischen Idealismus und Massendemokratie,* pp. 216 f. For the text, see K. D. Schmidt, *op. cit.* (1934), pp. 31–35.

Chapter VI

1. See Joachim Gauger, *Chronik der Kirchenwirren,* Part I, p. 130, for complete text.

2. For the complete text, see JK, No. 2, 1934.

3. Somewhat conflicting reports of this momentous meeting have been given. Cf. Theophile Wurm, *Erinnerungen aus meinem Leben,* pp. 91 f.; W. Niemöller, *Erinnerungen eines alten Mannes,* in StdG, No. 5, 1953, pp. 137 f.; *Macht geht vor Recht. Der Prozess Martin Niemöllers,* pp. 18 f.; and *Hitler und die evangelischen Kirchenführer; zum 25. Januar 1934.* Hein-

rich Hermelink, *Kirche im Kampf. Documente des Widerstandes und des Aufbaus in der evangelischen Kirche Deutschlands von 1933–45,* pp. 66–69, and others repeat the account given by the "German Christian" bishops Coch, of Saxony, and Oberheid, of Cologne. See Gauger, *op. cit.,* Part I, p. 138. English readers will find graphic yet accurate accounts in C. S. Davidson, *God's Man* (1959), pp. 56–59, and Dietmar Schmidt, *Martin Niemöller,* pp. 91–95.

4. Gauger, *op. cit.,* Part I, p. 138; cf. J. Beckmann, in KirchlJb 1933–44, p. 39.

5. Cf. Hermelink, *op. cit.,* pp. 70 f.; Wurm, *op. cit.,* p. 93; W. Conrad, *Der Kampf um die Kanzeln,* p. 92.

6. Gauger, *op. cit.,* Part I, p. 140; Beckmann, *loc. cit.,* p. 39.

7. Niemöller's congregation in Dahlem stood solidly behind him and refused to recognize the order for his exclusion from the Church.

8. Gauger, *op. cit.,* Part I, pp. 137–141.

9. Duncan-Jones, *op. cit.,* p. 75.

10. See Appendix V for a translation of the German text. Cf. *Freie reformierte Synode 1934,* ed. by Karl Immer; K. D. Schmidt, *Die Bekenntnisse des Jahres 1934,* pp. 22 f.

11. *Freie evangelische Synode im Rheinland. Vorträge und Entschliessung,* ed. by Heinrich Held; K. D. Schmidt, *op. cit.* (1934), pp. 36 f.

12. Gauger, *op. cit.,* Part I, p. 149; cf. JK, No. 5, 1934.

13. Gauger, *op. cit.,* Part I, p. 153; cf. JK, No. 6, 1934.

14. *Bekennde Gemeinde im Kampf,* ed. by Karl Immer; W. Niemöller, *Karl Koch. Präses der Bekenntnissynoden,* pp. 50 ff.; K. D. Schmidt, *op. cit.* (1934), pp. 44 f. According to W. Niemöller (*Kampf und Zeugnis,* p. 118) "perhaps never before had the communion of the Lord's Supper among Lutherans, Reformed, and United churchmen been so fervently observed" as at this Synod. Later this particular observance of the Supper was frequently mentioned when the question of intercommunion was discussed.

15. Karl Kupisch, *Zwischen Idealismus und Massendemokratie,* p. 232.

16. For the complete text, see K. D. Schmidt, *op. cit.* (1934), pp. 47–52, and KirchlJb 1933–44, pp. 50–55.

17. Gauger, *op. cit.,* Part I, pp. 170–172.

18. Hermelink, *op. cit.,* pp. 83 f.; Gauger, *op. cit.,* pp. 177–180.

19. For the text of the Ulm Declaration, see JK, No. 9, 1934; K. D. Schmidt, *op. cit.* (1934), pp. 62 f., and KirchlJb 1933–44, pp. 59 f. See Appendix VI for a translation.

20. Gauger, *op. cit.,* Part I, pp. 184–195.

Chapter VII

1. See Heinrich Hermelink, *Kirche im Kampf. Documente des Widerstandes und des Aufbaus in der evangelischen Kirche Deutschlands von 1933–45,* pp. 87 ff. For the text of the Ulm Declaration, see Joachim Gauger, *Chronik der Kirchenwirren,* Part I, p. 181. A translation is given in Appendix VI.

2. Gauger, *op. cit.,* Part I, p. 191.

3. *Ibid.*

4. Gerhard Niemöller, *Die erste Bekenntnissynode der deutschen evangelischen Kirche zu Barmen,* p. 60.

5. See Martin Niemöller, *Akte Bekenntnissynoden I, III, IV;* " Aufbau der Präsidialkanzlei in Bad-Oeynhausen." Cf. *Präsidium der Bekenntnissynode, Akte " Barmen "* in Bielefeld Archive.

6. Other recommendations had been prepared by Lücking, Müller, and Gräber, but they were not supported.

7. For a brief history of this congregation, see *Gemarke in den Jahren der Entscheidung,* by its present pastor, Robert Steiner.

8. See Appendix IX for a list of the members of the synod, according to their provincial Church (*Landeskirche*) and the positions they held at that time. The official list in the Bielefeld Archive gives only 138 names, lacking the name of Hans Asmussen. Actually he was not a commissioner from any of the Churches but was recognized as a delegate in virtue of his position as a reporter for the theological commission to the synod.

9. For a sketch of von Soden's life, see Alfred Niebergall in *Lebensbilder aus der Bekennenden Kirche,* pp. 100 ff.

10. For accounts of his life and work, see Hermannus Obendiek, *Paul Humburg* (Emil Müller Verlag, Wuppertal, 1947), and also in *Lebensbilder,* pp. 54–63.

11. See bibliography for a list of his writings dealing with the Synod of Barmen and its Declaration.

12. See Harmannus Obendiek, " Karl Immer " in *Lebensbilder,* pp. 63–73.

13. Wilhelm Niemöller, *Karl Koch. Präses der Bekenntnissynoden.*

14. See Robert Steiner, *Harmannus Obendiek,* 1955. This biography gives an eight-page list of Obendiek's publications. A volume of his sermons was published posthumously under the title, *Deine Zeugnisse sind meine Rede.*

15. *Und folget ihrem Glauben nach. Gedenkbuch für die Blutzeugen der Bekennenden Kirche,* ed. by Bernhard Heinrich Forck, pp. 65–77.

16. *Fritz Müller* in *Lebensbilder,* pp. 74–80.

17. Steil's widow, Gusti Steil, has written a moving account of her husband's life, which, she said, " reflected in miniature what our Church has experienced and suffered as a whole." See *Ludwig Steil. Ein Leben in der Nachfolge Jesu.* Of course, among the martyrs of Barmen should be reckoned all those who died for the sake of its Confession of Faith: Friedrich Weissler in Sachsenhausen Concentration Camp, February 19, 1937; Paul Schneider in Buchenwald, July 18, 1939; Martin Gauger in Buchenwald, July 14, 1941; Ernst Berendt, August 13, Paul Richter, August 13, and Werner Sylten, September 20 — all in Dachau during 1942; Erick Sack, January 24, Ernst Kasenzer, February 1, and Helmut Hesse, November 24, in Dachau, 1943; Hildegard Jacoby, June 2, 1944, in Berlin; Hans Buttersack, February 14, 1945, in Dachau, and Georg Maus two days later while being transported to Dachau; Dietrich Bonhoeffer, April 9, in Flossenburg; Ewald Dittman, April 19, in Kiel; Friedrich-Justus Perels and Hans Koch, April 23 and 24, in Berlin. Truly amazing was the way in which many who had been condemned to death were rescued at the last moment. Late in 1944 or early in 1945, Ernst Wilm, now president of the Synod of Westphalia, and seven others were released from the Dachau Concentration Camp. Others gained their freedom when the American troops moved in on April 29. Martin Niemöller, after being held for eight years as a prisoner, was taken to South Tirol to be " liquidated " along with other political prisoners. On April 30, German soldiers effected his liberation, and he was freed a second time by the American 7th Army on May 3.

18. The material for this section is based exclusively on the new transcription of the rediscovered stenographic record of the minutes of the synod. See Gerhard Niemöller, *Die erste Bekenntnissynode der deutschen evangelischen Kirche zu Barmen:* II, Texte-Dokumente-Berichte.

19. The text of the hymns sung during the meetings of the synod are also to be found in G. Niemöller, *op. cit.*

20. The text of Bishop Marahrens' meditation is also found in *Die Kirche vor ihrem Richter. Biblische Zeugnisse auf der Bekenntnissynode der deutschen evangelischen Kirche,* ed. by Karl Immer.

21. The text of this address is to be found not only in the minutes, but in *Bekenntnissynode der deutschen evangelischen Kirche Barmen 1934. Vorträge und Entschliessungen,* ed. by Karl Immer.

22. See Appendix VIII.

23. Printed in *Um Verkündigung und Ordnung der Kirche. Die Bekenntnissynoden der evangelischen Kirche der altpreussischen Union 1934–43,* ed. by Wilhelm Niesel (Ludwig Bechauf Verlag, Bielefeld, 1949).

24. G. Niemöller (*op. cit.,* I, p. 78) rightly points out that Asmussen is in error when he asserts (" Barmen 1934," in *Informationsblatt für die*

Gemeinden in den Niederdeutschen lutherischen Landeskirchen, Hamburg, February 26, 1954): " It was unfortunate that this synod of the Old Prussian Union was not binding upon the delegates to the synod of the German Evangelical Church and that they were not informed about it even in Barmen."

25. The original text of this address is to be found not only in the minutes but in the *Vorträge und Entschliessungen,* ed. by Karl Immer, pp. 28–37. See Appendix VII for a translation of the text of the Declaration.

26. The text of this address is also to be found not only in the minutes but in the *Vorträge und Entschliessungen,* pp. 38–48.

27. See Appendix VII.

28. These proposals are to be found in the minutes of the synod.

29. See the report of this meeting by Dr. Otto Schmidt in *Vorträge und Entschliessungen,* pp. 49 ff.

30. The text of Pastor von Bodelschwingh's sermon is to be found in the minutes and in *Die Kirche vor ihrem Richter,* pp. 21–24.

31. The text of this address is to be found in the minutes and in *Vorträge und Entschliessungen,* pp. 51–60.

32. The name is omitted in the minutes. G. Niemöller suggests that it probably was his brother, Gustav von Bodelschwingh.

33. The text of Asmussen's report is given in full in the minutes.

34. The members of the committee of the Lutheran Convention were Pressel, Breit, Merz, Kloppenburg, Meinzolt, Schempp, Beckmann, Sasse, Fischer, Vogel, Bosse, Ritter (of Marburg), von Arnim-Kröchlendorff, Hahn, Putz, Stratenwerth.

35. Actually there were five: Asmussen, Barth, Beckmann, Merz, Putz.

36. The reference is to the twenty-eight theses that had been composed by Dr. Grundmann, a member of the High Consistory, and which had been adopted by the Provincial Churches of Saxony, Brunswick, and Schleswig-Holstein. They are contained in essence in the new general directions published in December, 1933, by Dr. Kinder, the new Reich leader of the " German Christians." See K. D. Schmidt, *Die Bekenntnisse des Jahres 1933,* pp. 98–102, 176 f.

37. The verb is missing in the transcription of the stenographic minutes.

38. Again the verb is missing.

39. G. Niemöller remarks in a footnote to Vol. I of *Die erste Bekenntnissynode der deutschen evangelischen Kirche zu Barmen* (p. 170) that " unfortunately such was not the case. It was followed by an exchange of correspondence between Asmussen and Sasse, and the affair developed into a matter of personal honor." Sasse left the meeting of the commission and went home. Before his departure from Barmen in the night of May 31, he

handed President Koch a statement outlining his objections to the Theological Declaration. See Chapter VIII.

40. During the synod, the " laymen " had presented the following petition: " The undersigned Lutheran lay delegates and lay guests of the Confessional Synod of the German Evangelical Church request the Lutheran convention to bear in mind in their decisions that it would spell the end of the Evangelical Church in Germany if through a failure to arrive at a common declaration a *" bekenntnismässigen Kampfgemeinshaft "* did not come into existence at the synod. They earnestly beg the ministers of the Word not to endanger the basic cause of evangelical Christianity in the struggle for the existence of the Church by theological hairsplitting in the formulations." The petition was signed by twenty-seven laymen.

41. At the end of the First World War there was a fierce persecution of Christians by the Russians in the Baltic states. Forty-two ministers were put to death, among them Traugott Hahn, in February, 1918.

42. The synod recessed to meet in the Great Hall of the Hotel Vereinshaus rather than in the Gemarke Church, where it had been meeting.

43. The text of this report is to be found not only in the minutes but also in the *Vorträge und Entschliessungen,* pp. 61–70. See Appendix VII.

44. The minutes contain the text as read by Asmussen, and the *Vorträge und Entschliessungen* the final version. Cf. also K. D. Schmidt, *Die Bekenntnisse des Jahres 1934.* A handwritten draft by Asmussen exists, as well as a multigraphed copy of the final version for the Theological Commission signed by Asmussen, Flör, Putz, and Beckmann. See Appendix VII.

45. The text of Bishop Meiser's sermon is to be found in the minutes and in *Die Kirche vor ihrem Richter,* pp. 33 ff.

46. See Section 1, " Preparations for the Synod of Barmen."

47. Sasse was named to the committee on the motion of Bishop Meiser of Munich.

48. For further details, see a letter by Barth to Wilhelm Niemöller, dated Basel, October 17, 1953, which is in the Bielefeld Archive.

49. During a visit I had with him in Basel, February 14, 1958.

50. In a letter to Asmussen, dated Bonn a. Rhein, the twenty-third of May, 1934 (Bielefeld Archive). It was in this letter that Barth expressed surprise that he had not received any word about the meeting of the synod. " Or were only you [Asmussen] invited to report to the synod? I do not object because perhaps it would not be a bad thing if I did not appear in the synod in order to avoid all sorts of possible resentments. And you are man enough, if need be, to guard ' like a lion ' . . . against any attempts that might be made to water down the statement. Whatever

may or should be the case, I look back upon the day in Frankfurt with great joy and gratitude." Thereupon Asmussen telegraphed from Essen to President Koch in Bad-Oeynhausen at 11:55 P.M. as follows: "bart noch nicht eingeladen bitte nachholen. Asmussen." (Bielefeld Archive.)

51. It is possible that this draft is the one Prof. Hermann Sasse handed Asmussen in Erlangen and which the latter took back with him to Bonn. Cf. G. Niemöller, *op. cit.,* I, pp. 64 and 67.

Chapter VIII

1. For the text, see K. D. Schmidt, *Die Bekenntnisse des Jahres 1934,* pp. 102–104.

2. *Confessio Barmensis,* in AELK, June 29, 1934.

3. *Korrespondenzblatt für die evangelisch-lutherischen Geistlichen in Bayern,* No. 28, July 9, 1934.

4. Karl Barth and Gerhard Kittel, *Ein theologisches Briefwechsel* (Stuttgart, 1934).

5. Cf. Karl Barth, *Church Dogmatics* I, 2 (Eng. tr.), pp. 622 f.

6. The free Churches, such as the Methodist and Baptist Churches, were not represented because they were not affected by the Reich Church government and the errors of the "German Christians." Unfortunately the "established" and "free" Churches engage in little conversation except at the ecumenical level.

7. *Confessio Barmensis,* in AELK, June 29, 1934.

8. Karl Barth, *The Knowledge of God and the Service of God* (Hodder & Stoughton, Ltd., London, 1938), p. 226.

9. G. Niemöller, *Die erste Bekenntnissynode der deutschen evangelischen Kirche zu Barmen,* Vol. I, p. 171.

10. Hermann Sasse, *Wider das Schwärmertum,* in AELK, 1936, p. 781.

11. Dietrich Bonhoeffer, "Zur Frage nach der Kirchengemeinschaft," in EvTh 3, 1936, pp. 214 ff.

12. *Ibid.,* p. 224.

13. "Fragen," in EvTh 3, 1936, pp. 405 ff.

14. "Hans Asmussen und das Luthertum," in AELK, 1936, pp. 581–586, 610–661. This article was an especially vitriolic reply to an earlier article by Asmussen in AELK, 1936, pp. 443–446, entitled *Lutherisches Bekenntnis und Luthertum.* Christian Stoll had also answered Asmussen in JK, No. 13. Asmussen then sought to defend his position in *Wider die Luthertümer* in AELK, 1936, pp. 733–737. Sasse countered with *Wider das Schwärmertum* (pp. 773–781), in which he referred to the Confessing

Church as a sect and bitterly assailed Dietrich Bonhoeffer, Helmut Gollwitzer, and Karl Barth.

15. Hermann Sasse, *Konfessionelle Unbussfertigkeit,* in AELK, 1935, p. 266. Cf. " Eine Hochschule für reformatorische Theologie? " in AELK, 1935, pp. 418 f.; *Was heisst lutherisch?* Munich, 1934. Cf. Ernst Wolf's critical comments on these works in EvTh, November, 1934, pp. 325 f., and April, 1935, pp. 44 ff.

16. Karl Barth, *Die Möglichkeit einer Bekenntnisunion,* in EvTh, April, 1935, pp. 26 ff.

17. Sasse issued a final broadside against Barmen in seventeen theses, which he presented at a meeting of the Theological Working Committee of the Council of the Evangelical Lutheran Church held in Bethel, October 22–25, 1936. It was printed in AELK, 1936, pp. 1139–1143. It contributed nothing new to the debate and was never answered.

18. See Wilhelm Niemöller, *Die zweite Bekenntnissynode der deutschen evangelischen Kirche zu Dahlem.*

19. Wilhelm Niemöller, *Gottes Wort ist nicht gebunden,* p. 59.

20. A. S. Duncan-Jones, *The Struggle for Religious Freedom in Germany,* p. 108.

21. See KirchlJb 1933–44, pp. 109 f., for the text.

22. For a full account of this synod, see Wilhelm Niemöller, *Die vierte Bekenntnissynode der deutschen evangelischen Kirche zu Bad-Oeynhausen.*

23. See Wilhelm Niemöller, *Die bekennende Kirche sagt Hitler die Wahrheit.*

24. *Ibid.,* p. 18.

25. Heinrich Hermelink states in his *Geschichte der evangelischen Kirche in Württemburg von der Reformation zur Gegenwart* (Stuttgart and Tübingen, 1949), p. 480: " The Memorandum was kept strictly secret from their own comrades in the Lutheran Council, but not in foreign countries . . . and was released to the foreign press before it was handed to Hitler." Niemöller has shown that the truth is that at a meeting of the Council of Brethren on May 13, at which an early draft of the Memorandum was fully discussed, nearly all the Lutheran Churches connected with the Lutheran Council were represented. Moreover, the Memorandum had been delivered to Hitler six weeks before it appeared in the foreign press.

26. K. Barth, *Wünschbarkeit und Möglichkeit eines allgemeinen reformierten Glaubensbekenntnisses,* in *Die Theologie und die Kirche,* pp. 97 f.; cf. *Das Bekenntnis der Reformation und unser Bekennen,* in ThEx, No. 29, pp. 7 ff.

Bibliography

Abbreviations

AELK	*Allgemeine Evangelisch-Lutherische Kirchenzeitung*
BK	*Bekennende Kirche*
ChrW	*Die christliche Welt*
EKl	*Evangelisches Kirchenlexikon*
ELKZ	*Evangelisch-Lutherische Kirchenzeitung*
EvTh	*Evangelische Theologie*
JK	*Junge Kirche*
KirchlJb	*Kirchliches Jahrbuch*
RGG	*Die Religion in Geschichte und Gegenwart*
RKz	*Reformierte Kirchenzeitung*
StdG	*Stimme der Gemeinde*
ThEx	*Theologische Existenz heute*
ZwdZ	*Zwischen den Zeiten*

I. BIBLIOGRAPHIES AND ARCHIVES

1. Otto Diehn, *Bibliographie zur Geschichte des Kirchenkampfes* (Arbeiten zur Geschichte des Kirchenkampfes, Band I), Göttingen, 1959. Lists nearly six thousand items; has list of all previous bibliographies.

2. *Bielefeld Archive.* The founder and director is Dr. Wilhelm Niemöller. This archive contains the official papers, correspondence, etc., of the presidency of the Confessional Synod of the German Evangelical Church and the papers of the Westphalia and Hessen-Nassau Councils of Brethren, as well as those of the Pastors' Emergency League. In addition, there are the voluminous private papers of Hermann Hesse, Karl Lücking, Friederich Middendorf, Martin Niemöller, partial collections of the papers of Hans Ehrenberg, Wilhelm Jannasch, and Ludwig Steil, as well as the collections of Wilhelm Brandes, Eberhard Baumann, Hermann Diem, and Wilhelm Harnisch. Most valuable are the rediscovered stenographic reports of the most important Confessional Synods that have been retranscribed, namely:

> Barmen, 1934 (German Evangelical Church)
> Dahlem, 1934 (German Evangelical Church)
> Augsburg, 1935 (German Evangelical Church)
> Bad-Oeynhausen, 1936 (German Evangelical Church)
> Dahlem, 1935 (Prussia)
> Steglitz, 1935 (Prussia)

Halle, 1937 (Prussia)
Barmen-Gemarke, 1935 (Rhineland, 4th synod)
Dortmund, 1936 (Westphalia, 3d synod)
Siegen, 1935 (2d Reformed synod)
Conference of Churches. Gohfeld-Bergkirchen, May, 1935

A mimeographed listing covers sixty-eight pages and is being constantly revised and expanded. For a description of the archive, see Wilhelm Niemöller, " Ein Archiv der bekennenden Kirche " in EvTh (1954), pp. 527 ff.

3. *Archive of the kirchliche Hochschule in Berlin.* The director of the archive is Prof. Dr. Günther Harder. It contains the files of the Berlin-Brandenburg Church, the Württemberg Sozietät, the Old Prussian Union Church; extensive materials from the United Lutheran Church; files from the Pastors' Emergency League; correspondence of Günther Harder, M. Albertz, President Scharpf; data concerning Church trials. For a description of this achive, see Günther Harder, " Das Archiv für die Geschichte des Kirchenkampfes " in *Theologia viatorum* (Berlin, 1954).

4. *Hamburg Collection.* Prof. Dr. Kurt Dietrich Schmidt is in charge of this collection. It contains his own papers and records; those of Prof. Hans Freiherr von Soden (1881–1945), of Marburg, and of Bernhard Forck; also, valuable pamphlets of the " German Christians," the German Faith Movement, and the Confessing Church.

II. PERIODICALS, SERIES, AND PAPERS

Allgemeine Evangelisch-Lutherische Kirchenzeitung.
Bekennende Kirche, ed. by Theodor Ellwein and Christian Stoll. 1933 ff.
Christenkreuz und Hakenkreuz, ed. by Friedrich Coch. 1933 ff.
Die christliche Welt. Fortnightly Protestant paper.
Evangelische Theologie, ed. by Ernst Wolf, Wilhelm Niesel, Paul Schempp, and Wolfgang Trillhaas. 1934–1938. (Banned December 29, 1938. Reappeared 1946.)
Evangelium im dritten Reich. 1933 ff.
Junge Kirche. Fortnightly paper for Reformation Christianity. 1933–1941.
Licht und Leben. Evangelical weekly paper. (Banned July 6, 1938.)
Reformierte Kirchenzeitung. (Banned January 12, 1939.)
Der Reichsbote. German weekly newspaper for Christianity and the nation. (Banned May 27, 1936.)
Schriften zur deutschen Glaubensbewegung, ed. by Jakob Wilhelm Hauer. 1934 ff.

Theologische Existenz heute, ed. by Karl Barth and Eduard Thurneysen since 1933. Since No. 65, ed. by K. G. Steck.

Unter dem Wort. A Biblical weekly paper. (Banned December 8, 1936.)

Zwischen den Zeiten, ed. by Georg Merz, Karl Barth, Friedrich Gogarten, and Eduard Thurneysen. 1923–1933.

III. PUBLICATIONS OF DOCUMENTS AND SOURCES

Karl Barth zum Kirchenkampf. Beteiligung, Mahnung, Zuspruch, ed. by Ernst Wolf, in ThEx, new series, No. 49.

Beckmann, Joachim, *Kirchliches Jahrbuch,* 1933–1944. Gütersloh, 1948.

Bonhoeffer, Dietrich, *Gesammelte Schriften,* ed. by Eberhard Bethge. Munich. Three vols.: 1957, 1958, 1960; fourth in preparation.

Gauger, Joachim, *Chronik der Kirchenwirren I, Elberfeld* (1934), II (1935), III (1936).

Hermelink, Heinrich, *Kirche im Kampf. Dokumente des Widerstandes und des Aufbaus in der evangelischen Kirche Deutschlands von 1933–45.* Tübingen and Stuttgart, 1950.

Jannasch, Wilhelm, *Hat die Kirche geschwiegen?* A collection of materials in regard to the position of the Confessing Church toward the Third Reich, Frankfurt, 1945.

Klinger, Fritz, *Dokumente zum Abwehrkampf der deutschen evangelischen Pfarrerschaft gegen Verfolgung und Bedrückung 1933–45.* Nuremberg, 1946.

Niemöller, Wilhelm. *Bielefelder Dokumente zum Kirchenkampf.* Bielefeld, 1947.

–––––– ed., *Texte zur Geschichte des Pfarrernotbundes.* Bielefeld, 1958.

–––––– *Die vierte Bekenntnissynode der deutschen evangelischen Kirche zu Bad-Oeynhausen.* Göttingen, 1960.

–––––– *Die zweite Bekenntnissynode der deutschen evangelischen Kirche zu Dahlem,* Texte-Dokumente-Berichte. (Arbeiten zur Geschichte des Kirchenkampfes, Band III.) Göttingen, 1958.

Niesel, Wilhelm, ed., *Bekenntnisschriften und Kirchenordnungen der nach Gottes Wort reformierten Kirche.* Munich, 1938.

–––––– *Um Verkündigung und Ordnung der Kirche. Die Bekenntnissynoden der evangelischen Kirche der altpreussischen Union 1934–43.* (Collection of Documents.) Ludwig Bechauf Verlag, Bielefeld, 1949.

Schmidt, Kurt Dietrich, *Die Bekenntnisse und grundsätzlichen Ausserungen zur Kirchenfrage des Jahres 1933.* Göttingen, 1934. Vol. 2: *Das Jahr 1934.* Göttingen, 1935. Vol. 3: *Das Jahr 1935.* Göttingen, 1936.

Stoll, Christian, *Dokumente zum Kirchenstreit* I–VI. Munich, 1934.

Wolf, Erik, ed., *Zeugnisse der bekennenden Kirche. Das christliche*

Deutschland 1933 bis 1945. Dokumente und Zeugnisse. Tübingen, 1946–1947.
 1. *Der Kampf um die Kirche*
 2. *Der Kampf der bekennenden Kirche um das Recht*
 3. *Der Kampf der bekennenden Kirche um die Jugend*
 4. *Der Kampf der bekennenden Kirche wider das Neuheidentum*
 5. *Worte der bekennenden Kirche an den Staat*
 6. *Stimmen aus der Gemeinde für ihre geistliche Führer*
 7. Goldschmidt, Arthur, *Geschichte der evangelischen Gemeinde Theresienstadt.*
 8. von Dietze, Constantin, *Nationalökonomie und Theologie*
 9. Mie, Gustav, *Die göttliche Ordnung in der Natur*
10. Schlink, Edmund, *Bekennende Kirche und Welt*

IV. SELECTED LIST OF WORKS ON NATIONAL SOCIALISM

Baynes, Norman H., ed., *The Speeches of Adolf Hitler, April 22–August 1939.* 2 vols. Oxford University Press, London, 1942.

Bullock, Alan, *Hitler: A Study in Tyranny.* Harper & Brothers, 1952.

Butler, R. D., *The Roots of National Socialism 1783–1933.* Faber & Faber, Ltd., London, 1941.

Dulles, Allen, *Germany's Underground.* The Macmillan Company, 1947.

Heiden, Konrad, *Der Führer.* Houghton Mifflin Company, 1944.

—— *A History of National Socialism.* Alfred A. Knopf, Inc., 1935.

—— *Hitler — A Biography.* Alfred A. Knopf, Inc., 1936.

Hitler, Adolf, *Mein Kampf.* Unexpurgated edition in English, published by Houghton Mifflin Company, 1943.

Hofer, Walther, ed., *Der Nationalsozialismus. Dokumente 1933–45.* Frankfurt am Main, 1957.

Jaspers, Karl, *The Question of German Guilt.* Dial Press, Inc., 1947.

Lichtenberger, Henri, *The Third Reich,* tr. from the French and ed. by Koppel S. Pinson. Graystone Press, 1937.

Ludecke, Kurt, *I Knew Hitler.* Charles Scribner's Sons, 1938.

Neumann, Franz L., *Behemoth.* Oxford University Press, 1942.

Rauschning, Hermann, *The Revolution of Nihilism.* Longmans, Green & Co., Inc., 1939.

—— *The Voice of Destruction.* G. P. Putnam's Sons, 1940.

Reed, Douglas, *The Burning of the Reichstag.* Covici Friede, Inc., 1934.

Shirer, Wm. L., *The Rise and Fall of the Third Reich.* Simon & Schuster, Inc., 1960.

Trevor-Roper, H. R., *The Last Days of Hitler.* The Macmillan Company, 1947.

Ziemer, Gregor, *Education for Death.* Oxford University Press, 1941.

V. The Church Struggle: History and Critique

Althaus, Paul, *Die deutsche Stunde der Kirche*. Göttingen, 1933.

Barth, Karl, *Die bekennende Kirche in Deutschland im Jahre 1938–39*. Basel, 1940.

—— *Der deutsche Kirchenkampf*. Basel, 1937.

—— *Not und Verheissung im deutschen Kirchenkampf*. BEG-Verlag, Bern, 1938.

Beyer, Hans, " Das Altoner Bekenntnis vom 11. Januar 1933 " in *Ostdeutsche Wissenschaft,* Band V, 1958.

Brunotte, Heinz, " Kirchenkampf," in EKl II.

Buchheim, Hans, *Glaubenskrise im dritten Reich*. Stuttgart, 1953.

Buxton, Dorothy F., *The Church Struggle in Germany*. Kulturkampf Association. London, 1937.

Conrad, W., *Der Kampf um die Kanzeln*. Berlin, 1957.

Dannenmann, Arnold, *Die Geschichte der Glaubensbewegung " Deutsche Christen."* Dresden, 1933(?).

Drummond, Andrew L., *German Protestantism Since Luther*. The Epworth Press, London, 1951.

Duhm, Andreas ("German Christian"), *Der Kampf um die deutsche Kirche*. Gotha, 1933–1934. 7 pamphlets.

Duncan-Jones, A. S., *The Crooked Cross*. The Macmillan Company, London, 1940.

—— *The Struggle for Religious Freedom in Germany*. Victor Gollancz, Ltd., London, 1938.

Elmslie, W. T., *The European Churches*. S.C.M. Press, Ltd., London, 1944.

An English Christian: *The Church Struggle in Germany*. A Survey of Four Years. With a preface by E. S. Wood. Kulturkampf Association, London, 1937.

Frey, Arthur, *Der Kampf der evangelischen Kirche in Deutschland und seine allgemeine Bedeutung*. Zollikon, 1937.

Gurian, Waldemar (pseud.), *Hitler and the Christians*. Sheed & Ward, Inc., London, 1936.

—— (pseud.), *Der Kampf um die Kirche im dritten Reich*. Lucerne, 1936.

Hammelsbeck, Oskar, *Von Barmen bis Treysa* in *Der heilige Ruf*. Gütersloh, 1947.

Hauer, Wilhelm; Heim, Karl; Adam, Karl, *Germany's New Religion: The German Faith Movement*. Tr. by T. S. K. Scott-Craig and R. E. Davies. Abingdon Press, 1937.

Heim, Karl, *The Church of Christ and the Problems of the Day*. Charles Scribner's Sons, 1935.

Herman, Stewart, *It's Your Souls We Want*. Harper & Brothers, and Hodder & Stoughton, Ltd., London, 1943.

—— *Rebirth of the German Church*. Harper & Brothers, 1946.

Keller, Adolf, *Christian Europe Today*. Harper & Brothers, 1942.

—— *Religion and the European Mind*. Lutterworth Press, London, 1934.

Klotz, Leopold, ed., *Die Kirche und das dritte Reich. Fragen und Forderungen deutscher Theologen*. 2 vols. Gotha, 1932.

Koch, Werner, *Bekennende Kirche gestern und heute*. Stuttgart, 1946.

Krause, Reinhold, *Der " Fall Krause" und seine Folge. Von den deutschen Christen zur deutschen Volkskirche*. Berlin, 1933.

Künneth, Walther, *Der grosse Abfall. Eine geschichtstheologische Untersuchung der Begegnung zwischen Nationalsozialismus und Christentum*. Hamburg, 1947.

Kupisch, Karl, *Zwischen Idealismus und Massendemokratie. Eine Geschichte der evangelischen Kirche in Deutschland von 1815–1945*. Berlin, 1955.

—— " Das evangelische Jungmännerwerk und der Anbruch des ' Dritten Reiches ' "; in EvTH, new series, 1958.

Leiper, H. S., *The Church-State Struggle in Germany*. Friends of Europe Publications, London, 1935.

Littell, Franklin, *The German Phoenix*. Doubleday & Co., Inc., 1960.

Maarten, John, *The Abolition of Christianity. The Diary of a Disturbed Soul*. S.C.M. Press, Ltd., London, 1942.

—— *The Village on the Hill*. S.C.M. Press, Ltd., London, 1940.

Macfarland, Charles, *The New Church and the New Germany*. The Macmillan Company, 1934.

Martin, Hugh, *Christian Counter-Attack*. S.C.M. Press, Ltd., London, 1943.

Merz, Georg, " Bekennende Kirchen und Bekenntnissynoden "; in EKl I.

Micklem, Nathaniel, *National Socialism and Christianity*. Oxford University Press, 1939.

Niebuhr, Reinhold, *Europe's Catastrophe and the Christian Faith*. James Nisbet & Co., Ltd., London, 1940.

Niemöller, Wilhelm, *Die bekennende Kirche sagt Hitler die Wahrheit*. Bielefeld, 1954.

—— *Kirchenkampf im dritten Reich*. Bielefeld, 1946.

—— *Kampf und Zeugnis der bekennenden Kirche*. Bielefeld, 1947.

—— *Gottes Wort ist nicht gebunden*. Pocketbook report of the Church Struggle, Bielefeld, 1948.

—— *Die evangelische Kirche im dritten Reich. Handbuch des Kirchenkampfes*. Bielefeld, 1956.

—— *Hitler und die evangelischen Kirchenführer; zum 25. Januar 1934.* Bielefeld, 1959.

Niesel, Wilhelm, *Der Weg der bekennenden Kirche.* Zurich, 1947.

Nygren, Anders, *Church Controversy in Germany. The Position of the Evangelical Church in the Third Empire.* S.C.M. Press, Ltd., London, 1934.

Piper, Otto, *Recent Developments in German Protestantism.* S.C.M. Press, Ltd., London, 1934.

Rieger, Julius, *The Silent Church.* S.C.M. Press, Ltd., London, 1944.

Schmid, Hr., *Apokalyptisches Wetterleuchten.* Munich, 1947.

Schreiner, H., *Nationalsozialismus vor der Gottesfrage.* Berlin, 1931.

Steiner, Robert, *Gemarke in den Jahren der Entscheidung.* Barmen, 1952.

van Dusen, Henry P., *What Is the Church Doing?* S.C.M. Press, Ltd., London, 1943.

von Thadden-Trieglaff, Reinold, *Kirche im Kampf.* Zurich, 1947.

Wieneke, Friedrich, *Die Glaubensbewegung " Deutsche Christen."* Solden, 1933.

Wolf, Ernst, " Bekennende Kirche "; in RGG I.

The above list is not complete; it does not include articles found in symposia, collected works, and periodicals. See Diehn's *Bibliographie* for a complete listing. Among the general histories of the Church Struggle listed above, Wilhelm Niemöller's two volumes, *Kampf und Zeugnis* and *Handbuch des Kirchenkampfes,* are by far the fullest and more reliable that have appeared to date. A. S. Duncan-Jones, *The Struggle for Religious Freedom in Germany* (1938), was the best work in English prior to the war.

VI. Biographies and Autobiographies

Barth, Karl

Asmussen, Hans, *Begegnungen.* Wuppertal-Barmen, 1936.

Ehrenberg, H. P., *Der Bekenntniskämpfer;* in *Antwort. Karl Barth zum 70. Geburtstag.* Zurich, 1950.

Hesse, Hermann, "Mit Karl Barth in Kirchenkampf "; in RKz, 1956, pp. 23 ff.

—— *Wie ich Karl Barths Schüler, Freund und Bruder geworden bin.* Typescript in Bielefeld Archive.

Kupisch, Karl, *Begegnung mit Karl Barth;* in ThEx, new series, No. 62.

Mathias, W., " Barth, Karl "; in EKl I.

Niemöller, Wilhelm, " Karl Barths Mitwirkung im deutschen Kirchenkampf "; in EvTh, 1954.

von Bodelschwingh
Frick, Robert, " Bodelschwingh, Friedrich von "; in RGG I.
Trittelvitz, Walther, *Friedrich von Bodelschwingh der Sohn 1877–1946.* Bethel, 1953.

Bonhoeffer, Dietrich
Bethge, Eberhard, " Dietrich Bonhoeffer, Person und Werk "; in EvTh, 1955.
—— and Wolf, E., " Bonhoeffer, Dietrich "; in RGG I.

Ehrenberg, Hans
Ehrenberg, Hans, *Autobiography of a German Pastor.* London, 1943.

Humburg
Obendiek, Harmannus, " Paul Humburg als Zeuge des Herrn Jesus Christus "; in StdG, Nov., 1949.
—— *Paul Humburg — Der Zeuge. Die Botschaft.* Wuppertal, 1947.
—— *Paul Humburg;* in *Lebensbilder aus der bekennenden Kirche,* ed. by Wilhelm Niemöller. Bielefeld, 1949.

Immer, Karl
Obendiek, Harmannus, *Karl Immer;* in *Lebensbilder aus der bekennenden Kirche,* ed. by Wilhelm Niemöller. Bielefeld, 1949.

Koch, Karl
Niemöller, Wilhelm, *Karl Koch. Präses der Bekenntnissynoden.* Bielefeld, 1956.

Lilje, Hans
Lilje, Hans, *Im finstern Tal.* 2d ed. Nuremberg, 1948.

Marahrens, Bishop
Koch, Günther, " Was recht und billig ist "; in EvTh, 1958.

Meiser
Simon, Mt., " Landesbischof Meiser im Kirchenkampf "; in ELKZ, 1956.

Niemöller, Martin
Bartning, Ludwig, " Martin Niemöllers Berufung "; in BK, Munich, 1952.
Beyer, Franz, *Menschen Warten.* Siegen, 1952.
Davidson, C. S., *God's Man.* Ives Washburn, Inc., 1959.
Hildebrandt, Fr., *Niemöller and His Creed.* Hodder & Stoughton, Ltd., London, 1939.
Niemöller, Martin, *Vom U-Boot zur Kanzel.* Berlin, 1934. Eng. tr., *From U-Boat to Pulpit.* W. Hodge & Co., London, 1939.

Niemöller, Wilhelm, *Macht geht vor Recht. Der Prozess Martin Niemöllers*. Munich, 1952.

—— *Martin Niemöller. Ein Lebensbild*. Munich, 1952.

Schmidt, Dietmar, *Martin Niemöller*. Hamburg, 1959. Eng. tr., *Pastor Niemöller*. Doubleday & Co., Inc., 1959.

Steil, Ludwig

Steil, Gusti, *Ludwig Steil. Ein Leben in der Nachfolge Jesu*. Bielefeld, 1954.

Wurm, Theophil

Wurm, Theophil, *Erinnerungen aus meinem Leben*. Stuttgart, 1953; cf. Niemöller, Wilhelm, "Erinnerungen eines alten Mannes"; in StdG, No. 5, 1953.

General

Forck, Bernhard Heinrich, ed., *Und folget ihrem Glauben nach. Gedenkbuch für die Blutzeugen der Bekennenden Kirche*. Evangelisches Verlagswerk, Stuttgart, 1949.

VII. The Synod of Barmen: History and Critique

Albertz, Martin, "Barmen 1934–54," in *Die Zeichen der Zeit*, Evangelische Monatsschrift, Berlin, 1954, No. 5.

Althaus, Paul, *Bedenken zur theologischen Erklärung der Barmen Bekenntnissynode*. Lutherische Kirche, 1934.

—— *Die christliche Wahrheit, Lehrbuch der Dogmatik*, Vol. I, Gütersloh, 1947, 2d ed., 1949.

—— *Konfession und Union*. Lutherische Kirche, 1935.

Andler, Erich, *Barmen heute. Eine schlichte Auslegung der Barmen Theologischen Erklärung*. Berlin-Dahlem, 1947.

Asmussen, Hans, *Die konfessionelle Bedeutung der Bekenntnissynode der DEK in Barmen*, in JK, 1934.

—— "Konfessionalität," in JK, 1934.

—— *Kirche Augsburgischer Konfession*, in ThEx, No. 16.

—— *Barmen*, in ThEx, No. 24.

—— *Her zu uns, wer dem Herrn angehört. Warum doch Barmen?* Elberfeld, n.d.

—— "Lutherisches Bekenntnis und Luthertum," in AELK, 1936.

—— *Theologie und Kirchenleitung*, in ThEx, No. 31.

—— "Consensus de doctrina evangelii," in *Abendmahlsgemeinschaft*. Supplement No. 3 to EvTh. Munich, 1937.

—— *Soli fide*, in ThEx, Nos. 49 and 50.

—— "Wider die Luthertümer," in AELK, 1936.

Asmussen, Hans, "Eine neue Lage in der EKD," in ELKZ, 1949, No. 15.
—— "Barmen 1934," in *Informationsblatt für die Gemeinden in den Niederdeutschen lutherischen Landeskirchen*. Hamburg, February 26, 1954.
Barth, Karl, *Nein! Antwort an Emil Brunner*, in ThEx, No. 14.
—— *Das Bekenntnis der Reformation und unser Bekennen*, in ThEx, No. 29.
—— "Die Möglichkeit einer Bekenntnisunion," in EvTh, 1935.
—— *Die Kirche und die Kirchen*, in ThEx, No. 27.
—— *Church Dogmatics* I, 2, pp. 460, 620–660; II, 1, pp. 172–178; IV, 3, first half, pp. 95 f.
Karl Barth zum Kirchenkampf, ThEx, new series, No. 49.
Barth, Karl, "Barmen," in BK. *Martin Niemöller zum 60. Geburtstag*. Munich, 1952.
—— *"Barmen" — damals und heute*, in Kirche und Mann. Gütersloh, May, 1954.
—— "Volkskirche, Freikirche, Bekenntniskirche," in EvTh 11, 1936.
—— "Was bedeutet uns Barmen heute?" in JK, 1954.
Beckmann, Joachim, *Die unantastbare Grundlage der DEK*. Essen, 1936.
—— *Die theologische Erklärung von Barmen. Eine Auslegung für die Gemeinde*. Gladbeck, 1947.
Bell, G.; Kramm, H. H.; Cobham, J. O., *The Significance of the Barmen Declaration for the Ecumenical Church*. Society for Promoting Christian Knowledge. London, 1943.
Bonhoeffer, Dietrich, "Zur Frage nach der Kirchengemeinschaft," in EvTh, 1936.
Borngässer, Willy, *Die evangelische Kirche vor der Entscheidung*. Wiesbaden, 1952.
Breit, Thomas, "Bekenntnisgebundenes Kirchenregiment," in BK, No. 45.
Brunner, Peter, *Das lutherische Bekenntnis in der Union*. Gütersloh, 1952.
Brunotte, Heinz, "Die theologische Erklärung von Barmen 1934 und ihr Verhältnis zum lutherischen Bekenntnis," in *Luthertum*, No. 18, 1955.
—— *Die Grundordnung der evangelischen Kirche in Deutschland. Ihre Entstehung und ihre Probleme*. Berlin, 1954.
Diem, Hermann, "Schrift und Bekenntnis," in EvTh, 1935.
—— *Die Problematik der Konvention von Treysa; in Evangelische Selbstprüfung*. Stuttgart, 1947.
Ehrenberg, Hans, *Luthertum oekumenisch und deutsch*. Gütersloh, 1947.
Elert, Werner, "Confessio Barmensis," in AELK, 1934.
—— "Zur Frage eines neuen Bekenntnisses," in *Luthertum*, 1934.
Frey, Arthur, *Der Kampf der evangelischen Kirche in Deutschland in*

seiner allegemeinen Bedeutung. Zollikon, 1937.

Gollwitzer, Helmut, "Lutherisch, reformiert, evangelisch," in EvTh, 1934.

—— "Die Bedeutung der Bekenntnisbewegung und die Bekenntnissynoden für die Kirche," in EvTh, 1936.

—— "Zur Frage der Kirchengemeinschaft," in EvTh, 1936.

—— "Wollen wir heute lutherisch oder reformiert sein?" in BK. Munich, 1952.

Gloege, G., "Kirche und Bekenntnis," in AELK, 1934.

Hammelsbeck, Oscar, "Die Gegenwartsbedeutung der Barmen Erklärung," in JK, 1957.

Hopf, F. W., "Was ist 'Bekenntnis' nach evangelisch-lutherischer Lehre?" in JK, 1934.

—— "Barmen und das lutherische Bekenntnis," in AELK, 1938.

Immer, Karl, ed., *Bekenntnissynode der deutschen evangelischen Kirche Barmen 1934. Vorträge und Entschliessungen.* Wuppertal-Barmen, 1934.

—— ed., *Die Kirche vor ihrem Richter. Biblische Zeugnisse auf der Bekenntnissynode der deutschen evangelischen Kirche.* Kommissionsverlag, Wuppertal-Barmen, n.d. (1934?).

Iwand, Hans Joachim, "Lutherische Kirche," in EvTh, 1946/47.

—— *Die Neuordnung der Kirche und die konfessionelle Frage,* in *Evangelische Selbstprüfung.* Stuttgart, 1947.

Kimme, August, "Union und Konfession," in ELKZ, 1950.

—— "Barmen und die Ordnung der Kirche," in ELKZ, 1950.

Kittel, Gerhard, "Offene Frage an die Männer des Bruderrates der Bekenntnissynode der DEK," in AELK, 1934.

—— *Karl Barth und Gerhard Kittel. Ein theologischer Briefwechsel.* Stuttgart, 1934.

Klügel, Eberhard, "Die theologische Erklärung von Barmen und ihre Vorgeschichte," in ELKZ, 1954.

Koch, Günther, *Die christliche Wahrheit der Barmen theologischen Erklärung,* in ThEx, new series, No. 22, 1950.

—— "Doppelte Beurteilung von Barmen?" in ELKZ, No. 24.

Koch, Werner, *Bekennende Kirche gestern und heute.* Stuttgart, 1946.

Kolfhaus, W., "Die theologische Erklärung der Barmen Synode in Feuer theologischer Kritik," in RKz, 1934.

Kupisch, Karl, "Dahlem 1934," in EvTh, new series, 1959.

Lilje, Hans, "Kritik an Barmen," in JK, 1934.

Merz, Georg, "Die Barmen Kundgebung und das deutsche Luthertum," in JK, 1934.

Merz, Georg, "Barmen theologischer Erklärung 1934," in EKl I. Göttingen, 1956.

Niemöller, Gerhard, *Die erste Bekenntnissynode der deutschen evangelischen Kirche zu Barmen: I, Geschichte, Kritik, und Bedeutung der Synode und ihrer theologischen Erklärung; II, Texte-Dokumente-Berichte.* Arbeiten zur Geschichte des Kirchenkampfes, Bände V and VI. Göttingen, 1959.

Niemöller, Wilhelm, "Das war in Barmen," in JK, 1950.

―――― "Ein Blick nach rückwärts — Der Ruf nach vorwärts," in JK, 1954.

―――― "Vor fünfundzwanzig Jahren," in EvTh, 1958.

―――― "Vor fünfundzwanzig Jahren: Die Barmen Erklärung im Kampf der Kirche," in *Die Zeichen der Zeit,* No. 5, 1959.

Niesel, Wilhelm, "Die Bedeutung und die Rolle der Glaubensbekenntnisse in den reformierten Kirchen," in EvTh, new series, 1959.

Obendiek, Harmannus, "Um die Ordnung in der Kirche," in EvTh, 1934.

Sasse, Hermann, "Die Einigung der Kirchen und des lutherischen Bekenntnis," in *Luthertum,* 1935.

―――― "Konfessionelle Unbussfertigkeit," in AELK, 1935.

―――― *Was heisst lutherisch?* Munich, 1934.

―――― "Union und Bekenntnis," in BK, Nos. 41 and 42, 1936.

―――― "Hans Asmussen und das Luthertum," in AELK, 1936.

―――― "Credo ecclesiam apostolicum," in AELK, 1936.

―――― "Das Bekenntnis der lutherischen Kirche und die Barmen theologischen Erklärung," in AELK, 1936.

―――― "Wider das Schwärmertum," in AELK, 1936.

Schlink, Edmund, *Pflicht und Versuchung christlichen Bekennens,* in ThEx, No. 20.

―――― "Die Verborgenheit Gottes des Schöpfers nach lutherischer Verständnis der ersten Barmen These," in *Theologische Aufsätze. Karl Barth zum 50. Geburtstag.* Munich, 1936.

―――― *Der Mensch in der Verkündigung der Kirche.* Munich, 1936.

―――― *Gesetz und Evangelium. Ein Beitrag zum lutherischen Verständnis der zweiten Barmen These,* in ThEx, No. 53, 1937.

―――― *Theologie der lutherischen Bekenntnisschriften.* Munich, 1946.

―――― *Der Ertrag des Kirchenkampfes.* Gütersloh, 1947.

Schmauch, Werner, *Reaktion oder bekennende Kirche.* Stuttgart, 1949.

von Soden, Hans, *Artikel 1 der Verfassung der DEK von Juli 1933 und die Barmen theologischen Erklärung.* Giessen, 1937. Abstract in JK, 1937.

Steck, Karl Gerhard, *Fragen an das Luthertum,* in ThEx, new series, No. 13.

Stoll, Christian, "Konfessionen?" in BK, No. 23.

—— "Der deutsche lutherische Tag von Hanover," in BK, Nos. 31–32.

—— "Lutherisches Bekenntnis. Luthertum und lutherische Kirche," in AELK, 1936.

—— "Die Synode von Bad-Oeynhausen," in BK, No. 39.

—— *Die theologische Erklärung von Barmen im Urteil des lutherischen Bekenntnisses.* Munich, 1946.

Strathmann, Hermann, *Die Selbstüberschätzung der Kirche.* Bielefeld, 1947.

Thurneysen, Eduard, *Lebendige Gemeinde und Bekenntnis,* in ThEx, No. 21.

Vogel, Heinrich, *Wer regiert die Kirche?* in ThEx, No. 15.

—— "Erklärung über die 'Evangelische Antwort' und die 'Barmen Erklärung,'" in JK, 1934.

—— "Der 4. Artikel des Augsburgischen Bekenntnisses und die 1. These der theologischen Erklärung von Barmen," in *Theologia viatorum.* Munich, 1939.

—— *Lutherisch-reformiert heute,* in ThEx, new series, No. 5.

—— *Christologie I,* pp. 25 ff. Munich, 1949.

Weber, Hans Emil, "Das Bekenntnis und die Konfessionen in der evangelischen Kirche in Deutschland," in EvTh, 1947–1948, Nos. 1 and 2.

Wolf, Ernst, "Eine Antwort," in RKz, 1934.

—— "Zu Hermann Sasse, Was heisst lutherisch?" in EvTh, 1934–1935.

—— "Zu D. H. Sasse, Konfessionelle Unbussfertigkeit," in EvTh, 1935.

—— "Um die Ordnung der Kirche," in EvTh, 1936.

—— *Bekennende Kirche oder bekennende Bekenntniskirche?* Breslau, 1936.

Wolf, Ernst, "Zur Aufgabe des lutherischen Konvents der Bekenntnissynode der evangelischen Kirche der altpreussischen Union, in *Abendmahlsgemeinschaft* Supplement No. 3 to EvTh. Munich, 1937.

—— "Theologie am Scheideweg," in *Bekennende Kirche. Martin Niemöller zum 60. Geburtstag.* Munich, 1952.

—— "Barmen," in RGG, 3d ed., I.

—— *Barmen. Kirche zwischen Versuchung und Gnade.* Munich, 1957.

Index of Names

322